ANGLISTIK UND ENGLISCHUNTERRICHT

Herausgegeben von
Gabriele Linke
Holger Rossow
Merle Tönnies

Band 81

D1730803

ANETTE PANKRATZ
BARBARA PUSCHMANN-NALENZ (Eds.)

Portraits of the Artist as a Young Thing in British, Irish and Canadian Fiction after 1945

Universitätsverlag
WINTER
Heidelberg

Bibliografische Information der Deutschen Nationalbibliothek
Die Deutsche Nationalbibliothek verzeichnet diese Publikation
in der Deutschen Nationalbibliografie;
detaillierte bibliografische Daten sind im Internet
über *http://dnb.d-nb.de* abrufbar.

Herausgeber:
Prof. Dr. Gabriele Linke
PD Dr. Holger Rossow
Prof. Dr. Merle Tönnies

ISBN 978-3-8253-6059-7
ISSN 0344-8266

© 2012 Universitätsverlag Winter GmbH Heidelberg
Imprimé en Allemagne · Printed in Germany
Druck: Memminger MedienCentrum, 87700 Memmingen

Gedruckt auf umweltfreundlichem, chlorfrei gebleichtem
und alterungsbeständigem Papier

Den Verlag erreichen Sie im Internet unter:
www.winter-verlag.de

Contents

6

Anette Pankratz & Barbara Puschmann-Nalenz (Bochum)

Introduction. Portraits of the Artists in Context

Looking over the shoulders of artists and witnessing the creative process, reading about artists' struggles, failures and successes has attracted audiences and readers since the eighteenth century, when literature differentiated itself from religion, politics and the economy and emerged as a cultural system of its own. Recently, German cinema goers rediscovered Goethe as angry young man in *Goethe!* (2010). Movies about female artists usually do without exclamation marks and *Sturm und Drang*, but meet with equal public and critical success. *Frida* (2002), for instance, tells the story of Mexican painter Frida Kahlo; the German film *Geliebte Clara* (2008) presents the life of pianist Clara Schumann.

Nowadays, novels may be less popular and lucrative than biopics, but they provide equally fascinating, attractive and sophisticated representations of both male and female artists. Especially postmodern narratives tend to merge 'real' biography with meta- and intertextual games. In Jeff Noon's *Automated Alice* (1996), for example, the protagonist Alice is transported to Manchester in the late nineties. There she not only encounters strange wonderlandish characters, but she also meets her makers, a Mr Dodgson and the writer Zenith O'Clock with whom she cogitates the intricacies of words and worlds. More sombrely, John Cunningham's novel and Stephen Daldry's movie *The Hours* (1999; 2002) combine portraits of a chain-smoking, neurasthenic Virginia Woolf writing *Mrs Dalloway* with subplots set in the fifties and nineties respectively, which adapt and replay Woolf's novel. Contemporary novels in English often use artist figures, be they male or female, fictitious or (auto)biographical, in order to provide voyeuristic and sometimes satirical glimpses into the lives of the rich and famous as in Angela Carter's *Wise Children* (1991) with its feuding theatrical dynasties or Will Self's *Dorian* (2002) and its subculture of sex and drugs, or as framework for from-rags-to-riches narratives as in Jim Cartwright's *Supermarket Supermodel* (2008). More importantly, as in *Automated Alice* or *The Hours*, the postmodern portraits of artists offer reflections on creativity and the position of the artist in society.

The focus of the present volume will be on the depictions of female artists in British, Irish and Canadian novels, a topic which – rather surprisingly – has not been dealt with too often in systematic fashion, although both the (autobiographical) *Künstlerroman* and the *Bildungsroman* (formerly called 'apprentice novel' in English, which may focus on a literary figure that can be completely fictional and applies to a wider spectrum of protagonists and thematic models) have been in the centre of much scholarly attention. This introduction aims to situate the following essays first in literary studies and secondly to position the novels analysed in their literary and cultural contexts.

1. Portraits of the Artist in Research

Literary historian Maurice Beebe's monograph *Ivory Towers and Sacred Founts. The Artist as Hero in Fiction from Goethe to Joyce* (1964) has become a classic. It analyses a wide variety of artists' (self-)portraits by European writers from the late eighteenth to the early twentieth centuries as reflected in the genre of the *Künstlerroman*.

To Beebe it seems to go without saying that practically all of the hero artists and their creators are male and that female writers from Mme de Staël to Jane Austen, the Brontë sisters and Virginia Woolf are barely worth mentioning, even if they produced a work in this genre. Instead, woman as muse of the male artist serves as a figure firmly rooted in this male-centred universe. Beebe claims that "the most surprising fact about portrait-of-the-artist novels is their similarity", again referring exclusively to the male writers and their protagonists.[1] This gives evidence of the fact that in the sixties questions of gender were still regarded as hardly relevant by the male scholar. It was not before the early eighties, in the wake of feminist critical studies, that first Grace Stewart's *A New Mythos. The Novel of the Artist as Heroine* (1981) and shortly afterwards Linda Huf's *A Portrait of the Artist as a Young Woman. The Writer as Heroine in American Fiction* (1983) examined portraits of female artists in

8

novels in English.[2] The term 'heroines' in the subtitles of their books is reminiscent of both Beebe's study and of *Stephen Hero*, the title of an earlier version of James Joyce's *A Portrait of the Artist as a Young Man* (1916). While Grace Stewart includes British, American and Canadian late-nineteenth- and twentieth-century writers, Huf restricts her monograph to American fiction.

Not meaning to lament once again that most female writers were excluded from the Great Tradition of English or American literature, we cannot fail to realise that the question of literary canonisation arose when Grace Stewart and Linda Huf wrote their books on the female *Künstlerroman*. They focus on canonised authors, though both in their final chapters touch on women writers that had just been recently acclaimed such as Anaïs Nin (*Diaries*, 1966-1983) or Erica Jong with her protagonist Isadora Wing (*Fear of Flying*, 1973), or were gradually becoming famous, like Margaret Atwood.

Beebe, for whom the literary canon was unshakeable, combines the chronological with the typological. According to him the "Divided Self" characterises the artist as early as in the eighteenth century.[3] The artist, he says, feels separated from the world and lonely; he is introspective and self-absorbed. Life and art are contrasting, often incompatible for him. It was not before art came to be considered as self-sufficient and a cultural institution in its own right in the late eighteenth and early nineteenth centuries that the public's esteem of the artist rose to a level where artists could appear as literary protagonists.[4]

This concept of the artist, best exemplified by Johann Wolfgang Goethe's *Die Leiden des jungen Werthers* (1774) and *Wilhelm Meister* (1795/1829), is the root from which two different traditions emerged, one founded on "Art as Experience" and called by Beebe the "Sacred Fount Tradition",[5] the other taking "Art as Religion" and referred to as the "Ivory Tower",[6] a well-known symbol. Both traditions have their beginning in the early nineteenth century, in Romanticism and the Gothic, and continue into the first decades of the twentieth century. It is obvious that these metaphors indicate contrary sources for the artist's creativity, nevertheless they are not mutually exclusive and can merge.

Life, Beebe demonstrates, in its totality is essential and indispensable as the Sacred Fount by which the imagination is inspired. Since the artist is different from other humans, experience grants

him insights and visions inaccessible to the common man. Therefore, he is the best artist who lives most intensely. Samuel Taylor
Coleridge, Percy Bysshe Shelley and George Gordon, Lord Byron
are the most prominent representatives of this tradition where the
poet is a visionary and herald to his fellow men.

The artist in the Ivory Tower, however, does not care much
about mankind and life experience, because he is an individualist
and possibly a snob standing above it. He shares little with humanity at large. This leads to the concept of art for art's sake, to Charles
Baudelaire, Oscar Wilde and W.B. Yeats, and it results in the *hau-
teur* that the artist is often criticised for.

D.H. Lawrence (*Sons and Lovers*, 1913) and more distinctly
James Joyce are to Beebe two authors of the twentieth century who
successfully unite the two traditions in their protagonists. Joyce's
Portrait of the Artist, which is often considered the beginning of the
Künstlerroman, is seen by Beebe as its climax following a long development. But Joyce gives shape to an archetype, and therefore
still undisputedly marks the origin of the modernist artist novel in
English.[7] Exile and homecoming stand as symbolic situations of its
protagonist, Stephen Dedalus. Already in the myth of Daedalus, the
hero's namesake and the original artist of Western literature, these
states signify a breach with the environment, separateness and return through difficulties. Where art is religion the artist becomes
God; even if the authors do not believe in Him they tend to imitate
Him. For the modern artist "to express himself is more important
than to reflect the life around him".[8] Thus the Sacred Fount becomes subordinate to the self.

Beebe's study, which presents Honoré de Balzac, Henry James,
Marcel Proust and Joyce as "Four [Modern] Masters" in conclusion
of his analysis,[9] fails to ask if a similar tradition exists for portrayals
of women writers and thus implicitly points to the lack of research
in regard to the female artist novel. Both Grace Stewart and Linda
Huf try to close this gap. When Huf states on her first page that
women had written only few artist novels, which she defines as
"autobiographical novels depicting their struggles to become creative artists", this describes the state of the art in the USA 30 years
ago.[10] This opening already points to the concept of a complementary study, enlarging Beebe's field of research in her sample of narratives by not only devoting her investigation to novels by women
authors, but in spite of the book's subtitle simultaneously extending

it to the portrayals not only of women writers, but occasionally visual and musical artists, too.[11] In her introduction she specifies important distinctions – in opposition to its male counterpart – of the female *Künstlerroman*, which for her is not necessarily autobiographical.

The first of these differences is the gendered nature of the protagonists, which reveals itself as criss-crossing biological sex. While the male artist hero, according to Huf, displays features like sensitivity, shyness, passivity and even physical weakness – characteristics traditionally referred to as feminine – the female artist in American fiction appears as fearless, spirited and strong, thus illustrating long-established connotations associated with masculinity. Secondly, the central conflict, which for the male artist in fiction is the division of his persona between art and life, shifts for women to a self divided between her role as woman and her aspirations as artist. To this is added the exacerbating conflict between altruism and selfishness, because the wish for achievement and self-fulfilment generally deserves no other name.[12] Thirdly, to the woman artist is habitually added another, opposed female character, usually as a rival, who represents the Total Woman and provides a – sometimes satirical – foil.[13] Additionally, there exists no male muse that would correspond to the function of the female muse for a male artist. A man is presented rather as a despot or dictator.[14] Lastly, the female artist novel and its heroines are radical, directed against a patriarchal society. Therefore the reproach of 'selfishness' against the creative woman is one of the most frequent motifs.

It is obvious that the degree of difference claimed in this list between the male and the female *Künstlerroman* varies considerably and some of the statements would arouse controversial discussions in the light of more recent literary and critical developments.[15] Similarly, the imagery that Huf explores and ascribes as typical to the female narrative is often shared by both the male and the female artist novel: metaphors of flying or of hiding, of solipsistic isolation, separation and rupture. Only the observation that women monsters frequently occur in the female artist novel, thus pointing to the strangeness, even monstrosity of creative women, is peculiar to Huf's objects of research. At the end of her investigations she declares, following Virginia Woolf, Anaïs Nin as well as Sandra Gilbert and Susan Gubar's *The Madwoman in the Attic* (1979), that both the Angel in the House and the Monstrous Woman are 'killed' by those authors and their main characters who came to the fore in the feminist movement of the seventies.[16]

The results of her exploration of authors from Fanny Fern's *Ruth Hall* (1854) to Sylvia Plath's *Bell Jar* (1963), covering more than a century of writing the woman artist, are briefly stated in Huf's final chapter. The female artist eventually dares to "fly" and to "escape", albeit still threatened by possible failure – the fate of Icarus, often interpreted as punishment for hubris and high spirits.[17] Inspired and encouraged by Betty Friedan's sociopolitical analysis of American culture and her followers the woman artist is able to free herself from the "feminine mystique", especially from husband and home, thus offending the age-old unselfishness-command, but her future is still unsure.[18] If this seems a fragile state, the possibility of evolution of the female artist heroine has to be regarded with more optimism than the static condition observed in the male artist figure which shows no development.[19]

In regard to the gaps in criticism still present at the end of the first decade of the 21st century the most obvious consists of an investigation of postmodern British fiction and the question how the respective authors write the woman artist.[20] It was foreseeable that, once the postmodernist narrative had established itself, several boundaries would be extended, transgressed or blurred in the process. One very important borderline is gender, another ethnicity, and, last but not least, art itself. It is evident that – compared to Beebe's study – Huf's represents a brave, yet limited extension of the field of academic research to white female American novelists and their corresponding protagonists, who in some instances dedicate themselves to painting or making music instead of writing. Creative women with aspirations in the performing arts or male-dominated domains like composing music as central characters as well as 'anti-heroic' women artists in fictional biographies still offer a challenge to literary scholarship. Finally, novels dealing with female artists written by men constitute a field late discovered by criticism,[21] while narratives calling into question conventional images of masculinity and femininity, marginally hinted at by Huf, have meanwhile moved to the centre of research in literary and cultural studies. It is, however, perhaps not surprising that the nineteenth century and Victorianism have attracted significantly more critical attention since the seventies than any other period of British and American female artist fiction.[22]

A few years after the publication of Isabell Klaiber's monograph *Gender und Genie* (2004), which extensively deals with theories of gender and the ideological as well as cultural developments in nineteenth-century America, the recent collection of critical essays, *Gender and Creation* (2010) edited by Anne-Julia Zwierlein, follows the connection of gender, creation and authorship from the Middle Ages to the present.[23] In her introduction Zwierlein highlights the long tradition of "cross-gender narration".[24] She, however, implies that contemporary novels written by male authors about female artists as focalisers have been little acknowledged.[25]

Regarding the choice of illustrative narratives, Mary Eagleton's book *Figuring the Woman Author in Contemporary Fiction* (2005), which investigates female artists in literary texts published between 1973 and 2000 by contemporary American, British and postcolonial writers, for example, Margaret Atwood, J.M. Coetzee, Anita Brookner, David Lodge, A.S. Byatt and Fay Weldon, favours a strategy that is even more comprehensive than the one applied in this volume.[26] Visibly the barrier of gender has been ruptured: "[t]o insist on a special place for the woman author is essentialist, anachronistic and ties her to victimhood".[27] Eagleton initially states that there is a renewed interest in the female *Künstlerroman*, yet the figure of the fictional woman author may not be synonymous with woman artist, as her sample of novels and short stories also betrays. Consequently, the topic of the artist in fiction requires a broadened concept here, for women in times of feminism and a revised canon have also emerged as authors of writings as diverse as critical academic works, journalism, and romances; they may create quilts and fabrics or become the generators of oral narratives. Starting from the feminist criticism which celebrated the 'rebirth' of women authors simultaneously with the English translation of Roland Barthes's "Death of the Author" (1977), Eagleton claims that the female 'author' in the sense of originator has ceased to be victim to a heteronomous view of culture and gained authority. In seven chapters she groups the fictional characters around different relevant aspects or kinds of female authorship.

2. Contexts and Texts

While Maurice Beebe installs the white, male, upper- or middle-class writer as supposedly natural ideal and whereas Linda Huf conflates the gender of the author with her artist figures (and implicitly operates with an essentialised notion of a universal *écriture feminine*), the present volume assumes a broader perspective. Following Isabell Klaiber's and Anne-Julia Zwierlein's approach,[28] it understands gender as textual positionality, not necessarily autobiographical, not tied to the gender of the author or narrator, constantly exploring the dialectics of male and female, instead of assuming a natural opposition. Although the contributions focus on female artist figures, in most of the novels the spectre of Maurice Beebe's genial male artist still hovers over the plots, sometimes as Other, sometimes as complement. Constance Fenimore Woolson is clearly overshadowed by the 'master' Henry James in David Lodge's *Author, Author* (2004) and Colm Tóibín's *The Master* (2004); in Emma Tennant's *The Ballad of Sylvia and Ted* (2001) Plath plays Philomela to Ted Hughes's Tereus; in A.S. Byatt's *The Shadow of the Sun* (1964) Henry Severell succeeds as artist, while his daughter lacks the necessary visions. Occasionally, as in Jeanette Winterson's novels, the female artist claims the position of a Blakean poet/ prophet, fashioning herself as Beebean artist hero.

Most of the times, the ideals of male artistry implicitly serve as ridiculed, oppressive or threatening Other. Quite a few novels depict the female artists in their struggles against a patriarchal system and thereby reflect the discourses of second-wave feminism. Both painter Elaine Risley in Margaret Atwood's *Cat's Eye* (1988) and novelist Morag Gunn in Margaret Laurence's *The Diviners* (1974) emancipate themselves from their artist lovers. The personal also reflects the (socio)political and the artist becomes an integral, often central part of the Women's Liberation Movement of the sixties and seventies. The creative process serves to deal with trauma and restrictions. By rewriting or remembering, the women reinvent themselves, "telling li(v)es",[29] and creating "out of chaos, a new kind of strength", as Anna Wulf puts it in Doris Lessing's *The Golden Notebook* (1962).[30] Not seldom, the creative process is concomitant with ambivalent explorations of motherhood. On the one hand, pregnancy and childbirth reflect Hélène Cixous's ideal of *écriture feminine* written with "mother's milk",[31] an analogy taken up and developed further by Laurence's *Diviners* and especially by Bernard MacLaverty's *Grace Notes* (1997); on the other hand, they often endanger the artist's autonomy. Henry Perowne, for instance, worries about his pregnant daughter and her career at the end of Ian McEwan's *Saturday* (2005) and asks himself: "[w]hat's to become of Daisy Perowne, the poet?"[32]

Not all novels follow the trajectory of liberation through art. Penelope Lively's *Next to Nature, Art* (1982) satirises the female artist Paula as sham, who hides her egotism behind a liberated, feminist façade, and in Anita Brookner's *Hotel du Lac* (1984) the protagonist, romance author Edith Hope, is very far from both agency and independence despite her material safety and her profession as successful writer. She might cultivate her physical resemblance to Virginia Woolf, but *Hotel du Lac* exposes this as self-delusion when one of the guests realises that Hope really looks like "Princess Anne".[33] Virginia Woolf not only figures as patron saint of female writers in *Hotel du Lac* and more explicitly in *The Hours*, many artist novels appropriate her ideas about the nexus between "a room of one's own" and creativity as well as the androgyny of an ideal writer's mind. Artist figures like Lily Briscoe in *To the Lighthouse* (1927) or the shapeshifting, ventriloquising and sex-changing title character of *Orlando* (1928) provide models especially for postmodernist artist figures. As a bright young thing, Briony Tallis writes in the modernist style of Woolf, and McEwan's *Atonement* (2001) uses the intertextual references to also recreate the culture of the twenties and thirties. Many of Jeanette Winterson's protagonists transfer the bravado and zest of *Orlando* to present times.

It is also after the eighties that writers like Jeanette Winterson, Ian McEwan or Peter Ackroyd tend to forego the (strategic) essentialism associating women with a natural predilection for everything good, nurturing and pacifying, and enter the 'wilderness' of postmodernity. Influenced by or at least coeval with the theories of Judith Butler on gender as performance, "women writers turn self-consciously and deliberately to the parodic and the fantastic, to masquerade and monstrosity".[34] Their postmodern experiments attempt a queering of the artist figures, denying their narrators a stable gender as in Winterson's *Written on the Body* (1992) or, like Peter Ackroyd's *Dan Leno and the Limehouse Golem* (1994) as well as Sarah Waters's *Tipping the Velvet* (1999) depicting nineteenth-century music-hall culture as subversive world of male and female cross-dressing.

The wide spectrum of female artist figures, sociopolitical backgrounds and meanings produced by the texts concurs with the variety of formal approaches from the rather 'straight' realism of Lively and Brookner, Byatt's, Atwood's and McEwan's historiographic metafictions, the intertextual adaptations of Tennant and Zadie Smith to the experimental textual layers of Lessing or Winterson. The postmodern forms, the breaking up of chronology, the intertwining of discourses, texts and genres, do not serve as reliable indicators of female agency or the undermining of patriarchal structures. The romance form might stand for escapism and cheap titillation in *Hotel du Lac*, but in Byatt's *Possession* (1990), Atwood's *The Blind Assassin* (2000) or Winterson's *Sexing the Cherry* (1989) the generic norms of the romance become an integral part of the texts' *jouissance*. And although the patterns of the *Bildungs-* or *Künstlerroman* conventionally subscribe to the prevalence of male artistry, they are flexible enough to also depict women who intend to "forge in the smithy of my soul the uncreated conscience of my race",[35] as Stephen Dedalus so famously puts it in *Portrait of the Artist*.

As with Stephen Dedalus, who has to come to grips with questions of national identity, religion, and history, in the novels gender, class, ethnicity, national and regional identities intersect. The female artists represented in the novels are more than only female. Thus, MacLaverty's *Grace Notes* intertwines Catherine McKenna's career as composer with reflections on her identity as Northern Irish Catholic. Bernardine Evaristo's *Lara* (1997; 2009) explores the heavily hyphenated, hybrid identity of its protagonist, vying between paternal Nigerian-Brazilian and maternal Irish roots. Anna Wulf in *The Golden Notebook* comes to terms with her colonial past, while Atwood's and Laurence's texts probe into the Canadian past from a postcolonial perspective.

The articles in the present volume try to do justice to the complexity and variety of artist figures, shedding light on the structural intricacies and the cultural contexts as well as pointing out the sociopolitical potential of the novels. The essays are arranged in a loosely chronological order. Thus, trends become discernible (especially in the articles covering the complete or almost complete oeuvre of a single writer). But more often than not, it will transpire that lines of development are constructs, won from distinguishing between the typical and atypical, the canonical and the marginal (or rather, marginalised). Realism and postmodern experiments, feminism and conservatism appear as integral parts of a literature by and about women artists shaped by variety and polyphony.

The volume starts with Doris Lessing's *The Golden Notebook*, a classic, which signals both the beginning of the second wave of feminism and postmodern narratives. Ingrid von Rosenberg traces the development of protagonist Anna Wulf and how her assumption of a distinct stance as female writer merges with her textual experiments. The complex layers of the different notebooks are shown to allow a combination of political commitment, writing about the "overwhelming problems of war, famine and poverty",[36] coming to terms with psychic chaos and the need to liberate oneself from the restrictions of a capitalist, colonialist and patriarchal system. Anna can only overcome her writer's block once she stops compartmentalising and embraces chaos and uncertainties.

The themes of finding liberation through a blurring of boundaries between personal and political, art and life, past and present as well as male and female combined with the personal search for a role of one's own as artist also underlies many of the novels from the seventies and eighties. The articles by Alexa Keuneke, Christiane Bimberg and Brigitte Glaser analyse artist figures in Canadian literature. The novels of Margaret Laurence and Margaret Atwood are shown to merge the personal and political, as in the often explicitly historiographic metafiction the emergence of a national Canadian identity runs parallel to an understanding of the female identity of the artist figure. Keuneke's essay traces how Morag Gunn, the protagonist of Laurence's *The Diviners*, constructs her past self and the past of her ancestors through writing. By means of the creative process she retrospectively makes sense of her life and manages to find an identity of her own by means of her autobiography. Christiane Bimberg's analysis of Margaret Atwood's *Cat's Eye* points towards similar strategies and effects. It demonstrates how painter Elaine Risley uses the Retrospective of her paintings for a retrospective assessment of her life. Working through her childhood traumas not only helps her to forge her own identity, but, similar to Anna Wulf, to make sense of chaos. Brigitte Glaser's article on Atwood's *Alias Grace* (1996) and *The Blind Assassin* illustrates how the narrative and thematic patterns of the seventies and eighties evolved. The postcolonial elements in an artist's identity, hinted at in Morag Gunn's Scottish and in her lover's and her daughter's Métis heritage, are foregrounded in the historical setting of *Alias Grace* and the merging of autobiography, romance and science fiction in *The Blind Assassin*. The postmodern play with historiography, textuality and identity highlights fluidity and multiplicity. Thereby the artist figures Grace Marks and Iris Chase-Griffen undermine male authority and Atwood undercuts the dominant historiographic discourses.

Similar strategies, topics and trends can be discerned in the British novels by Jeanette Winterson or Peter Ackroyd. Marion Gymnich and Uwe Klawitter's essays, however, indicate that this was not the only way of presenting female artists. Gymnich's contribution focuses on Penelope Lively's *Next to Nature, Art* and its depiction of a Creative Study Centre peopled by pseudo-artists whose relaxed hippy pose contrasts sharply with their egotism and greed. The self-confident and charismatic, but talent-free and shallow sculptor Paula is compared to painter Lily Briscoe from Virginia Woolf's *To the Lighthouse*, and found wanting. Klawitter's essay analyses Anita Brookner's *Look at Me* (1983) and *Hotel du Lac*. Both artist figures, the writers Frances Hinton and Edith Hope, prove to be trapped by the expectations of the literary market and the traditional gender system. Hope produces popular romances; Hinton tries to turn her experiences into a comic novel. Unlike Lessing's Anna Wulf, they use their art not as means of self-expression, but try to compensate their empty lives by writing and getting public approval by male critics, a strategy, Klawitter points out, which stifles their creativity and feeds into a repressive gender ideology.

The contributions by Lena Steveker, Peter Childs and Susana Onega trace the development of one writer and his or her female artist figures over a longer period of time. Steveker's article focuses on solitude as essential factor for finding an artistic vision in A.S. Byatt's oeuvre from *The Shadow of the Sun* to *The Children's Book* (2009). Paradoxically, artists like Christabel LaMotte in *Possession*, Julia Corbett in *The Game* (1967) or Olive Wellwood in *The Children's Book* meet with the restrictions of a patriarchal society; at the same time, they often forego solitude themselves in favour of personal fulfilment. As in Brookner's novels, Byatt's texts seldom present successful female artists and emphasise the conflict between the wish for autonomy and the search for valid relationships with others. Childs's contribution highlights the changes in McEwan's representations of female characters. In the eighties they appropriate femininity as symbol of peacefulness and harmony. In *Atonement* and *Saturday*, however, this positive stereotyping (which Childs's analysis critically exposes as "womb envy"), gives way to more ambivalent and balanced portrayals. Especially Briony Tallis in *Atonement* serves to explore the connections between literary tradition, imagination and moral responsibility. Jeanette Winterson's novels, Onega's essay points out, use a different strategy. They self-confidently assume the position of Blake's poet/prophet, deconstructing patriarchy by leaving the strictures of realism and developing plural narratorial voices, moving from the lesbian protagonist in *Oranges are not the Only Fruit* (1985) to the refracted, complementary and shifting textual positions in *Art & Lies* (1994), *The.PowerBook* (2000) and *Lighthousekeeping* (2004). As in Atwood's and Laurence's texts, the artist creates herself through art, associating this transformative power with sexual dissidence and Virginia Woolf's ideal of androgyny.

Varying degrees of ventriloquism also stand in the centre of Jean-Michel Ganteau's and Silvia Mergenthal's articles. Both deal with "narratorial transvestism", to quote Mergenthal, i.e. they feature female artist figures in novels by male authors. Ackroyd's *Dan Leno and the Limehouse Golem* and MacLaverty's *Grace Notes* both first came out in the nineties, probably not coincidentally after the publication of Judith Butler's seminal *Gender Trouble* (1990). Ganteau's reading of *Dan Leno and the Limehouse Golem* indicates how Elizabeth Cree's career as music-hall artist, dramatist, diarist and murderer serves as instance of a nomadic identity and a performance of the "artist as disappearing act", as he puts it. Cross-dressing not only permeates Ackroyd's texts and appears centre stage in *Limehouse Golem*, it also indicates a subversion of Victorian gender norms and exemplifies Butler's notion of the constructedness and performativity of both sex and gender. Although MacLaverty's *Grace Notes* tells a more conventional story about composer Catherine McKenna's artistic emancipation reminiscent of the texts by Lessing, Laurence and Atwood, it also deconstructs binaries. Silvia Mergenthal's essay analyses how the a-chronological structure of the narrative ties in with the intermediality of music and literature on the meta-level and McKenna's compositional technique on the micro-level of the novel. In-betweenness undermines not only the opposition between male and female, it also destabilises the contrasts between East and West, public and private, Catholic and Protestant, Irish and English. Christian Schmitt-Kilb's article likewise focuses on the nexus of gender and hybridity. The comparison of the two versions of Bernardine Evaristo's *Lara* detects the importance of the matrilinear reconstruction of the protagonist's Irish identity. In addition, by comparing *Lara* to Woolf's *To the Lighthouse*, the analysis highlights the strong indebtedness to modernist models and thereby provides a complement to the usually postcolonial readings of Evaristo's work.

The last decade seems to have called a truce on sophisticated narration and experimental constructions of gender. Novels by McEwan or Lodge return to what some critics have interpreted as conservative "white backlash".[37] Without directly dealing with the political ramifications of this development, the articles by Anette Pankratz, Barbara Puschmann-Nalenz and Renate Brosch corroborate this trend. Pankratz's essay follows the development of the opposition between artists and academia. The analyses of the female artist as teacher of creative writing in Lodge's *Thinks...* (2001) and Smith's *On Beauty* (2005) find a return to the idea of genial creation as proposed by Beebe and liberal-humanist concepts such as truth, beauty or reality. Both Puschmann-Nalenz's and Brosch's contributions deal with biofictional texts, which likewise indicate a rediscovery of some kind of historical reality. Emma Tennant's *The Ballad of Sylvia and Ted*, however, refracts the biographical narrative with the myth of Tereus, Procne and Philomela as well as with the fairy tale of Little Red Riding Hood. Thus, Puschmann-Nalenz's reading shows, the narration manages to transcend boundaries, while the female artist figure Plath is depicted as confined by her personal situation and the patriarchal society of the fifties and sixties. Renate Brosch's essay on Colm Tóibín's *The Master* and Lodge's *Author, Author* brings the volume full circle: back to Beebe's hero artist. The female artist figure Constance Fenimore Woolson stands in the shadow of the 'master' Henry James. This, and the retrospective sexualisation of the relationship between Woolson and James, Brosch's contextualisation of nineteenth-century culture indicates, stems less from the meticulous reconstruction of facts, but from especially Tóibín's effort to represent and evaluate James's life from a contemporary perspective.

The essays collected in this volume cover a broad range of novels written after 1945, including most of the central male and female writers of the period. Due to the great proliferation of recent female artist figures, however, we did not even attempt completeness and the discerning reader will discover a certain predilection for the literary mainstream. Popular genres such as detective novels or chick lit are sadly missing.[38] So are forms of popular art: the female artists discussed are poets, novelists, composers, painters, sculptors and performers; the readers will find no pop stars like Vina, the protagonist in Salman Rushdie's *The Ground Beneath Her Feet* (1999), no punks, movie actors or comedians. With this decision to focus on Art and Culture (with firm capitals), we deliberately avoided asking the tricky question of "what is art?", which would justify more than a volume of its own, and we hope the readers will excuse this slightly myopic view considering the multiplicity of themes, genres and approaches offered nevertheless.

Finally, we would like to thank the contributors for their enthusiasm, erudition, reliability and cooperation; the general editors of a&e for their support. Last but not least, in a volume which often refers to female solidarity across cultures and generations, it is only fitting to evade the pose of the Editors as Heroes: many thanks to Anna Billmann and Nina Fremder for their proof-reading skills, computer wizardry, their sense of humour and their forbearance.

Notes

1 Beebe (1964: 5).
2 Stewart (1981); Huf (1983).
3 Beebe (1964: 21).
4 *Ibid.*, 23. Herbert Marcuse writes about the conditions of the origin of the *Künstlerroman* that "[it] is only possible when the union of life and art has been torn, the artist no longer merges in the life forms of his environment and awakens to self-consciousness" (1978: 12; trans. Barbara Puschmann-Nalenz).
5 Beebe (1964: 65).
6 *Ibid.*, 114.
7 *Ibid.*, 260.
8 *Ibid.*, 312.
9 *Ibid.*, 175.
10 Huf (1983: 1).

11 *Ibid.*

12 *Ibid.*, 5-6; 150.

13 *Ibid.*, 7-8.

14 *Ibid.*, 9-10.

15 See, e.g., Klaiber's critical assessment (2004: 15).

16 Huf (1983: 157).

17 *Ibid.*, 148; 149; 156.

18 *Ibid.*, 156-157. The proverb "wedlock is padlock", which Huf quotes as an experience made by female artists (*ibid.*, 159), seems at this point to be a retrograde step in argument considering that John Stuart Mill in *The Subjection of Women* (1869) makes a far more general acute statement, which releases especially husbands from the cumulative guilt of a "Bluebeard", about the conflict between gender and art in women when he writes that their creativity is handicapped since "they must always be at the beck and call of somebody, generally of everybody" (quoted in *ibid.*, 150).

19 *Ibid.*, 159.

20 Contributions on the writings of Virginia Woolf appeared in the knowledgeable comparative study edited by Jones (1991), in Jack Stewart (2009) and in White (2005). Grace Stewart's work additionally includes chapters on Dorothy Richardson and Doris Lessing; the latter is also taken account of in Lemon (1985), while Susan Gubar champions the birth of the artist in Katherine Mansfield's fiction (1983). In spite of these examples from Modernism it is striking that especially in connection with gender studies the preference for American fiction continues, as in Klaiber (2004) and Barker (2000). Very rarely do the studies give attention to post-seventies narratives on the subject by British authors. Several recent books about the *Künstlerroman* either again ignore novels on the female artist, e.g., Zima (2008); Seret (1992), or contemporary British fiction, e.g., Varsamopoulou (2002).

21 Klaiber (2004) superbly fulfils the requirements of applying the contemporaneous gender discourse as well as recent theoretical concepts of gender, gender transgression, gender crossing and performativity in fiction, but her cultural analysis and sample of narratives are restricted to nineteenth-century America.

22 See Klaiber (2004); Varsamopoulou (2002); Gilbert & Gubar (1979).

23 Zwierlein (2010).

24 *Ibid.*, 14.

25 Zwierlein explicitly points to the opposite: *Orlando* (1928) by Virginia Woolf or several of Jeanette Winterson's novels provide rare examples of male artists as internal focalisers in women's writing (*ibid.*).

26 Eagleton (2005).

27 *Ibid.*, 3.

28 See Klaiber (2004); Zwierlein (2010).

29 As the title of Brigitte Glaser's article in the present volume puts it.

30 Lessing (1973: 454).

31 Cixous (1991: 49). See also Susana Onega's contribution in the present volume.
32 McEwan (2005: 241).
33 Brookner (1993: 63).
34 Waugh (2006: 192).
35 Joyce (2000: 275-276).
36 Lessing (1973: 12).
37 See, e.g., Ribbat (2005: 19-20); Eckstein (2011).
38 Unfortunately, neither Agatha Christie's Ariadne Oliver nor Dorothy Sayer's Harriet Vane make an appearance, nor does an article take up the challenge suggested by Waugh (2006) and tackle Bridget Jones as writer of her own life.

Bibliography

Barker, Deborah: *Aesthetics and Gender in American Literature. Portraits of the Woman Artist*, Lewisburg, 2000.

Beebe, Maurice: *Ivory Towers and Sacred Founts. The Artist as Hero in Fiction from Goethe to Joyce*, New York, 1964.

Brookner, Anita: *Hotel du Lac*, London, 1993 [1984].

Cixous, Hélène: *"Coming to Writing" and Other Essays*. Trans. Deborah Jenson et al., Cambridge, 1991.

Eagleton, Mary: *Figuring the Woman Author in Contemporary Fiction*, London, 2005.

Eckstein, Lars: "Saturday on Dover Beach. Ian McEwan, Matthew Arnold, and Post-9/11 Melancholia", *Hard Times* 89, 2011, 6-10.

Gilbert, Sandra M. & Susan Gubar: *The Madwoman in the Attic. The Woman Writer and the Nineteenth-Century Literary Imagination*, New Haven, 1979.

Gubar, Susan: "The Birth of the Artist as Heroine. (Re)production, the *Künstlerroman* Tradition, and the Fiction of Katherine Mansfield". – In Carolyn Heilbrun et al. (Eds.): *The Representation of Women in Fiction*, Baltimore, 1983, pp. 19-59.

Huf, Linda: *A Portrait of the Artist as a Young Woman. The Writer as Heroine in American Fiction*, New York, 1983.

Jones, Suzanne W. (Ed.): *Writing the Woman Artist. Essays on Poetics, Politics, and Portraiture*, Philadelphia, 1991.

Joyce, James: *A Portrait of the Artist as a Young Man*, London, 2000 [1916].

Klaiber, Isabell: *Gender und Genie. Künstlerkonzeptionen in der amerikanischen Erzählliteratur des 19. Jahrhunderts*, Trier, 2004.

Lemon, Lee T.: *Portraits of the Artist in Contemporary Fiction*, Lincoln et al., 1985.

Lessing Doris: *The Golden Notebook*, St Albans, 1973 [1962].

Marcuse, Herbert: "Einleitung. *Der deutsche Künstlerroman*". – In H.M.: *Schriften, Volume I*, Frankfurt, 1978 [1922], pp. 9-19.

McEwan, Ian: *Saturday*, London, 2005.

Ribbat, Christoph: "The Windshield and the Rear-View Mirror. An Introduction to Twenty-First Century Writers, Books and Readers". – In C.R. (Ed.): *Twenty-First Century Fiction. Readings, Essays, Conversations*, Heidelberg, 2005, pp. 7-32.

Seret, Roberta: *Voyage into Creativity. The Modern* Künstlerroman, New York, 1992.

Stewart, Grace: *A New Mythos. The Novel of the Artist as Heroine, 1877-1977*, Montreal, 1981.

Stewart, Jack: *Color, Space and Creativity. Art and Ontology in Five British Writers*, Madison, 2009.

Varsamopoulou, Evy: *The Poetics of the* Künstlerinroman *and the Aesthetics of the Sublime*, Aldershot, 2002.

Waugh, Patricia: "The Woman Writer and the Continuities of Feminism". – In James F. English (Ed.): *A Concise Companion to Contemporary British Fiction*, Oxford et al., 2006, pp. 188-208.

White, Roberta: *A Studio of One's Own. Fictional Women Painters and the Art of Fiction*, Madison, 2005.

Zima, Peter: *Der europäische Künstlerroman. Von der romantischen Utopie zur postmodernen Parodie*, Tübingen, 2008.

Zwierlein, Anne Julia: "Introduction. Gender and Creation. Surveying Gendered Myths of Creativity, Authority, and Authorship". – In A.-J.Z. (Ed.): *Gender and Creation. Surveying Gendered Myths of Creativity, Authority, and Authorship*, Heidelberg, 2010, pp. 11-23.

Ingrid von Rosenberg (Berlin/Dresden)

"And Out of Chaos, a New Kind of Strength". The (Re)Birth of a (Still) Young "Authoress" in Doris Lessing's *Golden Notebook*

1. In Place of an Introduction: Doris Lessing's Portrait of Herself as a Young Artist

In comparison to other influential contemporary British writers Doris Lessing had an exceptional youth. Born in 1919 in Persia, she grew up in South-East Africa in the British colony then called Rhodesia, now Zimbabwe. Coming home from World War I, her father, despairing of a promising future in Britain, had followed the tempting call of the colonial administration spread at the Empire Exhibition of 1924 to make one's fortune by farming in the colonies. Alfred Taylor did not make a fortune, instead had to struggle with poverty and poor health all his life, while his wife became increasingly disappointed in her hopes for a comfortable, elegantly social life. But their daughter and her brother loved the free life in the hardly civilised wilderness of the *veld*. Doris opted out of school at fourteen, worked as a nursemaid and telephone operator, became a convinced Marxist and member of a communist group while producing her first literary texts, most of them never published. She married at nineteen and had two babies in quick succession, but left her family to have more freedom for her political and literary work. She married again soon, the German Gottfried Lessing, and had another baby boy with whom she moved to England after her second divorce in 1949.

All this and many more details the reader can learn from Lessing herself as she has written extensively about her younger years. Apart from smaller pieces, references in numerous interviews and the fact that all her early novels and stories are based on her own experiences and observations, she published two volumes of autobiography: *Under My Skin* (1994), covering the first 30 years of her life spent in Africa, and *Walking in the Shade* (1998), dealing with the period from 1949 to 1962, the beginning of her life in Britain as a professional author. Lately she has written a novel, *Alfred and Emily* (2008), dealing with two versions of her parents' lives, a virtual one and one based on reality. In all these texts Lessing registers her early literary work. For instance in *Under My Skin* she prints a poem she wrote at fourteen, mentions the sale of two stories to small South African magazines at fifteen and the writing of her first (unpublished) novel at seventeen.[1] These texts she later tore up in "transports of embarrassment" (Lessing 1995: 191), ashamed that she had tried to write "to suit the market" (181). But all this is only very briefly mentioned. Nowhere does Lessing go into an analysis of her impulse to write, or describe in detail the development of her literary skills. What she mentions are early literary stimuli: her mother's talent for storytelling, which the daughter apparently inherited, and her own avid appetite for reading which was satisfied by an impressive amount of literature ordered from England, for example the nineteenth-century Russian and French writers, Proust, some Americans, Sterne, Hardy, Meredith, Defoe, Austen, the Brontës, Woolf and Lawrence.[2] In her portrait of herself as a young woman artist Lessing is very discreet. Talking about her reasons for writing her autobiography at all she does not even mention her identity as a writer, but gives a historical-political motivation:

> [o]ne reason for writing this autobiography is that more and more I realize I was part of an extraordinary time, the end of the British Empire in Africa, and the bit I was involved with was the occupation of a country that lasted exactly ninety years. (Lessing 2008: 160)

Given her reluctance to publicly discuss the impulses behind her own writing, it does not seem surprising that only one of her texts focuses on an artist as the central figure: *The Golden Notebook* (1962). Yet in this novel, valued by most critics as her greatest achievement, Lessing deals at length with the growth of a female writer and the issue of female aesthetics in a particular time, the mid-twentieth century. It has remained her only metafictional work.

2. The Golden Notebook: a Künstlerroman of a Special Kind

In the famous "Preface" to *The Golden Notebook*, which Lessing only published in 1971, she pours scorn on the all-too-popular figure of the artist as presented by "every major writer" and "most minor ones": "this monstrously isolated, monstrously narcissistic, pedestalled paragon", "a creator with all excesses of sensibility and suffering and towering egotism".[3] Lessing's own protagonist Anna Wulf – the name, of course, is an homage to Virginia Woolf, although Lessing has never explicitly discussed any of Woolf's works in her criticism and very rarely even alluded to Woolf in her own work – was to be very different, a counter-figure so to speak, although she is equipped with no less sensitivity.[4] First of all, Anna is a woman, a rare figure among the artist heroes.[5] Secondly – and this may be characteristic of a feminine attitude to artistic work, indeed to any kind of work – she, in contrast to the male prototypical artist heroes described by Maurice Beebe, is not detached from life and the world, but involved with both in many ways.[6] Being a writer is only part of Anna's identity, her roles as a lover (of several men in sequence), as a mother, committed friend, working woman (Anna works in a communist publishing house, though without pay) and as a politically active person (as a member and later as a critic of the British Communist Party) are equally important to her. Moreover, Anna does not see all these other commitments as opposed to her artistic existence, but as the very stuff she draws on in her work. Thirdly, Anna is not presented as a gradually and smoothly unfolding talent, but – and Lessing in the "Preface" stresses the importance of the fact (Lessing 1973: 12) – is a writer with a block. In contrast to the majority of artist's novels *The Golden Notebook* is not a novel of adolescence, but the story of a woman writer of 40 at a crucial point in her development. One could perhaps say it is a novel of maturing as an artist, which is a stormy, painful and long-drawn process.

3. Anna's Block

When the reader first meets Anna Wulf, it is in the framing novel *Free Women*, which, as becomes apparent only at the very end of the text, has been written by Anna herself. The location is London, the time is the summer of 1957, and Anna is 40 years old. She has already published one novel, *Frontiers of War*, which was very successful, so that she can now live on the sales. In fact, Anna has achieved everything that Virginia Woolf in her famous essay *A Room of One's Own* (1929) had demanded for a woman writer: money and a room of her own. Anna's bestseller is based on her experiences as a young woman in Africa at the beginning of World War II. Surprisingly, however, Anna is not at all proud of her early work, though her lovers envy her the success. Her great love Michael, partner for five years, makes cracks "about the fact that I have written a book – he resents it, makes fun of my being 'an authoress'" (239). Even Saul Green, also a writer and closest to her in spirit, who later helps her to overcome her block, confesses: "[t]he truth is, I resent you for having written a book which was a success" (583). Anna herself feels uncomfortable about the mood she instilled into her first book: "the emotion it came out of was something frightening, the unhealthy, feverish, illicit excitement of wartime, a lying nostalgia, a longing for licence, for freedom, for the jungle, for formlessness" (82).[7] Anna recalls her feelings when she suddenly felt the impulse to write: "I remember very clearly the moment in which the novel was born. The pulse beat, violently; afterwards, when I knew I would write, I worked out what I would write" (81). It sounds more like an intoxication than an inspiration. From the distance of many years she asks herself why she did not simply report what actually happened, but fictionalised it, made a story out of it "which had nothing to do with the material that fuelled it" (*ibid.*). What the plot of the novel actually consists of the reader never gets to know, as she/he is only offered the parodistic version Anna writes "tongue-in-cheek" as a synopsis for a film with the schmaltzy title *Forbidden Love* (76). From the complex human relationships in wartime Southern Rhodesia later described in the Black Notebook Anna apparently distilled a melodramatic love story across the so-called colour bar, the rough outline of which runs as follows: a young English bomber pilot awaiting his call up to action in Africa falls deeply in love with a married black woman, the wife of a hotel cook. Given the political circumstances, the affair is bound to end unhappily. The young soldier has to leave for the front, while his love, thrown out by her husband, takes to the streets.

Apart from Anna's later shame about the spirit of her book, that "lying nostalgia", her dissatisfaction with her first published novel mirrors Lessing's own disillusionment with the traditional realist novel form which she had used in all her fiction prior to *The Golden Notebook* and would use again later. Lessing has a high opinion of the novelist's task: he or she should be able to catch "the intellectual and moral climate" of the time (11). In her essay "A Small Personal Voice" (1957) Lessing praises the realist novels of the nineteenth century, especially the French and Russian ones, as "the highest point of literature" because they fulfil this task and are moreover illuminated by compassion, humanity, love of people and faith in man.[8] Contemporary writers, by contrast, she sees in a predicament because they have to portray "a time which is dangerous, violent, explosive and precarious", but must not lose the vision "of a good which may defeat the evil" (Lessing 1994: 11). Lessing has always strongly held on to the belief that literature "should be committed", however disastrous the reality to portray may be (10). To her, most contemporary novels, however, do not live up to this standard. Many are "small, quite lively, intelligent" or "competent and infor- mative", bordering on journalism, but lack a philosophical dimen- sion (10; 18; Lessing 1973: 80). Her heroine Anna writes: "[o]ne novel in five hundred or a thousand has the quality a novel should have to make it a novel – the quality of philosophy" (Lessing 1973: 79). As to her own endeavours, Anna feels she has failed when facing the enormous task to cope with the "disparity between the overwhelming problems of war, famine and poverty" that haunt the twentieth century and "the tiny individual who was trying to mirror them" (12). She has given up writing because she feels "unable to write the only kind of novel which interests me: a book powered with an intellectual or moral passion strong enough to create order, to create a new way of looking at life" (80).

Does Anna, in the course of *The Golden Notebook*, reach this high aim? Yes, if we accept the assumption of an impressive num- ber of critics, who hold that Anna is not only the author of the fram- ing conventional novel entitled *Free Women*, but also of the whole *Golden Notebook*. The argument is that the first sentence given to Anna by her lover Saul as a start for a new book is both the begin- ning of *Free Women* and the opening sentence to the whole *Golden Notebook*: "[t]he two women were alone in the London flat" (25).[9] That Anna wrote *Free Women* is not in doubt, but it would in fact be rather a meagre result if this slim novel was all that she produced after the long and complex process of her rebirth as a writer. The obvious irony of the events in the last section of *Free Women* – bohemian Molly marries a rich man while Anna herself joins the Labour Party, stops writing and becomes a marriage counsellor, i.e. both women change their personalities from critical, creative spirits to social conformists – makes it even more unlikely that Lessing meant a novel with such a banal ending to be the climax of Anna's artistic development.

4. *The Shape of* The Golden Notebook

The entire *Golden Notebook* on the other hand is a very ambitious and innovative literary undertaking, in which the unusual narrative structure helps to convey the indeed philosophical message. In her "Preface" Lessing complains that her novel had been misunderstood by most readers and reviewers, friendly as well as hostile ones, who saw only the contents, above all a comment on the "sex war", while others mentioned only politics or mental illness (8; 22).[10] What was completely overlooked was the significance of the book's unusual structure, which, Lessing later underlined, had been "carefully planned":[11] "[b]ut my major aim was to shape a novel which would make its own comment, a wordless statement: to talk through the way it was shaped" (14). After Lessing had thus drawn attention to the importance of the novel's "shape", many critics plunged into its close scrutiny.[12] Lessing herself gives a rough outline at the beginning of the "Preface":

> [t]here is a skeleton, a frame, called *Free Women*, which is a conventional short novel, about 60,000 words long, and which could stand by itself. But it is divided into five sections, and separated by stages of the four Notebooks, Black, Red, Yellow, and Blue. [...] from their fragments can come something new, *The Golden Notebook*. (7)

The four notebooks (not diaries, as Anna stresses) form the weighty centre of the book and are all written in the first person. They deal with different aspects of Anna's life from her own intimate perspective. The Black Notebook is divided into two strands: under the heading "The Source" it presents her African memories that went into her first novel, and under the heading "Money" it deals with the book as commodity, i.e. contains reviews, ridiculous suggestions for TV adaptations, and other offers from the media. The Red Notebook tells of Anna's involvement and final disillusionment with the British Communist Party, which she joins out of a "need for wholeness, an end to the split", and her disappointment with the Soviet Union (171). The Yellow Notebook contains completed as well as sketched sections of a further conventional novel, *The Shadow of the Third*, in which parts of Anna's London life are fictionalised: the failure of her greatest love, her motherhood and the separation from her adolescent child, her close friendship with a woman, her work as an editor. Names are changed – Anna herself figures as Ella –, and significant, but easily recognisable changes in circumstances and events are made. Most important: Ella is also a writer, but one who does not suffer from a block. She is involved in composing a novel about a suicide, which she manages to publish in the course of the Yellow Notebook, "a quite good novel, nothing very startling", "a small, honest novel" (217). In this fiction based on autobiography Anna distances herself from her painful experiences and imagines alternative ways of coping. The Blue Notebook, finally, "tries to be a diary" and contains Anna's memories of her psychoanalysis with the Jungian therapist Mrs Marks and her current innermost thoughts and feelings. These four notebooks are gradually given up and followed by only one, in which the carefully separated aspects of Anna's life finally melt into each other as elements of her subconscious: the Golden Notebook. To avoid confusion Lessing herself in the "Preface" distinguishes this last notebook as the "inner Golden Notebook" from the "outer Golden Notebook", which means the whole novel.

The four earlier notebooks do not follow each other as completed texts, but are cut up each in four sections of varying length, which are organised in four chapters following the same order of arrangement. Roberta Rubenstein has convincingly argued that the sequence of the notebooks in each section is not arbitrary, but deliberate: it embodies a movement from "detachment or 'objectivity' toward the increasing immediacy and 'subjectivity' of the Blue Notebook/diary":

[e]ach larger unit of five segments [a section of *Free Women* plus sections from the four notebooks] forms a continuum, moving from exteriorized and shaped reportage of experience (*Free Women*) to the remoteness of recol-

31

lected past experiences or business transactions (Black notebook); to the public but contemporary political experiences (Red notebook), to the private, fictionalized projections of Anna's immediate past emotional life (Yellow notebook); to the current, totally introspective, and unshaped material of the diary (Blue notebook).[13]

Rubenstein also suggests that the figure four (of the notebooks) carries meaning as it refers to the four sides of a square, which in Jungian theory can symbolise the rational intellect.[14] One may add that the square – as well as the cross, a star or an octagon – may also figure as a symbol of totality in Jung's writings, while four is also the number of the ego's psychological functions (thinking, feeling, sensation, intuition), which Anna has to learn to combine rather than to separate. In Lessing's novel the square formed by the notebooks is complemented by the figure of the circle, which in Jungian terms stands for the mythical potentials of the subconscious: the repetition of the same pattern of the four sections may be called cyclical, but, more importantly, a circle is formed by the end of the novel folding back into its beginning. Molly Hite, writing ten years later, perhaps even more aptly compares this shape to a Möbius strip.[15] Thus the interconnection of Anna's rational side and her subconscious are symbolically mirrored by the very organisation of the text. Though the notebooks are held separately by Anna, there are many links and correspondences, repeated mentioning of the same emotional events from different perspectives. Patrocinio P. Schweickart speaks of "hinges" in a sense defined by Jacques Derrida. The novel is cracked, he argues, its parts have a "relative autonomy", but "are held together by folding-joints", are "hinged".[16] Lessing herself puts it like this: "[t]he point of that book was the relation of its parts to each other".[17]

The time pattern corresponds to these flexible links. Three of the notebooks cover the time from 1950 to 1957, while the Black Notebook refers to the distant past of the late thirties and early forties. The narrated time in *Free Women* reaches from summer 1957 into 1958 and partly overlaps with the fictional present in the last section of the Blue Notebook and the inner Golden Notebook. Time in the individual notebooks does not progress strictly chronologically, but Anna's thoughts and memories move freely backwards and forwards within the respective time frames.

Asked by several protagonists, most intensely by Tommy, the son of Anna's intimate friend Molly, why she keeps four notebooks instead of one, Anna replies: "[p]erhaps it would be such – a scramble. Such a mess" (265). When he insists: "[w]hy the four notebooks? What would happen if you had one big book without all those divisions and brackets and special writing", Anna answers: "I've told you, chaos" (272). Apparently Anna, scared, tries to keep the chaos she experiences at bay by means of compartmentalisation, partly through her own sensitivity, partly through the mad events in the world (on the private level the unsatisfactory gender relations, on the public level the failure of socialism, the wars, racism, the invention and testing of the H-bomb are themes which are raised again and again in the novel).[18] But Anna's escape route does not work.

When she realises that she is no longer able to come to terms with both her depressing private concerns and the terrible events in the world, she stops writing in the notebooks and just sticks newspaper cuttings containing more horror news in the Black and the Red Notebooks, before closing them altogether (509; 510). In the Blue Notebook she had done the same for a while in protest to her analyst, but had finally taken up writing again (241-251). Then a miracle happens. As Lessing declares in the "Preface": "[i]n the inner Golden Notebook things have come together, the divisions have broken down, there is formlessness with the end of fragmentation – the triumph of the second theme, which is that of unity" (7). What does that mean in terms of Anna's story?

Beginning in the last section of the Blue Notebook and continued in the inner Golden Notebook, which forms a chapter by itself after the four central sections, Anna describes her drifting into a breakdown, a collapse of her mental faculties to keep control over private and public nightmares. This process is triggered and supported by two events. First, Anna's conventional daughter Janet is leaving home to go to a boarding school, and with her disappears the necessity for Anna to structure her day. Secondly, Anna falls in love with her new lodger Saul Green, an American writer and refugee from McCarthyism. Saul, younger than Anna and in contrast to all her other lovers single, is, as she quickly perceives, a split personality showing signs of madness. Nevertheless, the two develop a deep relationship, marked by quick changes from closeness to distance, from happiness to mistrust and hatred. Above all, they share a very clear-sighted perception of what is going on in each other, they can actually read and enter each other's minds: "I had become part of him", Anna thinks (567). And she marvels: "I thought how odd it was that we two should be together at all, so close we should have become each other" (598). Lessing comments: "[t]hey are crazy, lunatic, mad – what you will. They 'break down' into each other" (7). While Saul keeps leaving the house to sleep with other women, Anna, "woman betrayed" (576), lies in bed or on the floor, writhing in agonies of jealousy, and has a number of (slightly too overtly) symbolic dreams: she becomes other people, an Algerian soldier, a young, pregnant Chinese peasant woman, two African politicians. She dreams of Saul as a tiger, beautiful and wild, but threatened by captivity (592-593). In another dream sequence he appears as a film projectionist who shows her the most important events of her life as film clips. And she dreams for the last time a recurring dream, which used to frighten her as long as she projected the spite expressed in it onto other figures, but now she accepts it as part of her own personality: she dreams of herself and Saul, "her counterpart", as malicious male-female dwarf figures, "the principle of joy-in-destruction", dancing and kissing "in some open place, under enormous white buildings filled with hideous, menacing black machinery which held destruction" (573).

Out of this chaos, unexplained and suddenly, friendliness, peace and harmony emerge which become the basis for both Anna's and Saul's new attempt at creativity. They give each other the first (rather gendered) sentences to a new novel and the confidence to succeed. Anna hands over the newly acquired (literally) golden notebook, which she had meant to keep for herself, to Saul and writes for him: "[o]n a dry hillside in Algeria a soldier watched the moonlight glinting on his rifle" (615). Saul gives Anna the famous first sentence to both *Free Women* and *The Golden Notebook*: "[t]he two women were alone in the London flat" (25).

Thus the "wordless statement" (14), the shape of the novel, supports the message that compartmentalisation and rationalisation did not help Anna. Instead – paradoxically – opening herself to the disorder of her subconscious saved her. Anna had to let all the different strands of her perception flow together in one notebook, expressed in long, often unstructured passages, distantly reminiscent of Molly Bloom's soliloquy in *Ulysses* (1922) (despite very different contents). She even had to melt into other people of both genders, i.e. transcend the borders of her personality; she had to succumb to chaos in order to reach a new form of agency: "sometimes when people 'crack up' it is a way of self-healing, of the inner self's dismissing false dichotomies and divisions", Lessing comments in the "Preface" (8). In Anna and Saul's special case it is also the pre-condition to regaining their creativity: "[a]nd out of chaos, a new kind of strength" (454). The reader may, however, have slight doubts whether Anna's breakthrough to new creativity was really so sudden. That her alter ego Ella, after all Anna's creation, writes and publishes a novel in the Yellow Notebook indicates that Anna has been thinking of writing again for some time.

Through the unusual structuring of her narration – later praised as one of the earliest examples of an English postmodern text –,[19] mirroring the movement from fragmentation to a new holistic view of reality, Lessing expresses a fundamental optimistic belief in the artist's ability to finally come to terms with the chaotic state of both society and the individual, however terrible they may be, an optimism which links her work more to Modernism than to the sometimes playful, sometimes cynical attitude of much postmodern writing. She has remained true to her old conviction that "literature should be committed".[20] On the level of contents this moralistic optimism is expressed in Anna and Saul's determination to stick to their fight for a better and more just world despite their disappointment in communism: "I won't accept that injustice and the cruelty", Anna reads in a dream, words she has written herself (611). They decide to remain "boulder-pushers" up "the great black mountain" of "human stupidity" (604). "We're a team", Saul says in their last meeting, "we're the ones who haven't given in, who'll go on fighting" (617).

If we accept the assumption that it is Anna who writes the whole of the outer *Golden Notebook*, then after much self-doubt and intro-spection she has reached a new, more sophisticated form of writing as an expression of her deeper understanding of the world. She has realised that despite its terrifying state she has "to preserve the forms", "create the patterns" (610). Anna has matured as an artist. Marjorie Worthington has argued that this does not mean that Anna as a person has also achieved coherence, but "Anna emerges as a fragmented subject who can create".[21] Thus, "*The Golden Notebook* represents the victory of form (or at least the attempt at form) over chaos, and the persistence of authorship in the face of contemporary fragmentation".[22]

Recently, Tonya Krouse has suggested a new theory concerning the aesthetics of *The Golden Notebook*. She maintains that Lessing, echoing Virginia Woolf's *A Room of One's Own*, has Anna develop a theory of androgynous aesthetics, effacing her gendered subjectivity and moving away from the traditional female aesthetic of self-expression towards "personal impersonality".[23] One might quote the merging of Anna and Saul, their mutual stimulation to creativity as well as Anna's identification with male figures in her hallucinations as arguments for this thesis (though Krouse does not do so). But the novels Anna and Saul produce after their moments of unity seem gendered in material and form again: Saul writes about male soldiers engaged in the Algerian War, and Anna about human relations in her African past and British present (both removed from actual scenes of war) with a focus on love affairs, and the unpolished, patchwork form of her text stands in sharp contrast to Saul's pointed short novel.[24] So the most one can say is that Lessing is ambivalent – as in several other aspects of the novel, for instance, female sexuality – concerning the new form of writing that Anna arrives at, leaving undecided whether it represents a specifically female or rather an androgynous aesthetic.

The new shape also means a broadening of artistic opportunities in practical terms. As Lessing herself has pointed out, the fragmented form, allowing the extensive exploration of so many facets of Anna's mind and aspects of the political and social state of the world, offers the chance to include much more material than the traditional realist narrative. The conventional novel, with third-person narrator, descriptions, dialogues and orderly chronology, as exemplified by Anna's three – published and drafted – novels *Frontiers of War*, *The Shadow of the Third* and *Free Women*, according to Lessing, inevitably frustrates the author by its limitations: "[h]ow little I have managed to say of the truth, how little I have caught of all that complexity" (14). *The Golden Notebook*, by contrast, achieves much more: "[h]ere it [the text of *The Golden Notebook*] is rougher, more close to experience, before experience has shaped itself into thought and pattern – more valuable perhaps because it is rawer material" (*ibid.*).

Claire Sprague has suggested the existence of a further meaningful structure in the arrangement of the novel: "a complex layer of doubling".[25] The layer, according to her, includes mixed as well as same-sex doubles or doppelganger of Anna. Sprague's interpretation (like Rubenstein's) is based on Lessing's knowledge of Jungian theory. According to Jung the "shadow" or the "double" is one of the four basic archetypal figures which together form the personality of an individual (the other three are animus/anima, persona and self). It consists of suppressed material, i.e. the demonic side and instincts of the individual, but is also the seat of creativity. To dissociate this "dark side", the subject often projects the shadow on other people. The well-known figure of the doppelganger in literature (for example Robert Louis Stevenson's *Dr Jekyll and Mr Hyde*, 1886; Fyodor Dostoevsky's story "The Double. A Petersburg Poem", 1846, and Edgar Allan Poe's story "William Wilson", 1839) are literary versions of the same idea. The problem with Sprague's suggestion is that usually the subject has to cope with only one double. "The second self", Sprague writes correctly, "normally exhibits displaced asocial characteristics that the public or the more compliant self does not acknowledge".[26] According to Sprague, Lessing, however, "develops her conception of the 'free' self with the primary self with wit and originality, in part accepting, in part contradicting, and in the process extending our conceptions of the double figures".[27] "No other writer", Sprague states, "has retained and burst the boundaries of twoness".[28] How convincing is this? Some doublings are obvious, first of all the protagonists in *The Shadow of the Third* (mark the title!) are quite openly Anna's projections, fictionalised versions of 'real' people in Anna's life, though they do not all embody negative characteristics. One might also argue that Molly is to a certain extent a double of Anna. "For a lot of people you and I are practically interchangeable", says Anna to her friend (25). And when Saul gives Anna the famous first sentence, he starts by saying: "[t]here are the two women you are, Anna. Write down: The two women" (615). They are both "free women" in the sense that they earn their own money, live without a permanent partner and bring up a child alone, and they are both politically committed. Yet in other respects they are opposites: Molly, working as an actress, has no creative talent, seems more extroverted, but also mentally more stable than her friend.

The most important and most obvious double is, of course, Saul. Long passages in the inner Golden Notebook express their unity:

> I felt towards him as if he were my brother, as if, like a brother, it wouldn't matter how we strayed from each other, how far apart we were, we would always be flesh of one flesh, and think each other's thoughts. (617)

As was explained, Saul's function is to confront Anna with her own destructive, "cannibalistic" impulses, but also to lead her to a new stage of creativity. In Saul's case Sprague's suggestion is convincing: he is almost a classical Jungian double with his destructive impulse, his intense sexuality, but also his creative potential. Yet to see practically all figures as Anna's doubles – Julia, Marion, the naive second wife of Molly's ex-husband, Maryrose from her African youth, Mrs Marks are all interpreted as further female doubles, all men as Anna's male doubles representing her destructive side – seems exaggerated and not really illuminating, if not meaningless.

Lessing's figures, I would like to argue, serve a variety of functions. Many of them, among which several minor ones, come across as lively characters with their own history and standpoints, for instance, the communist veteran Jack, who runs the communist publishing house, the Bowlbys, the hotel-owner family from Anna's African past, or Tommy, the bewildered young man who tries to shoot himself and paradoxically finds his peace after he is blinded. Others like the tycoon Richard, Molly's ex-husband, and his silly wife Marion or the media representatives seem social caricatures rather than projections of Anna's mind. And as to Anna's lovers, Michael, Nelson, de Silva and Milt – with the exception of Saul – do not appear as Anna's doubles, but rather seem invented to personify a certain type of male behaviour for which Anna invariably falls in a kind of compulsive repetition: they are intelligent, interesting, creative men, but womanisers unable to form a lasting relationship and to take responsibility. Lessing uses them to expose a certain type of gender relations which was widespread in the early years of women's emancipation. 'Free women' hung on to an old pattern from the times of unquestioned patriarchy: though independent in their lifestyles, they still longed for submission to a man and complete self-effacement in the sexual encounters with the lover. Anna, deeply wounded by Michael's desertion, gradually learns to recognise the type and to suffer less – however, she cannot give up the yearning for romantic love altogether. With self-irony she says to Saul: "[w]hat's my strongest need – being with one man, love, all that. I've a real talent for it" (602). She even wishes for her daughter, i.e. the next generation, that one day she might meet "a real man" (395). But despite this yearning Anna bravely stays by herself in the end, true to her decision taken at the end of her analysis: "[b]ut I've told you, I want to walk off, by myself, Anna Freeman" (458).

6. An "Inner-Portrait-of-the-Artist-as-a-Young-Thing"?

One side effect of the loose, but highly organised structure of *The Golden Notebook* is that some parts – despite their "hinges" – assume relative autonomy and contain pieces of narration that can be read as independent stories or essays. This may be one of the main reasons for the early misunderstandings about the text: readers could comparatively easily isolate passages that seemed most important to them. Thus, for instance, Ella's musings about sex, especially about the vaginal and the clitoral orgasm in the Yellow Notebook, and Anna's very private thoughts about menstruation and her body smells in the Blue Notebook could be picked out and discussed by feminists ignoring the context. Also several anecdotes from Anna's (and Ella's) love affairs can be read as independent stories or dramatic scenes: for instance, a party in the house of Anna's American lover Nelson, where he and his wife act out a fight in *Who's-Afraid-of-Virginia-Woolf* style, or Ella's encounters with Cy Maitland, an American brain surgeon, an uncomplicated, friendly man, successful in his work and "very sure of himself" (317), whom Anna meets during a near plane-crash and has a brief, reassuring affair with after the shock of her great love Paul's desertion. Anna's meetings with the TV representatives Reggie Tarbrucke and Edwina Wright in Paris can be enjoyed as semi-independent satires, and the story of the British communist teacher who met a very kind Stalin is a naive, but touching fairy tale. But the biggest independent section is formed by the first two parts of the Black Notebook, in which Anna remembers a crucial phase of her youth in Rhodesia.

It is an 80-page-long piece of narration, presenting the material that went into Anna's first novel, *Frontiers of War*, which, from the distance of about fifteen to seventeen years, she feels, falsified the events.[29] In 1954, when Anna starts the Black Notebook, she means to write down "the truth" of what had happened (82), but at the end of her endeavours she realises her failure, "although at the time I wrote it I thought I was being 'objective'" (163). One of the reasons for her dissatisfaction is the inevitable distortion by memory: "[a]nd I get exasperated, trying to remember – it's like wrestling with an obstinate other-self who insists on his own kind of privacy. Yet it's all there in my brain if only I could get at it" (148). A further reason is the welling up of nostalgia, which in her opinion already spoils her novel, a sick nostalgia for the fascination of war and death:

> [y]et it is so powerful, that nostalgia, that I can only write this, a few sentences at the time. Nothing is more powerful than this nihilism, an angry readiness to throw overboard, a willingness, a longing to become part of dissolution. (82)

But despite this self-criticism the reader gets a fairly clear impression of what Anna, at that time "twenty-three or twenty-four" years old, experienced (140). From the distance of many years and far removed in space, Anna writes impressively about the African setting, about the landscape and nature, about the social set-up and the political situation in the British colony Rhodesia with its colour bar and, above all, about the relationships among a small group of young people, a tiny sub-group of the Communist Party of (white) Rhodesia, who are already developing doubts about the Soviet version of Marxism. The group consists – apart from Anna – of beautiful Maryrose, traumatised by her brother's death in action, three young British bomber pilots, all ex-Oxford students training in Africa for the RAF, and Willi, a German-Jewish refugee, who is Anna's (asexual) boyfriend. From a certain moment on they all spend their weekends in the Mashopi Hotel, 60 miles from their town, where they get involved with a number of other people, among them the family of the hotel owner Bowlby, the (black) cook, his wife and her (white) lover. Among these people, all under the spell of the distant war, erotic relationships develop, which through misunderstandings, prejudices and jealousy have disastrous consequences: the cook loses job and house, the group breaks up, and the most glamorous and brightest of the young men, Paul, dies in a nasty accident. Anna at the time must have observed the people and their behaviour with acute attention, though she was not conscious of it. When Paul calls her "Anna of the tolerantly amused black eyes" (133), she is very surprised. Also in retrospect she remembers herself as very much caught up in her own affairs: "I don't think I really saw people then, except as appendages to my needs" (*ibid.*). Nevertheless she must have been very attentive, else she would not have been able to describe people and events in such a precise and lively manner years later as she does in the Black Notebook. And back in the forties she must have had good enough material to create a convincing novel.

At the end of the African events Anna remembers a decisive moment of her own life:

> [t]hat was the material that went into *Frontiers of War*. Of course, the two 'stories' have nothing at all in common. I remember very clearly the moment I knew I would write it. I was standing on the steps of the bedroom block of the Mashopi hotel with cold hard glittering moonlight all around me. [...] I was filled with such a dangerous delicious intoxication that I could have walked straight off the stairs into the air, climbing on the strength of my own drunkenness into the stars. (162-163)

This then is the moment when Anna, the writer, is born, even if she looks back on her exhilaration with self-irony and is soon ashamed of her first work. But she has reached the first step of her existence as an artist, and the road to it were her African experiences in her early twenties. So one may say that the first two sections of the Black Notebook contain indeed a portrait of the artist as a young thing. Just as there is an inner Golden Notebook there is also an inner portrait of the artist as a young woman in the outer *Golden Notebook*, even though Anna comes into her full maturity as a writer only several years later, at the age of 40, by writing the outer *Golden Notebook*.

7. Conclusion

It seems that, by dividing her heroine's artistic development into two stages, Doris Lessing means to convey a message concerning the role of the artist. Anna Wulf as a successful young writer becomes so embarrassed by her first novel because of the mood that triggered it, that she develops writer's block. She feels, as she tells her analyst Mrs Marks, that writing has become pointless: "I no longer believe in art" (235). And she asks: "[w]hy can't you understand that [...] I can't pick up a newspaper without what's in it seeming so overwhelmingly terrible that nothing I could write would seem to have any point at all?" (252) In a next step of her artistic development Anna, now in her early 40s, overcomes her block in a long, painful process, which, as we saw, is reflected in the very organisation of the text. She learns that just refusing to write is not good enough, that the gifted writer's task is rather to face up to the imperfect state of the world and its effects on the individuals and to try to portray it in an adequate manner. In order to be able to do that, Anna has to open her mind to all disturbing impressions as well as to her own destructive impulses instead of suppressing chaos by keeping her experiences separate in different notebooks. Most important is her determination despite all doubts, disappointments and anxieties "not to give in", to keep on struggling for a more just and peaceful world, to remain a "boulder-pusher". Thus Lessing confirms her conviction expressed five years before in "A Small Personal Voice" that the artist has a moral responsibility – which is indeed not so far off from Mrs Marks's conviction that "the artist has a sacred trust", which Anna at the time of her analysis ridicules (238). After her maturing process and at the height of her skills, Anna finally fulfils the writer's obligation, as Lessing understands it, by honestly reflecting the state of the world in the fifties and her own bewildered mind in the fragmented, but highly ordered shape that made the *Golden Notebook* famous.

Notes

1 Lessing (1995: 166; 181). Further references to this edition will be included in the text.
2 Lessing (2008: 185-186). Further references to this edition will be included in the text.
3 Lessing (1973: 12). Further references to this edition will be included in the text. Lessing's caricature corresponds amazingly closely to the characteristics of the typical artist figure Maurice Beebe lists in his classic study of the *Künstlerroman* from the eighteenth to the early twentieth centuries: "[t]he

person blessed (or cursed?) with 'artistic temperament' is always sensitive, usually introverted and self-centred, often passive, and sometimes so capable of abstracting himself mentally from the world around him that he appears absentminded or 'possessed'" (1964: 5).

4   See Sprague (1994: 3).

5   Beebe mentions only very few women writers who focused on artist heroines. Linda Huf in her study of portraits of young women artists in American novels confirms: "women have frequently balked at portraying themselves in literature as would-be writers [...]. Unlike men, women have only rarely written artist novels; that is, autobiographical novels depicting their struggle to become creative writers – to become, as the Romantics had it, as gods" (1983: 1).

6   Beebe (1964: 6-13).

7   Tonya Krouse in a recent article argues that Anna dismisses her first published work for being too personal: "Anna rejects the personality of her first novel" (2010: 40). To my mind this does not seem precise enough: Anna does not reject emotionality as a source for writing in general, but is embarrassed of the particular emotion that generated *Frontiers of War*.

8   Lessing (1994: 8; 10). Further references to this edition will be included in the text.

9   See, e.g., Rubenstein (1979: 177); Greene (1997: 118); Hite (1988: 65); Krouse (2006: 39).

10 Greene (1997: 93-97) gives a good overview of the early reviews of *The Golden Notebook*.

11 Newquist (1994: 55).

12 See, e.g., Mulkeen (1972: 262-277); Carey (1973: 437-456); Draine (1980: 31-48); Schweickart (1985: 263-279). A more recent study of the novel's structure is Worthington (2004: 59-78).

13 Rubenstein (1979: 75).

14 *Ibid.*, 107.

15 Hite (1988: 65).

16 Schweickart (1985: 267-268).

17 Newquist (1994: 55).

18 Lessing was particularly shattered by the appearance of the A-bomb and later the H-bomb. In an interview she gave in 1969 she said: "I feel as if the Bomb has gone off inside myself, and in people around me. That's what I mean by the cracking up. It is as if the structure of the mind is being battered from inside. Some terrible new thing is happening. Maybe it'll be marvellous" (Raskin 1994: 70).

19 See Waugh (1989: 201-204); Bradford (2007: 9-10; 118-119); Sage (1992: 16-17); Nünning (1998: 128-129); Seeber *et al.* (1991: 386-387).

20 Lessing (1995: 5).

21 Worthington (2004: 77).

22 *Ibid.*

23 Krouse (2010: 39).

24 Though Anna's African memories refer to the time of World War II, there was no fighting in Rhodesia itself.

25 Sprague (1986: 47).

26 *Ibid.*

27 *Ibid.*

28 *Ibid.*, 56.

29 There is a slight muddle about time here as in other instances in the book. Anna, musing about the unreliability of memories, writes: "[w]hat I remember was chosen by Anna of twenty years ago" (Lessing 1973: 248). Yet if Anna is 40 in 1957, then her African memories of the early war years can only be of fifteen to seventeen years ago.

Bibliography

Beebe, Maurice: *Ivory Tower and Sacred Founts. The Artist as Hero in Fiction from Goethe to Joyce*, New York, 1964.

Bradford, Richard: *The Novel Now. Contemporary British Fiction*, Oxford, 2007.

Carey, John L.: "Art and Reality in *The Golden Notebook*", *Contemporary Literature* 14:4, 1973, 437-456.

Draine, Betsy: "Nostalgia and Irony. The Postmodern Order of *The Golden Notebook*", *Modern Fiction Studies* 26, 1980, 31-48.

Greene, Gayle: *Doris Lessing. The Poetics of Change*, Ann Arbor, 1997 [1994].

Hite, Molly: "Subverting the Ideology of Coherence. *The Golden Notebook* and *The Four-Gated City*". – In Carey Kaplan & Ellen Cronan Rose (Eds.): *Doris Lessing. The Alchemy of Survival*, Athens, 1988, pp. 61-69.

Huf, Linda: *A Portrait of the Artist as a Young Woman. The Writer as Heroine in American Literature*, New York, 1983.

Krouse, Tonya: "'Anon', 'Free Women' and the Pleasures of Impersonality". – In Debrah Raschke, Phyllis Sternberg Perakis & Sandra Singer (Eds.): *Doris Lessing. Interrogating the Times*, Columbus, 2010, pp. 32-57.

–: "Freedom as Effacement. Theorising Pleasure, Subjectivity and Authority", *Journal of Modern Literature* 29:3, 2006, 39-56.

Lessing Doris: *The Golden Notebook*, St Albans, 1973 [1962].

–: "The Small Personal Voice" [1957]. – In Paul Schlueter (Ed.): *Doris Lessing. A Small Personal Voice. Essays, Reviews and Interviews*, London 1994 [1974], pp. 7-25.

–: *Under My Skin. Volume One of My Autobiography. To 1949*, London, 1995 [1994].

–: *Alfred and Emily*, London & New York, 2008.

Mulkeen, Anne M.: "Twentieth Century Realism. The 'Grid' Structure of *The Golden Notebook*", *Studies in the Novel* 4, 1972, 268-277.

Newquist, Roy: "An Interview with Doris Lessing" [1963]. – In Paul Schlueter (Ed.): *Doris Lessing. A Small Personal Voice. Essays, Reviews and Interviews*, London, 1994 [1974], pp. 49-64.

Nünning, Ansgar: *Der englische Roman des 20. Jahrhunderts*, Stuttgart *et al.*, 1998.

Raskin, Jonah: "Doris Lessing at Stony Brook" [1969]. – In Paul Schlueter (Ed.): *Doris Lessing. A Small Personal Voice. Essays, Reviews and Interviews*, London, 1994 [1974], pp. 65-81.

Rubenstein, Roberta: *The Novelistic Vision of Doris Lessing. Breaking the Forms of Consciousness*, Urbana, Chicago & London, 1979.

Sage, Lorna: *Women in the House of Fiction. Post-War Women Novelists*, Houndmills, 1992.

Seeber, Hans Ulrich *et al.*: "Die Zeit nach 1945". – In H.U.S. (Ed.): *Englische Literaturgeschichte*, Stuttgart, 1991, pp. 352-393.

Schweickart, Patricio P.: "Reading a Wordless Statement. The Structure of *The Golden Notebook*", *Modern Fiction Studies* 31, 1985, 163-179.

Sprague, Claire: "Multipersonal and Dialogic Modes in *Mrs Dalloway* and *The Golden Notebook*". – In Ruth Saxton & Jean Tobin (Eds.): *Woolf and Lessing. Breaking the Mold*, New York, 1994, pp. 3-14.

–: "Double Talk in *The Golden Notebook*". – In C.S. & Virginia Tiger (Eds.): *Critical Essays on Doris Lessing*, Boston, 1986, pp. 44-60.

Waugh, Patricia: *Feminine Fictions. Revisiting the Postmodern*, London & New York, 1989.

Worthington, Marjorie: "The Novel Construction of the Writer. Symbiotic Texts, Parasitic Authors in *The Golden Notebook*". – In Michael M. Meyer (Ed.): *Literature and the Writer*, Amsterdam & New York, 2004, pp. 59-78.

45

Alexa Keuneke (Bochum)

Writing the Self as a Life Narrative. Margaret Laurence's *The Diviners* as *Künstlerroman*

1. Introduction

Margaret Laurence's *The Diviners* (1974) is part of a long tradition of artist novels in Canadian literature, a tradition that particularly seems to favour the depiction of female artists, as Robert Kroetsch has noted in his essay "Beyond Nationalism. A Prologue".[1] Although feminist critics have observed that until the second half of the twentieth century male artists greatly outnumbered female artists in this genre, that the female artist "is notable for her absence", this is clearly not true of Canadian literature.[2] The female artist figures of Canadian literature are no longer the "paralyzed artist" that Margaret Atwood identified in her critical work *Survival*.[3] Instead, authors such as Alice Munro, Margaret Laurence, and Atwood herself have created strong female artists who, like the fictional writer and protagonist of *The Diviners*, Morag Gunn, use their art to gain power and independence, to understand their own identity and to achieve a better understanding of significant others in their lives.

The *Künstlerroman* typically traces the development and growth of an artist and is thus concerned with the question of the artist's identity formation. The artist's identity is typically represented as the outcome of that development, i.e. as a product of past experiences and encounters. Memories are usually employed in the narrative to show this development.[4] *The Diviners*, however, is not only a *Künstlerroman* about Morag Gunn, but also, as it turns out in the end, her fictional autobiography. Several hints in the novel alert the reader to the fact that what s/he has been reading can be seen as Morag Gunn's fifth novel, *The Diviners*. The most obvious of these hints is the novel's final sentence "Morag returned to the house, to write the remaining private and fictional words, and to set down her title".[5] The narrative form of the novel, too, is quite complex and it is only in the course of the novel that the reader comes to realise that, although it first seems as if *The Diviners* were narrated by a heterodiegetic narrator, certain features of the story suggest that it is really Morag herself who is telling the story and masking as a third-person narrator. We are actually reading what Leona Gom calls the "verbal transcription" of Morag's memories,[6] with Morag narrating her own story and the sections in italics representing her thoughts and comments on the writing process that seep into her narrative. The apparently heterodiegetic narration of the story points to a certain detachment of Morag not only from her past but also her current self – she appears to be in the process of self-analysis, past and present, and for this purpose distances herself from her self. This complex narrative situation enables Margaret Laurence to not only present the reader with the development of an artist, but also to concentrate on the processes at work when a writer sets out to put his or her life in writing.

The novel is divided into two narrative levels, a narrative 'now' in which the focus is on Morag as she is writing her fifth novel, and a narrative 'then' in which Morag's development is traced. When focusing on the narrative 'then', the typical linear *Künstlerroman* structure emerges. In it, the reader learns about Morag's childhood as the foster daughter of the town garbage man, her escape from the stifling small-town atmosphere to study at a university, her marriage to a university professor, and the failure of that marriage. Upon leaving her husband Morag begins to professionally pursue her lifelong passion of writing to support herself and her daughter. Both her role as an author and as a mother are depicted as "prime aspect[s] of her selfhood".[7] The narrative 'now' gives the *Künstlerroman* an innovative twist because it is on this narrative level that it takes on the form of an autobiographical novel and the focus is moved to the process rather than the product of writing a life.

By focusing on the writer, Morag Gunn, as she is writing a novel about her past rather than simply presenting the outcome of the writer's development, the novel is concerned with the retrospective construction of identity through writing. As Margaret Laurence herself stresses, "[f]or a writer, one way of discovering oneself [...] lies through the exploration inherent in the writing itself".[8] Morag undertakes to explore her identity in form of a life narrative, which, according to narrative psychologists, is "one way of defining the self".[9] The autobiographical novel that she is writing and that turns out to be the *Künstlerroman* the reader has just read presents the result of her exploration of her past. By piecing together her life story and presenting it to the reader as a life narrative, Morag retrospectively arrives at a sense of identity as defined by narrative psychology.[10]

While traditional novels about the development of an artist present the artist as a product of the past, *The Diviners* instead deals with the artist's retrospective construction of herself. This shift of focus results in a central importance of memories in the story. In the following, I will argue that the form of *The Diviners* as both a *Künstlerroman* and an autobiographical novel highlights the importance of Morag's profession for the development and construction of her identity. Furthermore, being a writer influences her awareness of the processes underlying the construction of identity.[11] It is memory that is of fundamental importance in this process and *The Diviners* therefore revolves around memories and remembering. Morag explores and to some extent creates her identity by writing an autobiographical novel and, because she is consciously setting out to review her life and write it into a narrative form, she becomes aware of the underlying memory processes involved, as well as the restrictions and limitations of memory.[12] Psychologists explain that the narratives people form about their lives are a "retrospective process of attributing meaning to a person's life events and actions" and are "more than a simple recounting of a person's life activities as they were experienced; rather, narratives present the meaning of these experiences from the present perspective of the person".[13] This implies that not only does the past influence the present, but the present also affects the way we look back on and interpret our past experiences. That Morag is aware of the reciprocal relationship of past and present is made explicit in the novel in a number of different ways, which I will describe in the course of this article. While many critics have focused on the novel's past level of narrative, some even going so far as to deny that the Morag of the present level of narrative is of any interest to the reader because she undergoes no development, I will follow Paul Hjartson in privileging the present level of narrative in which Morag's motivations for writing her autobiographical novel and the process of its creation are foregrounded.[14] It is on this level of narrative that the fundamental issues of the relationship between memory and identity, and the life narrative as a means of expressing one's identity, are addressed.

2. The Life Narrative as an Exploration of Identity and Relationships

The event that prompts Morag to review her life and write her life narrative in form of a novel is the departure of her daughter. Pique, who sets off on a journey of self-discovery, trying to make sense of her mixed heritage and identity as the daughter of a Scots-Canadian mother and a Métis father, has left home during the night, leaving only a note telling her mother not to worry about her (Laurence 1993: 3).[15] This causes Morag to contemplate how she herself was able to arrive at her own sense of identity and furthermore to reconsider the relationship with her daughter and her role as a mother. Although she warns herself of interpreting her daughter through her own experiences and of drawing parallels, which she thinks are "dangerous" because they prevent her from seeing her daughter as a person in her own right (195), the structure of the novel nonetheless encourages the reader to draw these parallels between mother and daughter. While Pique makes a physical journey into the West in order to visit places and people that might help her make sense of her identity, Morag begins a psychological journey into her past, recalling the formative episodes of her life that have shaped her own identity. As Pique rejects her mother and voices her mixed feelings about her, Morag recalls how she, too, wanted nothing to do with her foster parents (81). When Pique decides that she must leave her boyfriend, Gord, to be her own person, Morag draws a connection to the time when she came to realise that her marriage had led up to a dead end and that in order to be able to further evolve as a person, she had to leave her husband.[16]

As an artist, Morag undertakes her quest for an "understanding and acceptance of herself" artistically by writing her past into an autobiographical novel.[17] Pique's role in this process cannot be overestimated. She plays the role of a muse to her mother and only because "something about Pique's going, apart from the actual departure itself, was unresolved in Morag's mind" (5) does Morag set out to explore and write her own life and identity into a narrative.[18] What is unresolved in Morag's mind is what Pique will find out on her journey of discovery and how that will affect her relationship with her mother. Since Pique's birth, Morag has been plagued by feelings of guilt because she thinks that she is an inadequate mother. These fears resurface when Pique leaves, as Morag makes clear to her neighbour and friend, Royland:

> [s]he [Pique] hasn't had an easy life, Royland. I clobbered her with a hell of a situation to live in, although I never meant to. [...] But I chose to have her, in the first place, and maybe I should've seen it would be too difficult for her. You don't think of that, at the time, or I didn't, anyway. (81)

Much of the guilt Morag feels is related to being a writer and a mother at the same time. She feels that she is never able to do justice to her daughter or her writing. When she is unable to write because her daughter is ill, she contemplates how "getting back inside [the novel] will be torture" and "puts a mental hex on" writers "with private means" (303). Yet, when she is working, Morag also feels somehow remorseful: "[h]ow to change my hours to suit? What to do, Lord? How to cope with it all? Maybe I should be able to write evenings, late, so as not to inconvenience anyone? Goddamn, why should I not inconvenience anyone?" (306-307; emphasis in the text)

The guilt experienced by female artists about their conflicting roles of artist and mother is central to the female *Bildungs-* or *Künstlerroman*. Laurence obviously makes this role conflict a topic in *The Diviners*, but she also stresses the link between motherhood and creativity. In spite of Morag's feelings of guilt and her constant worries about her daughter, Pique is not only Morag's muse on the present level of narrative, but it is also through Pique's birth that "Morag realizes the fullness of her creative self".[19] Although Morag's recollections show that writing has been an important part of her life since childhood, her marriage to Brooke Skelton initially puts an end to this. Brooke stifles Morag's development not only as a writer, but also as a person. What attracts him to Morag in the first place is her "mysterious nonexistent past" which he likes about her because this makes it seem as if she "were starting life now, newly" (158). Brooke believes that Morag's lack of a past will enable him to give her a life and an identity. In the course of their marriage, Brooke tries to shape his wife according to his conceptions, denying her the wish of having a child and trivialising her writing ambitions. However, Morag refuses to be suppressed and as she is not able to communicate her feelings to her husband, she instead writes about them, although she is at first not aware of the close links to her own life: "[s]he has no idea where the character has come from. She has never in her life known anyone remotely like Lilac Stonehouse" (184). As a statement of her independence, Morag writes and submits her first novel without the aid of her husband, who is no less than a professor of English literature. When he is confronted with her published novel, he is hurt that his "reactions aren't any longer welcome", but Morag defends herself by explaining that "I know you know a lot about novels. But I know something, as well. Different from reading and teaching" (213). While her first publication already indicates strong frictions in the relationship of Morag and Brooke, it is only because she becomes pregnant by her childhood friend Skinner Tonnerre that Morag is able to leave her stifling marriage and pursue a writing career. Morag's birth as an author thus coincides with the birth of her daughter and both events empower her, giving her the strength to leave her husband and live an independent life.

All of Morag's novels, not only the autobiography that is *The Diviners*, show that writing is Morag's means of coming to terms with her past and they all amount to a form of memory work. Morag's first novel, *Spear of Innocence*, is written while she is married to Brooke. The novel is an expression of Morag's frustration during her marriage in which she is denied the future she wants. Instead, she writes about the past which is also unmentionable in the marriage with Brooke (184-188). The next novel, *Prospero's Child*, helps her come to terms with her marriage. In it she describes the story of a young woman who "virtually worships" her husband and later "has to go to the opposite extreme and reject nearly everything about him [...] in order to become her own person" (270). In her third novel, *Jonah*, Morag deals with her relationship with Christie Logan, her foster father, who is presented as the main character of the novel (299-300). Finally, the fourth novel the reader finds out about, *Shadow of Eden*, is a reworking of Christie's tales (341).[20] All of these novels thus show how Morag's past and her memories inspire her to write. Memory, the mother of the Muses, has thus been the prime source of inspiration for Morag.

In the narrative 'now', it is Pique's comings and goings and the frictions that mother and daughter continuously experience with each other that uphold and stimulate Morag's creative process of exploring the past.[21] This exploration in the end leads her to better understand not only herself, but also her daughter's situation, since she finally appreciates that Pique's search for identity is not so different from the one she went through and is still going through herself: "Pique's journey, although at this point it might feel to her unique, was not unique" (360). Like Morag, Pique, too, is an artist, albeit a singer, and explores her identity artistically by collecting the songs of her father and ancestors and creating new ones. And just as Morag ponders over the truthfulness of her own stories, she also wonders if Pique would "create a fiction out of Jules [Pique's father], something both more and less true than himself, when she finally made a song for him, as she would one day" (367). This concern with the nature of memories and their accuracy and truthfulness is a central element of the novel.

3. Time, Memory, and Truth

The creative process of self-examination is set in motion by Pique's departure. Morag's musings are directly related to her profession as a writer because they are part of her creative effort to produce an autobiographical novel. Two aspects are important in this respect: firstly, the way in which past, present, and future influence each other and one's identity, and secondly, the nature of memories and the role they play in granting us access to our past.

The relationship between past, present, and future is expressed by Morag's ponderings about the river that flows by her house. It becomes a central metaphor in Laurence's novel to express this interconnectedness of past and present. This metaphor appears in the first and final chapters of the novel and stresses the variability of the past and the merging of times. The very first sentences of the novel read:

> [t]he river flowed both ways. The current moved from north to south, but the wind usually came from the south, rippling the bronze-green water in the opposite direction. This impossible contradiction, made ap-

parent and possible, still fascinated Morag, even after the years of river-watching. (3)

At the end of the novel, the river is again described in a similar way: "[t]he waters flowed from north to south, and the current was visible, but now a south wind was blowing, ruffling the water in the opposite direction, so that the river [...] seemed to be flowing both ways" (370). A number of critics have analysed this as a metaphor of the "interdependence of past, present and future".[22] This interpretation is also supported by Morag's thoughts at the end of the novel: "[*l*]*ook ahead into the past, and back into the future, until the silence*" (*ibid.*; emphasis in the text). In this sentence, the normal order of things is inverted: instead of looking ahead into the future and back into the past, the past is something to look ahead to and the future something to look back at. Past, present, and future cannot be separated but are always interdependent. While subjective time, i.e. memory, moves backwards, objective time moves forward.[23] Morag's artistic examination of her life is based on the insight that in order to be able to face present and future, the past must be understood, and that furthermore the present and the future influence the way a person sees the past. The interdependence of time also has consequences for a person's understanding of self: though the events of the past have formed a person, one's present situation also influences the way one looks back and forward.

Morag also shows an awareness of the nature of memories and the role they play in granting us access to the past, and thus how they affect the writing of her autobiographical novel. She addresses an issue regarding the life narrative that psychologists have also commented on. Although the stories contained in the life narrative are "central to our experience of self", this "says nothing about its [the life narrative's] accuracy: memories may be vivid and meaningful and yet very substantially mistaken".[24] This phenomenon is made a topic in a very explicit manner, as the voice of the first-person narrator breaks into what is at first sight a straightforward third-person narrative account in order to undermine and call into question the memories that have just been presented. The central statement of the novel in this respect is the following: "[*a*] *popular misconception is that we can't change the past – everyone is constantly changing their own past, recalling it, revising it*" (49; emphasis in the text). This sentence draws attention to the fact that remembering is a creative process that includes the interpretation and revision of past experiences. The question whether any of the memories presented in the novel have been left unaltered presents itself not only to the reader, but also to Morag who wonders about the aptness of her profession for capturing truths: "[a] daft profession. Wordsmith. Liar, more likely. Weaving fabrications. Yet, with typical ambiguity, convinced that fiction was more true than fact. Or that fact was in fact fiction" (21).

Morag is aware that she has completely invented memories of her earliest childhood by describing and interpreting the snapshots that she has of this time. Her earliest childhood memories are entirely invented and based solely on photos, which she has kept "*not for what they show but for what is hidden in them*", namely stories otherwise shrouded in the fog of childhood amnesia that can be accessed only through these pictures (6; emphasis in the text). Under normal circumstances, i.e. if Morag's parents had not died, her earliest childhood memories would have been provided to her by her parents in form of shared remembrances and stories. As Morag does not have anybody who can share these early childhood memories with her, it is up to her to invent memories by searching for clues in the family photographs: "*I don't recall when I invented that one. [...] Looking at the picture and knowing what was hidden in it. I must've made it up much later on, long long after something terrible had happened*" (8; emphasis in the text).

Later childhood memories are not completely invented, but they do not seem to be any more accurate than her entirely invented memories: "[s]he could not even be sure of their veracity, nor guess how many times they had been refilmed, a scene deleted here, another added there. But they were on again, a new season of the old films" (23). These memories no longer take the form of "snapshots", but of "memorybank movies" thus alluding to the way these memories play in Morag's head. Each "memorybank movie" is also provided with a title, and in this way the fictional elements they contain are further stressed (for example, 11; 24; 25).

Since at least some of the memories presented in *The Diviners* constitute an altered past, the reader may wonder in how far they can be of any significance for a person's identity. However, although Morag's memories are "maybe true and maybe not" (7) this does not matter because "[w]hat really happened" is "[a] meaningless question" (49). The experiences an individual has made in the past cannot be changed, but their response to the past in the present, their interpretation of the past, is open to transformation.[25] Having lost her parents at an early age and thus lacking an identity based on her parents and parental heritage, Morag's invented memories of her earliest childhood are the only source she has on which to base her identity. Therefore, it is the psychological significance of her memories which is foregrounded rather than their historical accuracy.[26] The novel highlights that memories do not need to lay claim to truth, their value lies in satisfying the personal needs of the rememberer and in conforming to his/her self-narrative. This, however, is something that Pique needs yet to learn, since she still believes she needs to know the truth as a basis of her identity:

> "[b]ut some of those stories you used to tell me when I was a kid – I never knew if they happened like that or not."
>
> "Some did and some didn't, I guess. It doesn't matter a damn. Don't you see?"
>
> "No," Pique said, "I don't see. I want to know what really happened."
>
> Morag laughed. Unkindly, perhaps.
>
> "You do, eh? Well, so do I. But there's no one version. There just isn't." (287)

Although Morag stresses the constructed and changeable nature of memories, she does not question the significance these memories have for her own identity and that of others. She expresses the belief that a person's past is an important aspect for the understanding of that person: "Morag wants to know everything about him [Brooke Skelton, her husband], about his previous life, so that she will know all of him" (176).

4. Aestheticising the Past

Morag's profession as writer shows itself in the way she presents her memories. Her creativity and artistic nature lead to an aestheticised presentation of her past in form of a specific literary genre – the autobiographical novel. To begin, each memory unit is provided with a title that hints at the subject matter of that section. While most titles refer only to the contents of the memory, some of them are based upon other works of literature, thus situating Morag as an artist in a greater literary and intertextual context. The memories that deal with her pregnancy, for example, are entitled "Bleak House" (239), an allusion to Charles Dickens's novel and a fitting title for the memory, as it deals with the bleak outlook that Morag has as a single and pregnant woman at a run-down boarding house, and "A Portrait of the Artist as a Pregnant Skivvy" (242), a play on the title of James Joyce's influential *Künstlerroman*, and an expression of the hardships a female writer must endure to be both independent and able to live out her vocation of being a writer. Morag's stay at the "Bleak House" boarding house as a "pregnant skivvy" at least provides her with the most important thing for a female writer:

> [a] woman, if she is to write, Virginia Woolf once said (or words to that effect), must have a room of her own. The garret bit never appealed to Morag unduly, but by God, it is at least a room of her own. The only trouble is that she feels too tired and lousy most evenings to do any writing at all. (*Ibid.*)

By giving titles to her memories, Morag highlights their fictionalisation and also retrospectively structures and orders them, thus putting them into a logical sequence in which one memory unit leads up to and calls for the next one.

There are also elements of the memories themselves that show the author's retrospective influence on them. As Morag notes when she is recalling her early childhood, there are certain elements that are not likely to have been experienced the way which they are remembered:

> *I recognize anomalies in it* [the memory], *ways of remembering, ways which aren't those of a five-year-old, as though I were older in that memory (and the words bigger) than in some subsequent ones when I was six or seven, and partly because it was only what was happening to Me* [sic]. (11; emphasis in the text)

Morag's presentation of her memories to the reader often demonstrates "ways of remembering" that reveal an author's craft. Ironic interjections like "But hist! What have we here?" attest to the retrospective manipulations of the memory by the narrator (262). The transcription of sounds into words, too, shows a retrospective reworking, "ways of remembering" of an author who is putting her memories into words. Several times in the novel, Morag describes the sounds she heard in the past. In a memory of her childhood, Morag describes how "you have to chonk-chonk-chonk" the pump to fill the sink with water (12). As she is leaving Manawaka for college, Morag describes the sounds of the train wheels as "their steelsong *clickety-click-clickety-click*" (141; emphasis in the text), and the train taking her from Toronto to Vancouver when she leaves her husband makes the sound "*Clunk-a-clunk-clunk. Clunk-a-clunk-clunk*" (230; emphasis in the text).

Other memories are presented according to certain literary conventions, demonstrating an artistic and literary mind at work. The conversation Morag overhears between the teachers at her school, for example, is presented in the form of a dramatic dialogue and given a heading:

Conversation Overheard from the Teachers' Room All of Them in There Gabbing at Recess

Miss McMutrie: oh, Skinner's bad enough but at least he's far from school half the time and not much missed by me I can tell you   but Morag never misses a day   sometimes I wonder what on earth I'm going to do with her you find her same Ethel

Miss Plowright: how do you mean exactly

Miss McMutrie: well one day she's boisterous and noisy chewing gum in class whispering drawing dirty pictures *you* know and then heavens the next day she'll be so sullen not speaking a soul and you can't get a word out of her she won't answer just sits there looking sullen if you take my meaning. (50-51; emphasis in the text)

Similarly, Morag's conversation with her landlady Mrs Teffler about her pregnancy is also presented as drama, perhaps to highlight the helplessness with which Morag experienced the episode that she is now remembering. Rather than being an active participant, Morag is consigned to playing a predetermined role like an actor in a play:

Maggie T.: I thought I heard you coupla times before, upchucking. In the john. Wasn't sure it was you, Miss Gunn.

Morag: Yeh, it was me.

Maggie: (crudely, but with accuracy) I'd say you got a bun in the oven. Either that or the booze, and you don't have the signs of an alkie, as I should know, being probably the world's top authority on rubbydubs.

Morag: Huh? (240)

Finally, perhaps the most continuous example of a retrospective aestheticisation of Morag's memories is her characterisation and depiction of her foster father, Christie Logan. Christie is Manawaka's garbage man, or "scavenger", and "looks funny [...]. Sort of crooked in his arms or legs, or like that. He has a funny lump in his throat and it wobbles up and down when he talks" (24). He is also not very educated, but it is insinuated throughout the novel that he possesses a kind of wisdom that cannot be learned in school. Christie understands more about human nature than most people and tries to pass on this knowledge to Morag, who only begins to appreciate his wisdom later on in life. Christie's speech, though characterised by a colloquial register, is presented as that of a poet and philosopher. He explains to Morag that all people are equal, even if some imagine themselves to be worth more than others:

[l]et the Connors and the McVities and the Camerons and Simon Pearl and all them in their houses up there – let them look down on the likes of Christie Logan. Let them. I say unto you, Morag, girl, I open my shirt to the cold winds of their voices, yea, and to the ice of their everlasting eyes. They don't touch me, Morag. (38-39)

Christie has gained his knowledge about human nature from his experiences in war and also from reading people's garbage: "[b]y their christly bloody garbage shall ye know them in their glory, is what I'm saying to you, every saintly mother's son" (61). Like the prophecies of an oracle, Christie's wisdoms oftentimes need to be unriddled by Morag and even seem paradoxical:

"look here, it's a bloody good thing you've got away from this dump. So shut your goddamn trap and thank your lucky stars."

"Do you really think that, Christie?"

"I do," Christie says, knocking back the whiskey. "And also I don't. That's the way it goes. It'll all go along with you, too. That goes without saying."

But it has been said. The way it goes – it'll all go – that goes. Does Christie bring in these echoes knowingly, or does it just happen naturally with him? She has never known. (168)

However, the depiction of Christie as a poet and philosopher in spite of the menial labour he performs is fitting because Morag's retrospective evaluation of him shows that much of what Morag knows about life and people, she learned from her foster father, as she tells her friend, Ella, in a letter shortly after Christie's death: "Christie knew things about inner truths that I am only just beginning to understand" (341). Some of these inner truths were expressed by Christie in the stories that he told Morag, and that she also incorporates into her autobiographical novel.

5. The Ancestral Past and the Life Narrative

As Morag Gunn reviews her life and constructs her identity in the form of an autobiographical novel, she includes not only her personal memories but also stories and myths, pointing out the importance of narratives for the development of a writer. These deal with Morag's ancestral past, the deeds of her forefathers. They appeal to her creative imagination, giving her the first basis for her own attempts at writing, and also help to position her own life in a larger context, thus contributing to her sense of identity. Furthermore, they also reflect the growing interest in the sixties and seventies in the construction of a Canadian identity, thus representing a growing sense of national self-awareness. In this respect, *The Diviners* is again part of a Canadian tradition, in which, as Helen McWilliams has pointed out, the *Bildungsroman* or *Künstlerroman* is an "important literary tool in the forging of a Canadian identity".[27]

For Margaret Laurence family stories and history play a very important part in a person's sense of identity. In an interview with Graeme Gibson she stated that "[f]or me the past is extremely real. [...] the past goes back a long way. [...] it goes back not only as far as one's own parents, for example, but the grandparents and the distant ancestors, and a great deal is passed on".[28] I have already mentioned that Morag, as an orphan, is deprived of a parental heritage. As a result, Morag's identity as a child is grounded mostly in her invented memories and the social position of her foster parents, but there is also another source that she is provided with. Her foster father tries to create an ancestral and paternal heritage for Morag as a basis of her identity, which will allow her to shape and give meaning to her life. Christie's own sense of identity comes from his

Scottish ancestry. He often looks up his family name in *The Clans and Tartans of Scotland*, and stresses that his was an ancient family, making him worth no less than other people in Manawaka. Morag looks up her own family name in the book, perhaps hoping to find a family history as old as that of the Logans, but only finds out that "[t]he chieftainship of Clan Gunn is undetermined at the present time, and no arms have been matriculated" (40). Even Christie's book is thus not able to offer her a legacy.

It is for this reason that Christie begins to tell her stories of Piper Gunn, "the most famous Gunn of all", and his wife Morag (40-41). These stories give the child Morag a sense of worth that she does not receive from society and they become a basis for her identity. Morag instantly identifies with Piper Gunn's wife and invents further stories about her which show how Morag herself would like to be: "[o]nce upon a time there was a beautiful woman name of Morag, and she was Piper Gunn's wife, and they went to the new land together and Morag was never afraid of anything in this whole wide world" (42). The stories serve as a kind of creative input with which the young Morag begins to try her hand at storytelling and writing, which is at first something private for an insecure child like her: "[s]he thinks of the scribbler in her top dresser drawer. She will never show it to anyone, never. It is hers, her own business. She will write some in it tomorrow. She tells it in her head" (*ibid.*).

As she grows older, however, Morag begins to question Christie's stories of Piper Gunn and his adventures in Canada. Christie had been mixing them with elements of Canadian history, thus presenting Piper Gunn as a kind of Canadian founding father. These stories are, however, contradicted by what Morag learns about Canadian history in school and also by the stories that her friend Jules "Skinner" Tonnerre tells her about his forefathers (105-107; 117-120). As a teenager, Morag thus loses faith in the truth of these stories, and only comes to understand the true value they possess as a means of conceptualising the self and to foster the power of the creative imagination at a later stage in her life, when she is raising her own daughter and passes the stories of both her own family and the family of Pique's father, the Tonnerres, on to her.[29] Their inclusion in the autobiographical novel Morag is writing further attests to their significance as a means of identity construction.

Christie also tells Morag a story about her father, thus also giving her a "personal past", i.e. a paternal heritage.[30] He tells Morag about the Battle of Bourlon Wood in which Morag's father, Colin Gunn, saved Christie's life. The story of this battle is misrepresented in Christie's eyes in the regiment book: "'Oh Jesus,' Christie says, 'don't they make it sound like a Sunday school picnic?'" (73) Christie's version of the battle presents Morag with the possibility of looking up to her father as a hero (73-74). Christie also gives her a knife her father owned, thus also giving her "a lasting present" to remember Colin by (75). This story, too, turns out to be untrue, as Morag finds out from her foster mother, Prin:

> "[t]hat Colin," Prin says. "He never done that for my Christie. Saved him, like. Or maybe he done it, I dunno. He was a boy, just a boy, and that scared. Poor lamb. The poor lamb. He would cry, and Christie would hold him. Sh-sh. There, there. It's all right now. He's all right now, that Colin. Ain't he?"
>
> [...] Colin Gunn. Christie's tale of Gunner Gunn and the Great War. How Colin saved Christie, staved off his dying, that time away out there, on that corner of some foreign field that is forever nowhere. It hadn't happened that way, then, or probably not. (167)[31]

The circumstance that the story about her father and the stories about the Clan Gunn turn out to be not fact but fiction demonstrates that the veracity of a story is unimportant for a person's identity development – the needs one has in the present and the resulting interpretation of the past can be more important than what actually happened. Furthermore, it highlights the myth-making processes that are at work when people review their past. Morag comes to realise that she has been making legends out of certain people, such as her parents and her foster father. When she is looking at the photographs she has of her parents, she realises that "[s]he was not certain whether the people in the snapshots were legends she had once dreamed only, or were as real as anyone she now knew" (6). Christie is turned into a legend by Morag through the stories she tells about him to her daughter, but also because of the way Morag remembers him. After his death, she realises that Pique will never be able to know the real Christie, only the legend: "*I told my child tales about you, but never took her to see you. I made a legend out of you, while the living you was there alone in that mouldering house*" (337; emphasis in the text). Though Morag regrets that Pique did not have the chance to meet Christie, fictionalising the past and making people into legends is regarded as a natural process and Morag wonders if Pique, too, will make legends out of the people in her life: "[w]ould Pique create a fiction out of Jules, something both more and less true than himself, when she finally made a song for him, as she would one day, the song he had never brought himself to make for himself?" (367)

The myths, legends, and stories that are a part of the novel thus show how fact and fiction merge in the life narrative, just like past, present, and future do. They become an integral part of a person's life narrative and thus contribute to their sense of identity. As an author, Morag is concerned with the relationship of fact and fiction in her writing and thus also has a special awareness of how this relationship affects people's lives.

6. Conclusion

Margaret Laurence's *The Diviners* is not only a *Künstlerroman* about the development of an author, but also that fictive author's autobiographical novel, which focuses on the depiction of her retrospective construction of the past. The double form of the novel as both a *Künstlerroman* and an autobiographical novel enables Margaret Laurence to focus not only on how the past affects the present but also on how the present influences how people look back on the past, thus foregrounding the memory process and the limitations and possibilities of that process. In this way, *The Diviners* gives a new twist to a central element of the *Bildungs-* and *Künstlerroman*. Rather than viewing the artist as a product of his or her past, Laurence stresses the active role that the artist has of constructing his or her identity through the writing process.

Morag's profession is crucial to the novel because as an author she reviews her past artistically. The autobiographical form is thus used in one of its traditional functions, namely for the "Erschreibung einer Identität".[32] *The Diviners* constitutes Morag's life narrative, connecting her memories in such a way that they form a coherent whole that leads up to her present situation. In this way, Morag arrives at a sense of identity, if only a provisional one. This is due to another view that is expressed in the novel, namely that the past is not fixed, but changeable and closely interconnected with present and future. Morag's present situation and her profession influence the way she looks back on and, most importantly, how she interprets the past. While, on the one hand, the past helps her understand the present, on the other hand, the present influences the way that she sees the past. Therefore, the veracity and authenticity of memory are often questioned, since it is subject to interpretation and other changes. However, the truth of one's memories and the life narrative they add up to is less important than the role they play for one's understanding of self and identity.

The novel also focuses on another central element of the female *Künstlerroman*, namely the tensions between an artist's career and social expectations regarding her role as wife and/or mother, but this, too, is reworked. Although Morag is confronted with these conflicts, she manages to reconcile "her role as mother with that of writer".[33] Moreover, being a mother has a positive effect on her writing. Her daughter becomes Morag's muse, the frictions in their relationship serving to stimulate her creative projects. The birth of her daughter coincides with Morag's birth as a professional writer and Pique will continue her mother's artistic work as a different kind of artist, a musician. Her art will enable Pique to understand her past and her heritage and thus to give meaning to her life and define herself.

Margaret Laurence thus creates a *Künstlerroman* that is both in the tradition of the genre and also plays with its central elements. In doing so, she shifts the focus from the "growth of a poet's mind" (as William Wordsworth puts it in "The Prelude", 1805; 1850) to the retrospective construction of that development and makes the writer and the process of writing crucial for the act of self-definition.[34]

Notes

1 Kroetsch (1989: 66).
2 McWilliams (2009: 18); see also Huf (1983: 4).
3 Atwood (2004: 211).
4 Basseler & Birke (2005: 136).
5 Laurence (1993: 370). Further references to this edition will be included in the text. A number of critics have made the point that *The Diviners* is the novel that Morag is writing, see, e.g., Carrington (1977: 154); Greene (1990: 179); Warwick (1993: 18); Zimmermann (1996: 74). In an interview with Michel Fabre, Margaret Laurence also confirms this: "she is deliber-

ately setting out to construct her life and of course the novel she is writing is *The Diviners*" (1983: 205).

6 Gom (1976: 52).
7 Kuester (1994: 104).
8 Laurence (1977: 12).
9 Neisser (1994: 1).
10 Neisser & Libby (2000: 318) and Hinchman & Hinchman (2001: xviii).
11 Jutta Zimmermann has also noted that Morag's identity formation and search for the meaning of life are inextricably linked to her profession as an author (1996: 66).
12 Sherrill Grace points out that "it is memory which creates the self and the past in the act of remembering" (1978: 67).
13 Polkinghorne (2006: 9).
14 Leona Gom claims that "there is less reader interest in the older Morag than there is in the older Hagar" and that Morag "does not move toward a significant character development on the first level" (1976: 56). Paul Hjartson, on the other hand, stresses the importance of the novel's story of 'now', as it centres "on the *process* by which Morag composes herself in the stories she tells, by which, in the act of story-telling, she gives meaning and shape to the events of her life" (1988: 46; emphasis in the text).
15 The term 'Métis' was originally used to refer to "persons of Amerindian and French ancestry" and today refers to "all Amerindian/white admixtures" in Canada. Until 1982, when the Métis were formally recognised as an aboriginal people by the Canadian government, they suffered from an uncertain identity status since they were neither accepted as aboriginal nor as white (Dickason n.d.). In the Anglophone parts of Canada Métis with a French background, like Jules Tonnerre and thus also Pique in *The Diviners*, were outsiders in a double sense since they also lacked a common European background with the majority of the population.
16 In chapter seven of *The Diviners*, Pique returns home and tells Morag that she is no longer seeing Gord (Laurence 1993: 190). In the same chapter, Morag recounts how she left Brooke.
17 Warwick (1993: 11).
18 Buss (1988: 165-166).
19 *Ibid.*, 165.
20 Both Warwick (1993: 44-45) and Carrington (1977: 156-159) offer extensive interpretations of Morag's novels.
21 Kuester (1994: 115).
22 See, e.g., Greene (1990: 200).
23 *Ibid.*
24 Neisser & Libby (2000: 318).
25 Warwick (1993: 66-67).
26 Zimmermann (1996: 73).
27 McWilliams (2009: 21).
28 Gibson (1973: 204).

29 Greene (1990: 179).

30 *Ibid.*, 193.

31 This passage contains an allusion to Rupert Brooke's poem "The Soldier" (1914), again demonstrating how Morag's profession as a writer influences her recollections and ways of thinking.

32 Zimmermann (1996: 72).

33 Kuester (1994: 114).

34 This article is based on a paper I gave at the Canada Day conference held in Bochum, 23 July 2010. I would like to thank Burkhard Niederhoff, Maik Goth, and Raphaela Holinski for their helpful comments and suggestions.

Bibliography

Atwood, Margaret: *Survival. A Thematic Guide to Canadian Literature*, Toronto, 2004 [1972].

Basseler, Michael & Dorothee Birke: "Mimesis des Erinnerns". – In Astrid Erll & Ansgar Nünning (Eds.): *Gedächtniskonzepte der Literaturwissenschaft. Theoretische Grundlegung und Anwendungsperspektiven*, Berlin, 2005, pp. 123-147.

Buss, Helen M.: "Margaret Laurence and the Autobiographical Impulse". – In Kristjana Gunnars (Ed.): *Crossing the River. Essays in Honour of Margaret Laurence*, Winnipeg, 1988, pp. 147-168.

Carrington, Ildikó de Papp: "'Tales in the Telling'. *The Diviners* as Fiction about Fiction", *Essays on Canadian Writing* 9, 1977, 154-169.

Fabre, Michel: "From *The Stone Angel* to *The Diviners*. An Interview with Margaret Laurence". – In George Woodcock (Ed.): *A Place to Stand On. Essays by and about Margaret Laurence*, Edmonton, 1983, pp. 193-209.

Gibson, Graeme: "Margaret Laurence". – In G.G.: *Eleven Canadian Novelists*, Toronto, 1973, pp. 181-208.

Gom, Leona: "Laurence and the Use of Memory", *Canadian Literature* 71, 1976, 48-58.

Grace, Sherrill: "A Portrait of the Artist as Laurence Hero", *Journal of Canadian Studies/Revue d'études canadiennes* 13, 1978, 64-71.

Greene, Gayle: "Margaret Laurence's *The Diviners*. The Uses of the Past". – In Colin Nicholson (Ed.): *Critical Approaches to the Fiction of Margaret Laurence*, London, 1990, pp. 177-207.

Hinchman, Lewis P. & Sandra K. Hinchman: "Introduction". – In L.P.H. & S.K.H. (Eds.): *Memory, Identity, Community. The Idea of Narrative in the Human Sciences*, Albany, 2001, pp. xiii-xxxii.

Hjartson, Paul: "'Christie's Real Country. Where I Was Born'. Story-Telling, Loss and Subjectivity in *The Diviners*". – In Kristjana Gunnars (Ed.): *Crossing the River. Essays in Honour of Margaret Laurence*, Winnipeg, 1988, pp. 43-64.

Huf, Linda: *A Portrait of the Artist as a Young Woman. The Writer as Heroine in American Literature*, New York, 1983.

Kroetsch, Robert: "Beyond Nationalism. A Prologue". – In R.K.: *The Lovely Treachery of Words. Essays Selected and New*, Toronto, 1989, pp. 64-72.

Kuester, Hildegard: *The Crafting of Chaos. Narrative Structure in Margaret Laurence's* The Stone Angel *and* The Diviners, Amsterdam, 1994.

Laurence, Margaret: *The Diviners*, Chicago, 1993 [1974].

–: "Sources". – In William H. New (Ed.): *Margaret Laurence. The Writer and Her Critics*, Toronto, 1977, pp. 12-16.

McWilliams, Ellen: *Margaret Atwood and the Female* Bildungsroman, Farnham, 2009.

Neisser, Ulric: "Self-Narratives. True and False". – In U.N. & Robyn Fivush (Eds.): *The Remembering Self. Construction and Accuracy in the Self-Narrative*, Cambridge, 1994, pp. 1-18.

– & Lisa K. Libby: "Remembering Life Experiences". – In Endel Tulving & Fergus I.M. Craik (Eds.): *The Oxford Handbook of Memory*, Oxford, 2000, pp. 315-332.

Polkinghorne, Donald E.: "Narrative Psychology and Historical Consciousness. Relationships and Perspectives". – In Jürgen Straub (Ed.): *Narration, Identity, and Historical Consciousness*, New York, 2006, pp. 3-22.

Warwick, Susan J.: *River of Now and Then. Margaret Laurence's* The Diviners, Toronto, 1993.

Zimmermann, Jutta: *Metafiktion im anglokanadischen Roman der Gegenwart*, Trier, 1996.

Christiane Bimberg (Dortmund)

From Childhood to Retrospective. Portrait of an Artist in Margaret Atwood's *Cat's Eye*

1. Introduction

The essay studies the emergence of Elaine Risley as a Canadian painter in Margaret Atwood's *Cat's Eye* (1988), a novel that has stood in the shadow of her *Handmaid's Tale* (1985) up to now. *Cat's Eye* is both a *Bildungsroman* and a fictive autobiography. The central event is Risley's return to Toronto for a Retrospective of her work. The occasion triggers a retrospective by the protagonist and first-person narrator of her childhood and youth as the formative phases not only of her personal, but also of her artistic, identity. The reader is allowed to watch her development from a schoolgirl in Toronto in the forties to a successful middle-aged artist in Vancouver in the eighties.

The focus of this essay is on the interlinkage between artist and identity.[1] Identity construction is presented by Atwood in a very complex way,[2] conceptualising the body, art, biology, and the city, and employing postmodern narrative strategies.[3] The overarching thematic and organisational principle of the novel is a highly idiosyncratic concept of time:

> [t]ime is not a line but a dimension, like the dimensions of space. If you can bend space you can bend time also, and if you knew enough and could move faster than light you could travel backward in time and exist in two places at once.[4]

This space time is time in space. In visual terms, the image of time is that of a series of liquid transparencies laid on top of each other. As a consequence, one would not look back along time, but through it, like water.[5]

Risley's personal and professional identity formation are closely interlinked. Almost every important area of her childhood and youth impacts her development as an artist-to-be and the direction her art takes over time.[6] But this is an insight that, due to the fragmented, non-linear mode of presentation, the reader is only fully allowed towards the end of the novel, at the Retrospective. Elaine comes to celebrate her career, but also her personal and professional survival – finally physically returning to the traumatic site of her childhood.[7] The visit triggers all kinds of ambivalent feelings in her. She looks through Toronto's layers of time and understands what contributed to her emergence as an artist.[8]

It is especially the difficult parts of Elaine's childhood and youth that shape her identity and her painting. Among them are problematic relationships and traumatic experiences. Foremost here is Elaine's getting bullied by her girlfriends, in particular Cordelia. These experiences evoke images that later materialise in her paintings: the feeling of being driven over the edge, stepping off a cliff, or falling off a bridge or a cliff; the danger/temptation of (letting) her hand be caught in the wringer of her mother's washing machine; the feeling of sidestepping, leaving one's body, getting rid of it, floating.

Among the characters who have a deep impact on her is Mrs Smeath, the mother of Grace (one of the bullying girlfriends), who is resurrected in Elaine's paintings. She uses her illness to force her environment to treat her with consideration. This illness provides an endless source of secrecy, wonder and curiosity for Elaine. She visualises her bad heart in botanical terms and feels pain about it, but is also fascinated by it:

> [b]efore Valentine's Day we have to cut out hearts of red construction paper at school and decorate them [...]. While I am cutting mine I think about Mrs. Smeath's bad heart. What exactly is wrong with it? I picture it hidden, underneath her woollen afghan and the billow of her apron bib, pumping in the thick fleshy darkness of the inside of her body: something taboo, intimate. It would be red, but with a reddish-black patch on it, like rot in an apple or a bruise. It hurts when I think about it. [...] But the bad heart is also compelling. It's a curiosity, a deformity. A horrible treasure.

Day after day I press my nose against the glass of the French doors, trying to see if Mrs. Smeath is still alive. This is how I will see her forever: lying unmoving, like something in a museum, with her head on the antimacassar pinned to the arm of the chesterfield, [...] her scrubbed face, without her glasses, white and strangely luminous in the dim space, like a phosphorescent mushroom. She is ten years younger than I am now. Why do I hate her so much? Why do I care, in any way, what went on in her head? (Atwood 1989: 61-62)

The anatomical descriptions of Mrs Smeath anticipate Elaine's later artistic appropriations of them in her paintings (358). And perhaps her paintings reimpact the linguistic rendition of her childhood recollections. Elaine's hatred of Mrs Smeath stems from her complicity in the girls' bullying and, worse yet, her justification of it as God's punishment for her 'heathenness'. Elaine learns about it from a talk she accidentally overhears. From then on Mrs Smeath becomes her surrogate enemy:

I have a brief, intense image of Mrs. Smeath going through the flesh-colored wringer of my mother's washing machine, legs first, bones cracking and flattening, skin and flesh squeezing up towards her head, which will pop in a minute like a huge balloon of blood. [...] She is right, I am a heathen. I cannot forgive. [...]

Her bad heart floats in her body like an evil eye, an evil eye, it sees me. (193-194)

Another image which impressively reflects Elaine's personal dilemma is that of a little sparrow loved by God, which occurs in a Sunday school song and is represented on the church wall as well. The interaction of text and picture subtly suggests that the little sparrow is crushed by God's love:

[t]he picture is of a dead bird in an enormous hand, with a shaft of light coming down onto it.

I am moving my lips, but I'm not singing. I am losing confidence in God. Mrs. Smeath has God all sewed up, she knows what things are his punishments. He's on her side, and it's a side from which I'm excluded. [...]

I decide not to pray to God any more. [...]

If it means I will have to forgive Mrs. Smeath or else go to Hell when I die, I'm ready to go. (194)

71

Instead of praying to God, Elaine, in an act of defiance against Cordelia and Mrs Smeath, decides to "do something dangerous, rebellious, perhaps even blasphemous" (196) and pray to the Virgin Mary (the Smeaths always speak contemptuously about Catholic idolatry and worship, especially of the Virgin Mary). Again, it is the heart of the figure which is especially appealing to Elaine in a coloured paper she finds. The picture mirrors her own experience of torture:

> her heart is on the outside of her chest, with seven swords stuck into it. Or they look like swords. The heart is large, red and tidy, like a satin heart pincushion, or a valentine. Under the picture is printed: *The Seven Sorrows.* (195)

The Virgin Mary also appears in a hallucination to Elaine and even seems to rescue her when she is almost killed by her girlfriends in a ravine in winter. Only later does she understand that there was nobody. However, since the accident, which frees her mentally from her bullying friends, she visits churches and is interested in all kinds of representations of the Virgin Mary. It is neither religion nor architecture that is important to her, but the aesthetics and the authenticity of the representations. Later the figure of the Virgin Mary appears in her paintings. In one of them, Elaine depicts a feminist message, presenting the Virgin in an unorthodox interpretation of Christian iconography and as a very earthly, domestic figure – an overtaxed young mother. She calls the picture *Our Lady of Perpetual Help* (365).

A central role in the narrative is assigned to the eponymous cat's eye, Elaine's favourite marble:

> [t]he cat's eyes really are like eyes, but not the eyes of cats. They're the eyes of something that isn't known but exists anyway; like the green eye of the radio; like the eyes of aliens from a distant planet. My favourite one is blue. (67)

In her paintings eyes and cat's eyes abound. In *Unified Field Theory*, for example, a female figure, the Virgin of Lost Things, holds a glass object, an oversized cat's eye marble, with a blue centre (430).[9]

Last but not least, the image of a turtle's heart is significant. The animal is exhibited at the Conversat at the Zoological Building. The image complements a whole chain of association: Mrs Smeath's bad heart (like an evil eye), the sparrow being clenched by God's hand/ love, the turtle's heart (like an eye) being clenched, Elaine's psychological dilemma, and the cat's eye:

> [w]e come to a room where there's a cut-open turtle. [...] The turtle is alive; or it's dead, but its heart is alive. This turtle is an experiment to show how the heart of a reptile can keep on going after the rest of it is dead.
> The turtle's bottom shell has a hole sawed into it. The turtle is on its back so you can see down into it, right to the heart, which is beating away slowly, glistening dark red down there in its cave, wincing like the end of a touched worm, lengthening again, wincing. It's like a hand, clenching and unclenching. It's like an eye. (182)

However, Elaine's childhood and youth are also filled with pleasures. Both school and spare time offer her various occasions for artistic activities. Elaine's creative occupations in the various layers of time are minor, but significant influences that inspire her and lay the foundation for subsequent developments and professional decisions. They are expressive not only as to art objects, interests, teachers and their methods, but also of Elaine's awareness of the interaction between different media (texts, pictures), the nature of representation, the relationship between life and art, gender issues, social differences, power hierarchies, psychological games, appearance and reality, conventionality/unorthodoxy. The reader is allowed to watch Elaine develop her own strategies in life and art.

Life as presented in the workbooks and readers at school, for example, has no resemblance to Elaine's own life. In addition, the books mediate the typical gender and family pattern of the time, without considering the reality of World War II. Their appeal to Elaine is therefore rather exotic. Whereas her brother paints scenes from wars she imitates life as represented in the school readers. Books and her imagination make up for deficits in life. In her head she has elegant, delicate pictures of other little girls, but she has no idea what she would say to them if she were to actually meet them. By contrast, at home, in her own family reality, Elaine and her brother do the dishes, play war and continue their power struggles (31).

But school life also offers Elaine lots of occasions to test her own creativity, conventional and artistically undemanding as most of the artistic tasks may be. The teachers Miss Lumley and Miss Stuart form a binary opposition in terms of artistic concepts and methods – conventionality versus unorthodoxy. Miss Stuart, addicted to alcohol, really pays attention to the children, allows space for more demanding occupations, encourages the children, stimulates their imagination, curiosity and creativity:

> Miss Stuart likes art. She has us bring old shirts of our fathers from home so we can do messier art without getting our clothes dirty. [...]
> For her we make the familiar paper objects, the pumpkins, the Christmas bells, but she has us do other things too. [...] We draw pictures about foreign countries: Mexico with cactuses and men in enormous hats, China with cones on the heads and seeing-eye boats, India with what we intend to be graceful, silk-draped women balancing copper urns, and jewels on their foreheads. (173)

The belief in foreign countries that one could escape to is psychologically essential for Elaine's survival. She also favours Miss Stuart's open intercultural approach to foreignness to the restricted Christian-imperial one of Miss Lumley. Although the artistic representations of what children and teacher imagine to be typical qualities of foreign people and their cultures are not devoid of positive stereotyping, the images of the people are at any rate more friendly, the aesthetics more attractive. Miss Stuart defies negative labelling:

> I like these foreign pictures because I can believe in them. I desperately need to believe that somewhere else these other, foreign people exist. No matter that at Sunday school I've been told such people are either starving or heathens or both. No matter that my weekly collection goes to convert them, feed them, smarten them up. Miss Lumley saw them as crafty, given to the eating of outlandish or disgusting foods and to acts of treachery against the British, but I prefer Miss Stuart's versions, in which the sun above their heads is a cheerful yellow, the palm trees a clear green, the clothing they wear is floral, their folksongs gay. The women chatter together in quick incomprehensible languages, they laugh, showing perfect, pure-white teeth. If these people exist I can go there sometime. I don't have to stay here. (173-174)

It is no wonder that it is Miss Stuart who discovers Elaine's personal misery through her drawings – at a time when the psychoanalytical interpretation of children's drawings was not a standard method of diagnosis or therapy yet. Elaine's psychological revelations are triggered by the task to draw what the children do after school. She does a picture of herself in bed, black all over. Quite unexpectedly, Miss Stuart does not criticise her, but asks her kindly why the picture is so dark. When Elaine ridiculously answers "[b]ecause it's night" (174), the teacher only touches her on the shoulder – a non-verbal, silent acknowledgement of Elaine's personal misery. School parties also feel totally different with Miss Stuart. Whereas at Christmas the children eat the cookies brought from home silently at their desks in Miss Lumley's class, who supplies five jelly beans for each child, Valentine's Day is celebrated with Miss Stuart in a more sophisticated way in artistic terms and, yet more importantly, with a real party. The whole afternoon is a party, Miss Stuart brings dozens of heart-shaped shortbread cookies she has made herself, and the girls deliver the valentines.

Elaine even pursues her special interests – biology and art – when other subjects are on. While the history teacher is drawing a map of World War II Europe, elaborating on political details and showing himself to be moved by the end of an era, Elaine draws tulips and trees with their root systems and portrays a girl in class. She cannot understand what has changed politically, finds it hard to believe that she was a contemporary to all this. Although the historical explanations are beyond her comprehension at times, she feels inspired by some of them, represents the fashion of the time in her drawings and also trains her technique of doing body parts. But above all she is making the fullest use of biology lessons at school – scientifically and artistically. In grade thirteen, the children dissect worms, frogs and cats in the chemistry lab. Because she wants more than is offered at school, Elaine goes to her father's workplace, the Zoological Building, on Saturday afternoons to use the microscope in the empty labs. Here, she is attracted by the forms and colours of worms in section and by the bacteria; she is fascinated by the pictures she sees on the slides. She is already praised by Dr Banerji for her drawings at this early stage of her development.

Sunday school is also formative for Elaine. For the first time in her life she is exposed to religious instruction. Before she becomes more critical and stops praying to God because she feels excluded from God's mercy in the bullying, she feels really included, loved by God. Moreover, Sunday school contributes to Elaine's aesthetic and artistic development. Apart from the interanimation of text and pictures, there are two things that impress her: the stained-glass windows – they have light coming in behind them, which illuminates them so that she can hardly take her eyes off them (103) – and the coloured slides of the slide shows. They are reproductions of paintings and look old-fashioned. In one of them there is a knight whose description parallels the one of Mrs Smeath: white skin, his heart, his luminous face (*ibid.*).

In her spare time Elaine and her girlfriends colour in Grace Smeath's movie star colouring books. Grace's favourite movie star is Esther Williams, but Elaine has none because she has never been to a movie. Therefore she invents a figure whose name she likes: Veronica Lake. When the girls do the paper doll cutouts, Grace dictates: she never allows her girlfriends to cut out the outfits, but only to put them on and take them off. And in Grace's colouring books, the girls are only allowed to work away as long as they stay inside the lines. They are even told what colours to use and on which parts. Elaine conforms to this although she is aware that her brother would act subversively, disrespectfully, defying authority, demonstrating resilience: "I know what my brother would do – green skin for Esther, with beetle antennae, and hairy legs for Veronica, eight of them – but I refrain from doing it. Anyway, I like the clothes" (56).

The girls also study old *Eaton's Catalogues*, mail-order catalogues. Used as toilet paper in places that Elaine goes to with her parents in the north, they are treated with reverence by the girls here. The cut-outs – coloured figures, cookwear and furniture – are pasted into scrapbooks. The figures, always women, are called by the girls "my lady". The rule of the game is to belittle the quality of one's own scrapbook and praise those the others did. Elaine notices the false ring of the voices. She finds the game tiring and unrealistic anyway – her parents moved several times and it would be difficult to do that with all these possessions. She is practically-minded, whereas her friends Grace and Carol have never moved anywhere. Nor have "their ladies" (57). However, the revelation of a whole world of girls unknown to her before (she grows up with an older brother) has the effect that she begins to want things she never wanted before: braids, a dressing gown, a purse. Moreover, she notices that surviving in a world of males is more difficult because of the competition involved. In the world of girls eventually no effort is required from her: she just has to sit on the floor cutting out things and say she has done it badly. It is a false world of pretence and make-believe, but partly this is a relief also (56; 57).

Family life likewise offers infinite artistic inspirations to Elaine. For Christmas she gets a photo album to go with her camera. As she does not want to waste pictures, she thinks about what each picture will look like beforehand. She notices the reverse quality of colours in the negatives after the photos have been developed. The photos of her first roll of film show her girlfriends and her brother, but only one of herself standing in front of a motel door with a "9" on it (58). Although it was taken only a month ago she already recognises the change in herself, the development of her childhood self: "[a]lready that child seems much younger, poorer, farther away, a shrunken, ignorant version of myself" (*ibid.*). For another Christmas, Elaine gets a Barbara Ann Scott doll, which she had wanted because she did not have any girl-shaped dolls before. Elaine notices that the doll is "a slender stick" (136), a girl, who has no resemblance with the real woman, a famous figure skater who is muscular and has big thighs (*ibid.*). The doll only represents the sterile female beauty ideal of the time:

> [i]t had the worrying power of effigies, a lifeless life that fills me with creeping horror. I put it back into its cardboard box and tuck the tissue paper around it, over the face. I say I'm doing this to keep it safe, but in fact I don't want it watching me. (*Ibid.*)

When she is ill, lying in bed, she cuts things out of magazines and pastes them into a scrapbook, for example, pictures of women. With her personal scrapbooks at home, Elaine is much braver and less conventional than with Grace's. The pictures in the magazines represent the gender and family ideals of the forties, but Elaine creatively transforms them: "[i]f I don't like their faces I cut off the heads and glue other heads on. These women have dresses with puffed sleeves and full skirts, and white aprons that tie very tightly around their waists" (148). She particularly likes to cut out pictures of women who do things they are not supposed to do – gossip too much, are too sloppy or too bossy. She understands that whatever the women may do, there will be no end to imperfection: "[b]ut it pleases me somehow to cut out all these imperfect women, with their forehead wrinkles that show how worried they are, and fix them into my scrapbook" (149). Realism, subversion, emancipation, and artistic transformation (from fact to fiction) are important aspects here that will determine the quality of her emerging art as well.

Comic books figure largely in the novel. Elaine's brother is a collector of comic books and Elaine also loves to read them. Both the contents and the style of illustration fascinate her: "[i]n the comics there are people with round holes for eyes, others who can hypnotise you instantly, others with secret identities, others who can stretch their faces into any shape at all" (59). When Elaine's brother is later killed by terrorists on a plane she compares them to comic book characters:

> [i]t's hard to tell how many of them there are altogether, because of the identical pillowcases [over their heads]. They're like those characters in old comic books, the ones with two identities. These men have been caught half-way through their transformation: ordinary bodies but with powerful, supernatural heads, deformed in the direction of heroism, or villainy. (412)

The style of comics likewise informs the expression of Elaine's hatred of Mrs Smeath: "[i]f my eyes could shoot out fatal rays like the ones in comic books I would incinerate her on the spot" (193). The technique of comics is also used in Elaine's paintings of her: in the picture *Leprosy*, Mrs Smeath sits in front of a mirror with half of her face peeling off like the villain in a horror comic Elaine once read (372). Last but not least, Elaine does a series about her mother, employing a compositional feature of comics. The series is called *Pressure Cooker* and consists of six panels, like a double triptych or a comic book, arranged in two groups, three on top, three underneath (160).

Elaine's professional identity formation is eventually concluded by the victory of art/aesthetics over science, her preference of artist to biologist in her professional choice. Her father had sensitised her to botanical beauty during his field studies in the north,[10] on which his family accompanied him. In the middle of her biology exams it occurs to her that she is not going to be a biologist, but a painter (274). Her later art qualifies as applied biology, science with an aesthetic edge. For her father she is "a botanist manqué" (306). Whereas her brother becomes a scientist, moving away from biology to astrophysics, she also drops pure biology as a professional option, but integrates her skills from that area into her art, which is biologically focused and does not deny its scientific origins.

3. Identity: the Body, the Gaze, Clothing

Like time, the body is also conceptualised in various ways and expresses aspects of physicality, sexuality, identity, and aesthetics.[11] Atwood creates an aesthetics of the female body in social reality (the Canada from the forties to the eighties) as well as in visual/medial representations (in art history, popular culture, architecture; among them several representations of the Virgin Mary). The female beauty ideal is seen as temporally and culturally bound, and thus also as a gendered concept, the projection of a male-made aesthetics onto women.

The gaze at bodies also allows for psychological insights, even when looking at representations of bodies in paintings: at the opening of the Retrospective, looking at her pictures again, Elaine sees herself through the eyes of Mrs Smeath. She grasps the true character of that woman and of their ambivalent relationship:

> [i]t's the eyes I look at now. I used to think these were self-righteous eyes, piggy and smug inside their wire frames; and they are. But they are also defeated eyes, uncertain and melancholy, heavy with unloved duty. The eyes of someone for whom God was a sadistic old man; the eyes of a small-town threadbare decency. Mrs. Smeath was a transplant to the city, from somewhere a lot smaller. A displaced person; as I was.
> Now I can see myself, through these painted eyes of Mrs. Smeath: a frazzle-headed ragamuffin from heaven knows where, a gypsy practically, with a heathen father and a feckless mother who traipsed around in slacks and gathered weeds. I was unbaptized, a nest for demons: how could she know what germs of blasphemy and unfaith were breeding in me? And yet she took me in. (427)

This instrumentalisation of the gaze culminates in the function of the blue cat's eye. The marble serves as an instrument of vision, helping Elaine to an impassive, distanced, impartial, scrutinising gaze which reveals the truth beneath the surface, reality behind appearance:

> [s]he [Cordelia] doesn't know what power this cat's eye has, to protect me. Sometimes when I have it with me I can see the way it sees. I can see people moving like bright animated dolls, their mouths opening and closing but no real words coming out. I can look at their shapes and sizes, their colors, without feeling anything else about them. I am alive in my eyes only. (151)

Moreover, the marble becomes an instrument of empowerment for Elaine:

> I keep my cat's eye in my pocket, where I can hold onto it. It rests in my hand, valuable as a jewel, looking out through bone and cloth with its impartial gaze. With the help of its power I retreat back into my eyes. Up ahead of me are Cordelia, Grace, and Carol. I look at their shapes as they walk […]. They're like puppets up ahead, small and clear. I could see them or not, at will. (166)

Last but not least, clothes, which are closely related to body and skin, are functionalised by Atwood as an intimate marker of identity. Elaine's changing clothing styles over time, when she alternately either observes or neglects the decorum of outward appearance, indicate the ambivalence of clothing as a marker of identity, a means of disguise/device of deception (masking, counterfeiting) or a protective shield. Elaine keeps on literally re-fashioning herself. Her outward appearance is a reflection of her current identity, whether she likes it or not (including doubts, crises and transformations), an expression of her unorthodoxy or conformism. At the time level of the present Elaine has difficulties coming to terms with her appearance. This has to do with her being middle-aged, but even more so with her being insecure about her professional standing, particularly shortly before the opening of her Retrospective. Getting ready to have a first look at the gallery, she plays with various deceptive alternatives to avoid revealing her true identity as Risley, a painter:

> I pull on my powder-blue sweatsuit, my disguise as a non-artist, and go down the four flights of stairs, trying to look brisk and purposeful. I could be a businesswoman out jogging, I could be a bank manager, on her day off. [...] I don't intend to go in, make myself known, not yet. I just want to look at it from the outside. I'll walk past, glance casually, pretending to be a housewife, a tourist, someone window-shopping. Galleries are frightening places of evaluation, of judgment. I have to work up to them. (19-20)

Not sure how to react to the moustache drawn over her face on one of the posters, which deforms her identity, she reflects upon its meaning, its potential for disguise and concealment, power and diminishment, and, in the end, adopts a stance of self-affirmation: "I have achieved, finally [...]. A public face, a face worth defacing.

This is an accomplishment, I have made something of myself, something or other, after all" (20). Her final decision about the dress for the opening is even more difficult. The last preparations show her ending up resigned with her age, her supposed deficits and lack of artistic charisma, but at the same time eventually accepting herself as she is (425).

4. Elaine's Emergence as an Artist: Art Studies, Lovers, Feminism

In retrospect, it is still almost incredible for Elaine that she should have come all this way at all. Her current reflections about her profession demonstrate her conflict between the image of the artist in society and her self-image:

> [a]longside my real life [with her husband and two daughters] I have a career, which may not qualify as exactly real. I am a painter. I even put that on my passport, in a moment of bravado, since the other choice would have been *housewife*. It's an unlikely thing for me to have become; on some days it still makes me cringe. Respectable people do not become painters: only overblown, pretentious, theatrical people. The word *artist* embarrasses me; I prefer *painter*, because it's more like a valid job. An artist is a tawdry, lazy sort of thing to be, as most people in this country will tell you. [...] But I only make enough [money] to generate envy, even among painters, not enough so I can tell everyone else to stuff it.
>
> Most of the time though I exult, and think I have had a narrow escape. (15; emphasis in the text)

She approaches the Retrospective with mixed feelings, is sceptical about the exhibition, but also feels flattered and proud of herself. The exhibition is a retrospective both of her art and her life. The professional making of Elaine as an artist is first of all deeply influenced by her art studies. After graduation from high school she starts her art training at the Toronto College of Art and the University of Toronto. The reader sees her pass through the historical periods, experimenting with various visual media and art forms, ranging from classic to popular, trivial, commercial and avant-garde. All this has an impact on her emerging art and her developing personality. Elaine notices the historical changes in artistic representation and is particularly disturbed by the representation of women:

> [t]he naked women are presented in the same manner as the plates of meat and dead lobsters, with the same attention to the play of candle-light on skin, the same lusciousness, the same sensuous and richly rendered detail, the same painterly delight in tactility. [...] They appear served up. (346)

This is in fact a fitting description of her own role at the time of her affair with art teacher Josef Hrbik, when she is dining out in splendour with him. Later she gives up on oil paintings because she dislikes the thickness, the obliteration of line. Light, a luminous flatness, is the decisive quality that she envisages for her own style of painting (*ibid*.). Consequently, she starts to experiment with various techniques with coloured pencils or egg tempera, the technique of monks. Although she does not know yet what she will paint she is convinced that it will appear in coloured plates, in books – like the work of Leonardo da Vinci, whose representations of hands, feet, hair and dead people she studies very closely. She is fascinated by and studies the effects of glass and other light-reflecting surfaces in paintings. She spends a long time, for instance, over Jan van Eyck's *The Arnolfini Marriage*, intrigued by the pier glass on the wall behind the two figures (i.e. the view from behind, from a mirror), which reflects in its convex surface not only their backs, but two other people who are not in the main picture at all. This pier glass serves as a mirror and evokes the function of the blue cat's eye as an empowered instrument of vision:

> [t]his round mirror is like an eye, a single eye that sees more than anyone else looking: over this mirror is written, *Johannes de Eyck fuit hic. 1434*. It's disconcertingly like a washroom scribble, something you'd write with spray paint on a wall. (347)

Gradually, the direction of her art and her artistic credo take shape. She is aware that she is not fashionable, in line with current trends, supposedly being too mimetic. But she continues although her work is not even approved of by her new artist-lover Jon.

Elaine's artistic identity is obviously also shaped through her lovers. After her scientist-father and brother it is her two lovers, the art school teacher Josef Hrbik, a refugee from the Hungarian revolution, and the student Jon (who also becomes an artist and later Elaine's first husband), who influence her. The handing on of information, interests and skills from male to female and the respec-

tive shaping of an outlook establishes a parallel with Victorian patriarchal control over females. All the men strive to improve her;
she is, as it were, a postmodern Galatea. Almost all of them (with
the exception of Ben, her second husband, who is not an artist) are
busy carving out difficult artistic careers for themselves in a Canada
torn in the competition between Continental Europe, the US and
Britain. Yet they also try to mould her like material for an art object
(see the reference to the moulds and masks in Jon's studio, 18; parts
of the body are littered over his place – a parallel to the many fragmented lives and identities in the narrative) and fashion her. In the
long run, however, they do indeed advance her identity formation
tremendously by causing her to react either by following their models, distancing herself from them, and/or making use of the space
allowed to her by them. Her notions of love and sex, lifestyle, gender and art are thus constantly being re-defined. By the side of these
men she struggles through various severe identity crises, but finds a
way of embodying these experiences into her paintings. "With Jon
it's like falling downstairs" (391), is how she describes the relationship with her second lover. In the picture *Falling Women* she questions the traditional myth of the story of Adam and Eve and re-in-
terprets the meaning of 'fallen':

> [f]allen women were women who had fallen onto men and hurt them-
> selves. [...] Of course there was Eve and the Fall; but there was nothing
> about falling in that story, which was only about eating, like most chil-
> dren's stories.
> *Falling Women* showed the women, three of them, falling as if by
> accident off a bridge, their skirts opened into bells by the wind, their
> hair streaming upward. Down they fell, unto the men who were lying
> unseen, jagged and dark and without volition, far below. (286)

The feeling of constantly being dominated and manipulated by her
artist-lovers, being caught up in destructive relationships (jealousy,
manipulation, control) and forced also to stagnate artistically, almost suffocated her in her youth in Toronto. Her picture *Life Drawing* makes statements about her doubtful relationships with Josef
and Jon:

> Josef preserved in aspic and good enough to eat. He is on the left side of
> the picture, stark-naked but turned with a twist half away from the
> viewer, so what you get is the ass end, then the torso in profile. On the

right side is Jon, in the same position. Their bodies are somewhat ideal-ized: less hairy than they really were, the muscle groups in higher defi-nition, the skin luminous. [...] Both of them have wonderful bums.

Each of them is painting a picture, each picture is on an easel. Josef's is of a voluptuous but not overweight woman, sitting on a stool with a sheet draped between her legs, her breasts exposed; her face is Pre-Raphaelite, brooding, consciously mysterious. Jon's painting is a series of intestinal swirls, in hot pink, raspberry-ripple red and Burgundy Cherry purple.

The model is seated on a chair between them, face front, bare feet flat on the floor. She's clothed in a white bedsheet, wrapped around her below the breasts. Her hands are folded neatly in her lap. Her head is a sphere of bluish glass. (388)

The processes of maturation and emancipation discussed above are supported by Elaine's approaching feminism over time. This affects her private life, but also her self-image as an artist and her artistic credo. The beginnings of this development coincide with the time when her relationship with Jon is also crumbling to pieces. Elaine starts to attend all-women meetings with other female artists. They tackle the male-made beauty ideal for women, male violence, fe-male discrimination at work, financial discrimination of women. At a group show held in a small defunct supermarket, Elaine has her artistic breakthrough. She notices that her co-presenters make state-ments, have a confidence and assurance that she thinks is lacking her own paintings which are too highly finished, too decorative, too merely pretty. However, when a female moral-religious fanatic misreads the representational nature of one of her Mrs Smeath paintings, *White Gift*, and hurls a bottle of ink at it, the show attracts the media and she acquires a reputation of sorts. This minor, ambiguous reputation helps her in Vancouver where she tries to carve out a career for herself after having left her first husband with her daughter. After some time, she realises that she cannot fully share the rigid feminist convictions, the one-sided focus on female pain and male guilt. In addition, having been manipulated a lot in the past, she cannot stand being corrected and bossed around any more. She ends up torn between defiance and envy. Before she turns up in the gallery called Sub-Versions her doubts reflect her attitude towards feminism: she resists the impulse to excuse herself and leave, thinks she should be grateful for the honour done to her, but still feels excluded.

A highlight in this discussion is Elaine's desperate, even nonsensical interview done by the much younger Andrea before the opening of the Retrospective (92-95). The talk is exemplary of Elaine's attitude to feminism: it is an encounter between two women representing two different generations who live in two almost incompatible worlds of perception and have differing attitudes towards life, art, and gender. After Elaine's initial insecurity, she proves herself superior, mocking the apparent progressivity of Andrea's radical feminism and the relativity of societal developments. She exposes the interviewer's attitude of uncritically and ahistorically presupposing emancipation everywhere, at all times, in just everybody. She also corrects Andrea's historically incorrect assumption about her generation (the seventies when women were getting attention), fully unmasking the interviewer's naive presupposition of immediate and short-term influences, her ignorance of the importance of early socialisation on the long way to artistic success. Elaine makes clear that she was shaped by the war (not the Vietnam War, as Andrea naively assumes, but World War II), its memories, the colours of the forties, a different kind of behaviour. Last but not least, she corrects Andrea's ultra self-righteousness regarding the equality of the sexes for a better-informed view of the realities between men and women in life and art. The interview is totally incongruent because what Elaine has to say is not what Andrea wants to hear. A moderate, more realistic and authentically lived form of feminism stemming from experience is juxtaposed here to a more radical, theory-based, ideologised form of feminism very remote from the realities of life and art business.[12] Putting an end to the clash between concepts and reality Elaine eventually rejects the label of 'feminist painter', insisting on her right to paint women in her own unorthodox way.

5. Artistic Credo and Art Reception

The Retrospective offers the reader the possibility of seeing Elaine's art in its total perspective now. S/he is able to move across the time layers, decode the 'life on the wall' and learn something about the nature of artistic representation. The reader recognises all the influences of her life that inscribed themselves into those pictures. The process of their artistic re-creation and psychological re-appraisal has a tripartite structure: experience, recollection and artistic (re-) construction/appropriation. The chronological arrangement of Elaine's pictures reveals that particularly clearly. The pictures enclose the time layers: Elaine walks around the exhibition surrounded by the time she has made – she preserves time through her pictures. Moreover, this total view of her works shows the effects of the combination of all these ingredients and skills, disclosing the unique artistic credo underlying her works.

Any former impression of a male moulding of her art is now corrected once and for all: obviously Elaine has been resilient, independent and creative enough to distance herself from any simple imitation of male models in life, in her profession, and in her artistic practice. She has moved away from both Josef's conventional mimetic and Jon's pure avant-garde art and found her own style. In the same well-balanced way that she is capable of embracing a moderate form of feminism and criticising/mocking more radical forms, Elaine is sceptical about the current art business and yet able to deal with it successfully. Over decades, in fits and turns, through relationship- and motherhood crises and phases of fatigue and burn-out, she has developed her own style out of these highly diverse influences, evading *Zeitgeist* and trends.

In addition, instinctively, and, over time more aware of her aims, methods and skills, she has sought to create an art full of life and experience, a bodily art that she prefers to a neutral, sterile, antiseptic art.[13] Art for her is something which is still alive and in flux. Certainly, once pictures are hung on a wall the separation between life (the original impetus, a kind of energy which has inscribed itself into the pictures), artist/producer and art object/product is complete, but at the same time the communication between artist, work of art and recipient starts. In spite of mimetic elements in her paintings and nature as her point of departure, her art is not naturalistic, but surrealistic. Her methods of composition and painting merge reality and imagination, placing the objects in unusual, nonrealistic settings. She thus re-fashions and re-arranges them – another way of re-creating lives through the mix of fact and fiction. The ambivalent scientific-aesthetic appeal – a reunion of the principles of science and art in her paintings – and the surrealist technique which permeates temporal and spatial layers, polarise recipients.[14]

6. Conclusion

Atwood's treatment of artistic issues testifies to her vivid visual imagination, her expertise in the history and theory of Fine Arts and the art business. She proves herself a trained and cunning postmodernist when uniting the theory and practice of painting in the making of artist Elaine Risley. Risley as a postmodernist female Canadian artist is shown to emerge over several decades following World War II. She finds her individual path through perceiving and studying, but also setting herself off critically from art trends on the European continent, in Great Britain, Canada and the US. Her art is a postmodern multi- and intermedial synthesis inspired by nature and science, the composite result of ambivalent life and artistic influences. This is why she defies strict definitions and reductionist labels, why she resents being monopolised by trends and theories.

Risley's art is authentic, firmly rooted in life with its infinite material manifestations and precarious psychological experiences. She becomes a successful artist who survives in and through her art because she incorporates problematic experiences into her artistic (re-)constructions. As her life is mirrored, structured, shaped and appropriated in her paintings, transferred into a visual medium, female autobiography can be said to appear twice in the novel: in the narrative and in the paintings. The postmodernist portrait of the artist as a young thing is informed by the intermedial interaction of text and pictures, the integration of symbolic and iconic representations.

Notes

1   As to the concept of identity, it is important to see it as bound up with the subject-position of the individual: "[i]deology and language attempt to create a new representation or belief in the consciousness of the 'individual' – who, in (mis)recognizing her or his image (in *Discourse* as in a mirror) takes up a subject-position (assumes an 'identity'). Each person is therefore constantly interpellated or 'called' into a particular cultural position by discourses of gender, class, nationalism, '*Race*', sexuality, and so on" (Childs & Williams 1997: 234; emphasis in the text). Terms and concepts of postcolonial criticism are especially useful in current debates of identity because "it refuses an antagonistic or struggle-based model of politics in favor

of one that emphasises 'cultural difference', 'ambivalen[ce]' and 'the more complex cultural and political boundaries that exist on the cusp' of what 'modern' philosophy had imagined as the determinate categories of social reality" (Lazarus 2004: 4). For a discussion of the methodological and terminological advantages and limits of postcolonial theory and criticism see Gandhi (1998: 167-176).

2   On Atwood's general concern with questions of individual and national, female and Canadian identity, Canadianness, multiculturality, the role of history and memory and narrating the self, see Kuester (2002: 216-217); Kreutzer (2004: 454-455; 482; 487-488); Lucking (2003: 14; 15; 21; 163; 164; 168; 172); Howells (2003: 1-6; 8; 10-14; 18-20; 27-29; 32; 34; 37; 38; 40; 43; 203); Howells (2004: 201-203; 205; 206). For a general concern of contemporary Canadian literature in English with issues of Canadian identity see Renger (2005: 66-69; 361-379).

3   Some ideas from other essays of mine have been used for the present study, see Bimberg (2009) and Bimberg (2007). On postmodern narrative techniques (e.g. temporal disorder, erosion of the sense of time, pastiche, fragmentation, looseness of association, merging of the literal and the metaphorical) see Lewis (2005: 111; 113-115; 117; 118; 120).

4   Atwood (1989: 3). Further references to this edition will be included in the text.

5   For more details about this concept see Bimberg (2009: 134-139).

6   See *ibid.*, 125-134 on the formative impact of Elaine Risley's childhood experiences.

7   For parallels between *Cat's Eye* and *Bodily Harm* (1982) (Rennie's leaving Toronto, the place of her victimisation), *Cat's Eye* and *Surfacing* (1972) (the nameless narrator fears for her own sanity; she puts psychological and physical distance between herself and others), see Sheckels (2003: 13; 14; 93-94). Contrary to *Surfacing*, however, where the narrator is told that she cannot be a great artist because she is female and "she opts for the opposite extreme of a sell-out illustrator" (*ibid.*, 96), Elaine Risley makes it to the top.

8   Place is in fact an important marker of identity in the narration: "[b]y 'Place' we do not simply mean 'landscape'. Indeed the idea of 'landscape' is predicated upon a particular philosophic tradition in which the objective world is separated from the viewing subject. Rather 'place' in post-colonial societies is a complex interaction of language, history and environment. [...] Place is thus the concomitant of difference, [...]. Place therefore, the 'place' of the 'subject', throws light upon subjectivity itself, [...] so the discourse of place is a process of a continual dialectic between subject and object" (Ashcroft, Griffiths & Tiffin 1995: 391-392). For a fuller treatment of the interlinking of the city of Toronto and Elaine Risley's identity see Bimberg (2007: 80-93).

9   See also the illustration on the title page of the Bantam edition of the novel.

10 This is an autobiographical parallel to Atwood, whose father was an ento-
mologist who uprooted the family in the summer to follow him around the
bush country of northern Ontario and Quebec; see Sage (1999: 25); Kuhn
(2005: 10); Karrasch (1995: 25); Sullivan (1997: 63); New & Hengen
(2002: 49).
11 For more details, see Bimberg (2009: 139-145).
12 New describes this representation of feminism as characteristic of Atwood:
"[b]ehind all these books [*Cat's Eye, The Robber Bride, Alias Grace*] lies
the dystopian *The Handmaid's Tale* (1985), the resonant politics of feminism and its limits (the women in Atwood's novels are notoriously cruel to
one another)" (New 2003: 304). For an analysis of *Alias Grace* (1996), see
Brigitte Glaser's contribution in the present volume.
13 In that sense, Atwood seems to favour the so-called "Sacred Fount" tradition ("the assumption that the artist must 'live' in order to create"; "the equa-
tion of art with experience") to the "Ivory Tower" tradition ("art as a religion"; "the conflicting ideal of detachment") in her representations (Beebe
1964: vi). For an elucidation of these concepts, see the introduction to this
volume.
14 See Bimberg (2009: 145-151).

Bibliography

Ashcroft, Bill, Gareth Griffiths & Helen Tiffin: "Place. Introduction". – In
B.A., G.G. & H.T. (Eds.): *The Post-Colonial Studies Reader*, London &
New York, 1995, pp. 391-394.
Atwood, Margaret: *Cat's Eye*, New York *et al.*, 1989 [1988].
Beebe, Maurice: *Ivory Towers and Sacred Founts. The Artist as Hero in Fic-
tion from Goethe to Joyce*, New York, 1964.
Bimberg, Christiane: "Childhood and Postmodern Identity Construction in
Margaret Atwood's *Cat's Eye*. Body, Art, Biology". – In C.B. & Igor
Volkov (Eds.): *Textual Intricacies. Essays on Structure and Intertextuality
in Nineteenth and Twentieth Century Fiction in English*, Trier, 2009, pp.
125-153.
—: "Urban Space, City Life, and Identity Construction in Margaret Atwood's
Cat's Eye", *Izvestiya Juznogo Federalnogo Universiteta. Filologicheskiye
Nauki* Nos 1-2, 2007, 80-93.
Childs, Peter & Patrick Williams: *An Introduction to Post-Colonial Theory*,
London, 1997.
Gandhi, Leela: *Postcolonial Theory. A Critical Introduction*, Edinburgh, 1998.
Howells, Coral Ann: *Contemporary Canadian Women's Fiction. Refiguring
Identities*, New York, 2003.

–: "Writing by Women". – In Eva-Marie Kröller (Ed.): *The Cambridge Companion to Canadian Literature*, Cambridge *et al.*, 2004, pp. 194-215.

Karrasch, Anke: *Die Darstellung Kanadas im literarischen Werk von Margaret Atwood*, Trier, 1995.

Kreutzer, Eberhard: "Die neuen englischsprachigen Literaturen". – In Hans Ulrich Seeber (Ed.): *Englische Literaturgeschichte*, Stuttgart & Weimar, 2004, pp. 423-495.

Kuester, Martin: "Canadian Literature in English". – In Christa Jansohn (Ed.): *Companion to the New Literatures in English*, Berlin, 2002, pp. 202-232.

Kuhn, Cynthia G.: *Self-Fashioning in Margaret Atwood's Fiction. Dress, Culture, and Identity*, New York *et al.*, 2005.

Lazarus, Neil: "Introducing Postcolonial Studies". – In N.L. (Ed.): *The Cambridge Companion to Postcolonial Literary Studies*, Cambridge, 2004, pp. 1-16.

Lewis, Barry: "Postmodernism and Fiction". – In Stuart Sim (Ed.): *The Routledge Companion to Postmodernism,* London & New York, 2005, pp. 111-121.

Lucking, David: *The Serpent's Part. Narrating the Self in Canadian Literature*, Berne *et al.*, 2003.

New, William H. & Shannon Hengen: "Atwood, Margaret". – In W.H.N. (Ed.): *Encyclopedia of Literature in Canada*, Toronto *et al.*, 2002, pp. 48-51.

New, William H.: *A History of Canadian Literature*, Montreal *et al.*, 2003 [1989].

Renger, Nicola: *Mapping and Historiography in Contemporary Canadian Literature in English*, Frankfurt *et al.*, 2005.

Sage, Lorna: *The Cambridge Guide to Women's Writing in English*, Cambridge *et al.*, 1999.

Sheckels, Theodore F.: *The Island Motif in the Fiction of L.M. Montgomery, Margaret Laurence, Margaret Atwood, and Other Canadian Women Novelists*, New York *et al.*, 2003.

Sullivan, Rosemary: "Atwood, Margaret". – In Eugene Benson & William Toye (Eds.): *The Oxford Companion to Canadian Literature*, Don Mills, 1997, pp. 63-66.

Brigitte Glaser (Göttingen)

Women's Art of Telling Li(v)es. Female Artist Figures in Margaret Atwood's *Alias Grace* and *The Blind Assassin*

1. Introduction

With the two award-winning novels *Alias Grace* (1996) and *The Blind Assassin* (2000) and two non-fictional texts,[1] *In Search of* Alias Grace (1997) and *Negotiating with the Dead* (2002), Canadian novelist Margaret Atwood not only reached a new height in her creative output around the turn of the century but also presented in these texts her thoughts on Canadian history and historiography, on the art of writing postmodernist fiction, and on women's place in all of these. By looking back at two periods in history during which the loyalty of Canadians towards the British motherland was still strong, and at the same time alluding to subversive processes at work which suggest Canadian attempts to move towards a new sense of nationhood, Atwood participates in the postcolonial re-valuation of the country's past so prevalent in contemporary Canadian fiction.[2] Since in each of the novels the primary figure associated with challenging tradition, the old class- and race-based hierarchies as well as patriarchal structures is a woman, Atwood is able to unite her postcolonial and her feminist interests.

Known as a writer who is "most concerned with infiltrating traditionally male-centred literary genres and conventions and productively renegotiating the terms that define them",[3] Atwood displays in these novels a markedly feminist approach, especially when she has her two protagonists shape the rendition of their life stories in creative as well as subversive ways. At the centre of *Alias Grace* readers encounter the self-representation of Grace Marks, a historical character who, as a sixteen-year-old servant-girl, was convicted in 1843 of having assisted in the murders of Thomas Kinnear, her master, and of Nancy Montgomery, a fellow servant and Kinnear's mistress. After eighteen years in prison and, temporarily, in a mental institution, Grace takes the opportunity to present her version of the events leading up to the murders and beyond. In doing so, her skills in various arts and crafts emerge. Atwood's novel *The Blind Assassin*, by contrast, focuses on a woman's skill in one art only, writing, but it foregrounds this art in all its extraordinary complexity. This narrative revolves around Iris Chase-Griffen, an old lady presenting her memoir which, in addition to her and her family's lives, covers many of the social and political developments of twentieth-century Canada and is at the same time interspersed with segments of a scandalous romance novel, the product of her sister Laura, a young and budding artist. This soon-to-be notorious novel in turn contains an interpolated science-fiction narrative which, similar to the framing romance story, reflects on crucial events that are also narrated in the memoir. Iris eventually turns out to be the author of all of these interwoven and ultimately autobiographical texts. Both Grace and Iris may therefore be considered artists of a particular kind: women who, like Atwood on the authorial level, analyse the vagaries of private life against the background of public life and thereby also represent and assess historical circumstances and developments. The historical background against which each story unfolds is firmly marked by a colonial mindset, that is, a deference to the dominant British values and manners, the British social, legal and educational system and British political interests and loyalties. Hence it is not surprising that Grace's position as an Irish immigrant of the lower orders is a precarious one even before she is accused of her involvement in a crime against her betters, and that Iris's affair with a communist agitator would have been considered scandalous by her contemporaries, given her father's and her husband's connections to the Anglo-Canadian establishment.

Apart from the feminist agenda and the postcolonial stance, Atwood pursues her interests in the writing of postmodernist fiction. Not only do the two novels employ generic hybridisation, self-reflexiveness and intertextuality to emphasise issues of class, gender and politics as well as "the idea of the postmodern self as made up of different surfaces or veneers",[4] but the author also uses new approaches to historical fiction which draw attention to the scholarly insight that our understanding of historiography is informed by notions of constructedness, multiplicity of perspective, and elusiveness.

2. Historiographic Metafiction

With *Alias Grace* and *The Blind Assassin* Atwood presents narratives which Linda Hutcheon in *A Poetics of Postmodernism* (1988) refers to as 'historiographic metafiction' and defines as "novels which are both intensely self-reflexive and yet lay claim to historical events and personages" and as works in which the "theoretical self-awareness of history and fiction as human constructs [...] is made the grounds for [a] rethinking and reworking of the forms and contents of the past".[5] Hutcheon furthermore comments on the subversion of the notion that narrators tell the truth and points out that when postmodernist novelists render historical events in their fiction, it is usually in the form of "a dialogue with the past in the light of the present" and thus from a recognition that the past (or the 'truth') can never be fully known.[6]

This aspect of the inaccessibility of the 'truth' with regard to a subject matter, an individual or an event figures prominently in both novels and is conveyed by Atwood through using narrative techniques suggestive of the idea of a collage. Thus she uses, for instance, the notion of the patchwork quilt or the web for her own form of storytelling as well as her product, the piece of fiction, as both of them are constituted of a variety of elements: in both *Alias Grace* and *The Blind Assassin* there is a juxtaposition of perspectives, a mixing of generic traditions and the incorporation into the fictional texts of epigraphs, newspaper clippings, interviews, confessions, letters, the description of a photograph, and pieces from ancient history, legend or mythology.[7]

The aspect of 'versions' of history is furthermore reinforced through the juxtaposition of private and public life, since both novels are fictions in which "individual memory and experience and collective memory and experience come together".[8] In *The Blind Assassin*, for example, World War I, the Great Depression and the social upheavals of the thirties are rendered by Atwood in the form of the effects they have on the protagonists' private lives: through their acquaintance with the political activist Alex Thomas the two protected and privileged Chase sisters learn about the plight of working-class people (in their own country and elsewhere) as well as the social struggles occurring at that time in faraway places across the ocean. The female protagonist of *Alias Grace* is depicted as an Irish working-class girl who is judged by some against the background of William Lyon Mackenzie's 1837 armed rebellion in Ontario and the threat of further social upheavals.[9] She is above all portrayed as destitute immigrant woman, harassed daughter, exploited domestic and possibly innocent prisoner who is subjected to an increasingly hostile environment. The condescending treatment extended to her culminates in her exposure to the male-dominated medical establishment, as represented by the American psychiatrist Dr Simon Jordan, who wishes to gain fame and fortune by illuminating her role in the notorious murder case.[10]

3. The Protagonists as Young Women and 'Artists'

At the centre of the two novels are violence and trauma experienced by young women, which in turn induce these two females to later render their lives in art. The result is selves fashioned through various artistic and artful acts. Both Grace and Iris use their inventiveness and creativity to cope with the pain inflicted on them, thereby crossing the boundaries of public and private and making their life stories known to the world.

Atwood unfolds her narratives with the help of complex perspective. In *Alias Grace* she alternates between the first-person account of the 32-year-old Grace, who at that point has been a prisoner for half of her life, and a third-person narrative with a focalisation on Dr Simon Jordan, who wishes to unravel the mystery surrounding Grace's story by employing new scientific methods. Grace, as the organiser of her narration,[11] is an autodiegetic narrator addressing Dr Jordan and, when he is absent, speaking to herself: "she continues the story, complete with direct addresses, composing it in her mind as if he were still listening and anticipating his desires".[12] Eventually regarding Dr Jordan as her confidant, she even writes mental letters to him. While her perception of the dramatic events surrounding her life is represented as the dominant point of view, it is nevertheless accompanied by and contrasted with the evaluation of Grace by many other individuals, fictional as well as historical.

Compared to the polyphonic character of *Alias Grace*, *The Blind Assassin* is also presented as a heteroglossic text, but emerges as an ultimately monological narration.[13] Its complexity and seemingly multiperspectival approach lie in the Chinese-box design of the novel. While the framing narrative consists of the memoirs of the elderly Iris Chase-Griffen, this account is interspersed with sections taken from a romance novel supposedly written by Iris's sister Laura and published posthumously in 1947. Within this novel called *The Blind Assassin*, excerpts from yet another narrative, a dystopian tale, are given. All of the embedded narratives turn out to be closely linked to the frame story, in the sense that the fictional narratives mirror and comment on the confessional account of the protagonist.

In addition to the use of a prevailing female perspective meant to challenge the conventional male-dominated representation of history, Atwood foregrounds the historical victimisation of women by repeatedly alluding to the intersection of class and gender. While in *Alias Grace* the situation of the servant-class in mid-nineteenth-century Ontario is depicted in some detail, *The Blind Assassin* looks critically at the life of the colonial establishment in the first half of the twentieth century. In the earlier novel Atwood exposes, for instance, the sexual exploitation of servant girls in the representation of several other women who figure prominently in Grace's life and narrative. The first one is Mary Whitney, a fellow servant and friend, who had an enormous influence on her, as throughout her narrative Grace quotes Mary on politics and practical matters of daily life. Mary, seduced by her young master and left pregnant, dies after a botched abortion. Hoping that the future fellow servant Nancy Montgomery will, owing to their similar status, her kindness and knowledge of life, eventually fill Mary's place, Grace accepts the new position at Mr Kinnear's house: "[s]he resembled Mary Whitney, or so then I thought; and I'd been depressed in spirits ever since Mary's death. And so I decided to go".[14] The hitherto naive Grace Marks is severely disappointed when she is not greeted by Nancy on her arrival (Atwood 1996: 244), the other woman thereby insinuating a difference of class and position between the two of them. Only gradually does Grace become aware of the shameful relationship Nancy is engaged in with her master and realises that she herself has been used. At the heart of *The Blind Assassin* readers encounter the Chase sisters' victimisation at the hands of men.

While there appears to be romantic love only on Laura's part for the unconventional and subversive hero Alex Thomas, her sister Iris, after having been urged into a marriage of convenience with a rich and cruel industrialist by her father, engages in an affair with Alex. Hence Iris's memoir reveals also that which is the source of her sense of guilt: her betrayal of Laura, when she informs her of Alex's death while at the same time admitting her affair with him, these two pieces of information then leading to her sister's suicide. In turn, Iris later finds Laura's notebooks and is confronted with the revelation that her sister had been sexually abused by Iris's husband.

Given the problematic situations of the two protagonists and the external and internal pressures they are exposed to, art and artfulness become their means of coping with the nightmares haunting them and the guilt they feel. Taking the chance to gain her freedom if she cooperates with Dr Jordan, Grace deals with her traumatic experiences, such as the loss of loved ones, betrayal and disappointment, and the encounter of violence at a very early age, through a multi-facetted creative refashioning of her life story. As Atwood points out with regard to her protagonist, Grace has "strong motives to narrate, but also strong motives to withhold; the only power left to her as a convicted and imprisoned criminal comes from a blend of these two motives".[15] In contrast to this, Iris copes – by means of a palimpsestic text – with her victimisation at the hands of men, her need to camouflage the adulterous relationship with Alex Thomas and her sense of guilt after her sister's suicide, since both the incentive for fashioning her life-story and her addressees have changed over time. Having had her own needs in mind when she initially wrote the novel *The Blind Assassin* – "I wanted a memorial. That was how it began. For Alex, but also for myself" –[16] Iris later composes her memoir around segments of the earlier text in order to provide her granddaughter Sabrina with a new perspective on her family and thus also her own life.

4. The Form of Their Art

In both texts, the female protagonists stand out for a particular skill, that is, the combination of craft and creativity. They excel not only in writing, as is evident in Iris's production of an exceedingly complex narrative, but are also adept in the oral tradition of narration as well as in fashioning their lives with the help of a performance or through objects of art, as the example of Grace shows. Both characters are aware of themselves, or are perceived by others, as artists or 'crafty' individuals so that in Atwood's novels "the image of the woman as fabricator, seamstress, weaver, spider, becomes one with the image of tale-teller, writer".[17] Especially in *Alias Grace* scrapbooks, drawings, woven fabrics or quilts, conventionally associated with the female sphere, are repeatedly alluded to in the form of metaphors and leitmotifs, or are used as material objects which are described and commented on. Both female 'artists' tell their stories in covert and artistically modified ways: they change the known or official versions of their lives through the suppression and omission of some aspects, the obfuscation of other parts, and an inclination to allusiveness. Thus they present in their narratives "*creative confessions*" by fashioning their own version of truth for the purpose of "spiritual survival".[18] Iris goes to the extent of publishing *The Blind Assassin* as her sister's posthumous novel and thus shifts onto Laura the notoriety arising from the illicit affair being taken as autobiographical, only to claim later in her memoir joint authorship in a way that echoes Atwood's doubling of the self or "*double consciousness*" (Atwood 2000: 517; emphasis in the text):

> [a]s for the book, Laura didn't write a word of it. But you must have known that for some time. I wrote it myself, during my long evenings alone, when I was waiting for Alex to come back, and then afterwards, once I knew he wouldn't. I didn't think of what I was doing as writing – just writing it down. What I remembered, and also what I imagined, which is also the truth. I thought of myself as recording. [...]
>
> It was no great leap [...] naming Laura as the author. [...] it was merely doing justice, because I can't say Laura didn't write a word. Technically that's accurate, but in another sense – what Laura would have called the spiritual sense – you could say she was my collaborator. The real author was neither one of us. (512-513)

The possible motivations for this shift of authorship are various: turning Laura into the novel's author, Iris is able both to uphold her sister's memory and to exert control over it, she can defend Laura against criticism but she herself is responsible for Laura becoming the target of the same, and she can moreover take revenge on her husband by insinuating that the woman he had believed to have had a hold on had in fact had another lover.

Both female artists are skilful and crafty when it comes to the adaptation, alteration and manipulation of the facts that are known about them. As authors/narrators of their own stories they have recourse to various literary traditions and generic conventions which they juxtapose, merge or use as mirroring devices, assisting them in both the suppression on the surface level of the unmentionable facts while drawing attention to them in their artistically refashioned forms. Hence for a genuine decoding of their confessions these narrators require readers to transfer that which is revealed or alluded to in the work of art back onto the level of biography.

4.1 Narration

The artistic means both protagonists use most extensively is that of storytelling, either in the form of oral narration or as written and printed text. Both Grace and Iris turn to storytelling in order to challenge the representations and perceptions of their lives and personalities by others. They employ various aspects typical of narratives for fashioning their life stories. In terms of structure, each presents a roughly chronological account which, in Grace's case, is interrupted by flashbacks, dreams and visions, while Iris intersperses her narrative with segments of fiction. Grace's retelling of her life is intriguing when it comes to her selection of what she reports. Juxtaposed with an abundance of details and the occasional embroidery, that is, her adding "a touch of colour" (Atwood 1996: 424), she tends to draw her listener's attention to less important matters, as Dr Jordan correctly perceives: "he has an uneasy sense that the very plenitude of her recollections may be a sort of distraction, a way of drawing the mind away from some hidden but essential fact" (215). Especially towards the end of her narrative, when Dr Jordan, her confidant, no longer comes to visit her, the question of material selection weighs heavily on her mind. She appears to be obsessed with what she might later tell him (424), what he might want to hear (427), what Mr Mackenzie, her lawyer, has advised her to tell during the trial (429-430) and what others have written about her or have made of her story. The latters' "misconstruction" (431) she is now eagerly working to subvert.

Both narratives are composed of pieces that differ generically. In *The Blind Assassin*, the personal memoir is, in addition to the fiction, interspersed with excerpts referring to public history, such as newspaper clippings, many of them "pseudo-documents, which offer a pastiche of style and content of various Canadian newspapers, whereby narrative is shown to be an instrument of dominant ideology".[19] These references to the historical conditions by which the protagonists are influenced assist Atwood in voicing her criticism of Canadian colonial society. By revealing its downsides at different stages in history, and by identifying groups and individuals positioned at the losing end of its respective communities, the author exposes the existence of power structures modelled after the imperial centre and meant to strengthen its hold on the distant outpost. Another means applied by Grace Marks in her narration is that of embellishment. Thus Grace, who repeatedly comments self-consciously on her skills in presenting her version of the events, admits to sprucing up the tale she tells Dr Jordan out of gratefulness:

> [b]ecause he was so thoughtful as to bring me this radish, I set to work willingly to tell my story, and to make it as interesting as I can, and rich in incident, as a sort of return gift to him; for I have always believed that one good turn deserves another. (291)

Evidently knowledgeable with regard to those literary traditions that were particularly popular among readers in the early nineteenth century; Grace has recourse to elements of the Gothic and the sentimental to make her narrative more interesting. Through her description of dreams and nightmares, which the psychiatrist is immediately inclined to analyse and draw conclusions from, she achieves the desired response:

> Dr. Jordan is writing eagerly, as if his hand can scarcely keep up, and I have never seen him so animated before. It does my heart good to feel I can bring a little pleasure into a fellow-being's life; and I think to myself, I wonder what he will make of all that. (335)

Grace is furthermore skilful in hinting at what is to come, thus creating an atmosphere of foreboding: she describes, for example, the pleasant hot summer evening she, Nancy Montgomery, James McDermott and Jamie Walsh spent together in the absence of Mr Kinnear, only to associate the end of the evening with the fateful voyage she had experienced when coming to Canada and to hint at the sudden presence of an iceberg (273); or she cites, as she approaches the day on which the murders took place, Nancy's remark that she might give Grace notice since she is afraid of her and considers her a possibly mad woman (331-332). That Grace is playing with her addressee, Dr Jordan, becomes clear in her ironic comments on the effect her construction of a Gothic tale has on the listener: Grace is able to get the doctor's full attention and thus ensures that he will soon return for the continuation of the story. When she then, however, withholds detailed information about the actual murders, claiming amnesia, and is thus in danger of losing Dr Jordan's attention, she quickly turns to another genre. Through references to McDermott's sexual assaults on her which she successfully fends off through fainting fits, Grace places herself in the footsteps of eighteenth-century sentimental heroines. It is especially Samuel Richardson's Pamela and Clarissa, as well as Henry Fielding's Fanny (in *Joseph Andrews*, 1742) who are evoked in Grace's dramatic accounts of herself as persecuted damsel in distress.

In *The Blind Assassin*, by contrast, Iris Chase parodies the conventions of popular romance and science fiction as well as older texts, and uses them for her own purpose. By transferring constellations from ancient history and myth to a dystopian world and thus changing the context which her protagonists, the two unnamed lovers, evoke in their storytelling, Iris is, by implication, able to comment critically on the Canadian reality the young female writer experiences outside the text. Thus she likens the oppressive treatment of both women and members of the servant classes as represented in the mythical world of Zycron, and in particular the projected rape of the sacrificial virgin, who is rescued by the blind assassin, to her own suppression by her father, her forced marriage to the industrialist Griffen and her escape from the power structures imposed on her by means of the affair with the communist agitator Alex Thomas and through the writing of the scandalous piece of fiction.

Narrating in instalments constitutes another characteristic found in both texts. Iris deliberately alternates between autobiographical segments and excerpts from both romance novel and science-fiction tale, with the intention of indicating that the difficult situations the protagonists in the respective fictions are in resemble that of the central characters in the autobiographical account. As a result, the excerpts from the interpolated novel fill the lacunae of Iris's confessional text, that is, those significant facts about her life which she fails to give in her memoir. In the case of Grace, the episodic narration is linked by her former lawyer Mackenzie with yet another literary tradition: storytelling after the model of the *Arabian Nights*. Suspicious about the truthfulness of her account, Mackenzie warningly compares Grace with one of world literature's most accomplished storytellers when he discusses the young woman with Dr Jordan:

> [I]et me put it this way – did Scheherazade lie? Not in her own eyes; indeed, the stories she told ought never to be subjected to the harsh categories of Truth and Falsehood. They belong in another realm altogether. Perhaps Grace Marks has merely been telling you what she needs to tell, in order to accomplish the desired end. [...] To keep the Sultan amused, [...]. To forestall your departure, and make you stay in the room with her as long as possible. (452)

Grace's continuing fixation on Dr Jordan as her primary confidant even after he left Canada supports Mackenzie's argument that her narrative manipulations need to be seen within the context of her emotional condition. But this explanation may not suffice to explain her great need for self-representation by means of art and artfulness. Instead, in both texts, the desire to create a particular identity for oneself seems to be the driving force of the two artists' narrative endeavours, in addition to their need to deal with their sense of guilt. Both authors/narrators eventually allow for a splitting of their selves into two as a kind of coping mechanism which will help them endure the pain they suffered.[20] In *Alias Grace*, Atwood has her female protagonist reveal, during a scene of hypnotism, that she has for some time been inhabited by another self, the spirit of Mary Whitney, who declares: "[t]hey almost hanged her, but that would have been wrong. She knew nothing! I only borrowed her clothing for a time [...] Her earthly shell. Her fleshly garment" (482-483). This appearance of a "*double consciousness*" (517; emphasis in the text), whether induced by possession by a spirit, skilful performance or what would today be referred to as multiple personality disorder, provides Atwood with the opportunity of making "some startling revelations about Victorian hypocrisy, speaking the truth about a servant girl's situation of sexual and social oppression".[21] In *The Blind Assassin*, the protagonist is in a similar fashion changed by the death of a beloved person. Laura Chase's suicide by driving Iris's car over a bridge and wearing her sister's white gloves during the act constituted "a symbolic killing of Iris's social identity" and

101

has the consequence that Iris can continue with her life only by incorporating Laura into it:[22]

> [f]or Iris, writing her life becomes a prolonged negotiation with the dead, and constructing her identity means deconstructing her identity in the recognition that she has always been split, doubled, and defined by her close relationship with her young sister Laura.[23]

Not only does Iris suppress her own authorship of the romance novel titled *The Blind Assassin* and in turn render her dead sister a once promising young novelist, but through this act she also allows Laura to have a retrospective share in the illicit relationship with the man they both had been in love with. Iris is thus able to alleviate her sense of guilt and rewrite the two sisters' life stories. Hence Grace's meta-narrational comment made to divert the attention away from the possibility that she may in fact have been involved in the Kinnear murders is applicable also to Iris's situation after her sister's death:

> and today I must go on with the story. Or the story must go on with me, carrying me inside it, along the track it must travel, straight to the end, weeping like a train and deaf and single-eyed and locked tight shut; although I hurl myself against the walls of it and scream and cry, and beg to God himself to let me out.
>
> When you are in the middle of a story it isn't a story at all, but only a confusion; a dark roaring, a blindness, a wreckage of shattered glass and splintered wood; like a house in a whirl-wind, or else a boat crushed by the icebergs or swept over the rapids, and all aboard powerless to stop it. It's only afterwards that it becomes anything like a story at all. When you are telling it, to yourself or to someone else. (354-355)

Both stories will, so it seems, tell themselves, without their narrators knowing, at the point of telling, where they will lead them. Alternatively, they may have known the route and destiny all along but may have preferred not to let on.

4.2 Quilting

Atwood's deployment in *Alias Grace* of other forms of art in addition to oral narration in order to characterise her female protagonist's diverse skills highlights the significance of craft and craftiness in the novel. A craft traditionally performed by women, quilting figures prominently in *Alias Grace* both as a metaphor and a means of reassessing women's position in nineteenth-century Canada.[24] Traditionally an important aspect of a separate women's culture in North America which allows women to comment on their lives, quilting is appropriated by Atwood to engage with her novel in "current reconceptualizations of history and in a revaluation of a form traditionally associated with women and disassociated from the serious and valued realms of official history and art".[25] Quilts were originally made of scraps of fabrics sown together to form a large piece of cloth on which then a pattern may be discerned. A preliminary step towards quilting is the collection of material considered suitable for a subsequent reworking into a quilt. This act of collecting valuable pieces which would later be displayed was common also among those women in the nineteenth century who had taken up the fashion of having scrapbooks or keepsake albums and it constitutes a strategy pursued also by Atwood in her own piecing together of the narrative out of generically and thematically diverse parts. The idea of the novel as an album quilt is supported by Grace's reference to scrapbook collections early on in her conversations with Dr Jordan.[26] These collections usually consisted of newspaper cuttings or little pieces of gifts received from close female friends and they reflected on the themes of friendship, love and death. In *Alias Grace* the topic of crime is added since the prison governor's wife and his daughter have a special liking for reports on delinquents and their deeds, hence also display a great interest in the history of Grace whom they employ. Being the repositories of women's secrets and their most private thoughts and wishes, scrapbook collections and keepsakes hold a great fascination for Grace as she muses what her own keepsake album would be composed of:

> [a]nd as I knit, I think: What would I put into my Keepsake Album, if I had one? A bit of fringe, from my mother's shawl. A ravelling of red wool, from the flowered mittens that Mary Whitney made for me. A scrap of silk, from Nancy's good shawl. A bone button, from Jeremiah. A daisy, from the daisy chain made for me by Jamie Walsh.
> Nothing from McDermott, as I don't wish to remember him.
> But what should a Keepsake Album be? Should it be only the good things in life, or should it be all of the things? Many put in pictures of scenes and events they have never witnessed, such as Dukes and Niag-

ara Falls, which to my mind is a sort of cheating. Would I do that? Or would I be truthful to my own life.

> A piece of coarse cotton, from my Penitentiary nightdress. A square of bloodstained petticoat. A strip of kerchief, white with blue flowers. Love-in-a-mist. (459)

Grace's decision to be as inclusive as possible when it comes to the compilation of the significant aspects which make up her life not only points ahead to her subsequent integration of some of these aspects into the quilt she makes for herself but is also suggestive of the selective process at work in Grace's oral narrative as well as in Atwood's novel. In all of these selections, decisions have to be made as to which elements ought to be highlighted and which suppressed or left out. That the creation of a narrative is comparable to a piece of texture composed of different scraps of fabric emerges clearly also in Grace's comments on the constructedness of her tale when she ponders what she will tell Dr Jordan:

> [h]e will want to know about the arrest, and the trial, and what was said. Some of it is all jumbled in my mind, but I could pick out this or that for him, some bits of whole cloth you might say, as when you go through the rag bag looking for something that will do, to supply a touch of colour. (424)

Images deriving from quilt making serve the narrator here to explain her method, yet these images also hint at the problem Dr Jordan experiences with Grace's narration. Since quilt making is "a form of female discourse", the language and meaning of which Dr Jordan cannot understand, "Grace speaks in her own quilter's idiolect, and so while she is able to express her secrets, she can, at the same time, continue to conceal them from [him] and even from the readers of the novel".[27]

Atwood in fact uses Grace as a stand-in for herself within the novel which emerges through the overall design of the text as a huge quilt composed of parts drawing attention to the leitmotif of quilting. All the section titles recall the names of real quilt patterns and at the same time ironically allude to the content of the respective chapters. They are accompanied by grey and white illustrations of the quilt patterns as well as epigraphs in the form of excerpts from documented sources that either reflect on the subsequent fictional narratives or alternatively raise questions concerning their significance. Both Atwood and Grace are authors/narrators who create quilt stories the patterns of which appear to be immediately discernible, yet become less clear when inspected from a varying distance or different angles. At the end of the novel/narrative, readers are presented with the artistic products. Juxtaposed with the text *Alias Grace* is the object Grace is in the process of making, the quilt she has wished to have for such a long time. She is fashioning her own quilt, "a Tree of Paradise; but [is] changing the pattern a little to suit [her] own ideas" (551):

> [o]n my Tree of Paradise, I intend to put a border of snakes entwined; they will look like vines or just a cable pattern to others, as I will make the eyes very small, but they will be snakes to me; as without a snake or two, the main part of the story would be missing. Some who use this pattern make several trees, four or more in a square or circle, but I am making just one large tree, on a background of white. The Tree itself is of triangles, in two colours, dark for the leaves and a lighter colour for the fruits [...].
>
> But three of the triangles in my tree will be different. One will be white, from the petticoat I still have that was Mary Whitney's; one will be faded yellowish, from the prison night-dress I begged as a keepsake when I left there. And the third will be a pale cotton, a pink and white floral, cut from the dress of Nancy's that she had on the first day I was at Mr. Kinnear's, and that I wore on the ferry to Lewiston, when I was running away.
>
> I will embroider around each one of them with red feather-stitching, to blend them in as a part of the pattern.
>
> And so we will all be together. (551-552)

While her work on this quilt indicates her desire for leading the ordinary life of a married woman, the intricate plan for this specific design points also to her need to integrate all aspects of her traumatic experience into what will become symbolic of the whole of her life:

> [s]he thus stitches together pieces of cloth that mark different crucial events and persons from her life, creating a nonchronological, spatial representation of her life and of her self that is interwoven with the physical lives and selves of other women central to her life and that highlights subjectivity as itself always textualized.[28]

Apart from displaying her special skills in storytelling and quilting, Grace also excels in the field of acting. Aware of her theatrical competencies, she self-consciously comments now and then on the necessity to perform in particular situations. Having in the past played the roles of brutal madwoman – "[i]f they want a monster so badly they ought to be provided with one" (36) – and model prisoner, she is putting on a show for Dr Jordan when they first meet: "I look at him stupidly. I have a good stupid look which I have practised" (42). She later guesses correctly that he prefers to see her as "the heroine of a sentimental novel" (65) and assumes this role in the tale of how she kept MacDermott at a distance through her tearful demonstrations. Especially after her release from prison, Grace intensifies her acting activities as she senses that people expect her to behave in certain ways: "I could see she felt some tears were in order, and I shed several" (528) and

> [t]hat is it, I thought. I have been rescued, and now I must act like someone who has been rescued. And so I tried. It was very strange to realize that I would not be a celebrated murderess any more, but seen perhaps as an innocent woman wrongly accused and imprisoned unjustly, or at least for too long a time, and an object of pity rather than of horror and fear. [...] It calls for a different arrangement of the face. (529)

Her most accomplished performance occurs when she acts in a team with her old friend Jeremiah, the peddler, a fellow artist and shape-shifter who keeps changing his name and profession.[29] Jeremiah, who had earlier offered Grace the opportunity to perform together with him as a "medium clairvoyant" (318) and who had been taken into Grace's confidence,[30] presides in the role of Dr Jerome DuPont over the hypnotism to which Grace is subjected and during which she reveals herself as possessed by the spirit of Mary Whitney who in turn claims to have been accessory to the crimes and generally denounces the social conditions imposed upon lower-class people. Even though the source of the strange voice speaking in this scene remains unclear, the facts that Jeremiah had previously worked as a ventriloquist and that Grace exhibits an air of relief and lightness immediately following the event indicate that the people present in the room have just witnessed a successful performance.[31] If Grace, supported by Jeremiah, has indeed presented the portrait of an altered mental state in which boundaries, here of "the ordinarily sayable", are overstepped, then Atwood's comment that "portraying this process is deep power for the artist, [...] because it's a little too close to the process of artistic creation itself" is applicable also to her protagonist.[32] Given the various roles projected for women in the nineteenth century, some of them more desirable than others, Grace opts for an experimentation with almost all of them and seems to shape and use them to her own advantage: seduced and fallen women such as Mary Whitney and Nancy Montgomery serve her as warning examples and yet she integrates them into the quilt which is to reflect her life; regarded by some as a madwoman, she acts the part and yet she also fashions herself as a sentimental heroine to meet the admiring doctor's expectations; and, finally, Grace gains the most cherished role of all, that of wife but at the same time alludes to the dark sides of matrimony throughout her narrative.

5. Conclusion

While being consciously self-reflexive novels which foreground their protagonists as storytellers, authors and artists, *Alias Grace* and *The Blind Assassin* also display other features typical of historiographic metafiction, among them the questioning of historical knowledge and the relationship between fact and fiction. Since they "challenge the absolute 'knowability' of the past",[33] they evaluate historical situations from a contemporary and admittedly subjective perspective, thereby placing an emphasis on the changes that occurred between the respective periods described and the present. In each text, the artist-protagonist draws attention to some of the social ills afflicting her or her contemporaries. She does so in a slanted way, having her views presented by another voice which in fact originates within the context of her art: while Grace either appropriates, or is appropriated by, Mary's voice in order to comment on the problems of master-servant relationships as well as class- and gender-related discrimination, Iris, aware of her privileged and yet precarious position as a member of the Anglo-Canadian establishment, transfers her views on both the exploitation of the poor and weak by the wealthy and on women's victimisation owing to persistent patriarchal structures onto the level of the dystopian tale narrated in the interpolated novel. Margaret Atwood furthermore comments from a postcolonial point of view on historical events by showing how they affect her characters. Grace Marks, for example, experiences discrimination when, as an Irish immigrant, she is associated with notions spread within the context of the Mackenzie rebellion, while Iris Chase has to bear the consequences of her father's business failure during the years of the Depression.

Yet while in the two novels a general historical layer is indeed observable (and in the historical character of Grace Marks is even foregrounded), the 'truth' with regard to the protagonists' lives remains essentially elusive. Instead, since art and the artist are at the centre of attention, subjectivity and acts of creative re-modelling of experience, hence also the possibility of alternating between deception and revelation, figure prominently. Therefore, the reading or decoding of what is presented remains volatile and may well depend on the perspective of the beholder, as Grace's revealing comment on a quilt pattern, hence by implication one's narrative or one's life,[34] suggests:

> [a]nd the other quilt was called Attic Windows; it had a great many pieces, and if you looked at it one way it was closed boxes, and when you looked at it another way the boxes were open, and I suppose the closed boxes were the attics and the open ones the windows; and that is the same with all quilts, you can see them two different ways, by looking at the dark pieces, or else the light. (188)

The passage proposes that the interpretation of the art object "depends solely on the onlooker's ability to see 'differently'",[35] to challenge dominant versions of public and private history, and to permit the idea of a revisionary evaluation of supposed facts. In *The Blind Assassin* as well, readers are presented with confusion with regard to fact and fiction when, towards the end of the narrative, the inserted novel fragments, hence pieces of a text form which is conventionally seen as fiction are revealed as a version of reality, thus at once confirming and undermining the factuality of Iris's memoir. Iris's explanation, "I didn't think of what I was doing as writing – just writing down. What I remembered, and also what I imagined, which is also the truth" (Atwood 2000: 512), reveals a kind of trickster spirit which is at work in the narratives. Both the shape-shifting nature of the two protagonists and their dissident voices gradually emerge in the presentations of their life stories. And just as these protagonists employ their art to counteract dominant and oppressive discourses, thereby attempting to subvert the power relations imposed on them, Atwood fashions her fiction in ways that challenge traditional perceptions of Canada's past and thus proposes revisionist considerations, from a feminist-postcolonial point of view, of important episodes and aspects of Canadian history.

Notes

1   Atwood won the 1996 Giller Prize for *Alias Grace* and the 2000 Booker Prize for *The Blind Assassin*.
2   See also Wyile (2002).
3   McWilliams (2007: 122).
4   *Ibid.*, 122.
5   Hutcheon (1988: 6; 5).
6   *Ibid.*, 19.
7   Howells, e.g., identifies "all the classic ingredients of Victorian Gothic melodrama" (2003: 30) in *Alias Grace* and "discourses of the Victorian sensation novel, science fiction, modernist female romance, and American detective pulp fiction of the 1930s and 1940s" (*ibid.*, 28) in *The Blind Assassin*.
8   Atwood (1997b: 3).
9   Since the growing demands for democratic reform in Upper Canada were not met with concessions, the radical Reformers led by William Lyon Mackenzie attempted an armed rising in 1837.
10 Grace occasionally responds to Dr Jordan's impositions with self-defensive gestures: "I can't remember, Sir [...] I have little enough of my own, no belongings, no possessions, no privacy to speak of, and I need to keep something for myself" (Atwood 1996: 114).
11 Lovelady (1999: 38).
12 *Ibid.*, 39.
13 Szalay (2003: 174).
14 Atwood (1996: 236). Further references to this edition will be included in the text.
15 Atwood (1997b: 36).
16 Atwood (2000: 512). Further references to this edition will be included in the text.
17 Rigney (2000: 158).
18 Economou (2006: 145; emphasis in the text).
19 Staels (2004: 151).
20 See also Howells (2003: 59) and Howells (2004: 33-34).

21 Howells (2004: 35).
22 Staels (2004: 158).
23 Howells (2003: 41).
24 Wilson (2003: 125); see also Murray (2001).
25 Michael (2001: 426).
26 Rogerson (1998: 10).
27 *Ibid.*, 6.
28 Michael (2001: 439).
29 Lovelady states that "[h]e appears in the text as Dr. Jerome DuPont, 'Neuro-hypnotist', Jeremiah Pontelli, peddler, Gerald Ponti, magician, and finally, in the English translation of his symbolic surname, Gerald Bridges, medium" (1999: 43-44).
30 Jeremiah urges Grace: "[y]ou could be a medical clairvoyant; I would teach you how, and instruct you in what to say, and put you into the trances. I know by your hand that you have a talent for it; and with your hair down, you would have the right look" (Atwood 1996: 318).
31 Atwood describes this moment as follows: "Mrs. Quennell leaves the room with Grace, holding her by the arm as if she's an invalid. But she walks lightly enough, and seems almost happy" (*ibid.*, 484).
32 See Atwood (1997a). Atwood made this comment in a speech given at the Stratford Festival in 1997. She explicitly referred to the hypnotism scene in *Alias Grace* in the passage from which the quotation is taken.
33 Strolz (2009: 299).
34 Rogerson argues in the following way: "[t]his advice can be applied to a reading of Grace's story in the novel: what is seen at any one time depends on whether the pattern of her history is read by looking at the dark patches or the light ones" (1998: 15).
35 Szalay (2003: 179).

Bibliography

Atwood, Margaret: *Alias Grace*, Toronto, 1996.
–: "Ophelia Has a Lot to Answer For", 1997a, Stratford Festival, http://www.talkingpeople.net/tp/literature/atwood/ophelia.pdf (accessed 17 March 2011).
–: *In Search of Alias Grace. On Writing Canadian Historical Fiction*, Ottawa, 1997b.
–: *The Blind Assassin*, Toronto, 2000.
–: *Negotiating with the Dead. A Writer on Writing*, Cambridge, 2002.
Economou, Mary G.: "Weaving Women. Confessions and Identity in Margaret Atwood's *Alias Grace* and *The Blind Assassin*". – In Sylvie Mathé & Gilles Teulié (Eds.): *Cultures de la confession. Formes de l'aveu dans le monde anglophone*, Aix-en-Provence, 2006, pp. 143-158.

Howells, Coral Ann: *Contemporary Canadian Women's Fiction. Refiguring Identities*, New York, 2003.

–: "Margaret Atwood. *Alias Grace*". – In C.A.H. (Ed.): *Where Are the Voices Coming From? Canadian Culture and the Legacies of History*, Amsterdam, 2004, pp. 29-37.

Hutcheon, Linda: *A Poetics of Postmodernism. History, Theory, Fiction*, New York & London, 1988.

Lovelady, Stephanie: "I Am Telling This to No One But You. Private Voice, Passing, and the Private Sphere in Margaret Atwood's *Alias Grace*", *Studies in Canadian Literature* 24:2, 1999, 35-63.

McWilliams, Ellen: "Keeping Secrets, Telling Lies. Fictions of the Artist and Author in the Novels of Margaret Atwood", *Atlantis. A Women's Studies Journal/Revue d'Etudes sur les Femmes* 32:1, 2007, 25-33.

Michael, Magali Cornier: "Rethinking History as Patchwork. The Case of Atwood's *Alias Grace*", *Modern Fiction Studies* (MFS) 47:2, Summer 2001, 421-447.

Murray, Jennifer: "Historical Figures and Paradoxical Patterns. The Quilting Metaphor in Margaret Atwood's *Alias Grace*", *Studies in Canadian Literature* 26:1, 2001, 65-83.

Rigney, Barbara Hill: "Alias Atwood. Narrative Games and Gender Politics". – In Reingard M. Nischik (Ed.): *Margaret Atwood. Works and Impact*, Rochester, 2000, pp. 157-165.

Rogerson, Margaret: "Reading the Patchworks in *Alias Grace*", *Journal of Commonwealth Literature* 33:1, 1998, 5-22.

Staels, Hilde: "Atwood's Specular Narrative. *The Blind Assassin*", *English Studies. A Journal of English Language and Literature* 85:2, April 2004, 147-160.

Strolz, Andrea: "'True Stories' in the Course of Time in Margaret Atwood's *The Blind Assassin*". – In Stella Borg Barthet (Ed.): *A Sea for Encounters. Essays Towards a Postcolonial Commonwealth*, Amsterdam, 2009, pp. 287-306.

Szalay, Edina: "Quilting Her Story. The Resisting Female Subject in Margaret Atwood's *Alias Grace*", *Hungarian Journal of English and American Studies* 9:1, 2003, 173-180.

Wilson, Sharon R.: "Quilting as Narrative Art. Metafictional Construction in *Alias Grace*". – In S.R.W. (Ed.): *Margaret Atwood's Textual Assassinations. Recent Poetry and Fiction*, Columbus, 2003, pp. 121-134.

Wyile, Herb: *Speculative Fictions. Contemporary Canadian Novelists and the Writing of History*, Montreal, 2002.

Marion Gymnich (*Bonn*)

"A Time When Creativity Is Rated High". Penelope Lively's Satire on Art and Artists in *Next to Nature, Art*

1. Introduction

The contemporary British novelist, short story writer and author of children's fiction Penelope Lively has become well known for her subtle and multi-facetted explorations of the impact both the individual and the collective past have on the present. This interest is obvious in her children's novels as well as in the literary works that were written with an adult readership in mind, including her Booker Prize winning novel *Moon Tiger* (1987).[1] The preoccupation with history and with the collective past in a more general sense is already apparent in the professions many of Lively's protagonists share; her novels frequently feature "amateur or professional archaeologists, palaeontologists, architects, or historians",[2] who exhibit what Marie-Luise Egbert calls a "*déformation professionelle*" in terms of their perception of their environment.[3] The characters' complex reflections on individual and cultural memory have rendered Lively's works extremely interesting for studies focussing on historiographic metafiction as well as for memory studies in general.[4] Moreover, the preoccupation with the past is expressed in Lively's exploration of biography in her novel *According to Mark* (1984), which features a biographer as the main character, and in her two autobiographical works, *Oleander, Jacaranda. A Childhood Perceived* (1994) and the more recent *A House Unlocked* (2001). The focus on the past and the identification of its traces in the present is also one of the reasons why Lively tends to pay much attention to architecture in her novels. Buildings, streets and various architectural sites may, for instance, evoke a particular historical era for the beholder, or they may trigger personal memories; more often than not, architecture shows the impact of different historical periods by means of a mingling of period styles or later architectural modifications. In contrast to architecture, visual arts usually play at best a minor role in Lively's works. There is, however, one novel in which the author addresses art extensively, paying particular attention to visual arts, but also taking into consideration other types of artistic work: in one of her comparatively early novels, *Next to Nature, Art* (1982), Lively provides a "sharp satire focused on a trendy, for-profit arts-education course" in the seventies.[5]

Next to Nature, Art introduces a group of more or less successful artists and amateurs and mercilessly "skewers both instructors and students, debunking their mutual illusion that the pursuit of Art somehow raises one above the level of common humanity".[6] *Next to Nature, Art* arguably differs from Lively's other novels in several respects. Firstly, the focus on the past and on identifying its traces in the present certainly is not as prominent here as it is in the author's earlier and later works. Yet the interest in the past can be seen in this particular novel as well. In fact, it even contributes to the satire on art, as will be shown below. Secondly, as Mary Hurley Moran points out, *Next to Nature, Art* "lacks the depth of characterization and the intimate probing of consciousnesses" that is characteristic of Lively's other novels.[7] Thirdly, *Next to Nature, Art* can be regarded as Lively's "most comic novel".[8] Much of the comic and satirical potential of the text derives from a structural feature used repeatedly by the author, namely the juxtaposition of different perspectives which, usually unwittingly, discloses the characters' shortcomings – artistic and otherwise.[9] The impression of artists and of the creation of works of art that is projected in this novel is clearly a predominantly negative one. Instead of portraying artists in the process of creating works of art and pondering aesthetic choices, Lively clearly suggests that the supposed artists are hardly more than "a motley crew of self-centered pleasure seekers possessed of dubious quantities of talent, judgment, or taste".[10] In the following, the critical assessment of the artists and their shortcomings which is provided in *Next to Nature, Art* will be examined in more detail, with particular emphasis on the female artist Paula.

2. The Artists and the Amateurs

As was pointed out above, Lively's *Next to Nature, Art* provides criticism of the half-hearted attempts at creating works of art by a group of people who appear to have little or no talent. The novel is set in "nineteen seventy-four, a time when creativity is rated high",[11] and focuses on Framleigh Creative Study Centre, a privately owned institution which aims at offering people from the middle class a range of artistic experience. Yet the presentation of Framleigh Creative Study Centre suggests that the place is not conducive to encouraging artistic genius, but caters to the interests of potential 'customers'. Creativity may have been rated high in 1974, but the reader gets the impression that the artists and their more or less eager disciples who are assembled for a workshop at Framleigh are not all that creative, merely paying lip service to the spirit of the time. The Centre brings together writers, visual artists and a potter in "one of those residential art courses that were so popular during that era".[12] None of the teachers seems to be an artist in the true sense, however. The potter Bob, for instance, is a womaniser who also sells products that cater to low-brow tastes, including "toby jugs and thatched cottage honeypots" (Lively 1984: 169), in order to make profit, "while pretending to produce only carefully crafted William Morris-type pieces".[13] The owner of Framleigh Hall, Toby Standish, seems to be moderately successful as a visual artist, being

> known best as a lithographer and graphic artist. His allegorical studies, in which figures wander through odd mythical landscapes, and his more abstract swirling prints, called Nature Suites, have been seen in a couple of West End galleries. (5-6)

Although the passage above states that Toby's works have been exhibited in some galleries in London, the way his works are referred to hardly suggests that they are masterpieces. After all, both the use of the adjective "odd" and the description of the prints as "more abstract swirling prints" are likely to cause doubts concerning the aesthetic quality of Toby's works. Despite the fact that the reader has sufficient reason to doubt the artistic talent of the instructors, the latter never fail to strike an artistic pose, drawing upon a rhetoric that is meant to emphasise their special status as artists, which they try to cultivate in what Toby calls "[a] creative sanctuary" (68).

The instructors are not the only ones who know how to create a false impression, though. The participants in the arts workshop likewise are quite good at giving themselves an artistic flair. This is already alluded to in the very first description of the participants:

> [t]he women wear jeans, or long skirts of an Indian cotton in bright colours that, a few years back, would have been regarded as more suitable for bedspreads. They have long hair, for the most part, and look as though they have cultural or artistic connections – work in art galleries, perhaps, or small publishing houses, or in interior decoration. In fact they are a dentist's receptionist, a librarian, two teachers and two married women whose occupation is precisely that. The men are clad as though for a safari or a bout of guerrilla warfare, though this slightly aggressive look is tempered by a good deal of hair around head and face, suggesting aesthetic leanings. (7)

The use of social stereotypes is one of the crucial ingredients of the satire in Lively's *Next to Nature, Art*. The passage quoted above, for instance, immediately conjures up social stereotypes associated in particular with the late sixties and the seventies: middle-class, bourgeois teachers, librarians and housewives adopting the paraphernalia of the counterculture, such as long hair, brightly coloured Indian skirts or clothes that look as if they might be useful "for a safari or a bout of guerrilla warfare". The evocation of social stereotypes is not exclusively based on the description of the characters' appearance, however; their thoughts likewise echo what in 1982, when Lively's novel was published, but perhaps even more so from today's point of view, sounds very much like pseudo-artistic jargon. A case in point is the following reflection by one of the participants, Keith Harrap, who ponders his reasons for participating in the workshop:

> his own creativity is, well, undirected. Evening classes in this and that will no longer do. His potential, he knows, is as yet unrealized; the Framleigh course just might help him to see where he ought to be heading. (8)

Neither Keith nor any of the other characters experiences what might be seen as a genuine artistic vision during the workshop or manages to 'realise his/her potential'. Instead, disillusionment is lying ahead for all of them, since mediocrity rather than artistic genius is what the characters are thrown back upon during the time they spend at Framleigh. The participants who do pottery at least have something to take home with them, but their "ashtrays and mugs and bowls" (168) hardly look like art or as if they required much talent.

Juxtaposing a range of different artists and amateurs in *Next to Nature, Art* and using a "multiple-points-of-view approach" characteristic of many of Lively's novels,[14] provides the possibility of commenting on various branches of art. The reflections on writing stand out in so far as they almost inevitably assume a certain self-referential quality in a literary text. Keith has dabbled in just about everything, including writing. He has experimented with different literary genres – invariably, however, without the least success:

> [n]othing he'd ever taken up had seemed right for him, so far. Poetry. That bloody novel. Writing was the most unsatisfactory of all; in a poem you never could hit on the right word and in a novel something had to darn well happen and the problem was what. Oh, ideas were easy enough – what the stuff was about, one's responses and all that – it was how to get it down and anyway it all took so long. Something much more immediate is his scene, he suspects. (60)

Keith's assessment of the difficulties he encountered when he tried to write poetry and a novel clearly indicates that he is not driven by an impulse to be creative, to express something that is meaningful to him. Instead, he seems to be motivated by the more mundane desire to be recognised as a man with artistic interests. The passage quoted above reflects Keith's attitude towards art by means of the choice of words. His disgruntlement, which implicitly reveals his lack of talent, contributes to the comic effects produced by the passage. The expression "[t]hat bloody novel", for instance, is indicative of his dissatisfaction and his impatience with the creative challenge of writing a novel. Complaining about being unable to "hit on the right word" in a poem or about having problems with constructing a plot for a novel is bound to make sure that the reader does not take Keith's literary ambitions all that seriously. Beyond that, his statements presumably discredit his artistic efforts and interests on a more general level. The use of jargon in the last sentence quoted above reinforces the impression that Keith's attitude primarily pays tribute to the spirit of the age rather than emanating from a deep-felt desire to do artistic work.

Ironically, later on there is a scene in which the American poet Greg, who teaches poetry at Framleigh Creative Study Centre, expresses a somewhat similar impatience with regard to the task of 'hitting on the right word' when he accuses the writer Waterton of being too particular about the choice of words ("'You people,' says Greg kindly, 'really are into terminology, aren't you?'" 66). The apparent disregard for language expressed in Greg's utterance is not only reminiscent of Keith's unpleasant literary experience, but it is also apt to discredit Greg as a poet. There is a striking discrepancy between Greg's impatience with words and his own definition of what a writer must be like. He told the participants at the beginning of the workshop: "[b]eing a writer, being really into words, projecting, is either what you're about, or it isn't. If it isn't, then there's no way you're going to be" (37). Greg's encounter with Waterton suggests that he is incapable of living up to his own standards.

3. Paula: The Female Artist in the Seventies

All in all, the reader gets comparatively little information on the works of art that are produced by the artists and amateurs at Framleigh. The artistic work that is described in most detail in Lively's *Next to Nature, Art* is the work done by Paula, the only female instructor in the study centre. The descriptions of her work are hardly conducive to singling out Paula's talent for art or her attitude towards art, however. Instead, her artistic efforts are clearly discredited by the narrator throughout the novel, which reinforces the negative attitude towards artists that is characteristic of the entire narrative. Even when there is no explicit criticism of Paula's works, what is said about them as well as the lack of certain kinds of information turns out to be sufficient to brand her works as artistic failure. The following passage, for instance, introduces the reader to two of Paula's works which are on display in Framleigh Hall:

> [o]ne of Paula's own pieces, a huge appliqué-work picture of Adam and Eve in brilliant colours hangs above the (original) marble fireplace in the Common Room. The serpent, in puce nylon, coils round the trunk of a corduroy tree from which hang multi-coloured gingham apples. Some more of Paula's work, from her corrugated iron period, is in the hall, occupying the marble niches. Outside, at the apex of the woodland ride and upon the plinth where stood originally the Apollo that Toby's father was obliged to part with at an awkward time in the thirties, is her 'Intro-

spective Woman', an abstract sculpture of welded bicycle frames and silver-sprayed nylon fruit netting. (11)

The relatively detailed information concerning the material Paula's works of art have been made of which is provided in the passage above has a curious effect. In this context at least, specifying that the tree in *Adam and Eve* is made of corduroy and that the serpent in the same picture is made of puce nylon appears to be surplus information. Providing unnecessary information in this case amounts to exposing the works to ridicule. A puce nylon serpent and a corduroy tree in the Garden of Eden are hardly likely to inspire awe in the beholder. Moreover, they seem to be out of place above an old marble fireplace; the combination of the old and the new here does not seem to create a harmonious or even interesting combination.

It is not merely the contrast between the ordinary nature of the materials that are used on the one hand and the subject matter and setting on the other hand that discredits Paula's artistic efforts, though. In and of themselves the materials used by her are certainly not 'inartistic', as works by artists such as Jean Tinguely and other representatives of French New Realism in the sixties clearly illustrate. What discredits Paula's works in the descriptions quoted above is the exclusive emphasis on what her works are made of, since this stresses the striking lack of any kind of comment on the aesthetic quality or on the potential meaning of her works. While New Realism sought to explore the relationship between art and life, Paula does not offer any thoughts concerning her artistic choices. Thus, purely on the basis of the selection of information in the passage above, the reader is almost inevitably left with the impression that Paula's works are merely contrived efforts to imitate artistic trends. While the selection of information provides implicit criticism in the passage quoted above, there are also passages in the novel that render the criticism of the lacking artistic merit of Paula's works more explicit:

Paula's range is wide and includes anything she is herself up to at that moment: appliqué-work, a certain amount of straight painting, jewellery, *objets d'art* constructed from plaster of paris and bits of mirror, sculptures made from old tights stuffed with plastic foam fragments and arranged into contorted piles reminiscent sometimes of enormous turds and sometimes of intertwined draught excluders. She is also working out – and sharing her experiences with course members – a new technique involving chicken feathers, plastic flex, dayglo paint and lengths of bicycle chain. (20; emphasis in the text)

The list above suggests that Paula's choice of material is relatively random, perhaps vaguely influenced by current trends, but certainly not shaped by a personal artistic agenda and conscious aesthetic decisions. Although the participants in the workshop do not dare to criticise Paula openly, some of them at least have doubts about the quality of her work. Mary Chambers, for instance, "cannot for the life of her find in it [one of Paula's sculptures] anything to admire" (23).

A key to understanding the predominantly negative depiction of art in *Next to Nature, Art* can be found in a concept that is of the utmost importance in Lively's novels in general, the notion of the palimpsest. As Ruth P. Feingold points out, "the word *palimpsest* is used by Lively to denote the layers of experience, memory, and physical data that make up a place or a person".[15] Throughout Lively's novels the notion of the palimpsest serves to provide places as well as persons with depth and complexity. Given this background, it is striking how curiously one-dimensional Paula's works appear to be, despite the fact that her sculptures and her appliqué-work, which incorporate different materials, seem to lend themselves to expressing a palimpsest-like quality. Yet there is no hint that Paula's works might reveal any layers beneath the surface level. They thus appear to lack the specific quality of the palimpsest, namely that of providing layers of meaning one can perceive or at least imagine, which challenges the beholder's knowledge and imagination.

Paula's choice of subject matter – *Adam and Eve* and *Introspective Woman* – suggests that her work is meant to have a feminist bias. Thus, the reader is likely to conclude that her work has been shaped by the ideological framework of the Women's Liberation Movement, which began in Britain in the late sixties. Given the fact that Paula seems to lack artistic inspiration, one is further tempted to assume that she has exploited the contemporary interest in feminist issues in order to ensure her success rather than pursuing a genuinely feminist artistic agenda. Paula's biography arguably has feminist overtones, though, suggesting that she has experienced a personal process of emancipation. She married at the age of nineteen, but later split up with her husband, a doctor, thus avoiding "rot[ting] in Maidenhead as a suburban wife and mum" (60), as she herself puts it. In Paula's opinion, the role of (house)wife and mother, with "[d]inner parties for his [her ex-husband's] friends, and his parents to stay twice a year" (*ibid.*), would be incompatible with the role of an artist she has chosen for herself. Yet Paula at least is an artist and a mother, thus combining different female roles and, apparently, showing that it is possible to 'have it all': to be an artist, to be a mother and to enjoy the consequences of sexual liberation with changing lovers, without being socially ostracised. Thus, Paula can certainly be seen as a product of the process of Women's Liberation; yet, given the way she is characterised, it is doubtful whether female readers are likely to regard her as a potential role model.

Paula is shown to be an utterly self-centred and shallow character, one for whom modesty seems to be an alien concept. Paula is a woman who is conscious of the effect she has on others and who uses this effect to her advantage. For her being an artist seems to be one important ingredient in the image of herself she has created. Paula's extreme self-confidence is, for instance, revealed by the way she enters the party on the last day of the workshop, exposing herself intentionally to the male gaze, seeking to provoke admiration and, potentially, envy on the part of the women who are present:

> Paula is the last to appear. She slowly descends the main staircase, and those facing the door break off whatever they are doing to gaze for a moment. She certainly looks rather magnificent. Her hair is piled up in a vaguely Grecian way, with a good deal of it escaping in twists and coils; she wears a sea-green long dress, also indirectly classical though in fact made in Bombay [...]; the cut and texture of the dress make it clear that she has disposed of the problem of how to wear a bra under it by not doing so. She pauses for a moment under the broken pediment of Kent's double doors and looks round. "I could do with a drink," she announces. (173)

The way Paula descends the staircase suggests not only that she is perfectly aware of the fact that she is very attractive, but also indicates that she expects to be the centre of attention as soon as she joins the group. Throughout the novel Paula is shown to claim the right to be the centre of interest wherever she goes and to demand admiration for herself as well as for her work. In this respect she is very different from many earlier examples of female artists in literary texts.

In earlier works female artists tend to be presented as loners who more often than not are ill at ease with the expectations of society. At the same time, the female artists tend to take their artistic work very seriously and derive a deep sense of personal fulfilment from the creative process, although it is often seen as a mere pastime by others. The appearance of female artists in earlier literary texts frequently reflects their status as social outsiders. Virginia Woolf's novel *To the Lighthouse* (1927) is a case in point. Neither the painter Lily Briscoe nor her works are taken very seriously by the other characters, as the following description of Lily from Mrs Ramsay's point of view exemplifies:

> Lily's picture! Mrs Ramsay smiled. With her little Chinese eyes and her puckered-up face she would never marry; one could not take her painting very seriously; but she was an independent little creature, Mrs Ramsay liked her for it [...].[16]

Mrs Ramsay's attitude towards Lily Briscoe is clearly condescending; due to the fact that Lily seems to be unlikely to marry, she falls short of fulfilling Mrs Ramsay's expectations. The overall impression conveyed to the reader by the description of Lily Briscoe quoted above is that of an immature, perhaps even childlike character; she has "*little* Chinese eyes" and she is "an independent *little creature*" (my emphasis). Moreover, the passage suggests that Mrs Ramsay considers being an artist as an occupation that is quite suitable for women who are bound to remain unmarried anyway. The 'spinster' may dabble in painting, whereas the 'true woman' takes care of her family and her household. Lily even thinks of herself as "not a woman, but a peevish, ill-tempered, dried-up old maid" (Woolf 1977: 142), which shows that social expectations that were widespread at the time when the novel is set have left their imprint on her identity. Being a (female) artist apparently is not a valid alternative to being a 'woman', i.e. to being a wife and mother. The lack of respect for Lily Briscoe's painting is also indicative of a conservative notion of art. In Mrs Ramsay's world an "authenticated masterpiece by Michael Angelo" (32) certainly counts as art, but Lily Briscoe's painting is hardly more than the endearing effort of a 'spinster' to find something to do. In terms of her personality, the introverted and unassuming Lily Briscoe is the exact opposite of

Paula in *Next to Nature, Art*, but she is also Paula's opposite with respect to her attitude towards the creative process.

The fact that *To the Lighthouse* grants the reader insight into Lily Briscoe's thoughts means that there is a corrective to the condescending view others share of her. The reader realises that painting is very important to Lily Briscoe, that it stimulates her creativity and offers her a field for finding personal fulfilment. During a dinner, in a moment of vision, Lily becomes aware of how meaningful her painting is for her: "[s]he remembered, all of a sudden as if she had found a treasure, that she too had her work. In a flash she saw her picture, and thought, Yes, I shall put the tree further in the middle" (80). Pondering artistic choices obviously provides Lily Briscoe with a deep sense of personal satisfaction.[17] Repeatedly offering the reader glimpses of the aesthetic decisions made by Lily Briscoe lends importance to the artistic process; likewise, the fact that *To the Lighthouse* ends with her artistic vision, which serves as both climax and closure, is bound to render her painting important in the reader's eyes. In Lively's *Next to Nature, Art*, in contrast, there are no insights into any creative processes, impulses and visions that might motivate Paula's work. This contrast between Paula and Lily Briscoe is all the more striking because *Next to Nature, Art*, like *To the Lighthouse*, makes use of the female artist as a character focaliser. The complete absence of glimpses of creative processes in the case of Paula may arguably be regarded as an indication that her works of art are not based on aesthetic reflection, but simply pay tribute to the spirit of the times in so far as they exploit and reproduce ideas that are likely to 'sell'.

There is at least one female character in Lively's novel, however, who seems to have a certain amount of artistic insight and talent. Mary Chambers, who is "sensible, no-nonsense, knowledgeable about nature, and unaffectedly interested in art and ideas", is "the first of the course members to see through the Framleigh staff" and "the first to perceive their limitations as artists".[18] She is not deceived by pseudo-artistic jargon, as her thoughts on Toby's welcome speech indicate ("'doing your own thing' is of course an expression one hears a lot these days", Lively 1984: 81), but is actually shown to ponder aesthetic problems ("Mary wonders how to paint the flight of shadows across a hillside", 101). She firmly believes that true artists have a social responsibility and in this respect as well as in many others is clearly the opposite of Paula. Ulti-

mately, Mary Chambers appears to be the only one of the participants in the workshop who actually benefits from the time she
spends in the artistic commune:

> [t]hroughout the week, while most of the course members are busy in-
> gratiating themselves with the staff and while the latter are busy shoring
> up their egos, Mary is assiduously at work producing art: she creates
> some truly good sketches and watercolours and is the only one who ac-
> tually has something to show for her week at Framleigh.[19]

Moreover, Mary Chambers turns out to be an astute observer of
what is going on around her. She is also aware of the setting and
wonders whether there might be a connection between the atmosphere of the workshop and the "muddle" (81) which is characteristic
of the house and the garden today and which has replaced "the harmony and order of their conception" (*ibid.*). She, thus, reveals the
kind of perceptiveness regarding places that protagonists in other
novels by Lively typically display.

4. The Significance of the Setting

As was pointed out above, the setting generally tends to be of the
utmost importance in Lively's works.[20] The author clearly "likes to
explore the interactions of humans with both the natural and the
built landscape and to investigate the ways in which place constructs identity and informs relationships".[21] At first sight the significance of the setting in *Next to Nature, Art* is not as striking as in
City of the Mind (1991), for instance, but the setting still fulfils a
crucial function in Lively's satire on art, since the house where the
workshop takes place constitutes an ironic counterpoint to the contrived works of art produced by the novel's protagonists. The house
"was once itself a work of art, designed by William Kent to please
eighteenth-century aesthetic sensibilities".[22] Recognising the lack of
artistic insight on the part of most of the people gathered at Framleigh, the reader may have the suspicion that the house and its park
still are more of a work of art than the items which are created in
the workshop. At least when seen from certain angles, the house
and the park indeed look like a work of art, although there may be
flaws in the design:

Framleigh, revealed suddenly and with a flourish as the road twists, looks more appealing and indeed imposing at this distance than it will do in close-up. From here, the grand design of things is to be appreciated: the closing of the perspective to draw the eye towards the house, the grouping of trees, the use made of contours, the careful manipulation of nature. (62-63)

Although the description of the park of Framleigh Hall is not particularly detailed, it at least mentions aesthetic effects which create a unified impression for the beholder. While "the house itself is not perhaps outstanding" (9):

the park has always been considered a masterpiece, transcended only by Rousham and Stowe, the perfect manifestation of the picturesque: Hogarthian lines of beauty, sham ruins, cascade, grotto, the lot. Twenty-five acres in which the disordered was cunningly turned into a contrivance, in which the physical world was made an artistic product, in which nature became art. (*Ibid.*)

In the depiction of the various works of art that are mentioned in the course of the novel, in contrast, information on a possible aesthetic effect is conspicuously missing, which, as was pointed out above, expresses a clear judgment on the artistic efforts of the participants in the Framleigh workshop – instructors and amateurs alike.

One might even argue that a scene towards the end of the novel suggests that the house and the park are not only superior to the contemporary artists and their work in terms of their aesthetic value, but that they actually absorb the effect created by the current inhabitants into their atmosphere. In the following passage, the focaliser is an outsider, a character who otherwise does not appear in the novel and who is never involved in what is happening in the context of the workshop:

[o]ne of Lemniscaat Farms' stockmen, doing something to a calf in the park, looks across the ha-ha and up the prospect and sees them [the participants of the workshop] drifting there in the half-light; they seem some gilded product of the house itself, a manifestation of its style and age and detachment from real life – laughter, the tinkle of glasses, groupings and re-groupings. (173)

From the stockman's point of view, the temporary visitors seem to be part of the 'spirit' of the house, thus becoming subordinate to the place in a manner that is typical of the concept of place one encounters throughout Lively's novels. According to her works, the place is what will persist, in a palimpsest-like fashion integrating changes and new developments into its overall effect and thus constantly enriching its atmosphere. In comparison to the setting, the self-obsessed instructors in *Next to Nature, Art* are reduced in terms of their importance, ultimately serving as a temporary decoration rather than as the core of the place, as soon as they are seen from a (spatial or temporal) distance. Thus it seems suitable that the very last sentence of the novel is dedicated to the setting: "Framleigh sheds a few more flakes of stucco and settles to another day" (186).

5. Conclusion: Creativity, Reconsidered

As the paragraphs above have shown, throughout *Next to Nature, Art* the artists and amateurs reveal a deplorable lack of creativity and originality. Ultimately, the most creative and most original characters in Lively's novels seem to be the historians, palaeontologists, architects, journalists and biographers appearing in many of her works, rather than the artists. A prime example of this tendency is certainly the main character of Lively's *Moon Tiger*. Claudia Hampton is presented as a historian and journalist who possesses an extremely vivid imagination and who, even shortly before her death, is pondering various alternative ways of writing about history, stressing the significance of subjective approaches to examining the past.[23] A further crucial difference between Claudia and other protagonists interested in history on the one hand and the artists in *Next to Nature, Art* on the other hand concerns how passionate the characters are about what they are doing. The group around Paula and Toby in *Next to Nature, Art* hardly seems to be passionate about pursuing their own artistic work, let alone about teaching the workshop. Instead, they appear to be motivated by relatively mundane concerns, such as making money, seeking sexual gratification and perpetuating their "carefully contrived charisma".[24] Claudia Hampton, similar to other protagonists in Lively's novels, in contrast, "has been passionate about history since she was a child".[25] For her, the work she is doing is of the utmost importance; she thrives on intellectual challenges and is dedicated to what she is doing. While many of the characters in Lively's novels enjoy intellectual challenges and are devoted to their profession, the artists in *Next to Nature, Art* appear to lead a relatively pointless existence, one that is motivated solely by self-interest and by the desire to perpetuate the larger-than-life image they have created of themselves as artists. On the whole, thus, art, or at least a particular type of art, seems to be seen in a very negative way by Lively. Yet, even in Lively's satire on art, a character like Mary Chambers suggests that there may be other, more productive approaches towards art than those chosen by the instructors at Framleigh.

Notes

1 Lively has won several prestigious literary awards: in addition to the Booker Prize for *Moon Tiger*, she was awarded the Arts Council National Book Award for Fiction for her novel *Treasures of Time* (1979), the Whitbread Award for her children's novel *A Stitch in Time* (1976) and the Carnegie Award for another children's novel, *The Ghost of Thomas Kempe* (1973). Both *The Road to Lichfield* (1977) and *According to Mark* (1984) were shortlisted for the Booker Prize. Christina Kotte remarks that "comparatively few scholarly critics have concerned themselves with her [Lively's] work so far" (2001: 138) – despite the critical acclaim her works had received; ten years later, unfortunately, this still seems to be true. Moreover, most of the critical attention to date has focused on a single novel by Lively, *Moon Tiger*. The novel *Next to Nature, Art*, for instance, which will be discussed in the present paper, has received very little notice.

2 Feingold (1999: 164).

3 Egbert (2006: 206).

4 See, e.g., Le Mesurier (1990); Moran (1990); Nünning (1995); Kotte (2001); Ebel (2004).

5 Feingold (1999: 170).

6 *Ibid.*

7 Moran (1993: 70).

8 Feingold (1999: 170).

9 On the satirical bias of *Next to Nature, Art*, see also Moran: "this novel is more in keeping with a type of Lively's short stories: the crisp, pointed satire that exposes the pretentiousness of a particular class of people. Satiric scenes are sprinkled throughout Lively's other novels, but *Next to Nature, Art* is the only one in which the satiric predominates" (1993: 70).

10 Feingold (1999: 170).

11 Lively (1984: 5). Further references to this edition will be included in the text.

12 Moran (1993: 70).

13 *Ibid.*, 71.

14 Moran (1997: 103).

15 Feingold (1999: 164; emphasis in the text). On the use of the concept of the palimpsest in Lively's novels, see also Feingold: "[a]t a broad cultural level, an example of a Livelian palimpsest is the London of *City of the Mind* (1991), a long-inhabited city in which newer construction continually adds onto, yet never fully replaces, what has been built in generations past. At a more intimate level she may write of the palimpsest of personal experience: for example, in *Moon Tiger* (1987) the detritus of papers, small souvenirs, and memories that Claudia shuffles through in the course of her deathbed reverie about her life. The present is never simply the present for Lively but exists always as an accretion of past influences that must be continually reprocessed and accounted for" (*ibid.*, 164-165).

16 Woolf (1977: 21). Further references to this edition will be included in the text.

17 In Kate Chopin's *The Awakening* (1899) there is a female pianist who shows striking similarities to Lily Briscoe. The pianist Mademoiselle Reisz is also unmarried and a social outsider. She is described as "a disagreeable *little* woman, no longer young" (2003: 70; my emphasis). Moreover, similar to Lily Briscoe, she is depicted as a rather unattractive woman: "[s]he was a homely woman, with a *small* weazened face and body and eyes that glowed. She had absolutely no taste in dress, and wore a batch of rusty black lace with a bunch of artificial violets pinned to the side of her hair" (*ibid.*, 71; my emphasis). Both Mademoiselle Reisz and Lily Briscoe are described as being "small", which could presumably be translated as 'socially insignificant' in this context. Mademoiselle Reisz's glowing eyes, however, also suggest that, similar to Lily Briscoe, she derives personal satisfaction from art.

18 Moran (1993: 74).

19 *Ibid.*, 75.

20 On the significance of the setting in Lively's novels, see Erickson & Gymnich (1999).

21 Feingold (1999: 164).

22 *Ibid.*, 170.

23 Kotte says about *Moon Tiger* that "[t]he juxtaposition of elements that in the conventional writing of history are considered to be irreconcilable indicates that the reader is presented with an 'ex-centric' historiographic account – as 'ex-centric,' in fact, as the woman who writes it" (2001: 140).

24 Feingold (1999: 170).

25 *Ibid.*, 171-172.

Bibliography

Chopin, Kate: *The Awakening and Selected Stories*. Ed. Sandra M. Gilbert, London, 2003.

Ebel, Kerstin: *"...Something that People Can't Do Without". The Concepts of Memory and the Past in the Work of Penelope Lively and Other Contemporary British Writers*, Heidelberg, 2004.

Egbert, Marie-Luise: *Garten und* Englishness *in der englischen Literatur*, Heidelberg, 2006.

Erickson, Jon & Marion Gymnich: "'First of All, the Place'. Formen und Funktionen der Semantisierung des Raumes in den Romanen Penelope Livelys". – In Andrea Gutenberg & Ralf Schneider (Eds.): *Gender – Culture – Poetics. Zur Geschlechterforschung in der Literatur- und Kulturwissenschaft. Festschrift für Natascha Würzbach*, Trier, 1999, pp. 373-385.

Feingold, Ruth P.: "Penelope Lively". – In Merritt Moseley (Ed.): *British Novelists since 1960. Third Series*, Detroit, 1999, pp. 163-177.

Kotte, Christina: *Ethical Dimensions in British Historiographic Metafiction. Julian Barnes, Graham Swift, Penelope Lively*, Trier, 2001.

Le Mesurier, Nicholas: "A Lesson in History. The Presence of the Past in the Novels of Penelope Lively", *The New Welsh Review* 2, 1990, 36-38.

Lively, Penelope: *Next to Nature, Art*, Harmondsworth, 1984 [1982].

Moran, Mary Hurley: "Penelope Lively's *Moon Tiger*. A Feminist 'History of the World'", *Frontiers* 11:2/3, 1990, 89-95.

–: *Penelope Lively*, New York, 1993.

–: "The Novels of Penelope Lively. A Case for the Continuity of the Experimental Impulse in Postwar British Fiction", *South Atlantic Review* 62:1, 1997, 101-120.

Nünning, Ansgar: *Von historischer Fiktion zu historiographischer Metafiktion. Volume II: Erscheinungsformen und Entwicklungstendenzen des historischen Romans in England seit 1950*, Trier, 1995.

Woolf, Virginia: *To the Lighthouse*, London, 1977 [1927].

Uwe Klawitter (Bochum)

"Unsound Elements Seemed to Have Crept Into Her Narrative". The Representation of Female Writers in Anita Brookner's Novels *Look at Me* and *Hotel du Lac*

1. Introduction

The figure of the writing woman is particularly attractive to women novelists since it offers scope for the reflection of their own art as well as the exposure of the social and ideological factors influencing women's creative writing. Indeed, the cultural investment of art with autonomy and freedom turns representations of female writers into revealing sites of emancipatory effort and progress. As Rachel Blau DuPlessis points out, "[t]he figure of a female artist encodes the conflict between any empowered woman and the barriers to her achievement".[1]

In her distinguished career as a novelist, Anita Brookner has created two author-protagonists, Frances Hinton in *Look at Me* (1983) and Edith Hope in *Hotel du Lac* (1984), whose understanding of and approach to writing invite questions from a feminist angle. Brookner herself has rather discouraged the adoption of such a viewpoint.[2] The fact that a writer does not wish her novels to be read from a feminist perspective does, of course, not preclude the possibility of such a reading.[3] Indeed, critics have not refrained from approaching Brookner's novels in this way, but come to conflicting assessments. The two studies that specifically investigate Brookner's writer figures by Margaret Diane Stetz and Jennifer L. Holberg, for instance, identify a feminist agenda.[4] Critics with an interest in Brookner's overall novelistic achievement, however, frequently adopt quite a different position – a tendency which Dominic Head summarises as follows:

her writing might be said to be impervious to feminist ideas; indeed, to many readers Brookner's fiction promotes a conservative view of women's lot that colludes with traditional models of gender inequality.[5]

He himself wishes to mitigate this criticism by registering that

> the direction of her work has come to coincide with the post-feminist determination to fly by the nets of gender opposition, and to promote a world-view that is not required to be partisan in gender terms.[6]

In my view, Brookner's presentation of writer protagonists actually solicits gender-critical questions. Setting aside the problematic label of post-feminism, what can Brookner's representation of writer figures really tell us about female writing and its constraints? To answer this question it is necessary to pay more attention to generic frames and the function of narrative means than is usually found in discussions of her novels. What I propose then is a gender-orientated narratological examination of Brookner's representation of female writing.[7]

For a fair evaluation it is important to concentrate on the way literary means are employed in the text to convey insight into female writing. Accordingly, I will first consider the implications of genre, then look at relevant aspects of narrative composition, and, finally, turn to the extensive use of metafictional comments. The question of what is empowering and what is constraining in Brookner's portrayal of women writers – at the core of Joanne S. Frye's highly useful notion of a developing 'feminist poetics of the novel' – has to be somewhat broadened here.[8] What appears to be limiting in Brookner's presentation may after all be an 'intended' or 'potential effect' (subject to proof by narrative analysis) and be thus indirectly enabling.[9] Even where this is ostensibly not the case, it may be read against the grain. Lennard J. Davis's idea of resistance may be utilised here to explain the double perspective that is called for: Brookner's representation of writer protagonists can be understood as both a conscious and an unconscious resistance to social and ideological (possibly that includes also feminist) limitations imposed upon female writing.[10] As critical readers we may equally resist that resistance, though, by contesting assumptions, drawing attention to internal inconsistencies and questioning choices.

Writers of fiction who wish to create artist figures cannot escape already established genre conventions, as, for example, those developed in the history of the *Künstlerroman* or *Bildungsroman*. But they can decide whether these ideologically charged conventions can be adopted, have to be modified, or even subverted for their own expressive purposes.[11] With their strong focus on the perceptions, thoughts and emotions of the female writer protagonists, both *Look at Me* and *Hotel du Lac* can be regarded as female artist novels;[12] at least this is the generic frame that suggests itself most readily.

As is typical of the development of this genre in the second half of the twentieth century, the novels do not trace the artistic growth of the protagonists, but concentrate instead on a comparatively short phase, the impact of a crisis on their writing.[13] Both Frances Hinton, a budding writer with a couple of short stories published, and Edith Hope, a professional author of romantic fiction, have to overcome turmoil in close personal relationships. As in other women's novels, to mention another genre that applies here, the focus is very much on the protagonists' coming to terms with external and internalised social constraints. That the artistic work itself receives rather limited coverage is by no means unusual in artist novels.[14] Still, the paucity of information on formative experiences, endowment and personal growth is striking in both novels.

A generic expectation is certainly the struggle of the artist for self-realisation. However, Brookner does not create such artist heroines. Indeed, she rebalances the inner conflict of female artists between love/marriage/domesticity and art.[15] Her protagonists do not have to struggle for "leisure, and money, and a room to themselves".[16] Unrepresentatively privileged in all these respects, they are quite inclined to give up writing for private happiness. Their problem is not the choice between love and art,[17] but rather – as they see it – an unfulfillable desire for a relationship, which they seek to compensate by writing.

The economic independence of Brookner's writer figures does not mean, however, that they do not have to fend off encroachments on their work. In fact, both have to defend their own space at one time or another. Frances does not move in with her friends Alix and Nick Fraser, because she senses that this would distract her from writing.[18] Edith's one-time suitor Geoffrey Long would certainly have opposed her writing as a husband, because he "did not [...] approve of women working", and "teased her about the amount of time she gave to her books".[19] That Frances and Edith regularly encounter condescending and irritated reactions to their writing (Brookner 1983: 53; 54; Brookner 1985: 55; 57; 59; 93) draws attention to the fact that there are still reservations about female authorship.

While Brookner creates female figures that stick to their writing, she makes the quality and facility, even the continuation of their work psychologically dependent on relationships, especially on potential male partners. This certainly dampens high notions of agency. Privileging the desire for love, she seems to reject the idea that creativity assists self-liberation.

If Brookner's own choice and use of fictional genre(s) is revealing, so is that granted to her writer protagonists. Frances writes short stories that are thinly disguised, amusing fictionalisations of rather sad and unfortunate people working with her in a medical research library (Brookner 1983: 16; 71-72). This indicates a lack of empathy and a rather narrow range of subject matter. Her project to write a "comic novel, one of those droll and piquant chronicles enjoyed by dons at Oxford and Cambridge" (16) appears oddly out of touch with the fiction developed by women and unhealthily fixated on the judgment of male critics. Edith produces popular romances that are – judging by such parodic titles as *Beneath the Visiting Moon, The Stone and the Star, The Sun at Midnight* – formulaic, old-fashioned, and highly escapist; in short, the "most criticized" and "least recognized" genre fiction.[20]

Brookner does not provide specimens of her protagonists' fictional writing but confines them to 'private narration'.[21] Frances records her social experiences in a diary (again not directly quoted from), which is meant to serve as a collection of material for her prospective comic novel. Judging by the self-introduction of the narrator at the beginning of *Look at Me*: "[m]y name is Frances Hinton and I do not like to be called Fanny" (5), the serious and confessional account that follows is to be understood as an oral narration. That this account ends with the announcement "I pick up my pen. I start writing" (192) does not indicate a 'self-begetting novel' in the sense that Frances is "ready to begin writing the novel we have just finished reading",[22] but means that she is plunging into the comic novel she has been planning all along.

Edith remains similarly disempowered. During her 'exile' in a staid Swiss hotel on Lake Geneva, she tries to put in work on her romance *Beneath the Visiting Moon*, but also writes five letters to David Simmonds, her married lover in London. That both forms of writing are motivated by the same yearning for love is signalled by the way Edith alternates between them and arranges the scripts in folders. The skilful letters, which are interspersed into the main narrative, are written as if to give David an amusing account of events, but are never dispatched. This dead-end correspondence may be regarded as symbolic of Edith's writerly endeavours.

If the artist novel can expose the conflict between societal forces and the individual and give insight into artistic growth and identity formation, that potential is severely curtailed in *Look at Me* and *Hotel du Lac*. The consideration of narrative choices in the enactment of female authorship will show whether such narrowing down of possibilities could be understood as critical response to perceived constraints to women's scope for artistic development.

3. Central Narrative Options and their Effect on the Portrayal of Female Writing

3.1 Perspectivisation and Ironic Detachment

Both novels offer in various ways a privileging of the female perspective. While this is potentially empowering, it has to be carefully assessed in its functionalisation.[23] Other perspectives on the protagonists, usually offered in scenic presentation, can create ambivalence, especially when unsympathetic characters make valid observations or right things are said for the wrong reasons.

The construction of Frances as an autodiegetic narrator allows deep insights into the motivations and the psychosocial dynamics that influence her writing. Her perceptions, reflections and interpretations are responses to external and internal pressures which readers are bound to judge on the strength of their credibility and persuasiveness.

Although there is no reason to doubt her story of a dismal treatment by the people she had regarded as her friends, there are also signals of unreliability or at least diminished credibility. Discrepancies between events related in the mode of showing and the assessments of the experiencing I exhibit clear weaknesses in the protagonist's understanding of human relationships, but also of herself. As I will explain later, these have a negative influence on her writing.

Instability is also created by the not quite clear temporal relation between the narrative present and the related events. If these are, as the ending suggests, told from a short narrative distance, Frances would quite surprisingly display here a mode of storytelling that is markedly different from her publicly assumed voice. This discrepancy might be indicative of a well-known problem encountered by women writers: success in the world of publishing – at least the Oxbridge male-dominated one envisaged by Frances – seems only possible through the adoption of an artificial 'public voice' which denies authentic self-expression.[24]

For her portrayal of a writer of romantic fiction in *Hotel du Lac* Brookner chose a heterodiegetic narration with extensive internal focalisation.[25] With the exception of three brief focalisations involving male characters, events are perceived from Edith's perspective. Her view is also privileged by means of intradiegetic narration, her letters and a telegram. While this perspectivisation fosters sympathetic identification, it can be and is actually used to ironise the protagonist. If this is mainly achieved through shifts in perspective and free indirect discourse, one can occasionally also find overtly critical comments by the heterodiegetic narrator. To give an example:

> [t]hen taking up the folder containing *Beneath the Visiting Moon*, she pulled out her papers, re-read her last paragraph, and bent her head obediently to her daily task of fantasy and obfuscation. (Brookner 1985: 50)

Admittedly, Edith herself has no illusions about the compensatory and falsifying nature of her writing (27-28). But what the comment clearly indicates is the way her romance writing is meant to be understood – as a highly misguided endeavour.

The discussed arrangements on the level of discourse invite a critical reading of the female writer figures. They are ideally suited to give insight into internal constraints.

If Frances and Edith conform to the by now established formula of a Brooknerian female protagonist, "a middle-class spinster of means, disappointed in love and coming to terms with narrowing life options",[26] they also seem to counter stereotypes of writing women such as the 'Mad Girl' or 'Miss Eccentric Spinster' which have been used by male critics to denigrate female writing.[27] Through her work Frances is associated with mental illnesses, but certainly not highly strung. And Edith, though somewhat older and living on her own, is not really a spinster and surely not eccentric. Interestingly, she is seen in this way by others and actually cultivates that reputation to be left in peace to write.[28]

Both protagonists have telling names. "Hint(-on)" suggests that Frances is a somehow revealing, if not representative figure. "Hope" also invites an abstract reading and immediately introduces an ironic note. The question arises whether the hope of the character is justified. That Edith Hope writes under the pseudonym Vanessa Wilde points to the spuriousness of her fiction, but, above all, draws attention to the rift between her reality and her dreams. It is no coincidence that Edith's pseudonym has the same initials and number of letters as Virginia Woolf, a writer she is frequently compared with due to physical resemblance (8; 27). This is most likely an ironic comment on her lack of artistic aspiration, if not on her naivety in matters of female emancipation.

As regards the intra-figural and interfigural representation of the characters as artists, it is revealing for their isolation that most information is provided through their own reflections rather than the comments of other characters in dialogue. This is especially true of *Look at Me*. The rare comments by other characters show a lack of appreciation and respect. They question the quality of work or even the protagonists' competence as writers. Although most of these remarks are undermined by the selfishness or envy of the commentators, the main point of criticism, namely that the writer protagonists or their writings are devoid of a deeper knowledge of people (Brookner 1983: 68-69; Brookner 1985: 144), is justified, since it is confirmed by events.

The protagonists themselves are rather unsure or secretive about their work. Since their fictional writing caters for their psychic needs – for Frances it is a means of gaining attention (note the title

Look at Me) and for Edith basically a form of wish-fulfilment – it cannot be openly defended.[29] More importantly, the compensatory utilisation of writing imposes grave limitations on artistic development and precludes personal growth.[30] Writing is thus not a means of liberation but self-imprisonment.

What constrictions are shown to be in operation here? In how far does the characterisation of the writer figures advance a gender-critical perspective? To answer these questions, I would like to draw on research by Ansgar Nünning, who has examined the characterisation in Brookner's novels with respect to gender.[31] As he points out, Brookner questions existing gender stereotypes by mixing traits traditionally considered 'masculine' and 'feminine' in her female and male characters, also by introducing polarities in her constellation of characters that cut across the traditional gender dichotomy.[32] Considering these polarities and the resulting lack of reciprocity in the depicted relationships, which prevents Brookner's female protagonists from achieving private happiness, Nünning comes to the conclusion that Brookner goes beyond the mere representation of gender discrimination towards an exposure of the conventionality (and that implies malleability) of gender.[33] But, as he also points out, while drawing attention to her protagonists' plight of not being able to square their own needs with traditional gender expectations, Brookner does not offer any solutions.[34] While I can only agree, I would emphasise the message that is implied in the protagonists' dilemma. Does not the fact that they are and continue to be actuated by a conservative and clearly self-harming concept of gender (however relativised or obscured by their own personal dichotomies) set a deterring example? The inability of the protagonists to arrive at a more fundamental questioning of gender relations is even more glaring as they are economically independent and fairly free of social obligations. Frances's willingness to comply with social expectations: "I would do what was required of me" (Brookner 1983: 122) is already highly suspicious. That she judges herself in terms of attractiveness to others, finds herself wanting and therefore condemned to the role of passive observer and, if demanded, quaint entertainer, could be explained as legacy of a conservative gender upbringing. Edith, too, is "childishly anxious to please" (Brookner 1985: 62).[35] As Skinner has demonstrated, Edith's perception and thinking are dominated by a conservative gender ideology.[36] In both cases the restrictions on the protagonists' writing are clearly marked. To amuse others (the readership is envisaged as male) Frances produces fictional texts she herself does not like that much (Brookner 1983: 16). The stories avoid her own emotional concerns (19) and do not engage empathically with the lives of others (55; 69). Edith's romances are even, as indicated in psycho-narration, centrally concerned with gender decorum: "the question of what behaviour most becomes a woman" is "the question around which she had written most of her novels"; revealingly, this is "the question she had failed to answer" (Brookner 1985: 40). Surely, this is an aggravated case of internalised gender restrictions on female writing.[37]

3.3 Emplotment, Closure and Submerged Plots

As feminist narratologists have emphasised, the possibilities of female characters are limited by traduced plot patterns that support the patriarchal system. Frye, in fact, establishes a correlation between the entrapment of real-life women in gender scripts and the emplotment of heroines in fiction pervaded by cultural ideology.[38] Both novels discussed here actually encourage investigations along such lines, because the protagonists reflect on plots and use plot metaphors to assess their current situation or prospects. Frances, for example, expresses her surprise about becoming friends with Alix and Nick as follows: "[f]or the one thing I had not expected was to be written into the plot" (Brookner 1983: 82). But proleptically she also hints at the dark side of such emplotment: "[b]eginnings are so beautiful" (83). Edith "sometimes thought that the time spent working out the plots of her novels had prepared her for this, her final adventure, her story come to life" (Brookner 1985: 85). Revealingly, the moment she finds a resolution for her plots she feels "vividly unsafe" (117); most likely, because this removes the vicarious expectancy of fulfilment. As Andrea Gutenberg has demonstrated, Edith's holding on to notions of romantic love is thoroughly rejected in the novel by an undermining of the conventional romance pattern.[39] Her discussion of plot patterns in *Hotel du Lac* can be used here to answer the question of what further messages might be gleaned from the development of plot in the novels.[40]

Gutenberg takes up Carol P. Christ's notion of 'the women's quest',[41] namely "women's social quest" which "concerns women's struggle to gain respect, equality, and freedom in society" and "women's spiritual quest" which is (rather mystically, as Gutenberg notes) defined as "a woman's awakening to the depth of her soul and her position in the universe".[42] With respect to their writing – this should perhaps be mentioned first – both protagonists do not follow an artistic vision, but adopt a thoroughly pragmatic, even cynical stance (Brookner 1983: 132; Brookner 1985: 28; 152). They do not envisage writing as the cultivation of an individual talent or as vital self-expression, i.e. claim to an autonomous voice. One should beware here, however, of totalising the concept of the aspiring artist. But even if this is not applied, the term 'quest' sits uncomfortably with the characters' passiveness. Considering Christ's view that "[w]omen's spiritual quest provides orientation for women's social quest",[43] what 'spiritual quest' are Frances and Edith embarking on? I cannot follow Gutenberg's argument that Edith's 'exile' in Switzerland, organised by a patronising friend as penance for the scandalous jilting of Geoffrey Long, constitutes a 'spiritual quest'.[44] Both protagonists are too self-deceiving for such a quest. Their 'social quests', Frances's wish to escape from the boredom of her routine life and Edith's dreams of a romantic relationship, a domestic life with a husband (the preference for either or the compatibility of the two are not quite clear) remain therefore limited and limiting. I would rather emphasise Gutenberg's observation that Edith's tedious routine and aimless walking in the Swiss resort mirrors her lack of orientation.[45]

Both protagonists are for a time immersed in social life only to (presumably) resume their lonely writing existence. Significantly, this is not an autonomous decision in favour of writing, but one compelled by circumstances or effected by chance, because the prospective partners turn out to be incompatible. The protagonists' withdrawal into their old life of relative seclusion is motivated by disappointment, and evidently not a good solution.

That courtship plots are terminated in both novels (though less obviously so in *Look at Me*) could be, within limits, interpreted as rejection of the *telos* of marriage.[46] However, the painful experience of unfaithfulness (in Frances's case) and the last-minute rejection of selfish suitors (in Edith's case), have, as is revealed in flashbacks, happened before, and might – judging from the protagonists' persisting fascination for the wrong kind of partners – happen again. It is true that the resulting circular structure breaks away from traditional linear patterns of female emplotment, but whether this is really an emancipatory "writing beyond the ending" has to be assessed in conjunction with the inner development of the protagonists.[47] As already indicated, the protagonists do not really change attitudes. Although Frances's closing statement "I pick up my pen. I start writing" (Brookner 1983: 192) sounds like a new start into artistic self-determination, there is evidence which suggests that she will stick to her flawed poetics and self-isolation. Similarly, Edith appears to go back to her old lifestyle. The closures of the novels do thus not signal liberating departures.

The question arises whether there are "submerged plots" in the texts, for example, "a maternal subplot" which could shed some light on the protagonists' stance.[48] In many female artist novels, to apply the generic foil once more, the "daughter becomes an artist to extend, reveal, and elaborate her mother's often thwarted talents".[49] This is decidedly not the case in both of Brookner's novels. Frances's mother certainly encouraged her daughter's writing: "'[m]y darling Fan,' she used to say, her eyes widening, 'I think you have a gift'" (16). The mother seems to have had no artistic or professional ambitions of her own, but led a life surrounded by "men […] ministering to her" (30). Although Frances rejects such adoration for herself (*ibid.*), her craving for male attention may well have been conditioned by this example. So when she recalls her mother's words "[m]y darling Fan" at the end of the novel (192), one cannot help surmise (is there a pun on the name?) that the presumed new beginning is doomed to fail. Moreover, living with her mother's old servant Nancy, Frances remains something like an eternal daughter; hardly an enabling condition.

Edith recalls her mother as distant and unloving (Brookner 1985: 48). She believes that she took up writing romantic fiction because her mother, a Viennese flirt who experienced married life as disappointing and ageing as difficult to bear, read romances to console herself (104). Indeed, the dichotomy that informs Edith's writing is clearly indebted to her mother's anti-female attitudes (146). All in all, the mother's influence has therefore been rather negative. That Edith cannot understand the causes of her mother's discontent and define herself differently is by no means inevitable.

Brookner's writer figures are very perceptive in some respects, but appear oddly unable to learn from social experiences.[50] If they are slightly wiser after their trials of disappointed love, it does not translate into empowering action. Cheryl Alexander Malcolm's assertion that "Brookner [...] is depicting a world in which the oppressed are undeserving of their fate" appears only acceptable,[51] if one takes a highly deterministic stance on personal development.

4. The Thematisation of Writing

Both writer protagonists, particularly Frances, display a high degree of self-consciousness by reflecting extensively on their writing.[52] The comments deal mainly with their reasons for writing, their self-understanding as writers, the writing process, their subject matter and values, but they also extend into longer explanations of distinctions that inform their understanding of social life and thus their poetics. Many comments explore the relation between life and fiction. Indeed, both protagonists tend to understand life in terms of fiction and actually want to transform their lives through fiction (Frances) or hope their lives will turn out like fiction (Edith).

In the first chapter of *Look at Me* Frances gives a long explanation for the motives of her writing:

> [w]hen I feel swamped in my solitude and hidden by it, physically obscured by it, rendered invisible, in fact, writing is my way of piping up. Of reminding people that I am here. And when I have ordered my characters, plundered my store of images, removed from them all the sadness that I might feel in myself, then I can switch on that current that allows me to write so easily, once I get started, and to make people laugh. That, it seems, is what they like to do. And if I manage this well enough and beguile all the dons and the critics, they will fail to register my real message, which is a simple one. If my looks and my manner were of greater assistance to me I could deliver this message in person. 'Look at me,' I would say. 'Look at me.' But since I am on my own in this matter, I must use subterfuge and guile, and with a bit of luck and good management this particular message will never be deciphered, and my reasons for delivering it in this manner remain obscure. (Brookner 1983: 19-20)

Writing is for Frances an escape from, as she variously puts it, "boredom", "lack of company" (23), "loneliness" (70), "solitude" (53; 181) and a means to gain attention (85). It involves a suppression of her own feelings, but relieves her, as she describes elsewhere, of "heaviness" (18), "the weight of all that virtue" (31), that means the inculcated values that make her act according to other people's expectations rather than her own psychic needs. The writing process itself, which is repeatedly expressed in the metaphor of a 'current', makes her obviously feel alive, but leads "inevitably, to greater restlessness" (18), a clear sign that it merely alleviates symptoms. Instead of learning to relate to people in real-life situations, where she experiences a loss of words (92; 103), Frances suppresses her own feelings and tries to reach people by being entertaining. A deep sense of inadequacy as a woman ("[i]f my looks and my manner were of greater assistance to me") caused by a conservative gendering, and an inability to reach out to others ("I am on my own in this matter"), compel her to produce inauthentic writing ("I must use subterfuge and guile").

Frances bases her view of life on a social dichotomy between 'participants' and 'observers' (14; 132), regarding her friends Alix and Nick as belonging to the first group and herself to the latter. Casting herself as an observer due to a supposed lack of attractiveness (123), Frances cannot bring herself to fully acknowledge how much her fast-living and rude friends themselves are spectators that first thrive on her attention and admiration to be later entertained by her despair at being excluded from their circle. Nor does she realise her own very real social shortcomings and the destructiveness of her stance. Although valid to a certain extent, Frances's dichotomy is ultimately too simple and, above all, self-defeating.

When Frances notices a cooling off in her friends Alix, Nick and James Anstey, she turns to writing again, but this time as a means of protecting herself. This brings out another misguided conception of writing entertained by Frances, namely the idea that she could control life by means of fiction. If she has been trying to write herself into the lives of others all along, she returns now to the idea that she could "write [herself] into a new way of life" (31) and even persuades herself that she is "free to invent [her] life" (167). Deeply affected by the rejection of the people that fascinate her, indeed victimised by them, Frances hopes to retain control of the situation by turning other unfortunate people into material for her comic fiction: "I would write Miss Morpeth into my system of things: she would become a 'character', and in due course I would, by virtue of this very process, gain the upper hand" (134). In other words, she does in fiction what has been inflicted on her in real life.[53] The ethical problem of exploiting people for entertainment purposes has to give way to the sheer need of shoring up her brittle sense of identity:

> I performed some sort of surgery on myself and eliminated all feelings save those of mockery and judgment. I registered somewhere, but far away in my mind, that this was a terrible and decisive moment, and that I might never again recover my wholeness. But that wholeness now seemed to me so damaged that it was simply a question of safety, of survival, to protect the ruins, much as certain areas of faulty pavement are cordoned off while workmen heat and melt tar for resurfacing. If I could not ordain what went on below the surface, I would see that what was presented to the public gaze was unmarked. (135)

The strategy of self-concealment and the concomitant poetics of fiction are never revised. As Frances states at the end of the novel:

> I made notes for my novel, and I found that it was going very well and very fast, that the characters emerged quite naturally, and that, quite naturally, I found the right words with which to describe them. The words, in fact, which had previously deserted me, were pouring out. The fact that I was skating over the surface, jazzing things up, playing for laughs, may have had something to do with it. I laughed myself, at one point. It was quite easy, really. I managed to kill a couple of hours in this manner. [...] I thought of my lost hopes, and how lucky I was to be able to convert them so easily into satire. (190)

As the self-assuring use of adverbs betrays, this is whistling in the dark. The crisis in her private life is contained with the same old questionable instrument, an inauthentic fiction that keeps her trapped in self-isolation.

Edith's writing is also highly compensatory. Involved in a clandestine, long-running affair with a married man, her writing has been a means to fill the time between her partner's erratic visits (Brookner 1985: 180) or to overcome her jealousy when he was on holiday with his wife: "I wrote for ten hours a day to stop myself thinking of him" (74). As she also confesses to Philip Neville, a new suitor met in the Swiss hotel, she could not "write or even dream with any kind of energy in the absence of love" (98), meaning that she has to believe in love as an ideal. Aware that she has not found a fulfilling relationship yet, she hopes that she will be swept off her feet some day like the heroines in her popular romances (85).

Although Edith admits to herself "I make no claims for my particular sort of writing" (9), "[t]he facts of life are too terrible to go into my kind of fiction" (28), she does not grasp her emotional dependence on what she regards as "that illicit manufacture of a substance not needed for survival" (120). That Edith's writing is a questionable substitute for real-life relations is repeatedly indicated; for instance, when she is said to emerge "dazed and haggard from her room after several hours with *Beneath the Visiting Moon*" or when she is "mildly anaesthetized by her labours" and "highly charged with vicarious emotion" (51; 52). In an unsent letter to David, composed towards the end of the novel, she defiantly expresses her credo as follows:

> [y]ou thought, perhaps, like my publisher, and my agent, who are always trying to get me to bring my books up to date and make them sexier and more exciting that I wrote my stories with that mixture of satire and cynical detachment that is thought to become the modern writer in this field. You were wrong. I believed every word I wrote. And I still do, even though I realize now that none of it can ever come true for me. (181)

While this may be praised for spirit, it is ultimately a position which will keep her entrapped.

Like Frances, Edith bases her fiction on a dichotomy,[54] namely that between "hares" and "tortoises" (27), i.e. "ultra-feminine" (146) women who get what they want and women who are less attractive and therefore lose out. Edith sees herself as a "tortoise existence" writing "for tortoises, like herself" (30). Again, while her dichotomy is supported to some extent by the people she meets in the Swiss hotel, it is finally undermined by the fact that both groups of females are shown to be trapped in a pernicious gender ideology that restricts their agency to either shopping and eating or waiting and writing.

If Edith's public narration for women feeds illusions and, in sum, helps to perpetuate a conservative gender ideology, her private narration to her lover David is shown to be as similarly crippling as the comic fictionalisations Frances devises for an envisaged male audience. Interestingly, Edith herself senses that gender gets in the way of her amusing portrayal of women to her lover:

> Edith laid down her pen. This letter would have to be finished later, and even possibly revised. Unsound elements seemed to have crept into her narrative; she was aware of exceeding her brief. And was then aware of the restrictions that that brief implied: to amuse, to divert, to relax – these had been her functions, and indeed her dedicated aim. But something had gone wrong or was slipping out of control. What had been undertaken as an exercise in entertainment – for had not the situation seemed appropriate, tailor-made, for such an exercise? – had somehow accumulated elements of introspection, of criticism, even of bitterness. (114)

Here, Edith becomes aware of the restrictions the "brief", i.e. the assumed gender role, imposes on her, but, characteristically, engages in self-censure. That Brookner solicits feminist questioning becomes evident in the continuation of the just quoted passage:

> "[w]ell, darling, what news from Cranford?" David used to say, stretching out his long arm to gather her to him as they sat on the big sofa. And that had always been her cue to present him with her gentle observations, always skilfully edited, and to watch the lines of fatigue of his lean and foxy face dissolve into a smile. For that is how he saw me, she thought, and out of love for him that is how I tried to be. (*Ibid.*)

David's mocking reference to Elizabeth Gaskell's *Cranford* (1853), a novel representing a female community whose main protagonists are spinsters, invites a gender-critical reading of Edith's compliance. Brookner connects her female protagonists with male characters who exhibit patriarchal complacency (see the condescending behaviour of Nick Fraser and Philip Neville).

As further proof of Brookner's deliberate evocation of gender-critical questions, one could refer to the repeated thematisation of feminism in *Hotel du Lac*. When Edith, for example, tries to explain her dislike of the "ultra-feminine", "the complacent consumers of men" (146) to the strikingly chic but bulimic fellow-guest Monica (incidentally, a character who does not fit into her neat dichotomy of "hares" and "tortoises"), she declares herself dissatisfied with feminism for not criticising such women: "'I think perhaps the feminists should take a fresh look at the situation.' She stopped. What she was trying to say, although deeply felt, did not make much sense" (*ibid.*). Edith's criticism here is clearly marked as falling too short. Indeed, lack of sisterhood (inculcated by the patriarchal system) would be rather an argument in favour of feminist commitment than against it. To use a paternal saying frequently re-called by Edith and thus assuming the function of a leitmotif, her equations are false, because they do not address the more funda-mental questions raised by the inequalities of the gender system.

5. Conclusion

The protagonists' writing is determined by a sense of inferiority and emotional dependency that is at least partially caused, but certainly aggravated by gender constraints. That both figures develop dis-tinctions (in the suspicious form of binary oppositions) to explain their own life and their writing highlights the determining role of ideological thinking. The characters' dichotomies are shown to be false, because they cannot adequately explain the described gender reality. Significantly, the characters can to a certain extent recog-nise the inadequacies of their system, but are not able to change or transcend it, because they are emotionally dependent on their fic-tions for survival. Brookner thus draws attention to the reasons why women have difficulties to 'live new scripts' and 'to invent new sto-ries'. Fictions that compensate cannot liberate.

As has been demonstrated on various levels of the texts, Brook-ner cannot be accused of not addressing gender issues, in fact, gen-der-critical questions are clearly invited. Her writer figures could be regarded as negative examples of gender ideologisation. In many respects they are their own worst enemies. Through implied con-trast, they offer lessons to female writers, for example, not to con-form to dominant social and cultural expectations but to strive for authenticity and self-exploration,[55] not to seclude themselves from social life but to cultivate an empathetic understanding of others, not to engage in ideologically crippling forms of fiction but to de-velop their own voice.

Brookner's portrayal of female writing could, however, be faulted on three counts. First, her specific combination of economic independence and emotional dependence due to gender strictures cannot claim to be representative. One might rather expect the op-posite: a struggle to make ends meet and a more critical conscious-ness in matters of emancipation. Second, the conception of writing as compensation or, as becomes increasingly clear, self-imprison-ment appears unnecessarily reductive. Is it really impossible to turn the capable private narration into a self-asserting public narration? After all – this should be emphasised here – Brookner's own novel *Hotel du Lac* demonstrates that it is possible to reject traditional emplotments. And third, the sense of an inescapable destiny that pervades the characters' lives appears unconvincing, even in the light of the information we get in the novels. Frances is by no means unsupported. She has a loyal friend in Olivia and is integrated in Olivia's family. Olivia's mother could even be regarded as a role-model of a strong and independent woman.[56] The stifling situation in her flat could be easily remedied. And if Edith can call off her wedding at the last possible moment (Brookner 1985: 129-130), why should she not be able to create a more fulfilling life for herself? Or is Edith, as Watson suggests, after all, quite pleased with her life?[57] Brookner's portrayal of female writing elicits such polemical questions. The tensions between the characters' perceptiveness and blindness, their entrapment and passiveness are too exasperating. The same could be said about the author's functionalisation of generic and narrative means which is strangely unenabling. Brookner's representation of female writers certainly provokes critical reflection and comment through its bewildering mix of consciousness-raising and denial of empowerment, but it is difficult to align to the social reality of the majority of contemporary women writers and refrains from giving a more inspiring image of female authorship.

Notes

1   DuPlessis (1985: 84); see also Patricia Meyer Spacks's statement "[t]he woman as artist may help to illumine the woman as woman" (1976: 160).

2   As she stated in an interview with John Haffenden: "[y]ou'd have to be crouching in your burrows to see my novels in a feminist way", quoted in Skinner (1992: 83).

3   See Allrath (2005: 122).

4   Stetz takes Virginia Woolf's famous dictum in *A Room of One's Own* (1929) that "we think back through our mothers if we are women" (1991: 102) as her starting point. She interprets the fact that both figures' writing has been motivated by their mothers as proof of a feminist aesthetics that qualifies Brookner as a feminist, albeit a reluctant one. However, her reading plays down the arguably negative influence these mothers have had on their daughters' lives and creativity. As regards the intertextual references

in *Hotel du Lac*, which are also brought forward to support the idea of a feminist aesthetics (*ibid.*, 106-110), one has to admit that the mention of Virginia Woolf is highly suggestive, but significantly neither Edith Hope's writing seems to be geared towards qualities found in the women writers mentioned or alluded to in the text nor is her reading strongly oriented towards a female literary heritage. Holberg takes issue with the privileging of "an eccentric model of authorship" (1997: 157) in feminist criticism and reclaims Brookner by putting her into a minor novelistic tradition championing "the 'conventional' woman writer", i.e. characters that actually accommodate love, marriage and domesticity with successful writing (*ibid.*, 142; 10-12). While it is necessary to acknowledge the diverse realities of women's writing, Brookner's writer figures do not fit quite as nicely into the mould of 'conventionality' (a problematic term even in inverted commas) as their desire for love and – in Edith's case – also the prestige of marital status may suggest. Both certainly do not "spend their hours at the kitchen sink thinking of new stories to tell" (*ibid.*, 179).

5   Head (2002: 105).

6   *Ibid.*, 108.

7   I have been inspired here by two studies, namely John Skinner's *The Fictions of Anita Brookner* (1992) and Daphne Watson's *Their Own Worst Enemies* (1995). Skinner's study pays close attention to narrative means and convincingly demonstrates the fruitfulness of a feminist perspective (by way of the example of *Hotel du Lac*). His notion of *mise en abyme*, "a novelist writing a novel about a novelist who writes novels", does, however, not suffice to capture the complexity of Brookner's representation of female writing (1992: 83; 58). Watson's study draws attention to the persistence of formulaic and stereotypical elements in Brookner's novels that reinforce patriarchal structures. Her approach relates to patterns found in fairy tales and Gothic fiction, but does not consider the generic frame of the female artist novel, nor does she focus on the writer figures in particular (1995: 37-44). It should be mentioned here that Olga Kenyon had already moved in the direction of a generic approach by adopting the frame of the women's novel and arguing in favour of an ideological reading of narrative means. However, in the feminist assessment of some of her findings Kenyon is rather reserved (1988: 144-166).

8   See Frye (1986: 13-47).

9   For the terminological distinction between the author's 'intended effect', the 'potential effect' of textual structures (also the 'historical effect') see Sommer (2000); explained in Allrath (2005: 122-123).

10 See Davis (1987: 15-16).

11 As Fraiman points out with respect to the female *Bildungsroman*, "[w]hat we can do [...] is examine the patterns of inclusion and exclusion fostered by a given category, consider the explanations it is capable of yielding, identify the ideas and values on which it relies and that it reproduces, and evaluate these in relation to our own political commitments" (1993: 2).

12 To emphasise the originally male bias of the genre, which had to be overcome by female writers, it is appropriate to talk about the 'female artist novel'. For the late arrival of the 'woman's artist novel' see Huf (1983: 1-2).

13 See Würzbach (2004: 201).

14 This can be already observed in artist novels produced in the nineteenth century; see Noll-Wiemann (1977: 218).

15 Elaine Showalter refers to this conflict as "the immemorial choice of the woman artist" (1977: 301). Spacks observes that the conflict "is not peculiar to women, but women are likely to experience it with special intensity" (1976: 166).

16 As Virginia Woolf famously summed up the needs of female writers in her essay "Women and Fiction" (1966: 148).

17 Cheryl Alexander Malcolm states, "[t]ypical of Brookner's protagonists, Frances Hinton values personal relationships far more than career success" (2002: 45-46).

18 Brookner (1983: 71). Further references to this edition will be included in the text.

19 Brookner (1985: 119). Further references to this edition will be included in the text.

20 For this widespread negative attitude towards the genre of romance, see Fuchs (2004: 129).

21 For the distinction between private narration and public narration, see Lanser (1986: 352).

22 For this explanation of Steven G. Kellman's concept of the 'self-begetting novel', see Greene (1991: 16). If I am right in my assessment of the closure of the novel, Brookner does not make use of the enabling circular structure that can be, according to Greene, found in other female artist novels in the late twentieth century, namely in Doris Lessing's *The Golden Notebook* (1962), Margaret Laurence's *The Diviners* (1974) and Margaret Atwood's *Lady Oracle* (1976); see *ibid.* For an analysis of *The Golden Notebook*, see Ingrid von Rosenberg's contribution and for a reading of *The Diviners*, see Alexa Keuneke's contribution in the present volume.

23 See Greene (1991: 22).

24 Gilbert & Gubar have drawn attention to the various strategies women writers employed in the nineteenth century to overcome external and internalised constraints on female writing. If one applied their findings to the twentieth-century character Frances – which begs further questions – her strategy would appear to be some kind of 'male mimicry' at the cost of 'psychological self-denial' (1979: 69-71).

25 See Skinner (1992: 67).

26 Head (2002: 106).

27 See Couzyn (1985: 15).

28 See Holberg (1997: 174) and Sadler (1990: 61).

29 For a closer view of the psychological mechanism at work here, see Waugh (1989: 139-151).

30 Sadler talks in Frances's case of a "debasement of writing", since it "will hide the truth about life and merely amuse for the primary purpose of calling attention to herself" (1990: 43; 44).

31 Nünning (1993).

32 *Ibid.*, 256.

33 *Ibid.*, 266.

34 *Ibid.*, 263; 266.

35 See *ibid.*, 257.

36 See Skinner (1992: 77-82).

37 Considering the struggle of generations of female writers with 'anxiety of authorship', see Gilbert & Gubar (1979: 49); one is almost inclined to view Brookner's construction of a gender-conformist female writer figure as a provocation to feminist critics.

38 Frye (1986: 2; 29).

39 Gutenberg (2000: 245).

40 See *ibid.*, 245-253. Gutenberg's investigation into the plot patterns in women's novels is informed by possible-worlds theory (PWT) and highly useful, because her analytical distinctions provide access to the ideological meanings conveyed in plot constructions.

41 See *ibid.*, 246-248; 172-180.

42 Christ (1986: 8).

43 *Ibid.*, 11.

44 See Gutenberg (2000: 246-247).

45 See *ibid.*

46 For an interpretation of this ending in *Hotel du Lac* including its inherent circularity, see *ibid.*, 252.

47 DuPlessis (1985).

48 See Abel (1983: 163).

49 DuPlessis (1985: 93; see also 104).

50 As Sadler remarks, "Frances Hinton does not learn from 'human behaviour'" (1990: 45); see also Watson (1995: 41). Kenyon notices "a rational capacity to understand undermined by an emotional incapacity to adapt" (1988: 152), but does not follow up the questionable ideological implications of such a constitution of female characters.

51 Malcolm (2002: 17).

52 See Skinner (1992: 57; 59).

53 Frances's unethical behaviour could be related to Showalter's seventies comment, "the violation of private affection, the public exposure of someone else's suffering, has become almost a rite of passage for male writers, a display of manliness that critics take as a sign of true artistic dedication" (1977: 303). This supports the idea that Frances engages artistically in 'male mimicry' (see endnote 24).

54 The dichotomies point to a major flaw in the thinking of Brookner's female characters observed by Sadler: they can only see 'either-or' alternatives (1990: 41).

55 This is what Showalter identifies as a main step towards the "autonomy of the woman novelist" (1977: 318).

56 Sadler, who considers the function of foil characters, sees here the healthy middle ground of the novel (1990: 48).

57 See Watson (1995: 41).

Bibliography

Abel, Elisabeth: "Narrative Structure(s) and Female Development. The Case of *Mrs. Dalloway*". – In E.A. *et al.* (Eds.): *The Voyage In. Fictions of Female Development*, Hanover & London, 1983, pp. 161-185.

Allrath, Gaby: *(En)Gendering Unreliable Narration. A Feminist-Narratological Theory and Analysis of Unreliability in Contemporary Women's Novels*, Trier, 2005.

Brookner, Anita: *Look at Me*, London, 1983.

–: *Hotel du Lac*, London, 1985 [1984].

Christ, Carol P.: *Diving Deep and Surfacing. Women Writers on Spiritual Quest*, Boston, 1986 [1980].

Couzyn, Jeni: *The Bloodaxe Book of Contemporary Women Poets. Eleven British Writers*, Newcastle, 1985.

Davis, Lennard J.: *Resisting Novels. Ideology and Fiction*, New York & London, 1987.

DuPlessis, Rachel Blau: *Writing Beyond the Ending. Narrative Strategies of Twentieth-Century Women Writers*, Bloomington, 1985.

Fraiman, Susan, *Unbecoming Women. British Women Writers and the Novel of Development*, New York, 1993.

Frye, Joanne S.: *Living Stories, Telling Lives. Women and the Novel in Contemporary Experience*, Ann Arbor, 1986.

Fuchs, Barbara: *Romance*, London, 2004.

Gilbert, Sandra M. & Susan Gubar: *The Madwoman in the Attic. The Woman Writer and the Nineteenth-Century Literary Imagination*, New Haven & London, 1979.

Greene, Gayle: *Changing the Story. Feminist Fiction and the Tradition*, Bloomington, 1991.

Gutenberg, Andrea: *Mögliche Welten. Plot und Sinnstiftung im englischen Frauenroman*, Heidelberg, 2000.

Head, Dominic: *The Cambridge Introduction to Modern British Fiction, 1950-2000*, Cambridge, 2002.

Holberg, Jennifer L.: "Searching for Mary Garth. The Figure of the Writing Woman in Charlotte Brontë, Elizabeth Barrett Browning, E.M. Delafield, Barbara Pym, and Anita Brookner", *Dissertation Abstracts International, Section A. The Humanities and Social Sciences* 58:6, 1997, 2225.

Huf, Linda: *A Portrait of the Artist as a Young Woman. The Writer as Heroine in American Literature*, New York, 1983.

Kenyon, Olga: *Women Novelists Today. A Survey of English Writing in the Seventies and Eighties*, Brighton, 1988.

Lanser, Susan Sniader: "Towards a Feminist Narratology", *Style* 20:3, 1986, 341-363.

Malcolm, Cheryl Alexander: *Understanding Anita Brookner*, Columbia, 2002.

Noll-Wiemann, Renate: *Der Künstler im englischen Roman des 19. Jahrhunderts*, Heidelberg, 1977.

Nünning, Ansgar: "Formen und Funktionen der Auflösung von Geschlechterstereotypen in ausgewählten Romanen von Anita Brookner. Interpretationshinweise für eine Behandlung der Sekundarstufe II", *Die Neueren Sprachen* 92:3, 1993, 249-270.

Sadler, Lynn Veach: *Anita Brookner*, Boston, 1990.

Showalter, Elaine: *A Literature of Their Own. British Women Novelists from Brontë to Lessing*, Princeton, 1977.

Skinner, John: *The Fictions of Anita Brookner. Illusions of Romance*, New York, 1992.

Sommer, Roy: "Funktionsgeschichten. Überlegungen zur Verwendung des Funktionsbegriffs in der Literaturwissenschaft und Anregungen zu seiner terminologischen Differenzierung", *Literaturwissenschaftliches Jahrbuch* 41, 2000, 319-341.

Spacks, Patricia Meyer: *The Female Imagination. A Literary and Psychological Investigation of Women's Writing*, London, 1976.

Stetz, Margaret Diane: "Anita Brookner. Woman Writer as Reluctant Feminist". – In Suzanne W. Jones (Ed.): *Writing the Woman Artist. Essays on Poetics, Politics, and Portraiture*, Philadelphia, 1991, pp. 96-112.

Watson, Daphne: *Their Own Worst Enemies. Women Writers of Women's Fiction*, London & Boulder, 1995.

Waugh, Patricia: *Feminine Fictions. Revisiting the Postmodern*, London & New York, 1989.

Woolf, Virginia: "Women and Fiction". – In Leonard Woolf (Ed.): *Collected Essays, Volume II*, London, 1966, pp. 141-148.

Würzbach, Natascha: "Der englische Frauenroman vom Modernismus bis zur Gegenwart (1890-1990). Kanonrevision, Gattungsmodifikation, Blickfelderweiterung". – In Ansgar Nünning (Ed.): *Eine andere Geschichte der englischen Literatur. Epochen, Gattungen und Teilgebiete im Überblick*, Trier, 2004, pp. 195-211.

Lena Steveker (Saarbrücken)

"My Solitude Is My Treasure, the Best Thing I Have". A.S. Byatt's Female Artists

Artists feature strongly in all novels by British author A.S. Byatt. Except for the occasional painter, potter or sculptor, the majority of Byatt's artist characters are writers,[1] most prominently among them the novelists Henry Severell in *The Shadow of the Sun* (1964), Julia Corbett in *The Game* (1967) and Jude Mason in *Babel Tower* (1996), the poets Christabel LaMotte and Henry Randolph Ash in *Possession* (1990), the playwright Alexander Wedderburn and the poet Hugh Pink in what has become known as the 'Frederica Quartet',[2] and the writer of fairy tales Olive Wellwood in *The Children's Book* (2009). The characters of male authors in Byatt's fiction can easily be identified as being indebted to the romantic conception of the poet as a male visionary genius who is "fundamentally apart from, fundamentally separate from society" and the modernist idea that the writer lives in social "exile",[3] without any "fear to be alone" as James Joyce's Stephen Dedalus,[4] the prototypical modernist artist, remarks.[5] Byatt's woman writers, however, are more complex constructions as it is through them that her texts engage in discussions of female life in patriarchal society in general and of the female artist in particular. Byatt has claimed that her "books are about the woman artist";[6] she also stated that her "novels [...] think about the problem of female vision, female art and thought".[7] As I will argue in this essay, Byatt's concept of the female artist is fundamentally paradoxical as her novels portray women writers as depending on solitude which, however, they represent as being irreconcilable with either patriarchal society or human relationships.

The Shadow of the Sun portrays its protagonist artist as someone with visionary capacity; Henry Severell, "cast as an archetypically Romantic figure of artistic genius",[8] experiences frighteningly violent "attacks of vision" which enable him to write his novels.[9] His daughter Anna realises that her own hopes of becoming an author are doomed to fail because she is unable to have visions herself. She admits defeat, when, standing on a bridge,

> [h]er attention came sharply into focus on the whole scene [...]. She thought, this is important [...]. This will change me [into a writer], Anna thought, and waited for the sense of valuable loneliness [...]. And then the cutting edge of the vision melted [...] and Anna knew that whatever it was was over [...]. And that she had not been stirred out of herself [...]. She was still small, [...] and the possible glory was gone. [...] The desolation was chilling. (Byatt 1991a: 237-238)

This scene relates Anna's failure to develop into an author to her inability to have a vision, but, more importantly, it implies that seeing has to be preceded by solitude, "the sense of valuable loneliness" Anna waits for in vain. She is indeed repeatedly shown as longing for solitude, but failing to achieve it. The two almost-visions Anna experiences are interrupted by other people disrupting her loneliness (134; 151). Her wish for self-sufficient solitude remains likewise unfulfilled when, shortly after she has decided to start a new life, "[a]lone" (297; my emphasis), her lover Oliver prevents her from leaving, and she cannot think of a way she "could have [...] done without him" (298). Anna's description of her father as somebody who "saw all the time" (238), who "was with Wordsworth and Coleridge, [...] alone" (ibid.; my emphasis) also underlines the importance Byatt's novels ascribe to solitude, as do the characterisations of other male authors in her fiction. In *The Virgin in the Garden* (1978), for example, the playwright Alexander Wedderburn is portrayed as a man of "secretly acknowledged delicious solitude, which was both escape, energy and power",[10] whereas, in *Babel Tower*, the poet Hugh Pink composes a poem during a solitary walk through a forest.[11] Keeping these examples in mind, I would argue that Anna Severell, in *The Shadow of the Sun*, disqualifies as an artist not so much because she fails as a visionary, but because she lacks solitude.[12]

There are several dimensions to Byatt's conception of solitude as the defining characteristic of both male and female artist. The term not only denotes the mere experience of loneliness, which is denied to Anna Severell, but also refers to a writer's autonomy from the influences of the outside world and, moreover, to the notion of separate selfhood. While Byatt's male characters, both artists and non-artists, never seem to encounter any difficulty in achieving solitude in either of its three meanings, her female characters are constantly shown as struggling with fashioning themselves as either autonomous, separate subjects or feeling individuals. As my subsequent discussion of Christabel LaMotte (*Possession*), Julia Corbett (*The Game*) and Olive Wellwood (*The Children's Book*) will show,[13] Byatt's female writers are doomed to fail in either their creativity or their personal relationships because they do not succeed in reconciling art and life.

It is through the character of Christabel LaMotte that *Possession* explores the female artist's need for solitude within the context of mid-Victorian society. Christabel is a poet whose work is modestly popular for a brief period during her own life,[14] but fails to be subsequently canonised in the twentieth century (Byatt 1991c: 37). Until she falls in love with (married) Henry Randolph Ash, whose success as a poet, both with his contemporaries and in literary history, exceeds her own by far (403), Christabel has been living in social seclusion, sharing a cottage with her lesbian partner, painter Blanche Glover (37; 159; 186; 485). LaMotte is portrayed as an extraordinary woman who violates Victorian gender norms by "*renounc[ing] the [...] usual female Hopes (and with them the usual female Fears) [...] in exchange for [...] Art*" (187; emphasis in the text) as she writes in a letter to Ash.[15] Instead of contenting herself with a socially acceptable life of "*cramped Daughterly Devotion to a mother*" (*ibid.*) or an equally respectable existence as a middle-class wife and mother, she "*ha[s] fought for [her] Autonomy against Family and Society*" (189) in order to be an independent woman artist, thus stepping outside the norms of Victorian middle-class society. Christabel's hard-won autonomy enables her to lead the life of "*Solitude*" (137) she needs for writing poetry. She cherishes this solitude above anything, claiming that: "*my Solitude is my Treasure, the best thing I have*" (*ibid.*). Yet, LaMotte is to lose her autonomous solitude when she falls in love with Ash. At first she rejects his attempts at setting up an acquaintance, because she knows that even the merest shadow of doubt cast upon her respectability as a single woman might endanger her "*freedom to live as [she] do[es] [...] and work [her] work*" (184). Her initial hesitation notwithstanding, she eventually gives in to her feelings, embarking on a brief but passionate affair with him. Finding herself pregnant, however, she has no other option than to give up her self-determined life at her cottage and, in order to prevent herself and her daughter Maia from suffering the social stigma of illegitimacy, to move in with her sister Sophie and her brother-in-law who raise Maia as their own child. While Maia lives in ignorance of her biological parentage, LaMotte never contacts Ash again, the only exception being a single letter, written in old age when she learns that he is fatally ill, in which she tells him of both her personal unhappiness and her failure as a poet (499-503).

With Christabel repeatedly insisting on the fundamental importance of solitude for her identity as a poet, *Possession* applies romantic and modernist notions of (male) solitary subjectivity to its concept of the woman poet. At the same time, however, the novel problematises the very notion of female solitude which it conceptualises as a fundamental prerequisite for the woman artist. Drawing on the myth of Melusina, *Possession* represents the female artist's solitude as being incompatible with patriarchal society. This myth tells the story of the beautiful and powerfully creative water nymph Melusina, who, every Saturday, is doomed to turn into a creature that is half woman and half snake. This curse can only be lifted if Melusina marries a mortal who will agree to take a vow never to visit her on Saturdays, as this will enable her to hide her transformations from him. Melusina falls in love with the knight Raimondin, whom she marries after he has taken the necessary oath. However, their happiness is not to last, for, driven by curiosity, Raimondin eventually breaks his oath and spies on her in her bathroom, thus witnessing her transformation into a snake-woman. When he finally discloses her secret to other people, Melusina is doomed to turn into a dragon and is forced to abandon her husband and her children.[16] Embodying beauty, power and monstrosity, Melusina thus symbolises the female Other, feared and oppressed by patriarchal society.[17]

Possession refers to this myth in several ways. First, it presents the character of Christabel as a second Melusina who can only fashion her identity as an artist by separating herself from society.[18] LaMotte is not only described as "some sort of serpent, hissing quietly [...], but ready to strike" (366), but also compares herself to the snake-woman as she sees no other possibility than to abandon her daughter by passing her off as her sister's child (501). Second, *Possession* subtly reworks the myth's central metaphor, the fairy creature's bath. Since it is only in the privacy of her bathroom that Melusina is able to live as her 'true' self – half woman, half snake – this room symbolises the autonomy on which her identity as a monstrous, but powerfully creative being depends. Spying on her in the bathroom, her husband Raimondin not only breaks his oath, but also violates her autonomous space. Byatt's novel follows a similar strategy of negotiating female autonomy with the help of spatial metaphors. Christabel LaMotte describes the cottage she shares with Blanche Glover before she meets Ash as a place of female freedom from patriarchal society, "a place wherein we neither served nor were served" (186). What is more, she regards the cottage as a place that enables both her and Blanche to live independently as creative women (186-187). Read along the lines of the snake-woman's tale, the cottage is Christabel's Melusinian bathroom; the solitude it creates represents the woman artist's autonomy in patriarchal society. But although the novel's Melusinian space provides safety by closing off the outside world, it also shuts its inhabitants in, preventing them from partaking in social life.[19] Putting it with Christabel's words:

> [o]h Sir [Ash], *you must not kindly seek to* [...] *steal away my solitude. It is a thing we women are taught to dread –* [...] *no companionable Nest – but a donjon. The Donjon may frown and threaten – but* it keeps us safe – within its confines we [women] are free. (137; my emphasis)

Thus, *Possession* presents solitude, i.e. the autonomy necessary for the female artist, as both a means of liberating her from the stifling norms of Victorian society and, at the same time, a curse condemning her to the life of a social outsider.[20]

Critics have repeatedly celebrated Byatt's rewriting of Melusina's story, arguing that the novel uses the myth to "investigate the subject of a woman artist's autonomy",[21] in order to represent "women's potential for creative self-assertion and empowerment".[22] Although such readings are correct in that *Possession* indeed underlines the female artist's need for an autonomous life, such statements fail to comment on the fact that the novel marginalises the only female poet it features. It is after all Ash, not LaMotte, who is portrayed as "the central figure in the tradition of English poetry" (400) and as "one of the great love poets in our language" (403). As Susanne Schmid observantly notes, Byatt's novel eventually fails to put forward a successful concept of the female artist, since it denies LaMotte both emotional happiness and success as a poet.[23]

I would argue that the character of Christabel LaMotte is confronted with the paradoxical problem that patriarchal society denies her the autonomy on which her poetic self depends. When Christabel first gets to know Ash, she regards him as a "*Threat*" (187) to her autonomy and, consequently, to her identity as a poet. She states: "*I go to the Core* [...]. *The core is my* solitude, *my solitude that is threatened, that you threaten, without which I am nothing*" (195; emphasis in the text). Her initial refusal to invite him to her cottage is nothing less than an attempt to defend her autonomous space and, with it, her poetic talent. The fact that he calls at the cottage after all (197) foreshadows her failure as a poet – a failure in terms of both contemporary popularity and posthumous canonisation – for his visit represents the male violation of female artistic autonomy. For Christabel, her affair with Ash results not only in the birth of their daughter Maia, but also in the loss of her financial independence, her cottage and, consequently, her autarchy (500). Thus, it entails the destruction of her "*solitude* and self-possession" (502; emphasis in the text) on which her identity as an artist depends. In that last letter she writes to Ash, LaMotte wonders: "*if I had kept to my closed castle, behind my motte-and-bailey defences – should I have been a great poet – as you are?*" (*ibid.*) The spatial metaphor of the "closed castle" refers to Christabel's initial rejection of Ash's attentions to her (184; 197), but it also relates to her artistic autonomy as still being inviolate and intact before their affair. In short, Christabel's life at her cottage is a fictionalised version of Virginia Woolf's dictum that "a woman must have money and a room of her own if she is to write fiction".[24] Losing this "room of her own" because the moral norms of Victorian society force her to give it up, Christabel fails as a poet and loses the fundamental element on which her creative power depends. A woman artist's independence, the novel thus argues, is incompatible with Victorian patriarchal society.[25]

What is more, *Possession* also suggests that female autonomy is irreconcilable with female identity in a more essentialised sense. As I have mentioned above, LaMotte moves in with her sister's family after she has given birth to her daughter Maia. At first glance, she does so because it seems to be the only means of avoiding the life of a 'fallen woman'. However, she has apparently managed to keep her pregnancy a secret from anybody but a very small circle of necessarily discreet people, nobody of whom would have been likely to disclose their knowledge to the world. Putting it differently, Christabel might have been able to avoid giving up her cottage and, with it, her independent "*Life of the Mind*" (187) even after Maia's birth, whose very existence nobody seemed to be able to trace back to her. I make these conjectures about elements of the plot that have remained untold, because I would argue that the novel offers – in fact very subtly so – a second reason for Christabel's loss of autonomy: even if her daughter believes herself to be another woman's child, LaMotte is incapable of living without Maia – or putting it with Christabel's own words: "I could not let her go" (500). Having Christabel admit to a deeply felt "*need to see and feed and comfort my child, who knew me not*" (501), *Possession* implies that a woman who has given birth to a child – a "true mother" as Christabel calls herself (500) – is inseparably connected to her child. Thus, the novel suggests that the idea of autonomous selfhood is diametrically opposed to a woman's reproductive function. In other words, *Possession* can be seen as presenting autonomy as being unattainable for women who have born children. Maia's existence does not cause Christabel to stop writing, but while she can still lay claim to a certain reputation as a poet shortly before her daughter's birth (314), she confesses to "*ma[king] verses nobody wants*" after she has had Maia (450). A mother, the novel insinuates, cannot succeed as an artist, because her 'natural' connection to her child makes it impossible for her to retain the separate self on which the identity of Byatt's artist depends. Read along these lines, Christabel's motherhood does indeed put an end to her life as a female author, not only because the moral norms of Victorian society force her to give up her cottage and, with it, her autonomy in order to avoid social stigmatisation, but also because bearing a child – this "*monstrous catastrophe of body and soul*" (500) – is conceptualised as creating an irrevocable experience of bonding and relationality that destroys a woman artist's separate selfhood.[26] Hence, *Possession* follows, on the one hand, a feminist agenda since it criticises patriarchal society for oppressing women in general and female artists in particular. On the other hand, it pursues a patriarchal strategy itself in that it presents female art as being corrupted by female identity.

Portraying its female artist as being reliant on separate selfhood for her ability to write successfully, *Possession* both links back to

The Game and points towards *The Children's Book*, the two artist novels that precede and, respectively, succeed it. *The Game* also negotiates the woman writer's dependence on a separate self, but, unlike *Possession*, the novel does not comment on the consequences of the loss of autonomous selfhood, but on the need of establishing it. The novel features two female protagonists: the sisters Julia and Cassandra Corbett, the former a novelist, the latter an Oxford don. Due to a game of intricately imaginative power and highly escapist quality, which they used to play as children and adolescents, the sisters' relationship is deeply troubled. Each leads her own life, but they are bound to each other by the shared experience of mutual psychological control, oppression and, indeed, brutality. Therefore, they have been unable to develop into two separate individuals. As Jane Campbell observes, "[t]he overlapping of the sisters' lives [which they created as children] has continued, with unusual intensity, although they have seldom met as adults".[27] This psychologically damaging situation changes, however, when Julia writes *A Sense of Glory*, a novel that is – to her sister's intense embarrassment, anger and despair – clearly based on Cassandra's life. Although the act of writing this novel poses moral difficulties, because Cassandra commits suicide after she has read her sister's book, it is also Julia's means of ridding herself from Cassandra's influence. As she puts it: "I feel it has detached me from her".[28] What is more, this novel brings Julia into her own as a writer. "[I]t [*A Sense of Glory*] feels good", Julia remarks, "[i]t feels bloody good. [...] I've never really had that feeling before" (Byatt 1991b: 145). Praising Julia as a gifted novelist who "succeeds triumphantly in calling up sympathy for her central character" (219), critics celebrate her book as "good stuff" (145) and "a tour de force" (219). Significantly, it is this novel with which Julia "ha[s] achieved a new sense of identity [...], a detached [...] self" (169; 237) that sets her up, in both her own eyes and those of others, as a successful writer. Both literally and figuratively, *A Sense of Glory* has separated her from her sister, which then allows her to indulge in a new feeling of "solitude" and to "work in freedom" (235; 236). According to Campbell, *The Game* is based on the moral dilemma that Julia "fail[s] to achieve the freedom that [...] comes from really apprehending the separate existence of others";[29] but as my preceding discussion has shown, the novel indeed uses its protagonist to make a very strong, albeit morally problematic, claim to separateness of self as a fundamental prerequisite for the female artist. Thus, while *Possession* presents life as diminishing art, *The Game* depicts art as preying on life.[30]

Byatt's most recent novel, *The Children's Book*, takes up the discussion of the human cost of art, again linking it to the figure of the female writer. The novel's woman artist Olive Wellwood is "the author of a great many tales, for children and adults, and something of an authority on British Fairy Lore".[31] Although she is, like Christabel LaMotte, born in the Victorian age,[32] she is in many ways the complete opposite of *Possession*'s failed poet. While Christabel is forced to submit to the rules of patriarchal society, Olive is said to be a "matriarch" (Byatt 2009: 310). Indeed, Olive Wellwood is both the most emancipated woman and the most successful female author Byatt has created up to now. Not only is she able to earn a living as a writer, being her family's "breadwinner" (67), but due to her promiscuous love life she also has several children whose parentage she does not have to keep hidden from her – equally promiscuous – husband Humphrey. In short, Olive seems to be the only one of Byatt's woman authors who is able to reconcile art and life. Although Olive's sons and daughters do not prevent her from writing stories, children in *The Children's Book* nevertheless represent a potential danger to the female artist's creativity, as the following description of the pregnant Olive indicates: "[s]he found it hard to write when she was 'expecting'; the stranger inside her seemed to suck at her energy and confuse the rhythm of sentences in her blood and brain" (141). The baby inside Olive is clearly shown as diminishing her creative power. In addition, she feels the unborn child's "presence disturb[ing] her peace" (83), i.e. her inner calm she regards as essential for her ability to write (for example, 356). But although the novel conceptualises the relationship between mother and child – both unborn and born –[33] as a symbiotic connection, thus resembling *Possession* –, Olive is not shown as losing her autonomy of self as a mother: "[s]he took up her pen and *began writing* [...]. Blood flowed from heart to head, and into the happy fingertips, *bypassing the greedy inner sleeper*" (143; my emphasis). As this description of Olive implies, she has found a way – albeit one the novel fails to sufficiently explain – to remain a separate creative self whose solitude is not destroyed by the fact that her body is host to two human beings. Indeed, the novel's narrative voice insists that "[w]riting stories, writing books is fiercely solitary" (518), and Olive Wellwood can be seen writing both constantly and successfully throughout the book whether she is pregnant or not.

Due to her ability to both achieve and keep the autonomous self that allows her to write, Olive is shown as having overcome the paradoxical concept of the female artist which Byatt presents in *Possession*. Yet, *The Children's Book* problematises its figure of the woman author in that it criticises her for insufficiently caring for her family. She is said to "*ignore a great deal*, in order to persist in her calm, and listen steadily to the quick scratch of the nib" (301; my emphasis). The things she turns a blind eye to include her daughter Dorothy's distress upon discovering that Humphrey is not her biological father (343-347; 355-356), the traumatic reason behind her son Tom's troubled withdrawal from the company of others (233-236), and the sense of betrayal which Tom experiences when his mother turns the fairy tale she has written for him into a popular play (522-525) and which causes him to commit suicide (532-533). Perhaps worst of all, Olive has consciously withheld "the whole truth about the play" from her son (529), deciding not to look "into the cupboard in her mind when she had locked away any anxiety about Tom Wellwood [her son] and Tom Underground [the character in the play]" (524). In sum, the writer Olive Wellwood is portrayed as a fundamentally egoistic person who, the novel implies, does not really care about her family, but is "most complete in the act of reading and writing herself" (316). As Alexa Alfer and Amy J. Edwards de Campos observantly remark:

> [s]he [Olive] is a woman writer who has had the will to follow the life of the mind, who has literally and figuratively attained a room of her own, and paid for it by her own handsome earnings. And yet, she has [...] gained this at the expense of her immediate family. She has neglected her children [...] so that she can indulge herself in the imaginary worlds [...], and her perceptions of others [...] are tinged with narcissism.[34]

That is to say that *The Children's Book*, similar to *The Game*, features an autonomous woman writer who keeps her distance from her family, thus forcing her nearest relations to pay a high price for her disinterested self-sufficiency. In other words, art is again shown as preying on life in Byatt's latest novel.

In conclusion, *The Shadow of the Sun, The Game, Possession* and *The Children's Book* all problematise the female artist's need for solitude. Each of the four novels privileges a concept of the female artist which is inherently paradoxical in that it presents the woman author as depending on separate selfhood which is diametrically opposed to either the norms of patriarchal society or a woman's relationships to other people, most prominent among them the 'natural bond' that, according to *Possession*, exists between a mother and her child. Regardless of the fact that Byatt's novels criticise patriarchal society for restricting female autonomy, her female writers inevitably end up in a conceptual cul-de-sac: if they do not fail as artists because they have lost their autonomous selves to their children, they are criticised as human beings because they care more for their art than their families. In Byatt's novels, female art and female life thus remain irreconcilable.

Notes

1 *Possession* (1990), e.g., features Blanche Glover, a fictitious Victorian painter. Byatt's latest novel, *The Children's Book* (2009), includes two fictional potters, Benedict Fludd and Philip Warren, as well as the sculptor Auguste Rodin.
2 The 'Frederica Quartet' consists of *The Virgin in the Garden* (1978), *Still Life* (1985), *Babel Tower* (1996) and *A Whistling Woman* (2002).
3 Roe (2005: 659).
4 Joyce (2000: 208).
5 For analyses of Byatt's male author characters as following romantic and modernist conceptions of the (male) artist see, e.g., Alfer & Edwards de Campos (2010: 14-20); Franken (1997: 34-35; 93-103); Franken (2001: 39-44) and Steveker (2009: 44-47). Also see Plotz (2001) for a detailed reading of how Byatt's *The Virgin in the Garden* is indebted to the romantic notion of the visionary child as the embodiment of self-sufficient isolation from society.
6 Tredell (1994: 66).
7 Byatt (1991a: xiv). Byatt's *The Biographer's Tale* (2000) most certainly is not about the woman artist since it is, up to date, her only novel which features a single male protagonist. The 'Frederica Quartet' does not necessarily engage in discussions of female art, but it is concerned with female thought. For a detailed analysis of Byatt's notion of the 'thinking woman', see Steveker (2009: 65-73).
8 Alfer & Edwards de Campos (2010: 14).

9   Byatt (1991a: 58). Further references to this Vintage edition will be included in the text.

10 Byatt (1994: 454; emphasis in the text).

11 Byatt (1997: 2).

12 For a different, if problematic analysis of Anna, see Franken (2001: 49-60). Referring to a daydream in which Anna imagines herself a successful author (Byatt 1991a: 109-110), Franken claims that "[i]n this image Anna appears as an autonomous writer, capable of vision" (2001: 55) before arguing that "Anna Severell is not presented as a visionary genius who experiences a sublime of conquest. She experiences 'a sublime of nearness' and has visions which are not violent but 'embrace' their objects without possessing them. [...] This is the kind of visionary which might well be A.S. Byatt's ideal type of writer" (*ibid.*, 58). What Franken neglects to take into account, however, is that Anna does not create any art throughout the whole novel. Therefore, "Anna [...] is precisely *not* an artist, but an artist's daughter" (Alfer & Edwards de Campos 2010: 14; emphasis in the text).

13 Although Byatt's 'Frederica Quartet' also deals with questions of female autonomy, I will not include it in my discussion, because its female protagonists, the sisters Frederica and Stephanie Potter, do not qualify as artists. For a detailed discussion of the tetralogy's concept of female identity, female autonomy and the figure of the 'thinking woman' see Steveker (2009: 44-73).

14 Byatt (1991c: 501). Further references to this Vintage edition will be included in the text.

15 In *Possession*, LaMotte's as well as Ash's letters are given in italics. In all further quotes from this novel, italics do not function as markers of emphasis, but are part of Byatt's text if not otherwise stated.

16 For the tradition of this myth and its literary development see Frenzel (1963) and Lundt (1991: 41-184).

17 Lundt (1991: 30-37).

18 The novel's second female protagonist, Maud Bailey, is also likened to Melusina. For detailed readings of Christabel LaMotte and Maud Bailey as embodiments of Melusina see, e.g., Campbell (2004: 112-121); Chinn (2001); Franken (2001: 93-98); Maack (1999) and Schmid (1996: 120-124).

19 As LaMotte puts it: "*we* [Blanche and Christabel] *neither call nor receive callers*" (Byatt 1991c: 159).

20 Also see Schmid (1996: 123).

21 Franken (2001: 101).

22 Campbell (2004: 128; 146).

23 Schmid (1996: 124-125).

24 Woolf (1967: 6).

25 As I have argued elsewhere, *Possession* not only shows the woman writer's solitude as being incompatible with Victorian society, but also presents female autonomy in general as standing in opposition to patriarchal societies

of both nineteenth- and twentieth-century Britain (see Steveker 2009: 55-64).

26 *The Shadow of the Sun* also implies that children destroy a woman's solitude of self when Anna realises that she had – unknowingly – been pregnant during one of her abortive visions: "even on the bridge she had not seen, and that might have been to do with it: *femina gravida*, weighed down, weighed down" (Byatt 1991a: 289; emphasis in the text).

27 Campbell (2004: 45).

28 Byatt (1991b: 145). Further references to this Vintage edition will be included in the text.

29 Campbell (2004: 49).

30 Also see Alfer & Edwards de Campos who regard Julia as a "predatory" artist (2010: 25).

31 Byatt (2009: 10). Further references to this Chatto and Windus paperback edition will be included in the text.

32 The plot of the *Children's Book* spans three historical periods: the late Victorian age, the Edwardian age and World War I.

33 Olive feels that her favourite son "Tom was part of her, and she was part of Tom" (Byatt 2009: 203).

34 Alfer & Edwards de Campos (2010: 122).

Bibliography

Alfer, Alexa & Amy J. Edwards de Campos: *A.S. Byatt. Critical Storytelling*, Manchester, 2010.

Byatt, Antonia Susan: "Introduction". – In A.S.B.: *The Shadow of the Sun*, London, 1991 [1964], pp. xiii-xvi.

–: *The Shadow of the Sun*, London, 1991a [1964].

–: *The Game*, London, 1991b [1967].

–: *Possession*, London, 1991c [1990].

–: *The Virgin in the Garden*, London, 1994 [1978].

–: *Still Life*, London, 1995 [1985].

–: *Babel Tower*, London, 1997 [1996].

–: *A Whistling Woman*, London, 2003 [2002].

–: *The Children's Book*, London, 2009.

Campbell, Jane: *A.S. Byatt and the Heliotropic Imagination*, Waterloo, 2004.

Chinn, Nancy: "'I Am My Own Riddle'. A.S. Byatt's Christabel LaMotte, Emily Dickinson and Melusina", *Papers on Language and Literature* 37:2, 2001, 179-204.

Franken, Christien: *A.S. Byatt and the British Artist-Novel*, Amsterdam, 1997.

–: *A.S. Byatt. Art, Authorship and Creativity*, Houndmills, 2001.

Frenzel, Elisabeth: "Melusine". – In E.F.: *Stoffe der Weltliteratur*, Stuttgart, 1963, pp. 424-426.

Joyce, James: *A Portrait of the Artist as a Young Man*. Ed. Jeri Johnson, Oxford, 2000 [1916].

Lundt, Bea: *Melusine und Merlin im Mittelalter. Entwürfe und Modelle weiblicher Existenz im Beziehungsdiskurs der Geschlechter*, München, 1991.

Maack, Annegret: "Metamorphosen der Schlange. Zu A.S. Byatts Bildersprache", *Anglistik* 10:2, 1999, 67-78.

Plotz, Judith: "A Modern 'Seer Blest'. The Visionary Child in *The Virgin in the Garden*". – In Alexa Alfer & Michael J. Noble (Eds.): *Essays on the Fiction of A.S. Byatt*, Westport, 2001, pp. 31-45.

Roe, Nicholas: *Romanticism. An Oxford Guide*, Oxford, 2005.

Schmid, Susanne: *Jungfrau und Monster. Frauenmythen im englischen Roman der Gegenwart*, Berlin, 1996.

Steveker, Lena: *Identity and Cultural Memory in the Fiction of A.S. Byatt. Knitting the Net of Culture*, Houndmills, 2009.

Tredell, Nicolas: *Conversations With Critics*, Manchester, 1994.

Woolf, Virginia: *A Room of One's Own*, London, 1967 [1929].

Peter Childs (Cheltenham)

Ian McEwan's Venus Envy Revisited

Briony Tallis was born in Surrey in 1922, the daughter of a senior civil servant. She attended Roedean School, and in 1940 trained to become a nurse. Her wartime nursing experience provided the material for her first novel, *Alice Riding*, published in 1948 and winner of that year's Fitzrovia Prize for fiction. Her second novel, *Soho Solstice*, was praised by Elizabeth Bowen as "a dark gem of psychological acuity," while Graham Greene described her as "one of the more interesting talents to have emerged since the war." Other novels and short-story collections consolidated her reputation during the fifties. In 1962 she published *A Barn in Steventon*, a study of domestic theatricals in Jane Austen's childhood. Tallis's sixth novel, *The Ducking Stool*, was a best-seller in 1965 and was made into a successful film starring Julie Christie. Thereafter, Briony Tallis's reputation went into decline, until the Virago imprint made her work available to a younger generation in the late seventies. She died in July 2001.[1]

Looking back from the 21st century, Ian McEwan observed that "[i]n 1982 I had the rather romantic notion [...] that the problem with the world is actually men, and that everything would be all right if women ran it. I no longer hold that view".[2] After reviewing McEwan's "romantic notion" from the eighties, I want to look in this essay at the effects this shift in his viewpoint has arguably had on his portrayal of the female creative artist, particularly Briony Tallis in *Atonement* (2001). At the time he was working on *Atonement*, McEwan wrote the flyleaf biography given above for Briony, and though he decided against including it in the final novel, the life summary illustrates a portrayal of the female artist absent from his earlier work.

McEwan's third novel, *The Child in Time* (1987), begins with the disappearance of a little girl and ends with the birth of a baby. The sex of this newborn child is unknown, leaving the reader with a sense of open-endedness. The reason for this indeterminacy is made explicit in other work McEwan undertook in the eighties and while drafting *The Child in Time*, which he began in 1983. In particular, McEwan developed his thinking while working on the 1981 libretto for *Or Shall We Die?*, Michael Berkeley's oratorio.[3]

Or Shall We Die? was written partly as a response to the Soviet invasion of Afghanistan in 1980, a country McEwan had travelled around in 1972. The stockpiling of weapons on both sides of the superpowers' standoff during the Cold War created an atmosphere of mutually-assured destruction that McEwan felt had "a quality of nightmare" when it was presented in the media as "responsible deliberation on 'defence' policy by calm, authoritative men in suits".[4] In the libretto, opposition to war is explicitly presented in gender terms. The only characters are 'Man' and 'Woman' and it is just the latter who asks such questions as "[i]s the world redeemed / by shifts of power among men?" (McEwan 1989: 22) and "[a]re there men unafraid of gentleness?" (23) In terms that echo W.H. Auden's poem on the Spanish Civil War, "Spain" (1937), McEwan also places this gender binary in a context of male aggression distinct from female love: "[a]re we too late to love ourselves? Shall we change, or shall we die?" (24) The need for transformation for McEwan in the eighties was from a masculine world to a feminine one, symbolised in the libretto by the influence of the moon and its power for change. Consequently, the indeterminacy of the child's sex at the end of *The Child in Time* is McEwan's fictional equivalent to the central question in *Or Shall We Die?*: "[s]hall there be womanly times?" (17) He provides no answer to this in the libretto and also refuses to provide an answer in the novel, where the question of whether or not there shall be "womanly times" in the future, symbolised in the unrevealed sex of the child born in the final pages, is left in doubt.

In *The Child in Time* McEwan paints a society rooted in masculine times and nuclear threat that has created a culture of 'arms and the man' where authoritarianism characterises a harsh world of state-licensed beggars and an official childcare handbook overseen by the government. Pitted against this are the different Einsteinian temporal possibilities offered by the scientist Thelma Darke and a belief in the alternative of "constant flux" advocated by the grieving mother Julie, for whom hope lies "in endless mutability, in remaking yourself as you came to understand more".[5] This expresses the life-affirming feminine possibility that McEwan opposes to patriarchy, and is perhaps most clearly dramatised by Stephen Lewis's pregnant mother's decision not to abort Stephen when she sees his adult self in a moment of premonition across a curve in time. As in the "womanly times" of *Or Shall We Die?*, this is an assertion of life against the threat of nuclear proliferation, and McEwan writes in his introduction to the libretto how "[l]ove of children generates a fierce ambition for the world to continue and be safe, and makes one painfully vulnerable to fantasies of loss" (5). That fantasy of loss, of children and the future being suddenly taken away, is painfully dramatised at the start of *The Child in Time* in the unexplained disappearance of Julie and Stephen Lewis's child Kate.

In his introduction to *Or Shall We Die?* McEwan characterises his two posited world views as Newtonian and Einsteinian. The first is associated with masculinist imperial ambition. The second he describes, in anticipation of the physicist Thelma in *The Child in Time*, in terms of an alternative reality containing an emblematic woman who:

> believes herself to be part of the nature she studies, part of its constant flux; her own consciousness and the surrounding world pervade each other and are interdependent; she knows that at the heart of things there are limitations and paradoxes (the speed of light, the Uncertainty Principle) that prevent her from knowing or expressing everything; she has no illusions of her omniscience, and yet her power is limitless because it does reside in her alone. (15)

Passages such as this from McEwan's writing in the eighties, and *The Child in Time* in particular, prompted an attack from the writer Adam Mars-Jones in a 1990 tract entitled *Venus Envy. On the Womb and the Bomb*. Mars-Jones concludes that "McEwan may be one of the few literary examples of the New Man [...] but in his vision of the relationship between the sexes there is much that is atavistic, patriarchal, even patristic".[6] So, at the end of *The Child in Time*, Julie's new baby is delivered by Stephen in a scene that arguably depicts a shared moment between two parents at the birth of their child but is seen by Mars-Jones as a masculinist gesture that is appropriative and usurping of women's parturition. Mars-Jones decides that for McEwan, "even in a book that pays as careful a lipservice to women's perceptions as this one, male priorities must be defended".[7] Similarly, Mars-Jones thinks that the time-curve scene at the centre of the novel, when Stephen and his pregnant mother have a mutual vision of each other across the decades, makes "naked" the "fantasy that underlies the whole book": "that the desires of a man so taken up with the processes and privileges of reproduction actually move towards doing without women, or certainly minimising their part in the creation of life".[8] Mars-Jones concludes not that Stephen is presented as Oedipal, dispensing with his father and uniting with his mother, but that McEwan's writing exhibits a womb envy because Stephen wishes to be his own progenitor. Stephen thus usurps his mother's pro-creative role in Mars-Jones's reading just as at the end he usurps his wife Julie's in the birth of their new child. Stephen is also midwife to, and in that sense gives birth to, another person in the novel. After narrowly avoiding a road accident he helps a lorry driver to escape from his cab by delivering him from the wreckage through "a vertical gash in the steel" (McEwan 1988: 96). Mars-Jones argues that the use of the word "gash", "a piece of taboo slang", indicates a negative view of childbirth: "[a] man may think of childbirth as a mystery, as an apotheosis, or simply as an enviable power; or he may think of it as a piece of indifferent machinery, a bleeding trap, even an atrocity. This passage represents the second set of images".[9] At this point, Mars-Jones implies McEwan moves from "envy" to deep ambivalence, seeing the female act of childbirth as a Ballardian "atrocity".[10]

As Mars-Jones acknowledges, the anthropological term for what is colloquially known as 'sympathetic pregnancy' is 'couvade', a word coined in 1865 by the anthropologist E.B. Tylor to describe a near-universal spectrum of rituals across diverse cultures performed by husbands around the time in which their wives give birth. While there may be many physiological and psychological reasons for it, couvade in the modern world is thought to be a psychosomatic equivalent of ancient rituals of initiation into paternity.[11] Mars-Jones feels similarly that McEwan's new-man sympathy is in fact a covert usurpation of women's roles, a Trojan horse offering of identification: "McEwan tries to smuggle himself across the border of gender [...] seeking to align himself with qualities traditionally associated with women, with a certain tender-mindedness".[12] Effectively, the charge is that both women and children are used by men, eager to escape the bombs associated with their gender, as "handy screens for the projection of masculine emotion",[13] whether consciously positive or unconsciously negative.

Aware of a strong current of gender critique in McEwan's novels from *The Comfort of Strangers* (1981) to *The Child in Time* and

Enduring Love (1997), John McLeod also notes that "McEwan is a writer who seeks to unmask hegemonic masculinity" though his fictions seem unwittingly to reassert it at the same time by following male characters and logic.[14] Similarly, Rhiannon Davies sees *Enduring Love* as a conflicted text that concludes with the breakdown of Joe's "strategies of masculine self-fashioning" as he tries to assert the heroic triumph of his male adventure-ideal in the display of machismo that characterises his gun-toting victory over the "madman" threatening "his woman".[15]

McEwan's first publication of the new century was *Atonement*, his only novel to date with a female protagonist. As I noted at the start of the essay, by this time McEwan no longer held the "romantic" view of "womanly times" that he did in the eighties. That view evident in *The Child in Time* and *Or Shall We Die?* appeared to conform to a principal understanding of the female artist as creator of children; a familiar portrayal in many fictional characterisations (for example, in one of Rachel Cusk's novels, suburban mothers are described thus: "[e]ach of them had felt herself to be an artist, creating this girl, this daughter").[16] In *Atonement*, the simple contrast along gender lines between destructive forces and creative impulses is also replaced by McEwan's interest in the potential of the imagination to exert a manipulative as well as a sympathetic power, as portrayed in the central character of Briony Tallis.

Atonement presents itself as a third-person realist novel until its short final section, set in 1999. This millennial coda repositions the rest of the book as a part-fictionalised memoir written and reworked over nearly 60 years by Briony in reparation for ruining the brief lives of her sister Cecilia and Cecilia's lover Robbie Turner. In part, because Briony imagined Robbie a criminal she feels that her imagination should play a part in her atonement as she writes a future happiness that they never had for Cecilia and Robbie. McEwan has said in interview: "[t]he danger of an imagination that can't quite see the boundaries of what is real and what is unreal, drawn again from Jane Austen – another writer who is crucial to this novel – plays a part in Briony's sense that her atonement has consisted of a lifetime of writing this novel".[17]

Before the coda are three longer sections. The third of these appears to be the most fictionalised, in the sense that its focus is Briony's partial reconciliation in 1940 with the reunited lovers Robbie and Cecilia, who are in fact dead. Prior to that, the second section is an account, reconstructed from letters, interviews, and army records, of Robbie's part in the retreat to Dunkirk, where, we learn in the coda, he actually died from septicaemia. The first section is a much rewritten account of one summer day of calamity in 1935 in which Briony made her catastrophic mistake. As McEwan acknowledges above in his reference to Austen, Briony's fictional forebear is Catherine Morland from Austen's *Northanger Abbey* (1818), another heroine led astray by a love of fiction combined with an overactive imagination. Where Catherine falsely suspects with comparatively little consequence that General Tilney has murdered his wife, Briony's assessment of character leads her publicly to accuse Robbie of the rape of her cousin Lola, which results in his imprisonment and separation from his new lover Cecilia.

Equating with the number of sections, there are thus in the novel four different degrees of fictionalisation used by Briony as author. In Part One Briony writes her eyewitness account of real events that involved her in the third person as an extradiegetic narrator. Part Two is an entirely reconstructed narrative of Robbie's retreat to Dunkirk based on the official and personal accounts of other parties. Part Three mixes a based-in-fact but fictionalised third-person account of Briony's time as a nurse in 1940 with a wholly fabricated story of her visit to see Robbie and Cecilia in a London flat. The intradiegetic coda then moves explicitly to the first person and addresses the reader directly. In other words, the four sections appear like exercises in technique reminiscent of modernist experimentations in point of view and it would appear that McEwan's aim is to portray the approach of a postmodernist female author writing in the wake of authors like Virginia Woolf and Elizabeth Bowen. Indeed, Briony as a young novelist is given advice to find her own voice by Cyril Connolly when she sends in her first version of Part One, then entitled "Two Figures by a Fountain", to the journal *Horizon*.[18] Bowen is one of the readers of the manuscript and Connolly suggests too great an indebtedness to Woolf in Briony's writing.

It is Part One and Part Three of the book therefore that present a portrait of the artist as a young woman. In her final redraft of "Two Figures by a Fountain" the older Briony constructs a narrative around the formative traumatic experience of her childhood. Part One in particular is a story laced with allusions to other novels that give a picture of a writer's younger self, from L.P. Hartley's *The Go-Between* (1953) to Rosamond Lehmann's *Dusty Answer* (1927) (mentioned by Bowen to Connolly in connection with Briony's story). An author's confession, it is spiced with references to the Great Tradition from Jane Austen to Henry James.[19]

A comparison with another intertext for McEwan's novel, Dodie Smith's *I Capture the Castle* (1949), is salutary. Both are multi-part novels initially set in mid-thirties England and both feature a young, aspiring writer as protagonist: Cassandra Mortmain is writing "partly to teach myself how to write a novel",[20] while Briony Tallis at thirteen had already "written her way through a whole history of literature" (McEwan 2001: 41). Though one family is rich and the other poor, both the Tallises and the Mortmains live in impressive if cannibalised country houses. Each family consists of two daughters and a brother living with largely non-interventionist parents. In the characters of Robbie Turner and Stephen Colly, these families are also both supplemented by a semi-adopted cleaner's son who has fallen in love with one of the daughters. Both novels are also explicitly steeped in the fiction of Jane Austen (Smith's heroine pointedly shares the name of Austen's sister), but whereas Dodie Smith's book dwells on Austen's lighter social comedy, *Atonement* draws on such aspects as prejudice, class difference, and the perils of an overactive imagination. Also, while *I Capture the Castle* is written by Smith as Cassandra's first-person journal in the present, the first part of *Atonement* is presented by McEwan as Briony's personal experience refashioned 60 years later into the final draft of a many times re-written third-person narrative. Both novels consider the temptation of imagining how others are feeling: "Rose says I am always crediting people with emotions I should experience myself in their situation, but I am sure I had a real flash of intuition" (Smith 1996: 21); "only in a story could you enter these different minds" (McEwan 2001: 40). Both novels are also concerned with the danger of "a trick of the imagination" (177), as when Cassandra declares: "[w]hen I read a book, I put in all the imagination I can, so that it is almost like writing the book" (Smith 1996: 26). Again, in *I Capture the Castle* this suggests a view of the pleasures offered by classic Realism where reading and writing are fused by the reader's absorption in a believable world, whereas McEwan says he sees *Northanger Abbey*, for example, as a novel "about someone's wild imagination causing havoc to people around them".[21] While Smith nods to Austen's Gothic in the castle setting of her novel, McEwan takes its darker side into his portrait of the artist, who is also burdened with the weight of her modernist reading, which means that Briony as a girl, McEwan says, "is burying her conscience beneath her stream of consciousness".[22] This is the thirteen-year-old Briony we encounter in the novel who is sloughing off the eleven-year-old she was when she began writing in a phase of romantic dramatising that has culminated in her play "The Trials of Arabella" (Briony's protagonist takes the name of the sister of Richardson's eponymous heroine in *Clarissa*, 1748).

As mentioned above, Briony has in two years written her way through a "whole history of literature" to emerge as a writer indebted not to the Gothic imaginings of Catherine Morland (like the identically initialled Cassandra Mortmain) but to the failure of sympathy with character that McEwan feels is evident in the modernist writing of Bowen, Lehmann, and Woolf:

> [i]t was modernism that promoted the notion of the artist as a sort of severe high priest who belonged to a small elite [...]. Writers like Virginia Woolf saying, "Character is now dead," helped push the novel down some very fruitless impasses.[23]

In line with this, Briony thinks her childhood has "ended" (McEwan 2001: 160), or "closed" (116), meaning that she has moved from mere stories to what she takes to be a modernist conception of "[r]eal life" in which "truth was strange and deceptive, it had to be struggled for, against the flow of the everyday" (158). Born in the *annus mirabilis* of High Modernism, 1922,[24] Briony fails to realise that she is still in thrall to an authorial perspective, not of Gothic castles and romantic lakes but of deceptive facades, inner worlds, modernist depth readings: "[t]he very complexity of her feelings confirmed Briony in her view that she was entering an arena of adult emotion and dissembling from which her writing was bound to benefit" (113). A few pages on from this she sees Robbie and Cecilia making love in the library and senses "that her over-anxious imagination had projected the figures onto the packed spines of the books" (123). The reader is left to infer that the reverse has happened: Briony has projected a version of her "Two Figures", Robbie and Cecilia, from her reading of such books as line the library walls. Thus, Briony mistakenly reads what she sees taking place against the bookcase, like she misreads the earlier scene of "Figures by a Fountain", because she is in thrall to the Jamesian potential of art's imaginative power to transform the novel beyond its social, descriptive representation of reality into a higher realism character-ised by depth reading and the analysis of psychology.

The much older Briony, who is sculpting the prose we read, pre-sents her act of atonement less as a telling of truth than an admis-sion of the effects of her adherence to literary tropes. Briony writes Part One of the novel in the style of modernist writers such as Leh-mann, then the war scenes of Part Two in a more direct prose of 'masculine' writing associated with Ernest Hemingway, before of-fering a romance in Part Three – her epitaphic fantasy of Robbie and Cecilia's reconciliation – through the model of Lucilla An-drews's *No Time for Romance* (1977) (cited by McEwan in the ac-knowledgements for *Atonement*). Briony thus frames a literary atonement for the demotion of plot and realist character that was present in McEwan's own indebtedness to the Modernism of such writers as Franz Kafka in his early work. From Briony's point of view, her Promethean punishment is to "live in a kind of hell of imagining" for a crime of creative misprision in casting Robbie as villain.[25] Part of her atonement, she now sees 60 years later, is to restore the realism and the romance that her modernist reading took her away from. Briony as a long-established novelist now turns to the tropes of Impressionism and a "pointillist approach to verisi-militude" (359). Within the text, however, there are multiple com-plex maskings of authorship and gender in which, for example, the based-on-fact fictionalised wartime experiences of Robbie in Part Two are reconstructed by a third-person narrator, who is unmasked as a female novelist who is herself the creation of a male author. In addition to this layering, there are, because of the novel's stance of writing as penitence, important and unresolved questions of repre-sentation, self-knowledge, and motive attaching to authorship in the novel, reminiscent of the rehashed questions rejected by Foucault at the end of his essay "What is an Author?" (1979): "[w]ho really spoke? Is it really he and not someone else? With what authenticity or originality? And what part of his deepest self did he express in his discourse?"[26] Making the artist a simple function of the text is both the literal exercise undertaken in *Atonement* and an act that underpins the explicit ethical question that the novel asks about au-thorship, thus simultaneously endorsing in terms of textuality and refuting in terms of responsibility the question Foucault ends with: "[w]hat difference does it make who is speaking?"[27]

In words that describe both his and Briony's position well, McEwan says in an interview that "on the whole, it doesn't suit novelists to be collaborators. We are so used to playing God by ourselves".[28] The language is reminiscent of McEwan's take on masculinity in the eighties but here it is a portrait of the artist, who in *Atonement* McEwan initially makes a thirteen-year-old girl playing with the omnipotency of solitary creation. McEwan uses the expression "by ourselves" and it is notable that he puts Briony in a similar position where her imagination may run wild, largely unfettered by the society of siblings and peers. The ten-year age difference between Briony and her sister Cecilia is important in this regard (their brother Leon is several years older again) because McEwan effectively presents Briony as an only child. Not only is the age difference great but on the crucial day on which the novel opens in 1935, Cecilia is returned from university and Briony, while her sister has been at Cambridge, has grown from a pre-pubescent girl into a teenager asking herself questions of selfhood and sexuality that will be at the centre of McEwan's next sustained portrait of the female artist.

Since writing *Atonement*, McEwan has sketched two other young artistic women in the characters of Daisy Perowne in *Saturday* (2005) and Florence Ponting in *On Chesil Beach* (2007).[29] While Daisy is a newly-published poet, Florence is a violin prodigy.[30] The more detailed portrait is that of Florence. Like *Atonement*, *On Chesil Beach* rests on the events and aftermath of one summer day, now in 1962, and like the portrayal of the younger Briony, it is rendered in the third person. Here the artist is a violinist not a writer, but again the portrait is of someone closed off from an understanding of others. Florence Ponting thinks she is "sealed off in her everyday thoughts" and wonders if she lacks:

> some simple mental trick that everyone else had, a mechanism so ordinary that no one ever mentioned it, an immediate sensual connection to people and events, and to her own needs and desires?[31]

Like Briony, Florence believes she has "lived in isolation within herself" but also "from herself, never wanting or daring to look back" (McEwan 2007: 61). That final comment is never fully explained but the book hints repeatedly that it may be linked to Florence's father, Geoffrey, with whom she used to go alone on boat trips when she was twelve and more recently on

> journeys: just the two of them, hiking in the alps, Sierra Nevada and Pyrenees, and the special treats, the one-night business trips to European cities where she and Geoffrey always stayed in the grandest hotels. (54)

More than one critic has suggested that the text hints at Florence's abuse as a child by her father, but nothing explicit is stated and this is in keeping with the emphasis of the book on "a time when a conversation about sexual difficulties was plainly impossible" (1).[32] However, where Briony's life is transformed by an accusation based on imagining the sexual predation of Robbie Turner, Florence's "disgust" (7) at sex appears to be linked to experiences with her father. As her new husband Edward undresses on their wedding night, and she lies on the nuptial bed, Florence, who otherwise never dares to look back, finds:

> [h]ere came the past anyway, the indistinct past. She was twelve years old, lying still like this, waiting, shivering in the narrow bunk with polished mahogany sides. Her mind was a blank, she felt she was in disgrace. After a two-day crossing, they were once more in the calm of the Carteret harbour, south of Cherbourg. It was late in the evening, and her father was moving about the dim cramped cabin, undressing, like Edward now. She remembered the rustle of the clothes, the clink of a belt unfastened or of keys or loose change. Her only task was to keep her eyes closed and to think of a tune she liked. Or any tune. (99)

The passage's suggestion that Florence escapes into music echoes her reaction upon entering the honeymoon bedroom earlier, when "she had been aware of a stately, simple musical phrase, playing and repeating itself, in the shadowy ungraspable way of auditory memory, following her to the bedside" (79-80). Here, Florence tries to find refuge in music while also thinking that she should tell Edward of her deep fears: "she needed to speak up, the way she did at rehearsals" (81). Florence is baffled by the contrast between her assertive confidence when organising her quartet and her difficulty with expressing herself in words, particularly about sexuality. This duality is reflected in her ambivalence towards Geoffrey Ponting:

> her father arose in her conflicting emotions. There were times when she found him physically repellent [...]. But sometimes, in a surge of pro-

> tective feeling and guilty love, she would come up behind him where he sat and entwine her arms around his neck and kiss the top of his head and nuzzle him. (49-50)

Florence's repugnance for sexual contact on the wedding night – "[i]f she was sick into his mouth, was one wild thought, their marriage would be instantly over" (29) – is again linked back to her boat-trips with her father: while Edward undergoes "conventional first-night nerves, she experienced a visceral dread, a helpless disgust as palpable as *seasickness*" (7; my emphasis).

While Briony channels her imaginative power into a misreading of adult sexuality, Florence channels her sexuality into her violin playing, which is an activity in which she exercises considerable control. Though in other respects "she was surprisingly clumsy and unsure", of her string quartet she "was the undisputed leader" and when "the business was music, she was always confident and fluid in her movements" (15). Edward notices this and links it to Florence's control over her father: "[s]he knew her stuff, and she was determined to lead, the way the first violinist should. She seemed to be able to get her rather frightening father to do what she wanted" (17). The reader is thus encouraged by these inferences to harbour suspicions similar to those warned against by *Atonement* and its epigraph from *Northanger Abbey*: "[d]ear Miss Morland, consider the dreadful nature of the suspicions you have entertained. What have you been judging from?"[33]

Florence finds in music escape from the conflicted feelings she has for either Edward or her father. Art is for her, as it is for Briony, a parallel world in which she can exercise control. Thus, her final argument with Edward is considered by Florence with reference to music, and her retort to him is characterised as "the second violin answering the first" (144), while the argument itself is designated "only a minor theme in the larger pattern" (146). The couple separate forever after the quarrel and Florence goes on to become an accomplished and revered violinist with her quartet. One critic in 1968 says that "Miss Ponting, in the lilting tenderness of her tone and the lyrical delicacy of her phrasing, played, if I may put it this way, like a woman in love, not only with Mozart, or with music, but with life itself" (162).

In these two 21st-century portraits of the female artist, McEwan presents individuals who find a sense of control and power in art that sits at odds with what happens in their real lives. Both appear to have found their vocations not just after but through childhood trauma as avenues for their emotions and creativity. Neither Briony nor Florence ever has children and both remain fixed on a past they would otherwise choose to forget: Briony penitentially compelled, like a character in Greek mythology, to rewrite her 'crime' to the end of her life, and Florence scanning in vain for Edward in the audience at London's Wigmore Hall six years after their parting (Edward proves to be as lost to Florence as Robbie is to Briony). It thus seems that for McEwan's latter-day female artists, only self-expression through art provides atonement or compensation for their unalterable pasts.

As noted by the author himself at the start of this essay, McEwan's eighties view of female creativity as parturition and pastoral care in opposition to male destructiveness altered by the new century, and both Briony and Florence are figures whose creativity is not defined by reproductive biology, but by the relation their artistry has with personal history and experience. They are artists whose successes, akin to those of male writer protagonists such as Stephen Lewis or Joe Rose in McEwan's earlier writing, are bound up in guilt and shame, memory and forgetting.

In conclusion, it might be noted that Daisy Perowne is a figure who could be cast in either light. Daisy is a character who might be thought of in at least two different ways, emphasising McEwan's approach to female creativity from the eighties or his rejection of that portrayal which he says characterises his viewpoint in the new century. On the one hand, Daisy is a woman who argues with her father following her return from the anti-war march through London in protest against the forthcoming invasion of Iraq. Cementing a portrayal of her as life-affirming pacifier, that evening she disarms the knife-wielding intruder Baxter by reciting a poem by Matthew Arnold that, after he forces her to strip naked, casts "a spell" on Baxter and reminds "him how much he wanted to live" (McEwan 2005: 278). On the other hand, against this gesture towards a portrayal of her as seductress and life-force (she is also revealed to be pregnant), Daisy is herself an artist who has the "magic" of poetry (*ibid.*) and her performance for Baxter is presented in terms of the ritualistic power of the poet as magus, as a conjuror of words "attempting the seductive, varied tone of a storyteller entrancing a child" (221). Whereas in McEwan's earlier writing, Daisy might be expected to be rescued by someone else, as happens to Clarissa Mellon in *Enduring Love*, here it is she who effects the transformation in Baxter "from lord of terror to amazed admirer" (223). Most significantly for this understanding of Daisy as powerful artist is her father's indignant concern over her pregnancy by a boyfriend from Rome: "Italian men [...] expect their wives to replace their mothers, and iron their shirts and fret about their underwear. This feckless Giulio could destroy his daughter's hopes" (241). Faced with the prospect of his daughter's possible move into domesticity and motherhood, Perowne's question is this: "[w]hat's to become of Daisy Perowne, the poet?" (*ibid.*)

Notes

1   McEwan's biographical note, quoted in Begley (2009: 105).
2   Morrison (2008: 2).
3   McEwan said that from this work he "carried over a belief in the insufficiency of the intellect alone in understanding ourselves or our world", which is a comment that militates against attempts to rationalise the events of *The Child in Time* (1989: xxvi).
4   *Ibid.*, 4. Further references to this edition will be included in the text.
5   McEwan (1988: 54). Further references to this edition will be included in the text.
6   Mars-Jones (1990: 32).
7   *Ibid.*, 23.
8   *Ibid.*, 24.
9   *Ibid.*, 31.
10 The author J.G. Ballard explores the visceral and sexual attraction of violence and wounded bodies in books such as *The Atrocity Exhibition* (1970) and *Crash* (1973).
11 See Masoni *et al.* (1994: 125-131).
12 Mars-Jones (1990: 33).
13 *Ibid.*, 34.
14 McLeod (1998: 243). Lyn Wells argues that "[i]n all of McEwan's texts issues of gender are central to his representation of ethical relationships" (2009: 13). Certainly in the nineties McEwan pitched gendered world views against each other: in *Black Dogs* (1992), Bernard and June Tremaine are separated by his rationalism and her spiritual emotionalism while in *Enduring Love* (1997) Joe Rose and Clarissa Mellon are separated more by their divergent sensibilities than by Joe's persecution at the hands of Jed Parry.
15 See Davies (2003: 109-120).

16 Cusk (2007: 164). Another example occurs in the novel *The Bradshaw Variations* (2009), also by Cusk, when a man contemplating art thinks of his wife: "[s]he too, he realises, knows what it is to create. She created Alexa" (119).

17 Noakes (2002: 19).

18 McEwan (2001: 311-315). Further references to this edition will be included in the text.

19 In *The Go-Between* a writer remembers how he was asked as a boy one summer staying at a country house to take letters between a young woman and her working-class lover. In Lehmann's coming-of-age novel *Dusty Answer* the well-to-do only child of wealthy parents grows an attachment to a neighbouring family and the novel charts the development of her sexual and moral education.

20 Smith (1996: 4). Further references to this edition will be included in the text.

21 Omer (2001: 59).

22 Silverblatt (2002).

23 Lynn (2009: 153).

24 The *annus mirabilis* of 1922 alone saw the publication of many remarkable works, including T.S. Eliot's *The Waste Land*, James Joyce's *Ulysses*, Katherine Mansfield's *The Garden Party and Other Stories*, May Sinclair's *The Life and Death of Harriett Frean*, F. Scott Fitzgerald's *The Beautiful and the Damned*, Virginia Woolf's *Jacob's Room*, Claude McKay's *Harlem Shadows*, T.E. Lawrence's extraordinary war memoir *Seven Pillars of Wisdom*, Eugene O'Neill's play *The Hairy Ape* and E.E. Cummings's autobiographical novel *The Enormous Room*. What all these works have in common is an attempt to make sense of the modern world through art, to fashion chaos into literature, and to provide an aesthetic coherence to formless reality.

25 Remnick (2009: 165).

26 Foucault (1984: 119).

27 *Ibid.*, 120. For a robust discussion of such questions in relation to the female artist in novels since 1970, see Eagleton (2005).

28 Morrison (2008: 2).

29 With these, McEwan's portrait of women and creativity has altered to some degree since his early short stories, such as the Roth-inspired "Homemade" (1975) in which one girl is mythologised by the boy narrator as an "inter-galactic-earth-goddess-housewife, she owned and controlled all around her, she saw all, she knew all" (McEwan 1976: 20).

30 Florence is a musician who can be contrasted with the earlier example of Perowne's son Theo who plays the blues in *Saturday* just as Briony is a forerunner of the female writer reprised in poet Daisy. There is a sense in McEwan's work, however, that men remain the prestigious artists: Clive Linley, the famous composer in *Amsterdam* (1998), and Grammaticus, Daisy's grandfather in *Saturday*, are the powerful figures, while characters

such as Daisy, Florence, and Briony are introduced as precocious protégés (though in two cases glimpses are given of successful later careers).

31 McEwan (2007: 61). Further references to this edition will be included in the text.

32 See, e.g., Childs (2009: 33, fn. 45).

33 The quotation is taken by McEwan from near the end of chapter 24 of Austen's *Northanger Abbey*. It is perhaps also worth noting that the novel, though one of Austen's earliest to be written, was not published until after her death, as Briony's is to be.

Bibliography

Begley, Adam: "The Art of Fiction CLXXIII. Ian McEwan". – In Ryan Roberts (Ed.): *Conversations with Ian McEwan*, Jackson, 2009, p. 105.

Childs, Peter: "McEwan and Anosognosia". – In Pascal Nicklas (Ed.): *Ian McEwan. Art and Politics*, Heidelberg, 2009, pp. 23-38.

Cusk, Rachel: *Arlington Park*, London, 2007.

–: *The Bradshaw Variations*, London, 2009.

Davies, Rhiannon: "Enduring McEwan". – In Daniel Lea & Berthold Schoene (Eds): *Posting the Male. Masculinities in Post-War and Contemporary British Literature*, Amsterdam, 2003, pp. 109-120.

Eagleton, Mary: *Figuring the Woman Author in Contemporary Fiction*, London, 2005.

Foucault, Michel: "What is an Author?" [1979]. – In Paul Rabinow (Ed.): *The Foucault Reader*, New York, 1984, pp. 101-120.

Lynn, David: "A Conversation with Ian McEwan". – In Ryan Roberts (Ed.): *Conversations with Ian McEwan*, Jackson, 2009, pp. 143-155.

Mars-Jones, Adam: *Venus Envy. On the Womb and the Bomb*, London, 1990.

Masoni, Stefano *et al.*: "The Couvade Syndrome". *Journal of Psychosomatic Obstetrics and Gynecology*, 15 September 1994, 125-131.

McEwan, Ian: *First Love, Last Rites*, London, 1976 [1975].

–: *The Child in Time*, London, 1988 [1987].

–: *A Move Abroad*, London, 1989.

–: *Amsterdam*, London, 1999 [1998].

–: *Atonement*, London, 2001.

–: *Saturday*, London, 2005.

–: *On Chesil Beach*, London, 2007.

McLeod, John: "Men Against Masculinity. The Fiction of Ian McEwan". – In Antony Rowland, Emma Liggins & Eriks Uskalis (Eds): *Signs of Masculinity. Men in Literature 1700 to the Present*, Amsterdam, 1998, pp. 218-245.

Morrison, Richard: "Opera Gets Between the Sheets With Ian McEwan's *For You*", *The Times*, 9 May 2008, 2.

Noakes, Jonathan: "Interview With Ian McEwan". – In Margaret Reynolds & J.N. (Eds): *Ian McEwan. The Essential Guide*, London, 2002, pp. 10-23.

Omer, Ali: "The Ages of Sin. Interview with Ian McEwan", *Time Out*, 26 September 2001, 59.

Remnick, David: "Naming What Is There. Ian McEwan in Conversation With David Remnick". – In Ryan Roberts (Ed.): *Conversations With Ian McEwan*, Jackson, 2009, pp. 155-174.

Silverblatt, Michael: "Interview With Ian McEwan", *Bookworm*, KCRW, Santa Monica, 11 July 2002.

Smith, Dodie: *I Capture the Castle*, London, 1996 [1949].

Wells, Lyn: *Ian McEwan*, London, 2009.

Susana Onega (Zaragoza)

Portraits of the Artist in the Novels of Jeanette Winterson

In the Vintage edition of *Oranges Are Not the Only Fruit,*[1] Jeanette Winterson dedicates the novel to Philippa Brewster, the publisher who, in 1985, had recommended her novel for publication in the newly formed Pandora Press. As Patricia Duncker recalls, Pandora Press was "an imprint of a mainstream publisher, Routledge and Kegan Paul [which] had been set up in competition with the other feminist houses, Virago, Onlywomen, Sheba Feminist Publishers and The Women's Press".[2] As Simone Murray explains, the appearance of these feminist houses in the English-speaking world was a result of feminist activism and the increasing public demands for women's rights from the late sixties onwards. In Britain, together with Pandora Press, Virago Press and The Women's Press, this movement also gave rise to radical/lesbian/women of colour-identified imprints such as Sheba Feminist Publishers, Onlywomen and Silver Moon Books.[3]

The fact of appearing in Pandora Press automatically conditioned the reception of *Oranges*. For all its experimentalism, its reviewers unanimously described Winterson's first novel as a realistic and heavily autobiographical comedy of coming out, in line with the fictions that had begun to appear in the new feminist presses, which were novels that used the traditional hero's quest pattern of the *Bildungsroman* to represent the process of individuation of a heroine invariably at odds with the social roles of housekeeper, wife and mother allotted to her by patriarchal ideology. Formally, *Oranges* responds to this *Bildungsroman* pattern, as it is presented as the account of an autodiegetic narrator, a young lesbian woman teasingly called Jeanette, who tells her life story retrospectively from the perspective of her younger self. As has often been noted, the family background and childhood experiences of the fictional Jeanette have many traits in common with those of Jeanette Winterson, including the gift of storytelling, which proves essential for the fictional Jeanette's individuation process. In order to cope with the acute misery provoked by the brutality and neglect of her adoptive mother and the general hostility or incomprehension of the adults, Jeanette constantly tells herself stories with a strong fantasy element. Thus, when she falls ill with an inflammation of the adenoids and is left alone by her busy mother at the awe-inspiring Victoria Hospital with the only consolation of a few oranges, Jeanette transforms a sticky orange peel into an empty igloo and invents a truculent story about "How Eskimo Got Eaten".[4] Again, when her mother says of a radio programme on "The Family Life of Snails" that "it's an Abomination, it's like saying we come from monkeys", Jeanette imagines a story about "Mr and Mrs Snail at home on a wet Wednesday night; Mr Snail dozing quietly, Mrs Snail reading a book about difficult children" (Winterson 1990a: 21). And when she reaches the climactic point of having to decide between acknowledging her homosexuality, and so become a mature lesbian woman, or comply with the astringent morality of her mother and religious community, and so be unhappy and self-fragmented forever, Jeanette presents her crux in terms of having to choose between being a "priest" or a "prophet". As she reflects:

> I could have been a priest instead of a prophet. The priest has a book with the words set out. Old words, known words, words of power. Words that are always on the surface. Words for every occasion. The words work. They do what they're supposed to do; comfort and discipline. (161)

Unlike the priest, "[t]he prophet has no book. The prophet is a voice that cries in the wilderness, full of sounds that do not always set into meaning. The prophets cry out because they are troubled by demons" (*ibid.*). By choosing to be a prophet crying out her own truth in the wilderness of religious bigotry and social incomprehension, Jeanette situates herself in the position of William Blake's poet/prophet Los in *Jerusalem* (1804-1820) at the moment of his climactic declaration of individual creativity and freedom, when he tells his weeping Spectre: "I must Create a System or be enslav'd by another Man's / I will not Reason & Compare; my business is to Create".[5] Her decision shows Jeanette not so much as the protagonist of a lesbian *Bildungsroman* in the realist tradition of coming out, but of a modernist *Künstlerroman*, as Lynn Pykett acutely suggests when, comparing *Oranges* to James Joyce's *A Portrait of the Artist as a Young Man* (1916), she defines *Oranges* as "a portrait of the artist as a young working class lesbian who flees the nets of religion and community [in order to become] an artist/prophet".[6] Pykett's association of Jeanette with Stephen Dedalus and Jeanette's own description of herself as a prophet respond to Winterson's visionary conception of art and her definition of the writer as shaman, or mediator between the two worlds.

Winterson explains at length her conception of art in general and of literature in particular in *Art Objects. Essays on Ecstasy and Effrontery* (1995), a poetic manifesto where she presents herself as the inheritor of poets like T.S. Eliot, Robert Graves, Ezra Pound and W.B. Yeats, and of fiction writers like Gertrude Stein, Katherine Mansfield, Radclyffe Hall and Virginia Woolf. As the subtitle of the book suggests, Winterson rejects Realism and places herself in the visionary tradition initiated by Romanticism and continued by High Modernism:

> like Romanticism, Modernism was a poet's revolution, the virtues of a poetic sensibility are uppermost (imagination, invention, density of language, wit, intensity, great delicacy) and what returns is play, pose and experiment. What departs is Realism.[7]

Together with the centrality of language and the creative power of the imagination, Winterson defends the autonomy and independence of art (Winterson 1995b: 10), and its exclusive concern with "genuine aesthetic considerations and not politics, prejudice and fashion" (18). And she defines its function as a heightened form of knowledge aimed at providing an affective understanding of the human condition at large:

> [w]e know that the universe is infinite, expanding and strangely complete, that it lacks nothing we need, but in spite of that knowledge, the tragic paradigm of human life is lack, loss, finality, a primitive doomsaying that has not been repealed by technology or medical science. The arts stand in the way of this doomsaying. (19)

Winterson's conception of art situates her in the group of late twentieth-century writers that regard Postmodernism as a continuation, rather than a rejection or devaluation, of Modernism, while her critique of nineteenth-century Realism and the patriarchal values it represents may be said to stem from a vital need to create a new fiction capable of writing the (lesbian) woman self into existence. In this sense, Winterson follows the path inaugurated by Virginia Woolf when she brought to the fore the social and economic constraints that have prevented women in patriarchy from making a significant contribution to the literary canon. As is well known, in *A Room of One's Own* (1929), Woolf, after underlining the scarcity of women poets, argues that eighteenth- and nineteenth-century women had probably opted for writing novels, instead of poetry, because at that time "[t]he novel alone was young enough to be soft in her hands", and that not "even this most pliable of all forms is rightly shaped for her use", that woman needs "some new vehicle, not necessarily verse, for the poetry in her".[8] This reflection leads Woolf to predict a brighter future for women's writing that goes through the improvement of their material conditions and the recognition by the women themselves that:

> [t]he book has somehow to be adapted to the body, and at a venture one would say that women's books should be shorter, more concentrated, than those of men, and framed so that they do not need long hours of steady and uninterrupted work.[9]

Woolf's prophetic dream of a new generation of women with the intellectual and material freedom to express their bodily-felt sensibility and world view in a new, specifically feminine novelistic form provides a striking precedent for the demands of late twentieth-century feminism as well as for Winterson's own writing agenda, which, as I will attempt to show, is aimed at representing the role of the (lesbian) woman writer in the creation of a new feminine space of freedom, equality and love.

Jeanette Winterson wrote *Boating for Beginners* (1985) for the Methuen Humour List in a very short span of time after the success of *Oranges* and she usually labels it as "a comic book" or "a comic book with pictures".[10] However, this trenchant and surrealist novel offers a significant deconstruction of patriarchy through the sustained parodying of the distinction, made in *Oranges*, between power-seeking priests and prophetic poets. Situated in the mythical time before the Flood, *Boating* is narrated by a god-like author-narrator with the capacity to get in and out of the minds of the characters, particularly of Gloria, the purblind heroine intent on her individuation process. In keeping with the circularity of myth, Gloria lives in the modern yet ancestral Biblical city of Nineveh, under the rule of Noah, the mass-media tycoon who has risen from affluent owner of "a thriving little pleasure boat company called Boating for Beginners",[11] to "priestly" writer of religious bestsellers on the creation of the world. Noah, who exerts an iron-fisted control over the media, uses these religious bestsellers and other propagandistic creations, like large-scale documentary films and touring stage epics on the creation of the world, to enforce a raving patriarchal doctrine of his own device, called "Fundamental Religion" (Winterson 1990b: 85). Like the Jeanette of *Oranges*, Noah possesses in principle the visionary creativity of Blake's poets/prophets. But, like Gloria's mother, Mrs Munde, or also like Jeanette's mother and other fundamentalist bigots in Winterson's fictions, Noah has rejected the solitary and hard path of the visionary creator in order to become a spiritually blind and doctrinaire, theocratic ruler. According to Blake, the gods are the creation of the poets' imagination. Echoing this, Noah has created a god who lives with the angels in a cloud and calls himself "YAHWEH THE UNPRONOUNCEABLE" (13 and *passim*). However, this whimsical creature is not the product of Noah's imagination. As Desi, one of Noah's daughters-in-law, is astonished to discover, Yahweh, like Frankenstein's monster, was created by a combination of scientific hubris, chance and electricity (13; 83-84): he materialised out of "a slab of Black Forest Gâteau and a scoop of ice cream" left in Noah's refrigerator, after being reduced to "a state of nauseating decomposition" by a failure of current provoked by a thunderbolt (83). It is in order to please his evermore uncontrollable creature that Noah starts working

> on a manuscript that would be a kind of global history from the beginning of time showing how the Lord had always been there, always would be there and what a good thing this was, [... entitled] *Genesis or How I Did It*. (14)

In this task of writing/imagining into being his own patriarchal myth of origins, Noah has the invaluable collaboration of his fiancée Bunny Mix, the world-famous author of "two and a half thousand" romances, preaching "the purity of love between men and women, the importance of courtship and the absolute taboo of sex before marriage" (130; 16). Described by Emma Fisher as "an exaggeration of Barbara Cartland",[12] Bunny Mix has a deadly ascendancy over the thousands of Ninevehian women, including Gloria, who read her best-selling novelettes and who are ready to undergo all kinds of physical and spiritual sacrifices in order to attain the 'bunny-girl' standards of beauty embodied by her perfectly objectified and anorexic heroines. The feminist alternative to the repressive and life-denying priestly creativity of Bunny Mix is embodied by Noah's daughters-in-law, Rita, Sheila and Desi, three splendid women who are explicitly associated with "The Trivia" (21), the (parodic) mother-earth female trinity that ruled Nineveh before Noah's writing of *Genesis* precipitated its fall into history. The exuberance, assertiveness and freedom of these three women give purblind Gloria the stimulus she needs to shake off the repressive influence of her religious mother and of Bunny Mix's trashy romances and to develop into a visionary poet/prophet capable of imagining into being her own alternative to Noah's *Genesis*.

After characterising the role of the writer in these visionary terms in her first two novels, Winterson moves on to deconstruct the realist idea of the individual author and work in *The Passion* (1987) and *Sexing the Cherry* (1989). In *The Passion*, Winterson achieves this end by having two narrators, Henri and Villanelle, instead of one, and by making them not only lead parallel lives, but also and most significantly, by making them share the same words, expressions and refrains, thus creating an intricate pattern of repetition-cum-variation that suggests their ego-anima complementarity. This archetypal complementarity forcefully deconstructs the Cartesian notion of the subject as unitary and autonomous and sets into question the binary opposition subject-as-observer/object-as-observed. Given the fact that the main characters are a man and a woman and that Villanelle is bisexual, this deconstruction of the patriarchal binary also involves a redefinition of the oppositional logic that situates man in the position of subject and woman in that of objectified Other.[13] This basic presupposition, which suffuses the characterisation of woman in the realist novel from its very origins, has been systematically set into question by feminist writers and critics through the theorisation of alternative representations of sexual difference. Thus, in "Sorties" (1975), Hélène Cixous rejects the Lacanian model that privileges the phallus as the organising point of sexual identity and desire in the realm of the symbolic, and argues for the location of sexual difference at the level of sexual

192

pleasure, or *jouissance*. As Morag Shiach points out, this strategic move allows Cixous to remove any possibility of identifying femininity and masculinity with the certainties of anatomical difference, and to place sexual difference at the level of the libido, that is, in the realm of the unknowable.[14] Similarly, Judith Butler's postulation of the "lesbian phallus" as an alternative to the hegemonic patriarchal imaginary "constituted through the naturalization of an exclusionary heterosexual morphology", allows for "the displacement of the hegemonic symbolic of (heterosexist) sexual difference" and for the constitution of new "sites of erotogenic pleasure".[15] From this, Butler as well as Cixous move on to postulate the possibility of sustaining a bisexuality, not as a denial of sexual difference, but as a lived recognition of plurality, of the simultaneous presence of masculinity and femininity within an individual subject. As Shiach notes, such bisexuality is open to all subjects who can escape from the subjective and social effects of the dominant structures of desire. Yet "it is of particular relevance to women, since they have been the greatest victims of patriarchy".[16]

Winterson's interlacing of Villanelle and Henri's lives and narrations responds, then, to women's vital need to create an alternative feminine writing practice, an *écriture feminine* capable of imagining into being plural and shifting subjectivities as an alternative to the binary oppositions subject/object, man/woman that have structured Western thought since the pre-Socratic philosophers. In this sense, the fact that Villanelle is bisexual, rather than homosexual, is relevant, as it responds to Cixous's call for programmatic bisexuality, understood not principally as a form of sexuality, but as an embodied recognition of plurality, fluidity and coexistence of masculinity and femininity within individual subjects.[17] Still, the fact that Villanelle's bisexuality is marked as monstrous – since she was born with webbed feet, the exclusive attribute of male boatmen – points to her bisexuality as exceptional.

In the following novel, *Sexing the Cherry*, female monstrosity continues to be the price women have to pay for their sexual freedom and vital autonomy. The Dog Woman is a grotesquely huge creature of Brobdingnagian proportions, who, unlike women in patriarchy, does not need a sexual partner to feel complete and who is fully satisfied with the filial love of her adoptive son, Jordan, and the female friendship she shares with the nuns and whores living under Puritan rule.

According to Julia Kristeva, in order to gain admittance into Lacan's symbolic order, women must choose between virginity or motherhood, thus being forced to "atone for their carnal *jouissance* with their martyrdom".[18] Winterson sets into question this opposition, which defines woman in terms of sexual morality, by presenting the roles of nuns and whores as interchangeable. As Jordan is astonished to discover, the brothel was connected with the nearby Convent of the Holy Mother by a subterranean stream which, unknown to men, whores and nuns constantly used to visit and exchange places with each other.[19]

Jordan, who is a purblind hero in search of Fortunata, "the dancing part of [him]self",[20] enjoys from the start his mother's sexual fluidity and autonomy but without her tinge of monstrosity/exceptionality: disguised as a woman, he can enter the areas of brothels and convents forbidden to men and is allowed to see how women communicate "without words", in their own "private language. A language not dependent on the construction of men" (Winterson 1990c: 31). These women's collective language is what Lacan calls *lalangue*, the feminine language or mothertongue used by women in the unsymbolised realm of the imaginary, or, in Kristeva's terms,[21] the semiotic language of love that Jordan must learn if he is to develop into a mature visionary writer.[22]

Like every Winterson character immersed in a maturation process, Jordan is an artist in the making who must write himself into existence in the fluid and shifting terms of Winterson's programmatic bisexual subjectivity. Henri and Villanelle fail to round off their maturation process, since they drift apart at the end of *The Passion* and Henri is left at the St Servello madhouse, attempting to overcome his war trauma and his feelings of guilt for the murder of the cook, Villanelle's loathsome husband, in the only possible terms available to him: by planting Eliotean roses in the rocky wasteland outside his cell, and by re-reading and re-writing the notebook he jotted down during the war years, in the light of his love for Villanelle. As he explains, reviewing his future and his past in the light of this feeling of love "is as though I wrote in a foreign language that I am suddenly able to read. [...] I go on writing, so that I always have something to read" (Winterson 1988: 159).

As the qualification of "foreign" suggests, the language that Henri learns from Villanelle is the same pre-symbolic language of love that Jordan learns from his mother and the friendly nuns and whores. It is also the language Jordan employs to keep a private journal where he records his "hidden life" and which, as he explains, is written "with invisible ink" between the lines of the ordinary log book where he records his transatlantic journeys in search of exotic plants and fruits (Winterson 1990c: 10). Jordan compares this private journal with the invisible messages "written in milk" by the ancient Greek (*ibid.*), thus pointing to it as a piece of *écriture feminine*, which, according to Cixous, must be written with *languelait*, that is, with "white ink" or "mother's milk", in opposition to the phallogocentric writing of patriarchy, carried out, as she contends, with a pen/penis.[23] Jordan's distinction between his material and his imaginary journals and his suggestion that the invisible writing of his secret life is written with milk add a specifically feminine facet to his visionary act of writing/creation that is in keeping both with his suggested bisexuality and with Winterson's agenda of deconstructing the oppositional definition of man and woman in favour of more fluid and nuanced forms of subjectivity.

This attempt is given a further turn in Winterson's *Written on the Body* (1992), a novel that takes up and develops the issue of representing alternative forms of subjectivity from the point where *Sexing the Cherry* left it. Thus, where Jordan imagines his maturation process as a search for Fortunata/his female facet, in *Written on the Body* the gender and physical aspect of the autodiegetic narrator are never overtly stated, so that the protagonist is presented not only as bisexual but also as androgynous, in line with the eponymous protagonist of Virginia Woolf's *Orlando. A Biography* (1928); of Maureen Duffy's Kit, the autodiegetic narrator of *Love Child* (1977), whose gender and sexual orientation are never revealed; or also of Duffy's Al, the narrator of *Londoners* (1983), who, like the nameless narrator of *Written on the Body*, is a translator.

For all this, the narrator of *Written on the Body* still is an immature hero/ine engaged in a quest for individuation that, in his/her case, involves the giving up of his/her reckless promiscuity with partners of both sexes and the discovery of true love. As in Jordan's case, this aim is inseparable from the narrator's act of storytelling of his/her "inner" or emotional life in the "foreign" language of love. From the start, the narrator is perfectly aware that: "[l]ove demands expression", but s/he also knows that "'I love you' is always a quotation",[24] and that there are too many clichés surrounding the question of love (Winterson 1992: 10). The irony and cynicism with which s/he thinks of love make it impossible for the narrator to respond adequately to the true love offered her by Louise Fox, a beautiful Australian woman who is ready to abandon Elgin, her husband, for him/her. If s/he is to grow morally and spiritually, s/he will have to become aware of the seriousness of Louise's proposal and of the artificiality and wrongness of her/his reckless sexual behaviour.

After abandoning her husband, Louise and the narrator live "together in great happiness for nearly five months" (99), in their own private space, enjoying a relationship that the narrator describes in terms of subjective equality: "[n]either of us had the upper hand, we wore matching wounds. She was my twin and I lost her" (163). The twins metaphor substitutes the inequality of the self/Other opposition for a new pattern of equality, which I have compared elsewhere to the pattern the lesbian writer Nicole Brossard calls "desiring subject/subject of desire".[25] Their love relationship constitutes, then, an experience of pure *jouissance* in Cixous's interpretation of the term. However, this blissful situation comes to an abrupt end when Louise dies of cancer, leaving the narrator in the unbearable position of the split androgynes in Plato's *Symposium* (c. 385-380 BCE). As Aristophanes makes clear, the love that binds the split androgynes together is both a physical and a spiritual communion, a perfect understanding of each other's soul without the need of words.[26] Significantly, Louise and the narrator achieve this blissful state through their mutual act of writing and reading the body of the beloved:

> [y]ou tap a message on to my skin, tap meaning into my body. Your morse code interferes with my heart beat. [...] Written on the body is a secret code only visible in certain lights: the accumulations of a lifetime gather there. In places the palimpsest is so heavily worked that the letters feel like Braille. [...] I didn't know that Louise would have reading hands. She has translated me into her own book. (89)

This description reveals both protagonists as the joint authors of a piece of *écriture feminine* and of themselves as the visionary poets/prophets capable of imagining into being a new feminine space within the patriarchal symbolic order where they can share the same subjective position, as desiring subjects/subjects of desire.

In her next three novels, *Art & Lies* (1994), *Gut Symmetries* (1997), and *The.PowerBook* (2000), bisexuality is again taken for

196

granted and lesbian love presented as superior to the self-centred relationship offered to women by men. However, the general tendency of these novels is to present all kinds of human relations, including those of males and females, as complex, shifting and difficult to assess, and to depict subjectivity as a process of endless accretion and redefinition through interaction with other subjects. Therefore, in these novels, Winterson appears to move beyond the role of 'lesbian writer' towards the more comprehensive role of visionary writer, someone with the healing power to create art objects capable of revealing through their transcendental beauty the essential meaning of human life and to reconnect the split between self and world.

This agenda, which is programmatically detailed in *Art Objects*, is set into practice in *Art & Lies. A Piece for Three Voices and a Bawd*, a novel that is generally regarded as the extremely experimental and 'arty' counterpart to Winterson's poetic manifesto. Its epigraph, a quotation from F.H. Bradley defining the work of art as "A WORLD IN ITSELF, INDEPENDENT, COMPLETE, AUTONOMOUS", situates the complex action of the novel wholly within an imaginary space that has the form of a World/Book or Palace of Art. The novel combines the stories of two contemporary characters, Handel and Picasso, and of the ancient Greek poet Sappho. These stories are mirrored by an eighteenth-century embedded text entitled "The Entire and Honest Recollections of a Bawd".[27] This pornographic and comic text is contained, together with numberless other texts in the Western canon, in a fabulously old, yet unfinished book that Handel and Picasso find on the train that will take them at the time of their deaths from London to the Aegean sea/Sappho's Underworld. This infinite and all-encompassing World/Book, containing, among other things, the burnt volumes of the Library of Alexandria, is itself contained *en abyme* within *Art & Lies*. Therefore, by entering this book, the characters, and the readers with them, gain access to a transcendental and autonomous World of Art, presided over by Sappho, which, like Jorge Luis Borges's Library of Babel, is endlessly multiplying itself. Handel is perfectly aware that he lives in a linguistic universe, that what he takes for recollections of his lived experience might in fact be the product of somebody else's imagination: "[h]ow much of recollection is invention? / Whose invention?" (Winterson 1995a: 183) And he fears that he might be a fictional character existing only in somebody else's dream: "[l]ook

197

deeper: How much of your thinking has been thought for you by someone else?" (184) Given the fact that Handel is attempting to confer meaning on his existence by recalling and narrating his life story, these questions point to a disquieting distrust in his authorial autonomy and agency. Still, although he knows that he is "made up of other people's say so, veins of tradition, a particular kind of education, borrowed methods that have disguised themselves as individual habits" (*ibid.*), he also knows that he has the freedom to choose his master and to imitate the best: "[p]arrot may not learn to sing but he will know what singing is. That is why I have tried to hide myself among the best: music, pictures, books, philosophy, theology" (185). These words, which bring to mind T.S. Eliot's contention that no individual talent can flourish that is not firmly rooted in the tradition,[28] justify Handel's climactic decision to give up priesthood, thus rejecting the church's dogmas in which he had been educated, and devote himself to medicine – that heals the body, and art – that heals the spirit.

His choice of medicine and art over priesthood points to Handel as a poet/prophet in the making, like Picasso, the illegitimate daughter of Sir Jack Montgolfier, who has led an atrocious life of lovelessness and sexual abuse and who uses painting to work through her trauma. Indeed, both protagonists are victims of dreadful forms of sexual harassment: Picasso was repeatedly raped by her half-brother Matthew (42-46), and the chorus-child Handel was castrated and used as sexual toy by his Vatican tutor, Cardinal Rosso, with the argument that a castrato was the perfect man, the original androgyne (195-196). Needless to say, Handel's physical mutilation does not produce the cardinal's expected metamorphosis, for the unity and perfection of androgyny is spiritual rather than anatomical. Handel and Picasso are, then, deeply wounded characters striving for self-unification and healing by means of art. Handel attempts to round off his individuation process through the practice of medicine, the fruition of music and the writing of his life story, while Picasso, on the morning of Christmas 1997, after having been raped once more by Matthew, smeared her father's awe-inspiring Queen Anne mansion with bright coloured paint, poured whitewash on her half-brother's hair and clothes and covered her own naked body "in camouflage colours" (71). Her act, which is diagnosed as madness, is in fact an act of imaginative self-recreation that translates into the visual language of painting Cixous's injunction to women to use their bodies to write themselves into existence in their own terms. The novel ends with Picasso and Handel being led by Sappho to the transcendental train that will transport them from the world of common day to the atemporal World of Art. Sappho's appearance at this juncture reveals her as a shaman, that is, as a visionary artist with the capacity to connect the upper and the lower worlds. As the foremother of love, Sappho is perfectly equipped for this task since, according to Hermeticism,[29] love is the primal force that can bring about the reconciliation or "chymic wedding" of opposites that would give birth to the *filius philosophorum*, that is, the androgynous philosopher's child/precious stone.[30]

In her seventh novel, *Gut Symmetries*, Winterson further develops this hermetic aspect of the shamanistic role of the truly creative writer. As in earlier fictions, *Gut Symmetries* combines the narrations of several immature, complementary characters, in this case, of the love triangle composed of Alice, Jove and Stella. Stella, who is married to Jove, is a poet with a commonsensical German mother and a cabbalistic Jewish father. Jove is a university professor of String Theory, and Alice a postgraduate student of New Physics working on Paracelsus. Although Alice and Jove are both New Physicists, their attitudes to science are diametrically opposed. Jove is a rational materialist and an atheist,[31] and he starkly separates "honest science" from what "is not science at all. Call it alchemy, astrology, spoon-bending, wishful thinking" (Winterson 1997: 191). By contrast, Alice thinks of art, magic, religion and science as equally valid, alternative discourses for explaining the meaning of human life in the universe (73). In keeping with this, she shares with Stella a holistic approach to self and world that combines the discourses of hermetico-cabbalist magic, depth psychology and the New Physics. These discourses are all integrated at the narrative level in the quest structure of Stella and Alice's maturation processes, which take the form of the Fool's journey along the arcana of the Tarot.

As she herself suggests when she calls herself a fool (24), Alice plays the role of Tarot querent or quester in a life journey which is textual as well as physical and spiritual and which involves both a process of remembering/writing the intangible facts of her "broken past, named and not" (117), and the imaginative construction of a "vision in broken pieces behind the wall" (24). Similarly, Stella, at the beginning of the novel is a fragmented character in need of reconstructing/rewriting herself into a new and better person. Like other Wintersonian questers, Stella knows that this task involves the recovery of the intangible "inner life" and the mastery of "the other language" (45), which is the pre-symbolic, feminine language of love. Consequently, Alice needs Stella's collaboration in the creation of this language, as is suggested by Alice's repeated entreaties to Stella that she walk along with her and help her invent a common life story: "[w]alk with me, memory to memory, the shared path, the mutual view [...] as I invent what I want to say, you will invent what you want to hear. Some story we must have" (20; 25). Alice's invitation to Stella to participate in the writing/creation of their joint life story points to their archetypal complementariness as well as to their visionary capacity to imagine themselves into being. Stella describes this capacity in hermetic terms as a god-like act of creation, which she explicitly compares to God's creation of the first man (24).

In her next novel, *The.PowerBook* Winterson moves away from the scientific and esoteric complexities of *Gut Symmetries* to the apparently simple register of cybernetics. The main narrative line takes the form of a chat between a young woman called "Ali" or "Alix" and a customer,[32] a married woman whose alias is "Tulip" (Winterson 2000: 25). While in the earlier novels the protagonists envisage writing as an act of (self-)creation, Ali presents her writer's task simply as a way of earning a living. However, the impression that what she offers is sheer entertainment is delusive, for Ali asks her customer if she really wishes "to be transformed", and she explicitly says that the potential for self-transformation lies in the very act of storytelling: "[t]he alphabet of my DNA shapes certain words, but the story is not told. I have to tell it myself" (4). Furthermore, the fact that Ali and Tulip's dialogic storytelling is ruled by internet principles means that it is arranged as a web of thematically related stories that can be accessed, interacted upon, abandoned and reopened at will by narrator and narratee, thus giving them the possibility of inventing/living a potentially infinite number of stories/lives. This infinite potentiality situates the characters in a linguistic universe as autonomous and all-encompassing as Bradley's World of Art, but much more fluid and mutable, existing in a cybernetic space that denies the difference between the virtual and the actual. Still, even in this hyperreal universe, the task of the visionary writer continues to be decisive for, as Ali makes clear, only through the power of the individual imagination can one particular possibility be transformed into an actuality: "I can't take my body through space and time, but I can send my mind, and use the stories, written and unwritten, to tumble me out in a place not yet existing – my future" (53). Needless to say, within this space of infinite potentiality, there is no limit to Winterson's programmatic agenda of freeing the subject from the patriarchal constraints and inequalities of gender and sex and of creating subjectivities in her own fluid, multiple and changing terms.

In the following novel, *Lighthousekeeping* (2004), Winterson rounds off her portrait of the poet/prophet in the making. As in earlier works, the protagonist, Silver, is an orphan who has endured all sorts of Dickensian hardships, but unlike them she is lucky enough to draw the attention of Pew, the fabulously old and blind lighthousekeeper of Salts, who takes her as an apprentice. Pew, who considers eyesight a handicap, makes Silver live in pitch darkness, and he keeps telling her tales and asking her to close her eyes and watch the vision inside.[33] These tales are stories about Salts and its earlier inhabitants and about the construction of the lighthouses that pinpoint the coast of Scotland dispelling its dangerous darkness. As readers soon realise, Pew is a visionary storyteller and the lighthouse a transcendental ladder, like the train in *Art & Lies*, connecting the lower and the upper worlds. Silver's training in lighthousekeeping is, then, aimed at developing her visionary powers. This training ends the day she manages to transform the story Pew is telling her into a vivid mental picture: "I opened my eyes, and saw the waves and the ships and the birds. Pew let go of my hand. 'Now you know what to do'" (Winterson 2004: 206). After this, Silver takes up Pew's role as storyteller, recasting the stories he has told her in her own feminine terms and completing the story of Salts with her own life story, thus adding her own particular vision to what Blake called the One Central Form of the collective imagination.[34]

With this picture of the old shaman training a purblind child in the art of visionary storytelling, Winterson seems to have exhausted the topos she initiated in *Oranges*. As I have attempted to show, the picture of the woman artist that emerges out of the sequential reading of the novels displays the manifold nuances of a systematic rewriting of Blake's concept of the poet/prophet from a feminist and lesbian perspective that involves the deconstruction of the oppositional definitions of man and woman and the creation of a more fluid, varied and changeable concept of subjectivity, based on mutual relations of equality, freedom and the blissful fruition of true love.[35]

Notes

1 Winterson (1991).
2 Duncker (1998: 77).
3 Murray (2004: 4-5).
4 Winterson (1990a: 27). Further references to this edition will be included in the text.
5 Blake (1909: n.p.); see Onega (2006b: 28-30).
6 Pykett (1998: 58).
7 Winterson (1995b: 30). Further references to this edition will be included in the text.
8 Woolf (2001: 66).
9 *Ibid.*
10 See Winterson's website listed in the bibliography.
11 Winterson (1990b: 12). Further references to this edition will be included in the text.
12 Fisher (1985: 1228).
13 See Waugh (1989: 8).
14 Shiach (1991: 18).
15 Butler (1993: 91).
16 Shiach (1991: 16).
17 Cixous (1996: 84-85).
18 Kristeva (1989: 146).
19 Winterson (1988: 30). Further references to this edition will be included in the text.
20 Winterson (1990c: 40). Further references to this edition will be included in the text.
21 Kristeva (1982).
22 Onega (2006b: 91).
23 Cixous (1991: 49); see Onega (2006b: 87).
24 Winterson (1992: 9). Further references to this edition will be included in the text.
25 Onega (2006b: 121).
26 Plato (1998: 55; 57).
27 Winterson (1995a: 29; 165). Further references to this edition will be included in the text.
28 Eliot (1979: 2293-2300).

29 Hermeticism is a set of philosophical, religious and magical beliefs based upon the spurious writings of Hermes Trismegistus, a mythical figure built on the conflation of the Egyptian god Thoth with the Greek Hermes, the god who conducted souls to the judges of the Underworld where one's afterlife was determined.

30 Roth (2004: 144-147); see also Onega (2006b: 158).

31 Winterson (1997: 27). Further references to this edition will be included in the text.

32 Winterson (2000: 138). Further references to this edition will be included in the text.

33 Winterson (2004: 205-206). Further references to this edition will be included in the text.

34 Blake (2008: 651).

35 The research carried out for the writing of this article is part of a project financed by the Spanish Ministry of Science and Innovation (MICINN) and the European Regional Development Fund (ERDF) (code HUM2007-61035). The author is also thankful for the support of the Government of Aragón and the European Social Fund (ESF) (code HO5). As part of an ongoing research project, this paper takes up and develops ideas already tackled in Onega (1995; 1997; 2004; 2005; 2006a; 2006b; 2010).

Bibliography

Blake, William: *Jerusalem. The Emanation of the Giant Albion*. Eds. E.R.D. Maclagan & A.G.B. Russell, London, 1909 [1804-1820], http://www.archive.org/stream/propheticbooksof00blakrich/propheticbooksof00blakrich_djvu.txt (accessed 25 February 2011).

–: "Annotations to the Work of Sir Joshua Reynolds" [1804]. – In David V. Erdman (Ed.): *The Complete Poetry & Prose of William Blake*, Berkeley & Los Angeles, 2008 [1965], pp. 635-661.

Butler, Judith: "The Lesbian Phallus and the Morphological Imaginary". – In J.B.: *Bodies that Matter. On the Discursive Limits of Sex*, London & New York, 1993, pp. 57-91.

Cixous, Hélène: "Sorties". – In H.C. & Catherine Clément: *The Newly Born Woman*. Trans. Sandra M. Gilbert, London, 1996 [1975], pp. 63-132.

–: *"Coming to Writing" and Other Essays*. Trans. Deborah Jenson *et al.*, Cambridge, 1991.

Duncker, Patricia: "Jeanette Winterson and the Aftermath of Feminism". – In Helena Grice & Tim Woods (Eds.): *"I'm Telling You Stories". Jeanette Winterson and the Politics of Reading*, Amsterdam & Atlanta, 1998, pp. 77-88.

Eliot, T.S.: "Tradition and the Individual Talent" [1919]. – In M.H. Abrams (Ed.): *The Norton Anthology of English Literature, Volume II*, New York *et al.*, 1979, pp. 2293-2300.

Fisher, Emma: "'... and Before'. Jeanette Winterson, *Boating for Beginners*", *Times Literary Supplement*, 1 November 1985, 1228.

Kristeva, Julia: "About Chinese Women". – In Toril Moi (Ed.): *The Kristeva Reader*. Trans. Seán Hand, Oxford, 1989 [1986], pp. 138-159.

–: *Powers of Horror. An Essay on Abjection*, New York, 1982.

Murray, Simone: *Mixed Media. Feminist Presses and Publishing Politics*, London, 2004.

Onega, Susana: "'I'm Telling You Stories, Trust Me'. History/Storytelling in Jeanette Winterson's *Oranges Are Not the Only Fruit*". – In S.O. (Ed.): *"Telling Histories". Narrativizing History, Historicizing Literature*, Amsterdam & Atlanta, 1995, pp. 135-147.

–: "The 'Body/Text' as Lesbian Signifier in Jeanette Winterson's *Written on the Body*". – In Marita Nadal & M. Dolores Herrero (Eds.): *Margins in British and American Literature, Film, and Culture*, Zaragoza, 1997, pp. 119-129.

–: "Science, Myth and the Quest for Unity in Jeanette Winterson's *Gut Symmetries*", *Anglistik. Mitteilungen des Deutschen Anglistenverbandes* 15:1, 2004, 93-104.

–: "Jeanette Winterson's Visionary Fictions. An Art of Cultural Translation and Effrontery". – In Jürgen Schlaeger (Ed.): *The Yearbook of Research in English and American Literature* (REAL) XX, Tübingen, 2005, pp. 220-243.

–: "Writing, Creation and the Ethics of Postmodernist Romance in Jeanette Winterson's *Boating for Beginners*", *Récherches Anglaises et Nord-Américaines* 39, 2006a, 213-227.

–: *Jeanette Winterson*, Manchester, 2006b.

–: "Circularity and the Quest in the Novels of Jeanette Winterson". – In Christoph Henke & Martin Middeke (Eds.): *Symbolism. An International Annual of Critical Aesthetics* 9, 2010, pp. 193-216.

Plato: *Symposium*. Trans. & Ed. C.J. Rowe, Warminster, 1998.

Pykett, Lynn: "A New Way With Words? Jeanette Winterson's Post-Modernism". – In Helena Grice & Tim Woods (Eds.): *"I'm Telling You Stories". Jeanette Winterson and the Politics of Reading*, Amsterdam & Atlanta, 1998, pp. 53-60.

Roth, Remo F.: *The Return of the World Soul. Wolfgang Pauli, Carl Jung and the Challenge of the Unified Psychophysical Reality*, 2004 [2002], http://www.psychovision.ch/synw/pauli_fludd_flood_sync.htm (accessed 9 April 2011).

Shiach, Morag: *Hélène Cixous. A Politics of Writing*, London & New York, 1991.

Waugh, Patricia: *Feminine Fictions. Revisiting the Postmodern*, London & New York, 1989.

Winterson, Jeanette: *The Passion*, London 1988 [1987].

–: *Oranges Are Not the Only Fruit*, London, 1990a [1985].

–: *Boating for Beginners*, London, 1990b [1985].

–: *Sexing the Cherry*, London et al., 1990c [1989].

–: *Oranges Are Not the Only Fruit*, London, 1991 [1985].

–: *Written on the Body*, London, 1992.

–: *Art & Lies. A Piece for Three Voices and a Bawd*, London, 1995a [1994].

–: *Art Objects. Essays on Ecstasy and Effrontery*, London, 1995b.

–: *Gut Symmetries*, London, 1997.

–: *The.PowerBook*, London: 2000.

–: *Lighthousekeeping*, London & New York, 2004.

–: http://www.jeanettewinterson.com (accessed 21 October 2011).

Woolf, Virginia: *A Room of One's Own*. – In V.W.: *A Room of One's Own and Three Guineas*, London, 2001 [1929], pp. 1-98.

Jean-Michel Ganteau (Montpellier)

Non Serviam. Portraits of the Artist as a Young Performer

Summoning the name of Peter Ackroyd in a volume devoted to the visions of the artist as a young woman in the wake of Linda Huf's classic, may sound slightly unexpected. Ackroyd's tentacular oeuvre is notorious for its evocation of Englishness and more specifically a brand of Englishness very much associated with the Cockney imagination. Equally notorious is his fascination with a *genius loci* metonymically attached to the evocation of London as eternal metropolis. In unearthing the spiritual canon that he sees as the cornerstone of some submerged visionary Catholic English culture, as expounded in some of his most famous lectures and in most of his works of fiction – and as neatly encapsulated in his sixth novel, *English Music* (1992) – Ackroyd does handle a great deal of historical and cultural material, and presents the reader with a vast gallery of characters most of whom, admittedly, are men.[1] This is a point that Susana Onega confronts him with in a famous interview published in *Twentieth Century Literature*, triggering an edifying response:

> [i]t has nothing to do with homosexuality. It has nothing to do with my gender. I think it has all to do with the fact that I find it very difficult to ... You see, I am always writing about myself, [...] and I can't write about myself as a female, because I am not. It is a weakness which I regret actually, because in my fiction, when I create books, I find it very difficult to create sympathic or real, old female characters. Someone would say I can't create real characters at all.[2]

Although in his biographies Ackroyd has consistently explored a strictly male canon of Englishness (he did devote a biography to Shakespeare, and certainly not to the Bard's sister), it seems as if the above statement should be qualified since, in some of his recent novels, he does manage to draw convincing portraits of heroines who seem to have a fictional life of their own and whose contributions to the dynamics of the plot and to the success of the novel are more than strictly ancillary.

This is most notably the case with such novels as *The Lambs of London* (2002) or, more recently, *The Fall of Troy* (2006) and *The Casebook of Victor Frankenstein* (2008). In the first of these novels, Mary Lamb, Charles Lamb's sister, is portrayed at length as her enthusiasm and love for art evolve into an obsession. And with Sophia Obermann, the archaeologist's young Greek wife in *The Fall of Troy*, Ackroyd provides once again the portrait of an impassioned woman who is given considerable diegetic presence. Such a trend seems to be confirmed in his revisiting of the Frankenstein myth, as he devotes many pages to Mary Shelley, downplaying her role as the creator of *Frankenstein* (1818), and showing how she is created by the monster. It appears that, even if the feminine element has not been given pride of place in most novels or biographies, there seems to be a trend towards more salience in the recent production, and that the vulnerable yet strikingly generous and opinionated female figures already present in *The House of Dr Dee* (1993) or in *Chatterton* (1987) have lately evolved into full-throated, rounder characters.[3] In some of those novels the literary and cultural aspirations of female characters are present to a certain extent, as is the case of the fictional Mary Shelley or Harriet Scrope, the elderly novelist and forger whose dealings with Charles Wychwood fuel *Chatterton*'s contemporary plot. But nowhere is the figure of the female artist and creator more centrally exploited than in Ackroyd's seventh novel, *Dan Leno and the Limehouse Golem* (1994).

Interestingly, the American version of the novel is entitled *The Trial of Elizabeth Cree. A Novel of the Limehouse Murders*, underlining the female protagonist's central presence. As the subtitle signposts both the mysterious contents of the plot and the novel's revisiting of nineteenth-century London, by alluding to the Parr and Ripper murders, the title offers an alternative reading of the novel, displacing the focus from male protagonist – the late Victorian and Edwardian music-hall artist and female impersonator Dan Leno – to fictional heroine, and flaunting the chiasmic relation between the two, a relationship that Onega interprets in terms of polar opposition.[4]

In the following pages, I intend to focus less on Dan Leno than on Elizabeth Cree, though the dialectical relationship that binds them will have to be taken into account. My purpose will be to address the implications of Ackroyd's treatment of the female *Künstlerroman* in terms of what it reveals of a late twentieth-century vision of the late Victorian feminine subject. To do so I shall pay attention to the aspects and values of her multifaceted artistic credo, addressing the dissonant practice of her gender performances, and eventually envisaging her artistic constructions in terms of individual and collective trauma.

Dan Leno and the Limehouse Golem has attracted scarce academic attention. No full-length articles have been devoted to it, albeit a spate of allusions and references are present in the available articles and monographs. When considered in the light of Huf's criteria, what appears glaringly is that, even though it is staged in late Victorian London, it owes very little – not to say nothing – to the domestic novel and is concerned with the figure of the Angel in the House but marginally. To take up one of Huf's striking phrases, it is more especially concerned with the "slaying of the Angel in the House".[5] Granted, Elizabeth's ascension from pauper to respectable middle-class wife is one of the main characteristics in her social trajectory, but the narrative level devoted to the evocation of her life as Mrs Cree in her new house in New Cross and evoking the period closest to her execution as the murderer of her husband (among several other victims) is certainly no idyllic portrayal of domestic bliss. This is made perceptible through a fairly complex narrative structure juxtaposing several strata and partial testimonies, thus putting in perspective and puncturing the image of connubial bliss that she craftily puts together for the benefit of society.

As analysed by Onega, the narrative structure is fairly complex and summons an external, impersonal twentieth-century narrator whose self-assigned duty is to investigate into a series of murders taking place in late Victorian England, murders attributed to Elizabeth Cree, a former music-hall artist rescued from poverty by the immensely famous Dan Leno. In gathering material from the period, so as to throw some comprehensive light on the case, the narrator provides extracts from Elizabeth's trial, presented in the dramatic mode; extracts from what is presented as John Cree's – her husband's – diary; and excerpts from what looks like an autobiographical account written by Elizabeth herself, going over the main stages of her life from her early years in the poorest of households, with her reformed prostitute of a mother, when she used to work on the docks mending the fishermen's nets, to her years as respectable middle-class woman, through her stint on the London stage.[6] The four types of narrative are juxtaposed and alternate throughout, starting with the 'real' execution scene, and ending up with a replica of that scene transferred to the Victorian stage, in which the spectacular parody of the original turns into a metaleptic tour de force.[7] The juxtaposition of such heterogeneous fragments favours the emergence of a temporality that prefers *kairos* (or linked time) over *chronos* (a time dominated by strict linear progression), putting all temporal strata in relation to one another, and generating an impression of achrony evoking the permanence of the *genius loci* and the continuity of English culture in its popular form,[8] one of Ackroyd's most acute obsessions.

Elizabeth Cree's soaring is set against the background of the blighted Victorian metropolis, in which utilitarian models have wreaked havoc on the lower classes. The humanistic principles advocated by Thomas Carlyle and Charles Dickens and emblematised by George Gissing or Dan Leno are evoked alongside Karl Marx's revolutionary proposals – Marx and Gissing being two of the historical characters imported into the world of the novel.[9] From her early years as pauper of the Dickensian type, Elizabeth aspires, Icarus-wise, to fame and independence, and the least that can be said is that Ackroyd's novel stages no wavering between domesticity and artistic vocation: the heroine knows from the beginning where her destiny lies. Seen from the vantage point of the late twentieth century, she appears to be in a class of her own, taking advantage of one of the very few loopholes in Victorian society that allows her to secure her radical independence. The evocation of the music-hall community as space of freedom and subversion and as permanent carnivalesque space is thus instrumental to the heroine's portrayal.[10] *Dan Leno and the Limehouse Golem* might as well be dubbed *A Portrait of the Woman as Escape Artist*, to take up one of Huf's most sticking formulae.[11]

Elizabeth Cree's ways of escape are various, each soaring being envisaged as rebirth. When escaping from the hovel where her mother is lying in the throes of death, she attends a performance by Dan Leno and his friends, becomes acquainted with them, and joins the group as soon as her mother has breathed her last. On the first night when she meets the artists, she spontaneously slips into a role, sloughing off her former skin, complete with identity and name change:

> "What's your moniker?"
>   "Your name, dear."
>   "Lizzie, Sir." Then as I looked around at all of them, I suddenly felt that I must also step into a character. "Lambeth Marsh Lizzie."[12]

After this initial conversion, which marks the beginning of her "second life" (Ackroyd 1995: 215) Elizabeth is going to experience a series of changes, on stage, by stepping into the lives of the various characters that she impersonates, thus emulating the great Dan Leno's talent for plasticity. This leads her to another stage in her career in which she becomes a male impersonator – in chiasmic relation with Dan Leno as dame, or female impersonator – by stepping from Little Victor's Daughter's shoes into Little Victor's Elder Brother's: "I had become a man, from tip to toe [...]" (150), thus confirming her initial discovery: "[i]t was as if I had some other personality which walked out from my body every time I stood in the glare of the gas, and sometimes she even surprised me with her slangster rhymes and cockney stuff" (106). Elizabeth Cree, short of becoming the epitome of the Cockney monypolylinguists that haunt the pages of Ackroyd's oeuvre, turns into professional impersonator as escape artist, adopting a model of nomadic identity based on the principle of ceaselessly becoming Other.[13] The consequence is a blurring of ontological spheres, the magic of the stage spreading to the city and invading domestic space, as one of Elizabeth's later roles is that of self-fashioned lady, an identity she adopts for the sake of appearances, reverting to the impersonation of a feminine part, as carefully constructed as that of her music-hall characters.

In her assumed identity as respectable wife, Elizabeth chooses yet another way of artistic escape by getting promoted from the status of actress to that of stage manager, as seen when she hires Aveline Mortimer, a former actress in want of a job, to play the part of the maid in her home: "by the time she had put on her black cotton collar, she looked every inch the lady's maid. 'A change of dress works wonders,' I said. 'A new woman is born'" (223). Aveline is subsequently given a notebook with specific phrases in it, so that she may perform Elizabeth's script (224), in an overtly metafictional novel saturated with the idea of the text, written or performed.

The next step leads Elizabeth from playwright to author. As indicated before, her autobiographical narrative constitutes one of the main components of the plot. On top of that, the reader soon realises that she is also a forger, and that she is the author of the diary attributed to her husband in which he confesses in details to his murder of two prostitutes, an old Jewish scholar and the greater part of the Gerrard family in their Ratcliffe Highway dwellings (273). The motif of the forger as artist, which runs through Ackroyd's works and is best exemplified in the figure of Chatterton as genius, is given a twist here, Elizabeth standing in between the Marvelous Boy acclaimed by the romantics and the already mentioned Harriet Scrope. In her trajectory, forging is yet another means towards independence.

However, Elizabeth's take-off strip towards emancipation assumes other, connected artistic forms, when she acts as ghost writer for her husband, for instance. In fact, when she finds her role as a lady uninspiring, her ambition to start a new career on "the legitimate stage" (214) leads her to complete *Misery Junction,* the play that her husband, an aspiring artist with philanthropic intentions, fails to bring to a close. As she wants to take on the leading role in the play, she works on it secretly, officially to please her husband, and in actual fact with a view to managing her own career and destiny (230-242). Quite clearly, instead of instrumentalising and obliterating her, her ghost-writing practice is a way of playing the cuckoo in her husband's nest. Putting herself in his place and impersonating him in this fashion is but a means to reject any access to alterity, couched in terms of a *non serviam*.[14] The fact that this ends up with failure and ruins her social ambitions is of little consequence as her main way of escape is through the artistic practice of murder which, in consonance with Thomas de Quincey, she considers as one of the fine arts.

Not only does Elizabeth perform the part of a murderer on stage (178) but she becomes a specialist in foul play, as suggested in the diary allegedly written by her husband. Through a series of recurrences in her autobiographical sketch, the reader cannot but realise that she is in fact the one that murdered her mother, and also, possibly, her father-in-law (189) together with a series of cumbersome witnesses, among whom Doris (155), Little Victor (102) and Uncle

(186). At one point, she even comes close to strangling Dan Leno himself (182). That she is a serial killer and may well be the Golem holding sway over the Limehouse area is corroborated in a passage when a mesmerist hypnotises her and, horror-struck, tells her "[i]t couldn't have been you, Lizzie" (156). Despite the authorised version of her autobiography, and in spite of her rhetoric of denial, or precisely because of it, Elizabeth tells more than she means to say and lets the holes in the text signal themselves and lead the reader onto the right trail, a version confirmed in her last confession to the priest before her execution, when she confesses to her criminal record while refusing to be shriven (272-273). One of the entries in the forged diary points at the analogy between murder and art, insisting particularly on murder as performance, as indicated in the following words evoking the murder of the Gerrard family:

> I did truly mourn their passing, since they had left the world without having the chance to acclaim my artistry – the flick of the knife, the pressure of the artery, the whispered confidence, are all, to quote Lord Tennyson, "unknown to name and fame." That is why I have come to detest this phrase, the "Limehouse Golem;" it is no true title for an artist. (260)

Usurpation is not something that Elizabeth is willing to tolerate, as escape artist and independent woman who makes room for herself in the world by carving people and society with a knife. Interestingly, most of her performances as a murderer are seen as so many stages in her development, as underlined by Onega.[15] As Elizabeth indicates after nearly strangling Dan Leno, "I am not playing, I am real" (183). Becoming an artist implies no scruples for her and is a matter of survival. If *Dan Leno and the Limehouse Golem* qualifies as female *Künstlerroman*, it is certainly because it provides the ever mutable portrait of an ever mutable self, that of a chameleon-artist, in Keats's terms, an artist always on the wing, sloughing off self after self and resorting to performance as ontological multiplication and demise. In conformity with Huf's demonstration, the artist's rebirths are seen as a series of self-births, with the difference that this process is endless. Elizabeth Cree becomes the epitome of rebirth as process, a device made all the more striking through the image of dressing up, either as drag artist or as transvestite.

Ackroyd's fascination with cross-dressing as expression of the English imagination crops up in most of his novels and historical texts. In *Albion* (2002), he sees it as part of the spontaneous drive towards assimilation and imitation that he considers inherent in the English genius,[16] and traces a pattern of continuity from the mummers of the Medieval English stage to the contemporary pantomime. Most of his novels rehearse this theme and stage secondary characters indulging in this practice. This is the case of one of Matthew Palmer's friends in *The House of Dr Dee* who shifts identities to turn into a transvestite at night.[17] Still, the transvestite is not such a recurrent figure, unlike the drag artist that may be said to assume the status of a motif to be encountered in *First Light* (1989), with Joey and his malaprop wife as mummers, or in *Chatterton*, with Pat as domestic cross-dresser.[18] The historical figure of the Chevalier d'Eon is summoned in *Dan Leno and the Limehouse Golem*, a narrative that goes further in its analysis of gender bending and performance by importing the figure of the androgyne as borrowed from the esoteric tradition through allusions to Adam Kadmon (67; 154), a time-honoured figure of primal man and of original androgyny. The fascination with dressing up might be said to seep into the novels from Ackroyd's early study *Dressing Up. Transvestism and Drag. The History of an Obsession* (1979), in which he documents the persistence of the practice through the ages and summons essential historical figures, transvestites or drag artists from d'Eon to Dan Leno through Julian Eltinge.

In the third chapter of his study, "Transvestism Rejected", he devotes a few pages to Victorian England and to the pressure on what he calls "the two sexes" who had to conform to strict sartorial codes in a context which could put up with very little manifestation of cross-dressing and gender bending: "[a] society which represses sexuality, but welcomes prurience, is not one to welcome transvestism in any form except that of comic or lurid drag".[19] It is to such a cultural context that the novel brings us back, and its exploration of the music-hall stage and circles may be considered fairly realistic, and documented in many historical or cultural studies. In their book-length definition of gender, David Glover and Cora Kaplan do allude to the place reserved for the drag artist or performer in the context of eighteenth- and nineteenth-century England and America, mentioning "self-subsistent enclave[s] whose members compulsively mime and parody the conventions of the straight world around them".[20] In traditional fashion, dressing up is seen as a mode of resistance and even of subversion in a community at odds with dominant sexual morality and gender conventions. This is where the study of the literary evocation of the young woman as (escape) artist may prove relevant, in that in the introduction to *A Portrait of the Artist as a Young Woman* Huf insists on the artist heroine's early description as characterised by male attributes, essentially psychological ones that, in Ackroyd's novels, seem to be literalised into bodily aptitudes.[21] From the beginning of the novel, on account of her lowly extraction which gets her to earn her living mending the nets on the banks of the river, Elizabeth is metonymically characterised by her large raw hands:

> even my leather gloves could not keep the cloth and the needle from chafing my hands. Look at them now, so worn and so raw. When I put them against my face, I can feel the ridges upon them like cart-tracks. Big hands, my mother used to say. No female should have big hands. (12)

The big raw hands become an uncanny motif recurring throughout, a darker version of Villanelle's webbed feet in Jeanette Winterson's *The Passion* (1987), and the indication that her social assignation is written on her body.[22]

However, what might be seen as the emblem of an imprisonment becomes the instrument of a disruption and the very means to introduce further dissonance. In other words, the portrayal of the young woman as escape artist follows the convention of the female artist's self portrait as freak.[23] Still, while such a characteristic is largely compounded with opprobrium – or at least uneasiness – in the early novels studied by Huf, in *Dan Leno and the Limehouse Golem* no such scruple seems to haunt the protagonist who uses what turns out to be a gift to fairly literally carve her way through the world. From this point of view, Elizabeth Cree is less to be associated with the positive, healing figure of the androgyne than to that – freakish, biologically instable and faintly menacing – of the hermaphrodite.[24] On top of this biological specificity, the character, as already mentioned, is a specialist in the art of impersonation, whether it be on or off stage.

That cross-dressing is an act of rebirth and self fashioning brooks little ambiguity. In *Dressing Up*, Ackroyd refers to the common practice among transvestites of sending photographic portraits of themselves, with their 'femme' names printed underneath, as "artificial act of rebirth".[25] Now, even if Elizabeth Cree does not resort to such narcissistic props, her identity as drag artist is an essential modality of her trajectory as escape artist. In *Dressing Up*, Ackroyd analyses the element of political or social dissent inherent in the practice of cross-dressing. He also takes pains to underline the fact that in times past, female cross-dressing was more often than not "a natural and ambitious attempt of women to overcome the conditions of the 'inferior' sex".[26] As might be expected, he stresses the subversive power of cross-dressing, or more precisely the refusal to abide by the gender roles imposed by society, taking an example from the late seventeenth century of a female transvestite who "was not made for the pleasure or delight of Man and decided that since she could not be honoured with him she would be honoured by him in that garb and manner of raiment she wore".[27] Female cross-dressing as performed by Elizabeth Cree becomes an obvious way of exposing and challenging the superiority of male culture. Granted, by assuming men's roles, she might be said to strengthen such a superiority. Yet, within the music-hall community staged in *Dan Leno and the Limehouse Golem* and within the democratic world of the stage whose leader, Dan Leno, makes sure that a "woman's voice was always heard" (225), the ubiquity of female cross-dressing assumes some revolutionary potential that challenges role models and gender conventions through the dissonant resort to performance.

Dan Leno and the Limehouse Golem is unique in the Ackroydian corpus for the centrality of its treatment of cross-dressing, both male and female, both on stage and off stage. Dan Leno, the great music-hall dame, is unanimously admired for his ability to shift from one character to another without stopping, in an endless flux, this being the true mark of the monopolylinguist, which leads one of the secondary characters to pronounce him "endless" (109), even while he manages to remain himself, as the impersonal narrator insists: "Dan was only fifteen then, but he played so many parts that he hardly had time to be himself. And yet, somehow, he was always himself" (108). One of the reasons why the dialectic tension between being oneself and being Other is suspended – to the benefit of the first proposition – may reside in the fact that his cross-dressing is confined to the stage, making him a famous drag artist, but holding in check his ability to keep escaping from himself. In Dan Leno, as white, positive impersonator, the openness to alterity is permanent and remains rooted in some stability of the self that is vulnerable to the Other and never colonises the Other through identification or mere possession. Dan Leno's practice of impersonation remains ethical.

Conversely, Elizabeth Cree's practice is of a darker, more truly endless type, as she moves from one character to the next after perpetrating a series of crimes: she impersonates Little Victor's Daughter after killing Little Victor, one of the actors in Dan Leno's group, and has to kill the character that she is impersonating before being able to move on to another one: "I grew sick of Little Victor's Daughter. She was just too sweet, and I longed to kill her off by some violent action" (150). Similarly, she will play the leading role in her husband's play after appropriating the play itself and acting as ghost writer, as mentioned above. Her character is thus in polar opposition to that of Dan Leno, in that her relation to the other is of an eminently violent type and, in Levinasian terms, unethical, as Levinas posits that the ethical relation is a non-violent encounter with the other.

What unites the two performers, though, is the fact that, precisely, they are performers. As drag artists, they never allow the spectator to forget about their playing with gender, as the man remains visible under the dame's costume, while the woman can be identified under Little Victor's Daughter's Older Brother:

> [e]veryone knew that I was also 'Little Victor's Daughter', but that was the joy of it. I could be girl and boy, man and woman, without any shame. I felt somehow that I was above them all, and could change myself at will. (153)

In such passages, gender is thus seen to be performed and, one step further, to be a matter of performance, as indicated by Judith Butler, in one of the pithiest passages devoted to her analysis of gender trouble:

> [t]he performance of drag plays upon the distinction between the anatomy of the performer and the gender that is being performed. [...] then the performance suggests a dissonance between not only sex and performance, but sex and gender, and gender and performance. [...] It also reveals the distinctness of those aspects of gendered experience which are falsely naturalized as a unity through the regulatory fiction of het-

erosexual coherence. *In imitating gender, drag implicitly reveals the imitative structure of gender itself – as well as its contingency.*[28]

Said differently, the practice of drag in *Dan Leno and the Limehouse Golem* provides an image of identity as made up of surfaces, as underscored by Gibson and Wolfreys.[29]

I would argue that this is the truer for the character of Elizabeth Cree since, as argued above, she never returns to the stability of what might be seen as her 'true' self. This is confirmed towards the end of the novel when, after the failure of her performance on the "legitimate stage", she becomes an empty self, a void, unable to return to a core or, more precisely, "to be returned" (243). When comparing Dan Leno and Elizabeth Cree then, one could claim that one – Dan Leno – is more selfless in the traditional, moral sense than the other, but that the character whose self is more truly nomadic and elusive, always on the move and always under construction, is Elizabeth Cree. Within the context of a female *Künstlerroman*, this may be seen as a radical way of resisting the location of identity, to take up a phrase of Julian Wolfreys's –[30] a way of radicalising the image of the female artist as escape artist, through an affirmation of difference and dissonance that destabilises social and heterosexual conventions.[31] In Gibson and Wolfreys's evocation of the Ackroydian text, such process is envisaged in terms of "affirmative resistance",[32] a process that no doubt goes well beyond and subverts the very idea of rebirth that Huf sees as instrumental in the fashioning of the female artist.

Another difference between Dan Leno and Elizabeth Cree is that the latter does not confine her cross-dressing to the sphere of the music-hall stage, but haunts the London streets:

> [i]t must have been two or three months after the Older Brother was born that I had a sudden fancy of my own: it might be a piece of fun to take him out into the streets of London and see the other world.
> (153)

In so doing, Elizabeth Cree shifts from drag artist to transvestite, literalising the Woolfian notion of street haunting ("*I* am the London phantom", 272; emphasis in the text). As explained by Ackroyd and other commentators, what allows to discriminate between the drag artist and the transvestite is that the latter's purpose is to produce an almost perfect illusion that he is a woman or she is a man, as the case may be. Without achieving the transsexual's illusion of perfect illusion, though, the transvestite "will, unconsciously or surreptitiously, leave clues to his male [or her female] gender even in the most complete dressing up".[33] This may well be what happens in *Dan Leno and the Limehouse Golem* as Elizabeth, when walking in the streets in male attire, is recognised by Doris and most possibly by Dan Leno, when he turns detective and tries to identify the author of the Ratcliffe Highway murders: "[w]ell, it's a very funny thing, Peggy. But, believe me or believe me not, I think you saw the shadow of a woman along the Ratcliffe Highway" (208). Transvestism, in a more muted and thereby more uncannily efficient form than drag, thus helps retain the dissonant effect that Butler sees at work in drag, showing that what is generally taken as the essence of identity is in fact a fabrication.[34] One step further, Elizabeth Cree's ubiquitous practice of dressing up as both drag and transvestism situates her and the narrative of which she is the protagonist in a context to which the conventional vision of identity does not apply any more, i.e. in a post-identity context.[35] The performativity of gender that Elizabeth Cree keeps privileging and, precisely, performing is yet another escape lane. For when admitting that identity is a construction, just another type of discourse, one is in a position to act on this discourse through a process of counter-interpellation.[36]

The gender performance privileged by Elizabeth Cree may be said to be the very means by which she manufactures her identity as an artist, by subverting patriarchal order, substituting for men and placing herself over men, as she confesses to the Roman Catholic priest prior to her execution: "I have no need to beg pardon or absolution from you. I am the scourge of God" (266). By becoming what the popular press and the Londoners call the Limehouse Golem, she achieves some form of release beyond identity, her hubris becoming in turn the most radical expression of her *non serviam*.

The emptiness that has come to colonise Elizabeth Cree after impersonating a spate of characters and failing in her long wished-for attempt to triumph on "the legitimate stage" (214), may be evocative of the void that comes to affect and haunt the traumatised subject. This may well be what the reader of *Dan Leno and the Limehouse Golem* is ultimately presented with, i.e. a dissolution of the subject submitted to the pressure of traumatic effraction, the outcome of a series of psychic shocks and reactions that give free rein to trauma symptoms and transform the subject into an empty husk. From this point of view, the heroine could be seen as a figure of the young woman as escape artist in a peculiar acceptation, her escape looking like some tragic descent into pathology. Seen in this light, her performances and impersonations assume an even more disquieting shade and become the symptoms of some psychic fragmentation at work in the traumatised character. Indeed, it looks as if one part of her had become encysted within her psyche without her having access to the information, in accordance with the fundamental rules of trauma – as evinced by the pioneering works of Pierre Janet, Sigmund Freud or Sandor Ferenczi whose intuitions are taken up by many contemporary followers.

Such an interpretation may be substantiated by textual references to sexual effraction, as appears in the first pages of Elizabeth Cree's autobiography:

> [t]here is a place between my legs which my mother loathed and cursed – when I was very little she would pinch it fiercely, or prick it with the needle, in order to teach me that it was the home of pain and punishment. (13)

Another allusion to such a practice crops up later on, when Elizabeth evokes the reason why she will not let her husband have sex with her (224-225). Yet, this would provide too pat an explanation, as the characteristic of trauma is that its presence and action are unknown to the reader who is literally haunted by an internal foreign body.[37] In fact, such references are meant to put the reader onto the trail of trauma while leaving the question of its origin open to conjecture.

What remains obvious is that the drag heroine is used as trope to emphatically signal the presence of psychic fragmentation, as indicated in various passages in which the character alludes to herself with different pronouns, a tendency that is amplified in her writing of the melodrama that she transforms her husband's play into: "[c]an this be me who lies here? No, I am not here. It is someone in my place whom I do not know. [...] I have some dark life that is hidden from me" (232).[38] This does not mean that the character does not have access to the memory of her murders, but rather that she is haunted by some internal foreign body that wields sway over her actions and compels her to repeat in the present an action that cannot be remembered or situated in the past,[39] in perfect accordance with what Cathy Caruth defines as "collapse of [...] understanding".[40] The novel would thus qualify as trauma narrative, presenting a fairly realistic evocation of how trauma haunts the subject without her knowing (and without the external narrator ever revealing it). This could lend a double justification to the fact that the various murders perpetrated by the protagonist are never evoked directly (13), as if she were not conscious of them or as if she denied them. Such a reading would account for the reason why Elizabeth Cree is compelled throughout to repeat in the present an action that she is unable to assimilate, being dominated by a compulsion to repeat, possibly the initial, unconfessed, inassimilable matricide that would thus be rehearsed in each one of her murders. Of course, such a view of the female artist as traumatised serial killer would lead us to reconsider her career as escape artist less in terms of choice than of compulsion. It could then be said that Elizabeth Cree does not choose gender performance but is compelled to choose gender performance. The trauma hypothesis may thus cast new light on her gender politics and justify the emergence of the female artist as compulsion.

On an altogether different plane, the heroine could also be envisaged as emblem of a trauma of a more collective, historical type, and the Golem that haunts the Limehouse streets would thus appear not as an emanation from the character (from a bottom-up perspective), but as the angry spirit of the age crushing the most helpless individuals (in a top-down movement). The shock of the second Industrial Revolution and of rampant urbanisation, and its consequences on the squalid living conditions of the London poor – a topos of Victorian studies –, may be seen to register in the demeanour and psyche of the most vulnerable citizens, the poorest, and among them, women. From this point of view, the story of Elizabeth Cree's artistic vocation in all its dimensions, complete with its Icarus-like falling trajectory, would be illustrative, in Françoise Davoine and Jean-Max Gaudillière's terms, of the individual and "social convulsions that tend to eliminate the subject".[41] Elizabeth Cree as self-fashioned and traumatised female artist would thus provide a metonymy for the subject of history as partly erased but also relentlessly existing, in a socially and historically conscious novel documenting woman's challenging and challenged rights as an individual artist at the turn of the twentieth century, a far cry from the vision of Ackroyd as uniquely concerned with male heroes.

Notes

1   For more information, see Ackroyd (1992) and more especially Ackroyd (2001a: 328-340; 2001b: 341-351).
2   Onega (1996: 216). In his lecture "London Luminaries and Cockney Visionaries", Ackroyd himself comments on the maleness of contemporary London authors, welcoming all the same such a novelist as Jeanette Winterson as one of the luminaries of visionary Englishness (2001b: 341). Interestingly, when envisaging the books that Ackroyd reviewed over the two decades preceding the publication of *The Collection* (2001) one realises that the quasi totality of them were written by male authors. He did review some of Virginia Woolf's collections of essays, though, in which he comments that she was essentially entrusted with women's books to review. That there is a gender role and practice inherent in reading and writing seems to be implied by consciousness of one's institutional practice of literature, but one of the purposes of this article is to insist on Ackroyd's bending of such conventions, as will be apparent in the following pages.
3   I am thinking of Dr Dee's clever perceptive wife in *The House of Dr Dee* whose contemporary avatar might be said to be Vivienne Wychwood in *Chatterton*.
4   Onega (1996: 143).
5   Huf (1983: 157).
6   Onega (1999: 131-134).
7   For a close analysis of that fragment, see Ganteau (2008: 153-164).
8   Letissier (2004: 320).
9   For an in-depth analysis of the Victorian context, see Onega (1999: 135-138).
10 It may also be reminiscent of Angela Carter's unforgettable *Nights at the Circus* (1984), in which the heroine, Fevvers, a winged female aerialist with apparently magical powers, is in full charge of her destiny in the context of turn-of-the-century Cockney England, and provides a decrowning literalisation of the Angel-in-the-House image.
11 Huf (1983: 156).
12 Ackroyd (1995: 55). Further references to this edition will be included in the text.
13 For more information on the "monopolylinguist" or "monypolylinguist" as impersonator going through a series of impersonations, shifting effortlessly from one to the other as one of the emblems of Englishness and of the English genius for imitation and assimilation, see Ackroyd (2001b: 344). A re-

lated notion is that of "pantomimesis" as indicated by Gibson & Wolfreys (2000: 68).

14 Needless to say, the image, borrowed from James Joyce's *A Portrait of the Artist as a Young Man* (1916), is taken up by Huf (1983: 150).

15 Onega (1999: 42-143).

16 Ackroyd (2004: 116).

17 Ackroyd (1993c: 48; 81).

18 See Ackroyd (1993b: 68) and (1993a: 50-53).

19 Ackroyd (1979: 60).

20 Glover & Kaplan (2000: 92).

21 Huf (1983: 4).

22 For a more sustained analysis of *The Passion*, see Susana Onega's contribution in the present volume.

23 Huf (1983: 150-151).

24 I would like to thank Justine Gonneaud for drawing my attention to this distinction present in the literature devoted to androgyny, and more especially in Delcourt (1992).

25 Huf (1983: 24).

26 *Ibid.*, 74.

27 *Ibid.*, 72.

28 Butler (2006: 187; emphasis in the text).

29 Gibson & Wolfreys (2000: 46-48).

30 Wolfreys (1997: 2).

31 *Ibid.*, 2.

32 Gibson & Wolfreys (2000: 49).

33 Ackroyd (1979: 18).

34 Butler (2006: 185).

35 Glover & Kaplan (2000: 120).

36 Butler (1997: 34-35).

37 Press (1999: 69-75).

38 On pronominal hesitation, see also Onega (1999: 142).

39 Press (1999: 69).

40 Caruth (1995: 9).

41 Davoine & Gaudillière (2004: 25; 47).

Bibliography

Ackroyd, Peter: *Dressing Up. Transvestism and Drag. The History of an Obsession*, Norwich, 1979.
–: *English Music*, Harmondsworth, 1992.
–: *Chatterton*, Harmondsworth, 1993a [1987].
–: *First Light*, Harmondsworth, 1993b [1989].
–: *The House of Dr Dee*, Harmondsworth, 1993c.

–: *Dan Leno and the Limehouse Golem*, Harmondsworth, 1995 [1994].

–: "The Englishness of English Literature". – In P.A. & Thomas Wright (Eds.): *The Collection. Journalism, Reviews, Essays, Short Stories, Lectures*, London, 2001a, pp. 328-340.

–: "London Luminaries and Cockney Visionaries". – In P.A. & Thomas Wright (Eds.): *The Collection. Journalism, Reviews, Essays, Short Stories, Lectures*, London, 2001b, pp. 341-351.

–: *The Lambs of London*, London, 2004.

Butler, Judith: *Gender Trouble. Feminism and the Subversion of Identity*, New York & London, 2006 [1990].

–: *Excitable Speech. A Politics of the Performative*, New York & London, 1997.

Caruth, Cathy (Ed.): *Trauma. Explorations in Memory*, Baltimore & London, 1995.

Davoine, Françoise & Jean-Max Gaudillière: *History beyond Trauma. Whereof One Cannot Speak ... Thereof One Cannot Stay Silent*, New York, 2004.

Delcourt, Marie: *Hermaphrodite. Mythes et rites de la bisexualité dans l'antiquité classique*, Paris, 1992.

Ganteau, Jean-Michel: *Peter Ackroyd et la musique du passé*, Paris, 2008.

Gibson, Jeremy & Julian Wolfreys: *Peter Ackroyd. The Ludic and Labyrinthine Text*, Houndmills, 2000.

Glover, David & Cora Kaplan: *Genders*, London, 2000.

Huf, Linda: *A Portrait of the Artist as a Young Woman. The Writer as Heroine in American Fiction*, New York, 1983.

Letissier, Georges: "Biographie d'une ville, temporalities d'une oeuvre. Londres selon Ackroyd". – In Ronald Shusterman (Ed.): *Des histoires du temps. Conceptions et représentations de la temporalité*, Pessac, 2004, pp. 303-322.

Onega, Susana: "Interview with Peter Ackroyd", *Twentieth Century Literature* 42:2, 1996, 208-220.

–: *Metafiction and Myth in the Novels of Peter Ackroyd*, Rochester, 1999.

Press, Jacques: *La perle et le grain de sable. Traumatisme et fonctionnement mental*, Lausanne, 1999.

Wolfreys, Julian: The Rhetoric of Affirmative Resistance. Dissonant Identities from Carroll to Derrida, London, 1997.

Silvia Mergenthal (Konstanz)

Visceral Music. The Female Composer in Bernard MacLaverty's *Grace Notes*

Bernard MacLaverty was born in Belfast in 1942, and lived in Northern Ireland until 1975, when he moved to Scotland. After periods spent in Edinburgh and on the Isle of Islay, he settled in Glasgow, where he still resides. *Grace Notes*, published in 1997 and short-listed for the Booker Prize, was the third of his four novels to date; it was preceded by *Lamb* (1980) and *Cal* (1983), and followed by *The Anatomy School* (2001). In addition, MacLaverty has published several collections of short stories, the first of which, *Secrets & Other Stories* (1980), contains a story entitled "My Dear Palestrina"; this testifies to MacLaverty's lifelong interest in music and prefigures, in the relationship between a young boy and his (female) music teacher, some of the themes and motifs which will later re-emerge in *Grace Notes*. MacLaverty has also written what he himself calls "versions of his fiction for other media",[1] that is, screen, television, and radio plays; among these are, for instance, a film adaptation of *Cal*, television and radio adaptations of "My Dear Palestrina", and a radio version of *Grace Notes*.

After the "predominantly masculine" worlds of *Lamb* and *Cal*,[2] *Grace Notes*, as a number of critics have noted,[3] presents itself as an extraordinary piece of narrative transvestism:[4] it employs a third-person limited point of view, with long passages narrated in free indirect discourse – occasionally shading over into stream of consciousness – and uses as its focaliser young Northern Irish composer Catherine McKenna.[5] Questioned on his decision to use a female voice, MacLaverty has commented:

> I think there is a level of shared humanity between the genders. We are all fifty per cent our sex and maybe fifty per cent human, so there is an overlap. Those aspects of creativity, making things up and music would have come out of me. I have researched the other aspects, but I did not

want just to create a handbag female; somebody described with lipstick and tampons.[6]

However, MacLaverty also links his choice of a female focaliser to having grown up in a feminised environment, and to a seminal conversation with a female writer:

> [m]y background information came from the women who had surrounded me in my childhood: I was brought up in a house where I had a mother and a grandmother and a great aunt. Across the street was my Aunt Cissie, and Cousin Anne. I was surrounded by strong, talking women! The novel was sparked off by a friend who is also a writer. She had to balance her writing with having babies. I think that was a starting point, and in a throwaway remark she made was the whole of the novel. She said, "It's all right for you – you don't have to have the babies." Biological production can get in the way of creativity and I was all right because I didn't have to have the children.[7]

Catherine McKenna is heavily pregnant with her daughter Anna; she has been living on the Isle of Islay with Anna's father Dave, an Englishman, for some time now, and has taught music in the local school. Anna's birth – for which Catherine had to be air-lifted from Islay to Glasgow – plunges her into post-partum depression, and deprives her of the ability to compose music. However, after her abusive partner has hit her, a walk on the beach of Islay with Anna, in the course of which she experiences a kind of spiritual rebirth – while Anna takes her first, faltering steps –, restores Catherine's creative abilities. She also finds the strength and determination to leave Dave and return to Glasgow, where she has spent formative years at the School of Music. Catherine's first long orchestral piece *Vernicle*, which has emerged from her Islay epiphany, is successfully premiered in Glasgow.

Several weeks after the premiere, Catherine is recalled to the small town in County Derry, where she grew up as a member of the Catholic community, for the funeral of her father. Catherine has been estranged from her parents for five years, and has neither told them about the birth of Anna, nor let them know that they could have listened to *Vernicle* on the radio. After the funeral, the prodigal daughter is confronted by her mother, who is horrified both by Catherine's status as a single mother, and by the fact that she has quit her secure job as a music teacher to concentrate on her work as composer. The two women do come to some kind of rapprochement just before Catherine's departure for Glasgow; even so, and not surprisingly under these circumstances, Catherine suffers a setback in terms of her medical condition, and relapses into depression. This time, however, she can still contemplate new musical projects, chiefly, a set of piano pieces ("*haiku* for piano"),[8] and a mass: "'[t]here's not too many masses written by women.' Catherine laughed. 'It's a way of getting my own back because they wouldn't let me serve at the altar'" (MacLaverty 1997: 111). On her return to Glasgow, Catherine is united with Anna, now eighteen months old, who has uttered her first word – predictably, "Mama" (137) – in her mother's absence.

Within this chronological frame, there are a number of flashbacks, chiefly to Catherine's childhood in Northern Ireland, but also to various stages of her career as a composer, and to her encounters with various mentors. The most important of Catherine's childhood musical experiences is her first conscious awareness of Lambeg drums (which she will later integrate into *Vernicle*), an instrument associated, as her father explains, with Northern Irish Protestantism and the annual July 12 marches to celebrate the victory of William of Orange at the Battle of the Boyne: "[o]n the Twelfth they thump them so hard and so long they bleed their wrists. Against the rim. Sheer bloody bigotry" (8). Catherine's father, incidentally, provides Catherine with another of her early musical memories: his taste tends towards the operatic – he venerates Irish classically-trained singers such as John McCormack (24) –, and he forbids her to listen to pop music, which he refers to as "noise pollution" (25).

As regards Catherine's mentors, the first of these is Miss Bingham (a Protestant music teacher), who, in one of her first lessons, asks Catherine to clap her own name:

> Then she understood. And clapped the rhythm of her name perfectly. Seven little claps in all – spaced out as her name was spoken. That was her.
> "Very good. But shouldn't it be six?"
> "My music name is my full name, Catherine Anne McKenna. Seven claps are better than six." (31)

This passage indicates that already for a very young Catherine music is bound up with a sense of selfhood and self-representation: the seven syllables of her name will later recur in the Credo ("*Cre* / *Do* / *In* / *Un* / *Um* / *De* / *Um*", 132-133; emphasis in the text) and in the Kyrie ("*Kyrie Eléison.* / *Christe Eleíson.* / Seven syllables answered by six syllables", 73; emphasis in the text) of the mass she is composing. At the same time, Catherine's clapping demonstrates that music, for her, is quite literally embodied in the human *physis*: not only does Catherine possess an almost preternaturally acute sense of hearing – the most frequently repeated words in the novel are "sound" and "noise" – but she is also taught, by her first male mentor, Chinese composer Huang Xiao Gang,[9] to improvise by "alternating 'breath sentences'" (35). Catherine herself will later compose what she calls "visceral music" (124; 274).

Huang Xiao Gang, like Catherine's second important male mentor, Ukrainian composer Anatoli Ivanovich Melnichuk – who bears a certain resemblance, at least in musical terms, to Arvo Pärt – represents a non-Western musical tradition which is very strongly rooted in ritual:[10] we learn that the only music Xiao Gang "had heard before reaching manhood was ritualistic – funeral music, wedding music" (33), while Melnichuk and his wife take Catherine, who visits them in Kiev, to an Orthodox church service where "all would be revealed about the source of his music and its spiritual intensity" (121). Melnichuk, in particular, also serves as an example of the political dimension of making music when he discusses Dmitri Shostakovich's *Babi Yar Symphony*, composed in commemoration of the 1941 massacre of 35,000 Jewish inhabitants of Kiev by the Germans (127). Catherine, remembering this conversation with Melnichuk,

> thought of the geography of the places of death in her own country – it was a map which would not exist if women made the decisions – Cornmarket, Claudy, Teebane Crossroads, Six Mile Water, the Bogside, Greysteel, the Shankill Road, Long Kesh, Dublin, Darkley, Enniskillen, Loughinisland, Armagh, Monaghan town. And of places of multiple deaths further to the east – Birmingham, Guildford, Warrington. (*Ibid.*)

On a somewhat different scale, Catherine's experience of listening to music, and eventually of composing music, is, as we have already seen in the instance of the Lambeg drums, embedded in the specific sociopolitical and cultural contexts of eighties and nineties Northern Ireland and Scotland. These contexts provoke some of Catherine's acts of musical rebellion, as when Miss Bingham takes her to a performance of Handel's *Messiah*, and she refuses to stand for the Hallelujah Chorus: "[c]an you imagine how I felt?" reminisces Miss Bingham, "[m]y little charge – sitting – while the whole of Ulster's concert-going public stood" (108). Later, Catherine will insist on calling a piece she has written for her pupils on Islay "Suite for Trumpetists and Tromboners", although her headmaster, "a business studies graduate", repeatedly suggests to her that she should correct her title to "Trumpeters and trombonists" (100). She will also, vis-à-vis the patriarchal tradition of the Catholic Church in Ireland, choose the mass – "[i]t's a great form, a great structure" (89) – for her next composition, and she will symbolically inscribe herself into the male-dominated tradition of classical music when she prints her name onto a poster entitled "The Masters of Classical Music": "[w]hat a testosterone brigade. The only woman, at the very bottom of the tree trunk, did not have a picture. Hildegard of Bingen, 1098-1179" (229).[11]

As Gerry Smyth has pointed out in *Music in Irish Cultural History* (2009), *Grace Notes* is only one of many novels published in recent years – "by an army of literary *galacticos*" –[12] to which music is of central importance: in Britain alone, there are Louis de Bernières's *Captain Corelli's Mandolin* (1994), Jeanette Winterson's *Art & Lies. A Piece for Three Voices and a Bawd* (1994),[13] James Kelman's *How Late It Was, How Late* (1994), Hanif Kureishi's *The Black Album* (1995), Kazuo Ishiguro's *The Unconsoled* (1995), Alan Warner's *Morvern Callar* (1995), Nick Hornby's *High Fidelity* (1995), Ian McEwan's *Amsterdam* (1998), Jackie Kay's *Trumpet* (1998), Salman Rushdie's *The Ground Beneath Her Feet* (1999), Vikram Seth's *An Equal Music* (1999), Rose Tremain's *Music and Silence* (1999), Jonathan Coe's *The Rotters' Club* (2001) Michel Faber's *The Courage Consort* (2002), Janice Galloway's *Clara* (2002), Zadie Smith's *On Beauty* (2005),[14] Russell Hoban's *My Tango with Barbara Strozzi* (2007), and A.N. Wilson's *Winnie and Wolf* (2007). Smyth refers to these texts as "music novels" as they engage "with musical matter through the medium of prose", often, though not invariably, attempting "to invoke musical effects and to incorporate musical form into [their] own structure".[15] So far, critics have linked *Grace Notes* to McEwan's *Amsterdam* and to Seth's *An Equal Music*, but an instructive point of reference – though unfortunately beyond the scope of this essay – might also be provided by

Janice Galloway's *Clara* (2002), a fictional biography of pianist and composer Clara Schumann, neé Wieck.

In *Grace Notes*, musico-literary intermediality is from the very beginning achieved through, in MacLaverty's own phrase, "assaulting" readers by noise:[16] on the first two pages alone, they are made to listen, along with the protagonist, to the noise of a car going past in the wet, a man whistling, airport chimes, flight announcements, the scream of a power-saw, a baby crying (3-4). At the same time, the novel encourages its readers to pay attention not only to the visual shape of words on paper, but also to how words sound: there are numerous examples of onomatopoeic words such as "tintinnabulation" (124), "screech", "clunk", "creak", "click", "glugg" (49), "tinkle" and "jingle" (50). More importantly, as will become apparent later, Catherine is fascinated by phenomena such as homophony – "Lynn C. Doyle and linseed oil", "Bartók and bar talk" (25) – and polysemy: in both cases, the same sound produces different meanings, which, if only for a brief moment in time, the mind is able to hold simultaneously, making homophony and polysemy the auditory equivalents of picture puzzles (275). Finally, *Grace Notes* is full of references to 'real' composers and their compositions, both as influences on Catherine's own work, and presumably as indicative of what her music would sound like. Catherine does take Scottish and Irish influences on board: *Vernicle*, her submission to a European Broadcasting Union contest which "would look favourably on works which included an instrument more associated with music of ethnic origins" (261), will, after all, include Lambeg drums. But her musical taste is wide-ranging enough to stretch to Purcell and Bach, or to Schumann and Mahler. Among twentieth-century composers she prefers Janácek, Shostakovich or Messiaen to Schönberg and Stockhausen, which of course suggests that her compositions are more likely to be tonal than atonal. Taken together, this plurality of musical references, as well as Catherine's choice of non-Western mentors, also helps to dissociate her from the systematic association of Irishness with musicality, which, as Gerry Smyth has shown, has for centuries brought "a socio-political agenda to bear upon musicological discourse".[17] Smyth shows how, from the eighteenth century onwards, music became an important measure of Irish identity both in Ireland itself and in the Irish diaspora, so that, by what he calls a "reciprocal maneuvre [...], Irishness soon became a measure of music"; he goes on to ask:

> [w]hat systems – institutional and otherwise – exist for demarcating the gradations of musical identity (*non-Irish, Irish, Irisher, Irishest*), and, when these gradations have been established, to reward the worthy and sanction the undeserving?[18]

According to Smyth, one of the key works in the process of mapping Irish music on to Irish cultural identity, and vice versa, is Thomas Moore's collection *Irish Melodies* (1808-1834). MacLaverty, incidentally, plays a (as it were, nicely polysemous as well as intermedial) trick on his readers when he has Catherine refer colloquially to "Silent O' Moyle" (73; 253): "Silent O' Moyle" is a well-known song from *Irish Melodies* and is alluded to repeatedly by James Joyce (in *Dubliners*, 1914; *Ulysses*, 1922 and *Finnegans Wake*, 1939). In *Grace Notes*, it also nods towards what is one of the most influential modern *Künstlerromane*, Joyce's *A Portrait of the Artist as a Young Man* (1916).[19]

This, finally, raises the question of how Catherine herself works as a composer, music-making being, perhaps – at least to non-musicians – a much more mysterious creative activity than either painting or writing. Catherine, it seems, relies on her auditory memory, that is, a repertoire of sounds – and silences – which she can use as building blocks for her own compositions, but she is also engaged in what might be called, in analogy to life-writing, life-composing,[20] in the dual sense of drawing upon the experiences of her own life, and of giving that life shape and meaning.

Thus, for instance, *Vernicle* originates in the liminal landscape of a beach at Islay and proceeds from pre-hearing, which segues into inner hearing (213), to something which Catherine will eventually commit to paper, and eventually to its triumphant first performance. In the closing pages of the novel Catherine herself listens to this premiere, and re-identifies the motifs which she has integrated into the textured tale of her composition: the walk on the beach with Anna; other "everyday stuff" (270) such as her mother's bread-making, weaving, the ornaments in the *Book of Kells*, fingers locked in prayer, becoming pregnant, giving birth to a child and suffering from post-partum depression, the Lambeg drums of her own childhood, the bells she has heard at Kiev, and so on: "[i]t had shaped itself into two long movements – the *yin* and *yang*, so to speak. The first was male, the second definitely female" (223; emphasis in the text). The result is a creative synthesis:[21]

> [e]xhilaration comes from nowhere. The bell-beat, the slabs of brass, the whooping of the horns, the battering of the drums. Sheer fucking unadulterated joy. Passion and pattern. An orchestra at full tilt – going fortissimo – the bows, up and down, jigging and sawing in parallel – the cellos and basses sideways. The brass shining and shouting at the back. The orchestra has become a machine, a stitching machine. The purpose of training an army is to dehumanise, to make a machine of people yet here all this discipline, all this conformity was to express the individuality and uniqueness of one human being. Catherine Anne's vision. A joy that celebrates being human. A joy that celebrates its own reflection, its own ability to make joy. To reproduce.
>
> The orchestra soars in conjunction with the Lambegs, and the Lambegs roar in response to the orchestra and the effect is as she had hoped for. Her baby. *Deo gratias.* Anna's song. (276; emphasis in the text)

As various critics remind us, *Grace Notes* was written, and *Vernicle* presumably composed, in the nineties, during a time in which "the Peace Process was creating a cultural dividend in Northern Ireland while also revising the image of the Irish as a benighted, unforgiving race".[22] Although Catherine herself resists a political interpretation of her music (105), it is, of course, in the context of the Northern Irish situation that her use of the Lambeg drums is particularly significant: they appear in the two symmetrical movements of Catherine's composition – in the first part, with the effect of "[a] brutalising of the body, the spirit, humanity" and "utter despair" (273), in the second with the effect described above, "sheer fucking unadulterated joy". This act of de-contextualisation and re-contextualisation, in the course of which the drums are deprived of their "sheer bloody bigotry", is due to homophony, "an optical illusion in sound":

> [t]he same thing could be two things. Transubstantiation. How could the drum battering of the first movement be the same as the drum battering of the second movement – how could the same drumming in a different context produce a totally opposite effect? The sound has transformed itself. Homophones. Linseed oil. Lynn C. Doyle. Bar talk. Bartók – the same sound but with a different meaning. (275)

At this point, and in light of such remarks as "[h]er baby. *Deo gratias*. Anna's song" – or, elsewhere in the account of Catherine's listening experience: "[s]ound shaking the blood from the walls of her womb. The rhythm of a woman's life is synchronised with the moon and the moon is synchronised with the sea, ergo – a woman is synchronised with the tides" (274) – one needs to address the question to what extent Catherine's creative vision is shown to be determined by her gender, and specifically, by her reproductive role, which appears to tie her to natural forces. To rephrase the title of a famous essay by Sherry B. Ortner,[23] is Catherine to male composers as nature is to culture?

Grace Notes has, in fact, been described as stressing "a re-visioning of silence and the gaps between sounds as the basis of bringing an essentialist understanding of female cultural and corporeal identity out of the histories and narratives that have silenced them".[24] It is, perhaps, hardly surprising that an act of life-composing by a female composer – who, moreover, expressly writes "visceral music" – should also include giving birth among the formative experiences it draws upon. However, while the novel is indeed situated, as Wondrich has claimed, at the "crucial nexus of opposition and integration between [...] two forms of creativity",[25] namely, (literally) giving birth to a child and (metaphorically) giving birth to a piece of music, it tends to conceptualise the former in terms of the latter rather than the other way around.[26] In other words, *Grace Notes* seems to suggest, once again through a cluster of motifs involving homophony, polysemy and optical illusion, that these two activities, and the creative forces expressed through them, are held in a precarious balance, a suggestion which is borne out by the various implications of the title of the novel, and by its structure.

The first part of the title, 'grace', is, to state the obvious, a word with several layers of meaning which range, on the one hand, from beauty or charm of form to the unmerited love and favour of God towards humanity, and, still in a theological frame of reference, to God's influence acting on human beings to make them pure and morally strong. In musicology, on the other hand, 'grace notes' are notes which are not necessary to the melody of a piece, but are added for ornamentation and usually printed as smaller notes in between the 'main' notes which they are supposed to embellish. As Stephen Benson explains:

> [t]wo elements stand out: that the grace note is supplemental to a given piece of music, and yet an integral part of its effect, and that its status in relation to the text of music is either non-existent (unnotated, so immaterial) or visibly marginal.[27]

Both the theological and the musicological dimensions of grace (notes) are exploited in the novel: Melnichuk, Catherine's Ukrainian mentor, describes music as "a way of praying, [...] a way of receiving God's grace" (125), while a secularised version of grace in the sense of being made pure and morally strong is experienced by Miss Bingham when she listens to Catherine's music (112), and by Catherine herself, listening to her own piece being performed: "[f]illing herself with her own grace" (271).

As for the musical aspects of grace notes, Huang Xiao Gang quite explicitly associates them, once again, with the composer, and with the composer's body, when he asks his students: "[d]o you compose the music or does the music compose you? Where are the notes between the notes? Graces, grace notes or, as the French would have it, *agréments*" (33; emphasis in the text). This suggests, ultimately, that Catherine herself, in and through her life-composing and as a "reluctant embodiment of a grace note",[28] drifts towards a precarious position in-between: this in-betweenness can either be construed as a source of weakness, relegating her, as a female composer, to the ornamental margins of a male tradition writ large – or, as a Northern Irish Catholic woman, to the margins of a patriarchal society – but it can also become a source of strength, as in Catherine's most extended meditation on grace notes when she has begun to compose her *Credo*. Like *Vernicle*, the credo will achieve a (by definition, precarious) synthesis:

> [g]race notes – notes which were neither one thing nor the other. A note between the notes. Notes that occurred outside time. Ornaments dictating the character of the music, the slur and slide of it. *This is decoration becoming substance*. Like a round in Granny Boyd's kitchen. Or Purcell's Songs of the Tavern. Soarings. Voices slipping. Joining folk music and art music. East and West. Male and female. (133; my emphasis)

At this point, and deliberately late in this essay, the structural oddity of *Grace Notes* needs to be addressed, namely the novel's startling discrepancy between plot – as in a sequence of events presented in a literary text – and story – as in a sequence of events which the reader reconstructs on the basis of their arrangements in the narrative: in terms of the events which they chronicle, the two parts of the novel are presented in reverse order.

On the plot level, the novel opens with Catherine's return to Northern Ireland for her father's funeral, and thus mid-way in the story, and it ends with the first performance of *Vernicle*. In other words, and still on the plot level, Catherine travels from Glasgow to Northern Ireland and back again, and from Islay to Glasgow – or else from the nadir of her father's funeral to the triumphant height of musical success, surmounting her post-partum depression in the process. On the story level, however, it is the triumphant heights of musical success from which, relapsing into depression, Catherine travels to her father's funeral, and her story does not end with her success as a composer, but with her reunion with her daughter. On the plot level, then, Catherine appears to be cast as a composer, who also happens to be someone's daughter and mother – on the story level, she is a daughter and mother, who also happens to be a composer. The contradictory movements of plot and story are encapsulated in the opening and closing sentences of the novel – "[s]he went down the front steps" (3) and "[s]he rose" (277): does Catherine descend at the beginning in order to rise at the end, or does she rise only to have to descend once again? And, in what MacLaverty himself calls the "hinge" between the two parts of the novel,[29] in Catherine's life, will "Credo" (the last word of the first half; 138) forever be echoed by "Day Grow" (the first words of the second half; 141), or is it actually the other way around? As for the situation in Northern Ireland, this is certainly not resolved allegorically by the musical re-contextualisation of the Lambeg drums in Catherine's scallop-shaped composition: when Catherine travels from Glasgow to Northern Ireland for the funeral, she is treated like a potential terrorist by airport security, and she returns to a "place of devastation" as the centre of her home town has been destroyed by a bomb and is "nothing but a *shell*" (10; my emphasis). She also re-enters a community which is still deeply divided and in which Protestant mourners still "wouldn't be seen dead in a house where the Rosary was being said" (55).

And, finally, if MacLaverty's novel is, like Catherine's orchestral piece of music, a vernicle composed of two symmetrical halves, the one a musical rendering of despair, the other of hope, or one successfully fusing the discordant parts of Catherine's experience, the other representing their disintegration – which of the two halves of MacLaverty's book is represented by which half of *Vernicle*, the first or the second? 'Vernicle', incidentally, is yet another word the various meanings of which are exploited to the full in the novel: a vernicle is a medieval pilgrim's badge – scallop-shaped (like Catherine's composition and MacLaverty's novel) in the case of pilgrims returning from Santiago de Compostela – but also "a representation of the face of Christ impressed on Veronica's handkerchief. Or any image of Christ made by an artist and used for devotional purposes" (245; see 104).

MacLaverty's novel, then, both suggests the interrelatedness of narratives of Northern Irish pacification,[30] and of female artistic emancipation (from patriarchal Northern Irish society as well as from patriarchal musical tradition), and resists facile appropriation by either of these celebratory discourses. At best, to reiterate a persistent theme of the novel and of this essay, centripetal and centrifugal forces can be held in a precarious balance: one of the "*haikus* for piano" which Catherine is composing is entitled "*Woman Holding Balance*" (109; emphasis in the text), but "the slightest carelessness could bring her down on one side or the other" (121).

Notes

1 See MacLaverty's homepage listed in the bibliography.
2 Monteith, Newman & Wheeler (2004: 109).
3 See, e.g., Ganter's rather snide remarks in his review of *Grace Notes*: "[b]y giving voice to a young woman on her quest for female selfhood, MacLaverty has dared to broach a topic for which a male writer can easily get into hot water" (1997: 114). And: "[i]t is a stirring book on the immeasurable power of music and an important piece on womanhood – although written by a man" (*ibid.*, 116); see also Wondrich (2000: 141).
4 The term "narrative transvestism" was initially coined by Madeleine Kahn in her influential monograph on the eighteenth-century novel (1991) and adapted, with slight modifications, for nineteenth-century canonical texts such as Charlotte Brontë's *Shirley* (1849) and Charles Dickens's *Bleak House* (1852) by Ina Schabert (1997: 483-490).
5 Catherine is a fictitious character, but is said to resemble Scottish composer Judith Weir; see Benson (2006: 144).
6 MacLaverty in an interview conducted by Morales Ladrón (2000: 206).
7 MacLaverty in Monteith, Newman & Wheeler (2004: 110).

8   McLaverty (1997: 109; emphasis in the text). Further references to this edition will be included in the text.

9   Huang Xiao Gang is based on Chinese composer Tan Dun. As MacLaverty explains in the Monteith-Newman-Wheeler interview, he attended a composer's workshop, where Tan Dun, like Huang Xiao Gang in the novel, "worked on a stage with about ten music students. There were no musical instruments and he used breath and voice to compose – along with mouth pops and hand claps. He talked about pre-hearing and inner hearing. I was sitting rapt on the edge of my seat in a lecture on composition listening to people breathing" (Monteith, Newman & Wheeler 2004: 111).

10 See Benson (2006: 114).

11 See also the conversation Catherine has with yet another of her male mentors, Helmut Lemberg, in which she recounts a conversation she has had with a BBC producer, whom she asks "'how a composer could get their first work performed. Do you know what he said?' Lemberg shook his head. 'He should try the Society for Promotion of New Music. Can you imagine?' 'And what was wrong with that?' 'He's a she. He's me'" (McLaverty 1997: 64-65).

12 Smyth (2009: 140; emphasis in the text).

13 For Winterson, see Susana Onega's contribution in the present volume.

14 For Smith, see Anette Pankratz's contribution in the present volume.

15 Smyth (2009: 140). For a comparison between Seth and MacLaverty, see Ruge, who discusses both novels as texts which draw on established narratives about classical composers and musicians, namely, the pathography and the wunderkind story (2005). For a comparison between *Grace Notes* and *Amsterdam* see Benson (2006: 129-140) and Bushnell (2007: 60-99).

16 Monteith, Newman & Wheeler (2004: 111).

17 Smyth (2009: 4).

18 *Ibid.*; emphasis in the text.

19 See Seret (1992: 91-116).

20 Harte & Parker refer variously to Catherine's "aural self-translation" and her "self-composure" (2000: 243; 249).

21 The phrase is Barry Sloan's; see Sloan (2006: 313).

22 Smyth (2009: 96). On the Northern Irish context of *Grace Notes*, see also Harte & Parker (2000: 232-233).

23 "Is Female to Male as Nature is to Culture?" (1974).

24 See Peach (2004: 218).

25 Wondrich (2000: 141).

26 In the delivery room, Catherine muses "it was a bit like composing music, really, parading the personal as they all stood at the bottom looking at the pain which was now cracking her open and which was responsible for her yelling so that a nurse who seemed to be orchestrating the whole thing came to her to hold her hand" (MacLaverty 1997: 161-162). For an analysis of these and similar passages, see Bushnell; she concludes: "[t]aken to-

gether, these examples suggest not that art is natural but that what is natural (birthing) is artistic (music)" (2007: 96-97).

27 Benson (2006: 130).

28 *Ibid.*, 131; on Catherine's role as a kind of grace note personified, see also Sloan (2006: 311); Bushnell (2007: 88-89) and Watt (2002).

29 MacLaverty in his interview with Morales Ladrón (2001: 203-204).

30 Smyth (2009: 142).

Bibliography

Benson, Stephen: *Literary Music. Writing Music in Contemporary Fiction*, Aldershot, 2006.

Bushnell, Fae Cameron: *Imagining Other Worlds. Literary Constructions of Alterity Through Music*. Unpublished PhD thesis, 2007. http://drum.lib.umd.edu/bitstream/1903/7145/1/umi-umd-4385.pdf (accessed 6 May 2011).

Ganter, C.J.: "Bernard MacLaverty. *Grace Notes*", *The International Fiction Review* 24, 1997, 114-116.

Harte, Liam & Michael Parker: "Reconfiguring Identities. Recent Northern Irish Fiction". – In L.H. & M.P.: *Contemporary Irish Fiction. Themes, Tropes, Theories*, Basingstoke, 2000, pp. 232-254.

Kahn, Madeleine: *Narrative Transvestism. Rhetoric and Gender in the Eighteenth-Century Novel*, Ithaca, 1991.

Ladrón, Marisol Morales: "'Writing is a State of Mind not an Achievement'. An Interview with Bernard MacLaverty", *Atlantis* 23:3, 2001, 201-211.

MacLaverty, Bernard: *Grace Notes*, London, 1997.

–: http://www.maclaverty.com (accessed 6 May 2011).

Monteith, Sharon, Jenny Newman & Pat Wheeler: *Contemporary British and Irish Fiction. An Introduction Through Interviews*, London, 2004.

Ortner, Sherry B.: "Is Female to Male as Nature is to Culture?" [1974]. – In Jessica Munns & Gita Rajan (Eds.): *A Cultural Studies Reader. History, Theory, Practice*, Harlow, 1995, pp. 491-508.

Peach, Linden: *The Contemporary Irish Novel. Critical Readings*, Basingstoke, 2004.

Ruge, Enno: "Angry Young Musicians. Vikram Seth's *An Equal Music* and Bernard MacLaverty's *Grace Notes*". – In Lilo Moessner & Christa M. Schmidt (Eds.): *Anglistentag Aachen 2004. Proceedings*, Trier, 2005, pp. 261-272.

Schabert, Ina: *Englische Literaturgeschichte. Eine neue Darstellung aus der Sicht der Geschlechterforschung*, Stuttgart, 1997.

Seret, Roberta: *Voyage Into Creativity. The Modern* Künstlerroman, New York, 1992.

Sloan, Barry: "The Redress of Imagination. Bernard MacLaverty's *Grace Notes*". – In Emily Griesinger & Mark Eaton (Eds.): *The Gift of Story. Narrating Hope in a Postmodern World*, Waco, 2006, pp. 303-315.

Smyth, Gerry: *Music in Irish Cultural History*, Dublin, 2009.

Watt, Stephen: "Beckett, Late Modernism, and Bernard MacLaverty's *Grace Notes*", *New Hibernia Review* 6:2, 2002, 53-64.

Wondrich, Roberta Gefter: "The Pain Within. Female Bodies, Illness and Motherhood in Contemporary Irish Fiction", *Textus* 13, 2000, 129-148.

Christian Schmitt-Kilb (Rostock)

Re-Reading the Re-Written Portrait of the Young Artist.
Bernardine Evaristo's *Lara*s

1. Introduction

Bernardine Evaristo's novel in verse *Lara* (1997; 2009) is a semi-autobiographical growing-up novel, or novel of transformation,[1] featuring a young Nigerian-Irish-Brazilian-English-German mixed-race woman growing up in sixties and seventies London. Evaristo, herself a typical exponent (if there is such a thing) of a "hyphenated identity" in a postcolonial world,[2] traces her fictional alter ego's family history and consequentially evokes "the history of the European conquest of South America and the colonization of Africa" together with the "population movements these imperial enterprises induced".[3]

There are two versions of the text in existence, the 1997 original version and an extended 2009 edition with roughly 40 pages added to an original 140 pages. In the earlier version, Lara is literally born into the story after less than a third of the total text while in the 2009 edition readers have to consume half the book until Evaristo makes good on the promise of the novel's title. The additional material in the new version mainly elaborates on the maternal Irish side of Lara's family tree, aspects relatively underrepresented in the 1997 edition which mainly concentrates on the history of the Nigerian father. In the new edition, *Lara*, and Lara, are 50 percent history.

Lara's quest to uncover the history of her family in order to find herself follows a non-chronological pattern which is mirrored by the structure of the book itself. The narrative is delivered through the voices of many characters – from ancestors' spirits to Lara's forefathers and -mothers to Lara herself. What might at first glance appear as an example of deliberately chosen techniques of postmodern aesthetics – fragmentation, a-chronological narration, multi-perspectivity – turns out, in the context of Lara's quest, to be a historical and geographical necessity. Lara's transcultural character and identity emerge through "plaiting together different strands of culture and ancestry" – and geography, I would like to add – "into a linked yet by no means homogenizing narrative".[4]

Most readers and critics of the novel have either remarked upon the original narrative form of the novel,[5] highlighted Africa as a key reference point for an understanding of Lara's quest,[6] and/or, rightly and understandably, read the novel in a postcolonial framework focusing upon politics, racism and discrimination as major factors in the protagonist's often painful search for her identity.[7] The novel genre, Dominic Head writes in 2002, "has proved to be a fruitful site for investigating the hybridized cultural forms that might be produced in an evolving, and so *genuinely*, multicultural Britain".[8] Critical interpretations of *Lara* (1997), a text which definitely bears out Head's claim and deserves investigations of the kind he mentions, have made extensive use of the analytical terminology provided by postcolonial studies in general and key thinkers such as Frantz Fanon, Edward Said, Homi Bhabha, Gayatri Spivak *et al.* in particular: hybridity and the third space, transculturality, transnationality and translation, the subaltern and (post)colonial subject(ivity), to name but the most current. The results of many of these readings have been fruitful and impressive and not much remains to be uncovered about Evaristo's debut novel, it seems, from this critical perspective.

There are aspects of the novel, though, which have not so much been in the centre of interest in discussions about the book. I will start with a reading of *Lara* which places emphasis on the protagonist's steps towards becoming an artist and the obstacles posed by tradition, family, peers and society to developing her imaginative skills. Following this, I am going to add some thoughts on the rather unlikely relationship between Bernardine Evaristo and Virginia Woolf, or between *Lara* and *To the Lighthouse* (1927). While novels which were written at about the same time as *Lara* are usually invoked as comparative and concept-forming intertexts (Andrea Levy, Kiran Adebayo, Zadie Smith), I am going to suggest a reading of *Lara* in the context of modernist portraits of the artist with Woolf's novel *To the Lighthouse* as a reference text. This is pertinent, I find, in order to widen the critical horizon and to more fully appreciate Evaristo's impressive achievement. A comparison of both versions of *Lara* and a special appreciation of the additions in the second version will lead to the suggestion that some key ideas of Woolf are still being powerfully reworked in contemporary women's fiction.

The essay at hand is of course heavily indebted to the aforementioned interpretations, most of all to Mark Stein's brilliant analysis. My first aim is to do critical justice to the achievements of *Lara* (2009), which has not been discussed extensively because of its very recent date of publication;[9] my second aim is to provide some material for a bridge-building between postcolonial concerns and more traditional attempts at making sense of contemporary fiction. Thus the following thoughts ought to be taken as a long footnote to the current postcolonial interpretations of *Lara*.

2. Imagination and its Repression

2.1 Lara

Before Lara is allowed (and allows herself) to make artistic expression her main aim and occupation in life, she has to negotiate a long history of imagination and its repression which runs through the family. Fantasy, imagination and history are fundamentally linked in the novel. The first evidence of Lara's vivid imagination – and its critical observation by her parents – is when she sees the "Daddy People in the garden singing me", a recurrent (day-)dream of Lara's which makes her mother Ellen angry: "[t]oo fanciful, too boisterous / and too much silly imagination for her own good. / [...] It had to stop".[10] Lara's father Taiwo commands a strict, often cruel and violent regiment in the family, particularly over his eight children. His mantra is discipline. He is convinced that in order to make his children fit for the "harsh harsh world" he has to "show them the ropes". They "will not swim in a lake of lost dreams, / with discipline they will flourish" (Evaristo 1997: 50; Evaristo 2009: 105). He takes particular issue with playing in the street and, accompanied by growls of "[d]iscipline! [...] Discipline! Discipline!" (Evaristo 1997: 52; Evaristo 2009: 107), punishes Lara severely when she transgresses that law. A climax is reached at Lara's seventh birthday party when she happily dances through the garden trying to summon the Daddy People with "her magic wand, a branch" until she is interrupted by Taiwo who "furiously snatches the wand, breaks it clean in two" (Evaristo 1997: 54; Evaristo 2009: 109). For the first time, Lara resists her father's aggression, talks back and as a consequence is beaten with the broken wand. For the first time also, she is not afraid but angry: "[t]hat night in bed she called the Daddy People to her, / said farewell, willed them away forever" (*ibid.*).

What has the suppression of the child's urge to play got to do with the development of the artist? The nexus between the child's play, imagination and the artist's creativity has been described and analysed by Sigmund Freud. In his essay "The Relation of the Poet to Daydreaming" (1908), he writes that

> we ought surely to look in the child for the first traces of imaginative activity. [...] Perhaps we may say that every child at play behaves like an imaginative writer, in that he creates a world of his own or, more truly, he rearranges the things of his world and orders it in a new way that pleases him better. [...] He takes his play very seriously and expends a great deal of emotion on it. The opposite of play is not serious occupation but – reality. [...] The writer does the same thing as the child at play; he creates a world of phantasy which he takes very seriously.[11]

Willing the Daddy People away marks Lara's involuntary entrance to the world of the grown-ups governed by the law of the father ("[d]iscipline!"), a world in which she "breathed a life of rules instilled through fear" (Evaristo 1997: 54; Evaristo 2009: 110). The suppression of playing equals the attempt to suppress the freedom of the imagination with the aim to replace 'serious' play with the reality principle. Lara does not stop daydreaming, though, but her dreaming has to find different outlets. Narratologically speaking, her imaginations begin to cluster around new ideas and issues on the level of story, while on the level of discourse, the novel itself is the result of the protagonist's redirected creative energy.

On the story level, riding her bike offers room for imagination: "she rode her imagination [...] pretending to free wheel down country hills" (Evaristo 1997: 59; Evaristo 2009: 113). But most importantly, she discovers the library and the world of books and begins to identify with characters in fiction: "Lara became the beautiful Maisie in 'The Orphan Girl' / a story she'd made up, like Dickens" or "Captain Scott / a brave lone figure conquering the vast desolate white" (*ibid.*), while Thor Heyerdal sailed her to Fatu Hiva (Evaristo 1997: 71; Evaristo 2009: 125). In a classic case of what Roman Jakobson has described as the poetic principle of language, alliteration and contiguity turn library and liberty into a cross-referencing, semantically related pair: "[e]xpeditions in books borrowed from the *library* / *liberated* her from the environs of Arundel Road" (Evaristo 1997: 59; Evaristo 2009: 113; my emphasis).[12]

So long as Lara is able to identify with fictional characters, these flights of the imagination suffice to compensate for the child's urge to play. This changes dramatically during puberty. Noticing her physical difference in comparison with her age-mates goes hand in hand with a challenge to her innocence at the experience of racial abuse instigated by friends of her best friend Soo. Lara is shocked and wants to go home, but the feeling of home is not an easily available concept for a person who cannot find herself "on the screen, billboard, books, magazines, / and first and last not in the mirror". Searching for "an image, / a story, to speak me, describe me, birth me whole" (Evaristo 1997: 69; Evaristo 2009: 121) she realises that the representational images which the majority society has to offer do not fit her. At precisely this moment, she distances herself from the books she used to like so much. They lose their potential for identification. As a result, she longs to be invisible and to draw attention to herself at the same time. A few years later, art will give Lara the chance to accomplish that trick. Then she will be able to express her identity through paintings while keeping her distance from the self-representations at the same time. But for the time being, the antithetical wish to be simultaneously "invisible" and "noticed" (Evaristo 1997: 70; Evaristo 2009: 124) must be endured.

Lara's artistic expression is obviously triggered by the necessity to let her imagination come into its own and to write/paint/express herself in order to fill the identification gap. There are strong parallels to be observed between Lara and the author. Talking about herself in interviews, Evaristo has argued that growing up in a time "where images of people of colour were almost unknown in the UK", when "the local library had no books by black people" and the available images of people of colour in public were negative, "the cumulative effect was almost total invalidation by society at large". She continues:

> [p]eople in the majority culture of a society often don't understand this need for validation. Over the years I've heard such people say, "I don't read fiction to see myself in it!" Well neither do I now, but don't we all look for writing that explains ourselves to ourselves when we're younger? When the gap between our own cultural backgrounds and those portrayed in literature is a chasm, we can fall into it, screaming, sometimes silently or sometimes noisily, as I did. I loved literature, but literature, it seemed, did not love me.[13]

Artistic expression for Lara and, as it appears, also for her author, is a consequence of a disappointed love affair with the literary canon. Evaristo acknowledges that after having come into contact with African-American writing in the years after school, she "blocked out" everything she had read before, especially the canon: "Shakespeare? Dickens? They had nothing to do with me. I was on another mission altogether". As a young reader, Lara also opens herself up to the figures she encounters in world literature but she has to realise that they do not open up to "a mixed-race girl growing up in a devastatingly dull suburb of Woolwich in south east London".[14] Coming back to the story/discourse dichotomy: on the level of discourse the willing away of the Daddy People consists in the writing/telling of the story itself. When Lara begins to "travel the former colonial routes" as a postcolonial subject "in a mythopoeic quest for origins",[15] the journey together with the telling/writing of it serves to trace her own roots and to exorcise the repressive legacy of her father.

2.2 The Parents: Taiwo and Ellen

In the case of Lara's father Taiwo, Evaristo emphasises right from the start the role which artistic and media representations – literary texts, radio, films, TV – have played in his construction of London, England, Britain. Taiwo is introduced listening to the radio and watching British films which fuel his dreams of a better life in England. The England he nourishes in his mind is shaped by readings of classic literature (William Shakespeare and Percy Bysshe Shelley are explicitly mentioned) and by clichés according to which he imagines himself strolling "through the city with bowler and brolly" (Evaristo 1997: 132; Evaristo 2009: 182). When he finally arrives in Liverpool in 1949, a year after the passing of the British

Nationality Act, he tries hard and largely unsuccessfully to reconcile the England of his mind with the actuality he encounters on the streets of Liverpool. Once he has moved to London and met his future wife Ellen, films continue to be important for them (Evaristo 1997: 9; Evaristo 2009: 25). Even though Taiwo works hard to suppress manifestations of childishness, playfulness and imagination in himself and in his daughter Lara, he also is a man of the imagination. On the page before his speech about discipline and the need to escape "the lake of lost dreams", we overhear his own poetic voice on the bus on his way to work where he laments his fate metaphorically and comments with self-irony on his own literary potential:

> Life is a boxing ring without referee, judge or prize.
> How I tire of defending my right to exist on these
> great British isles. How I ache with invisible bruises.
> How I long to saunter casually down the road
> without tensing my stomach muscles, ready for foes.
> Hey! What a speech! I will write a play. One to rival
> Saint Joan. "The Tired Boxer" by Taiwo da Costa,
> the brilliant new Bernard Shaw from the colonies.
> (Evaristo 1997: 49; Evaristo 2009: 25)

There will be no Taiwo the playwright, he knows, even though he keeps on reading and dreaming about a better life. He has to provide for his family in a job where his "imagination dies and [his] soul suffocates" (*ibid.*).

Shortly before that passage, we witness Lara's mother Ellen imagining herself as a poet. In an extended metaphor of Miltonesque length, she describes her average Saturday night household chores through the filter of associations other people may have thinking about that particular day of the week: a recreational night out, fun and love making. Down at her "psychedelic disco", she makes "passionate and intimate love with some hard green soap" seducing the children's clothes before her "final flirtation [...] with an iron and ironing board [...]! By 12 the party's over" and only sleep seems to redeem her, but "just as I nod off my youngest starts screaming" (Evaristo 1997: 47; Evaristo 2009: 102).

Just as Taiwo and Lara, Ellen has a vivid imagination ("[i]f I were a poet", *ibid.*) which was simultaneously encouraged and rejected early on in her life. Her mother Edith (in the 2009 *Lara* her name is Peggy) pours "dreams onto Ellen like syrup on treacle tart"

247

and forbids "playing in the street" (Evaristo 1997: 16; Evaristo 2009: 28) at the same time. For Edith/Peggy also, discipline and cleanliness are more than secondary virtues, and hard work the only path to the fulfilment of dreams. Ellen likes to read as well, but when she does so she is told that she is "being lazy sitting around doing nothing" and that she will "end up in a factory if I do not do what she says" (Evaristo 1997: 23; Evaristo 2009: 60). Evaristo's method to accredit the different characters with their own voices blurs the lines between Lara's discourse, authorial stance and individual perspectives. The reader feels distant from and close to Taiwo and Ellen at the same time because it is difficult to decide whether we hear Lara retroactively investing her parents with her own voice, or whether the parents themselves conceive of their situations in poetic form.

In the added passages of the new *Lara* a tradition of reading is indicated which runs through that part of Lara's ancestry. It finds its culmination in Lara herself, and brings into focus the specific difficulties of women who try to develop in themselves their imaginative potential. Her mother's grandmother Emma, an Irish servant in a manor house, believes in the power of words (Evaristo 2009: 36) and is shown reading *Pride and Prejudice* by candlelight (37), her daughter Mary Jane, Ellen's mother and Lara's grandmother, enjoys reading *The Picture of Dorian Gray* (50) to her mother Emma.[16] What hinders these women to live their creativity more fully is the work they have to do as mothers and organisers of their households.

The topic comes to the fore in a passage which is essential to understand Lara's path towards finding her identity. It is one of the rare scenes which are related to alternating points of view. When Lara is about sixteen years old we overhear her mother Ellen who feels unconsoled and almost paralysed in her role as worrying mother. The kids grow up and "run off into adulthood" while Ellen remains in the house, "a Russian Doll, peering, down the dark street" (Evaristo 1997: 78; Evaristo 2009: 132). She feels betrayed not so much by life as by the sentimental stories she has fed herself with in form of romantic novels ("Barbara Cartland has betrayed me", *ibid.*). Helpless in the face of her mother's melancholia, Lara suddenly realises that apart from racial discrimination, her prospective role as wife and mother in a society organised along the lines of a patriarchal matrix will stand in her way towards self-fulfilment.

Her conclusion: "[t]hat's it! No marriage for me, no begetting of sprogs" (*ibid.*).

Shortly after her emotional decision not to follow in her mother's tracks, Lara takes up her studies at art school. It seems that the decision against marriage and motherhood and the determination to make art her profession are more than merely chronologically linked. Art stands between herself and the world; at this stage in her development, she uses art as a weapon and her "large portfolio an aggressive advance guard" (Evaristo 1997: 87; Evaristo 2009: 140) on her way to school. When her first boyfriend and lover, a fellow student from Nigeria, confronts her with the idea of marriage, she shouts at him that she loves "the f-word too much, you know...freedom!" (Evaristo 1997: 90; Evaristo 2009: 143) Sexual experiences, radical emancipatory ideas, the will to freedom and self-expression in painting happen all at once to culminate in her first "masterpiece, oops! / mistresspiece, yeh!" (Evaristo 1997: 93; Evaristo 2009: 143) The fact that she tells the incorrectly spelled Jean-Michel Basquiat (whom she calls "Jean Michel-Basket"), one of the first black artists whose works achieved top prices on the market, to "eat [his] art out" (Evaristo 1997: 95; Evaristo 2009: 148) emphasises her growing self-confidence. The pun also demonstrates a simultaneous distancing and acknowledgement of her postcolonial legacy.

The addition of substantial parts about the maternal Irish side of the family tree in the 2009 version of *Lara* has widened the historical scope of the novel by addressing the colonial history of Ireland. When asked why she had not written about the Irish side of her ancestry in the first edition, Evaristo replied that she "hadn't thought of it" and that she "was shocked because it seemed such an obvious thing to explore".[17] It is true that Ireland's history of immigration and colonialism are prominent in the added parts. Britannia, from the point of view of Lara's Irish ancestry, figures as "the Protestant Conqueror who'd long ago / throttled Catholic Hibernia between her two / mammoth hands and stamped it to the ground" (Evaristo 2009: 31), a colonial power which attempts to "cut out our own sweet Gaelic tongue at the root" (32). Nevertheless, the surplus Irish genealogy is more than an addition to topics which were already essential in the first edition. I agree with Pilar Cuder-Dominguez, who has remarked in an essay about the first *Lara* that Evaristo's "reconfiguration of Englishness goes beyond a mere inclusion of the (post)colonial, or even beyond a historical glance on their presence in London".[18] This widening of the perspective is even more obvious in the new edition. Whereas Cuder-Dominguez emphasises the relevance of class, next to race, as a theme of major importance in the novel in general and for the growing-up of the protagonist in particular, I would like to point to the fact that the addition of the maternal genealogy has helped to embed Lara's search for identity in the context of twentieth-century female literary struggles for artistic freedom.

3. Bernardine Evaristo and Virginia Woolf

One obvious point of departure to conceptualise these struggles is Virginia Woolf's collection of seminal lectures *A Room of One's Own* (1929), particularly her elaborations on the androgynous mind and the need to consider the importance of a female tradition. *Lara* (2009) clearly highlights both the necessity to "think back through our mothers",[19] and the imperative to reject current role models of motherhood in the genesis of the independent artist. In order to understand and to overcome the patterns and behaviours that restrict them, women need to listen to their female ancestors. Enlarging on the female lineage makes it easier for the protagonist of the 2009 version to arrive at a point of departure from which she is able to transform the productive and the destructive power of her mother's ancestry into her own creative energy. As to the idea of the artist's androgyny, Woolf has pointed out that "in each of us two powers preside, one male, one female".[20] An androgynous equilibrium and a spiritual co-operation between the two principles are necessary in order for a great mind to be born. Only "when this fusion takes place [...] the mind is fully fertilized and uses all its faculties".[21] As has been shown, Lara reconsiders her mother's ancestry in *Lara* (2009) and acknowledges its importance for her own intellectual, emotional and artistic development.

Considering both versions of *Lara*, one has to concede that the fictional character has not changed. The last 80 pages or so of both books are identical and judging by the outcome, the Laras emerging from both texts are identical as well (unless Jorge Louis Borges's Pierre Menard is right after all).[22] Well, they are and they are not. As readers, we are invited to interpret both Laras against the backdrop of what we have been told about them, and what we have been told about them is different. I would like to claim, admittedly with a grain of presumptuousness, that *Lara* (2009) is the better book because Lara's mind is here fertilised in equal measure by both parents' histories. This is not so much a matter of an androgynous mind in Woolf's sense of the term but of an androgynous history which needs to be acknowledged first before the artist's imagination can construct unity from it.

There is another point of contact between Evaristo and Woolf which I would like to hint at in order to underline the potential to read Lara not 'merely' in a postcolonial framework but also in the context of the twentieth-century female *Künstlerroman*. As already mentioned, I suggest that *Lara* may be meaningfully read against the backdrop of Woolf's novel *To the Lighthouse*.

Why *To the Lighthouse*? The many authors Bernardine Evaristo has mentioned in various interviews as formative for her thinking about books, writers and writing range from Sophocles via Chaucer and Shelley to Toni Morrison and Kazuo Ishiguro. Virginia Woolf does not figure at all as far as I know. Nevertheless, besides the fact that both novels are portraits of young female artists/painters and besides the superficial similarities constituted by the names Lara and Lily as well as the fact that both novels are dealing with families with eight children, there are a number of more substantial thematic parallels between *To the Lighthouse* and *Lara* which deserve closer investigation. Both Lara and Lily are symbolically associated with water imagery. In both novels, the young artist protagonists emerge as painters from the experiences they underwent in the course of their stories, Lily on the last page of *To the Lighthouse* adding the finishing touch to a painting she started ten years earlier, Lara on the last page of the story carrying her name resolved to paint her past. Both books are self-reflexive in the sense that they perform this act verbally. Telling their own stories, their own histories, painting their own pictures are acts of self-authorisation which take the protagonists beyond the scope of possibilities they had hitherto envisioned for themselves. Both Lily and Lara have to overcome social, cultural and gender obstacles in order to realise their potential as artists. In the context of my argument, though, the most important cross-reference between Woolf and Evaristo consists in the conflicting relationship between the protagonists and their real (in Lara's case) and symbolic (in Lily's) mothers.

One point of contact consists in the idea of wholeness and unity. Creating unity is one of the major issues in *To the Lighthouse*. In the opening chapters Mrs Ramsay acts as the Angel in the House whose redeeming faculties prevent disintegration from happening: "[n]othing seemed to have merged. They all sat separate. And the whole effort of merging and flowing and creating rested on her".[23] The climax of part one is the dinner party at which, for the last time, Mrs Ramsay manages to bring about coherence from social chaos and a sense of stability from flux and change. She enjoys her success in being social putty and experiences peace and rest: "[o]f such moments, she thought, the thing is made that remains for ever after" (Woolf 1969: 121). Already at this stage the aspiring artist Lily Briscoe, the author's alter ego, senses that "directly she [Mrs Ramsay] went a sort of disintegration set in" (129). In the last of three parts, Lily acquires the position of her symbolic mother Mrs Ramsay and fuses the fragments of what she conceives to be a "house full of unrelated passions" (168). But even if her role as artist enables her to create unity from chaos, the circumstances have fundamentally changed. The unity Lily creates is the abstract unity of the work of art. In order to emerge as an autonomous female artist, Lily needed to sacrifice the oppressive "spectre of Victorian respectability",[24] with its accompanying ideology of the woman as Angel in the House. Virginia Woolf killed her twice: once theoretically in a paper called "Professions for Women" (1931), which is the origin of the phrase ("[k]illing the Angel in the House is part of the occupation of a woman writer")[25] and four years earlier in *To the Lighthouse*, where the killing was done kindly but uncompromisingly.

Marriage and art are incompatible concepts for women in *To the Lighthouse*. "An unmarried woman has missed the best of life" (58): Mrs Ramsay is obsessed with the idea of marriage and believes that fulfilment for a woman can only be achieved in marriage and motherhood. She sums up her impression of Lily and her preoccupation as follows:

> Lily's picture! Mrs. Ramsay smiled. With her little Chinese eyes and her puckered-up face, she would never marry; one could not take her painting very seriously; she was an independent little creature, and Mrs. Ramsay liked her for it. (21)

The apparently haphazard nexus of independence, marriage and art is not without deeper meaning after all. In a recent essay on "Female Developments in the Twentieth Century" (2010) Lisa Downward has expanded on Marianne Hirsch's argument that in the twenties' female *Künstlerroman*

> connection between mother and daughter becomes possible and even necessary in spite of the fact that the daughter-artist herself still does not become a mother. After the daughter explores the mother's life it becomes incorporated into the daughter's vision.[26]

What Woolf began in the twenties finds its repercussions in fiction until today. In the surroundings of eighties London still marriage and art are difficult to reconcile for the aspiring female artist. In the 2009 version of *Lara*, the young protagonist incorporates her mother's (and mothers') lives, hopes and frustrations into her artistic vision. Her triumph to step out of history and into her future as a painter is marked by the fact that she can now deal creatively with her father's oppressive heritage. This triumph appears more plausible, though, in a book into which Lara has written the Mummy People with equally colour-rich strokes as the ones with which she plans to paint "the Daddy People onto canvas" on the last page. Androgyny, albeit differently understood, is a model which points towards the future both for Lara and for Lily.

4. "The Family are Like Water": Back to the Sources and Into the Future

Lara's full Yoruba name is Omilara (Omolara in 2009), translated in the text as "the family are like water" (Evaristo 1997: 43; Evaristo 2009: 98). Water imagery and water symbolism run through the whole novel (as well as through *To the Lighthouse*). Thrice in the story, a baptismal situation in a transcultural setting triggers a sense of fullness, unity and identity. Travelling Europe with her friend Trish, Lara goes "for a midnight dip" (Evaristo 1997: 139; Evaristo 2009: 187) into the Turkish sea, the grey zone between Europe, Asia and Africa. Here her memory becomes dislocated, she watches her old ego "bob off" and she finally emerges "the sum of all [her] parts" (*ibid.*). The second 'baptism' happens towards the end of the novel when Lara travels up the Amazon. After having showered "in brown river water" she expresses a feeling of unity and identity with her parents: "[t]he river calms me: I become my parents, my ancestors, my gods" (*ibid.*). The Yoruba proverb which marks the epigraph to the novel – "[h]owever far the stream flows, it never forgets its source" – rounds off the meaning of that final passage. Lara's journey and her quest for identity have come full circle in South America. Water is Lara's element; the Amazon river as well as the Turkish sea provide neutral ground, places where she can forget history ("[t]he past is gone, the future means transformation", *ibid.*) and live fully in it, be her own history, at the same time. She has travelled far and not forgotten the source, or rather, not forgotten the sources. From this reconstructed basis she can set out towards a future which will necessarily mean transformation.

The claim that Lara becomes her parents is more deeply motivated and thus more convincingly implemented in the second version of the novel than in the first because of the intensity with which the importance and the different impacts of both branches of the family tree are explored. The identification with the parents has to be read against the backdrop of the lived transculturality which Lara experiences in Brazil. Right after the 'baptism' in the Amazon, Lara is present when an Indian congregation performs "Catholic hymns hybridized by drums" (*ibid.*), a reminder of the presence of both her mother's Irish Catholicism and her father's Nigerian-Brazilian traditions. Watching that scene from the door she sees her own multicultural identity reflected and feels instantly at home in the presence of "one culture being orchestrated by another" (*ibid.*).

On the last page of the novel, Lara explicitly states that she is baptised after stepping into the waterfall at Cachoera do Taruma. Finally she is ready and resolved to return to London and to step into her future.

5. Summary

Lara's quest for her identity as a young woman and as a young artist is triggered by her longing for "an image, / a story, to speak me, describe me, birth me whole" (Evaristo 1997: 69; Evaristo 2009: 123). Not yet able to raise the strength in herself to conjure up that vision, she has to literally and symbolically travel a long way before she emerges from the Turkish sea, somewhere between Europe, Asia and Africa, "the sum of all my parts" (Evaristo 1997: 97; Evaristo 2009: 150). Even though this emergence is already expressed in the original *Lara*, the reader of both versions may get the impression that not all of her parts had been equally well explained, and that some pieces of essential information were missing in the original version. The supplement (in Jacques Derrida's terminology) of *Lara* (2009) may at first appear as an interesting but rather informational addendum, the more so as the second half of the text remains exactly the same. Nevertheless, the addition of the new parts reinforces a thinking back through Lara's mother's side and it challenges the preexisting totality of the original. This totality, indicated in the phrase "the sum of all my parts", is overwritten with a slightly different concept of wholeness, unity and identity. Reading the supplement in this manner underlines the provisional and contingent status of identity formation. Moreover, the reader of both *Lara*s is a first-hand witness to the reconstruction of identity through personal history. Reading both texts parallel to each other also adds a strong gender dimension to a novel which has been predominantly analysed in the context of race and, less often, of class. The gender dimension gains intertextual depth and theoretical complexity when considered against the backdrop of Virginia Woolf's fictional portrait of a young artist in *To the Lighthouse*. Moreover, the gender dimension is carried over into the parts which deal with Lara's early explorations into painting. The new *Lara* helps the reader to conceptualise the difficulties of a young artist writing/painting her identity as a palimpsest of (family) history, gender and race in postcolonial London.

Notes

1 See Stein (2004).
2 Baumann (1999: 70).
3 Stein (2004: 80).
4 McLeod (2004: 178).
5 Sauerberg (2004); Burkitt (2007).
6 Msiska (2009).
7 Stein (2004); Oyedej (2005); Cuder-Dominguez (2005).
8 Head (2002: 156; emphasis in the text).

9 The first chapter of Sebnem Toplu's forthcoming *Fiction Unbound. Bernardine Evaristo* apparently discusses both Lara novels. Unfortunately, it was not available when the current paper was written.

10 Evaristo (1997: 48; 2009: 103). Further references to these editions will be included in the text.

11 Freud (1999: 124).

12 Etymologically, library and liberty are no relatives; fittingly, though, the child (*liber*) and liberty have the same linguistic roots. The children in the Roman family were considered free (in opposition to the unfree slaves). Lara's childish excursions into the free land of the imagination are thus sanctioned by etymology.

13 All quotes Evaristo (2006).

14 All quotes *ibid.*

15 Stein (2004: 89).

16 Why these two books? *Pride and Prejudice* (1813) might be considered the Irish servant Emma's equivalent for Ellen's Barbara Cartland (see passage below), a novel about the improbable social rise of a woman by marriage; *Dorian Gray* (1890) on the one hand suits Emma who uses words as a weapon (Evaristo 2009: 36); on the other, it is written by an Irishman who suffered under English jurisdiction; lastly, it is a book about the power of books. Dorian Gray falls under the spell of a book he is given by Lord Henry, presumably Joris Karl Huysman's *A rebours* (1884).

17 McCarthy (2010).

18 Cuder-Dominguez (2004: 188).

19 Woolf (1977: 83).

20 *Ibid.*, 106

21 *Ibid.*

22 In Jorge Louis Borges's famous story "Pierre Menard, Author of the Quixote" (1939), the fictional late French writer Pierre Menard immerses himself in the life and masterpiece of Cervantes in order to re-create *Don Quixote* line by line from a twentieth-century perspective. The resulting text is identical with the 1602 prototype, but, we are told, it is nevertheless much better, more subtle, infinitely richer than the original. Evaristo's case is more down to earth. Rewriting her own *Lara*, she is not concerned with postmodern investigations into the nature of authorship and originality. Her re-authored *Lara* is different – even the identical passages are different – not because the literary text is never ever self-identical, but because the identity of the protagonist emerges as a different one from a more fully fleshed-out family background.

23 Woolf (1969: 96). Further references to this edition will be included in the text.

24 Showalter (1972: 339).

25 Woolf (2011).

26 Downward (2010: 146); see also Hirsch (1989).

Bibliography

Baumann, Gerd: "Britain. To Each Its Own", *Harvard International Review*, Spring 1999, 68-72.

Burkitt, Katharine: "Imperial Reflections. The Post-Colonial Verse-Novel as Post-Epic". – In Lorna Hardwick & Carol Gillespie (Eds.): *Classics in Post-Colonial Worlds*, Oxford, 2007, pp. 157-169.

Cuder-Dominguez, Pilar: "Ethnic Cartographies of London in Bernardine Evaristo and Zadie Smith", *European Journal of English Studies* 8:2, 2004, 173-188.

–: "(Re)Turning to Africa. Bernardine Evaristo's *Lara* and Lucinda Roy's *Lady Moses*". – In Kadija Sesay (Ed.): *Write Black, Write British. From Post Colonial to Black British Literature*, Hertford, 2005, pp. 300-313.

Downward, Lisa: "Female Developments in the Twentieth Century". – In L.D. & Giovanna Summerfield (Eds.): *New Perspectives on the European Bildungsroman*, London, 2010, pp. 143-167.

Evaristo, Bernardine: *Lara*, Tunbridge Wells, 1997.

–: "New Writing Worlds. Writing and the Past", http://www.newwriting partnership.org.uk/fp/aspen/public/getFile-21.asp, 2006 (accessed 19 September 2011).

–: *Lara*, Highgreen & Tarset, 2009.

Freud, Sigmund: "The Relation of the Poet to Daydreaming". – In James M. Thompson (Ed.): *Twentieth Century Theories of Art*, Carleton, 1999, pp. 124-131.

Head, Dominic: *The Cambridge Introduction to Modern British Fiction. 1950-2000*, Cambridge, 2002.

Hirsch, Marianne: *The Mother/Daughter Plot. Narrative, Psychoanalysis, Feminism*, Indiana, 1989.

McCarthy, Karen: "In Conversation. Bernardine Evaristo on Updating *Lara*", *Open Notebooks*, 2010, http://opennotebooks.co.uk/category/bernardine-evaristo (accessed 19 September 2011).

McLeod, John: *Postcolonial London. Rewriting the Metropolis*, London, 2004.

Msiska, Mpalive-Hangson: "Remembering Africa. Africa as the Sign of the Transnational in Black-British Writing". – In Walter Goebel & Saskia Schabio (Eds.): *Locating Transnational Ideals*, London & New York, 2009, pp. 175-190.

Oyedej, Koye: "Prelude to a Brand New Purchase on Black Political Identity. A Reading of Bernardine Evaristo's *Lara* and Diran Adebayo's *Some Kind of Black*". – In Kadija Sesay (Ed.): *Write Black, Write British. From Post Colonial to Black British Literature*, Hertford, 2005, pp. 346-374.

Sauerberg, Lars Ole: "Repositioning Narrative. The Late-Twentieth-Century Verse Novels of Vikram Seth, Derek Walcott, Craig Raine, Anthony Burgess, and Bernardine Evaristo", *Orbis Litterarum* 59, 2004, 439-464.

Showalter, Elaine: "Killing the Angel in the House. The Autonomy of Women Writers", *The Antioch Review* 32:3, Autumn 1972, 339-353.

Stein, Mark: *Black British Literature. Novels of Transformation*, Columbus, 2004.

Toplu, Sebnem: *Fiction Unbound. Bernardine Evaristo*, Newcastle, forthcoming.

Woolf, Virginia: *To the Lighthouse*, Harmondsworth, 1969 [1927].

–: *A Room Of One's Own*, London, 1977 [1929].

–: "Professions for Women" [1931], http://ebooks.adelaide.edu.au/w/woolf/virginia/w91d/ (accessed 19 September 2011).

Anette Pankratz (Bochum)

"Nothing That Is Worth Knowing Can Be Taught". Artists and Academia in Novels by A.S. Byatt, David Lodge and Zadie Smith

1. Introduction

"Nothing that is worth knowing can be taught".[1] This aphorism from Oscar Wilde's *The Critic as Artist* (1891) seems to hold especially true for the art of fiction; it is a divine gift, a blessing of nature, the result of human genius.[2] At least, this view can be inferred from classical *Künstlerromane* such as James Joyce's *A Portrait of the Artist as a Young Man* (1916). Stephen Dedalus does not take creative writing classes, and in his quest for artistic fulfilment, he has to escape from family, society, friends, religion and, last but not least, "more mud, more crocodiles" associated with university.[3] Academia provides erudition, but has to be left in favour of life and literature. In his career, Stephen represents the archetypal male, white "Hero with Creative Genius",[4] combining intellectual capacity, an encyclopaedic knowledge and talent,[5] which implicitly favours "the male quality" as "creative gift",[6] or, put more bluntly, the "upspurt of sperm [...], the form-creator".[7]

Significantly, the then almost exclusively male-dominated space of Oxbridge serves as starting point for Virginia Woolf's *A Room of One's Own* (1929). Gaining access to university runs parallel to women claiming a literary heritage and getting the opportunity to produce fiction. A complementary way to undermine the notion of the natural-born or cultured genius was the institution of creative writing.[8] It is no coincidence that it flourished both at the end of the nineteenth century and in the seventies, both periods associated with changes in Western mentality towards more openness, liberality and inclusiveness. By offering to teach the craft of writing,[9] the workshops undercut the myth of genial creation. Another development also questioned the notion: although diametrically opposed to the hands-on approach of creative writing, post-structuralism, feminism and postcolonialism similarly denaturalised the act of creation. The new theories exposed liberal bourgeois aesthetics as ideology promoting the patriarchal status quo.[10] They replaced the concept of authorship by shifting discursive positions and broadened the range of what was to be considered art.

Literary representations of women, university and writing would not wholly subscribe to the story told in the last two paragraphs. In them, academia is neither conducive to the liberation of women nor to the democratisation of literature, but serves as sometimes merely whimsical, sometimes outright inimical, and always muddy background to the female artist figures. This dichotomy also pertains to the representations of creative writing, which is presented as harm- and useless in the best case, detrimental to creating art in the worst. The present article aims to show how contemporary campus novels (in the widest sense) use the opposition between art and academia to appropriate the traditionally male figure of the Hero as Creative Genius. The developments in this discursive framework will be shown in two steps: A.S. Byatt's *The Game* (1967) and *Possession* (1990) foreground the restrictions female writers have to undergo, at the same time the two novels intertwine essentialised notions of female creativity with a critique of the sterility of academic research. This paradigm has undergone some changes in the last ten years: David Lodge's *Thinks...* (2001) and Zadie Smith's *On Beauty* (2005) suggest a more liberal and egalitarian society as far as questions of gender are concerned. By focusing on artists who also teach creative writing, it will be shown that what might suggest a breaking up of the contrast between creation on the one side, teaching and research on the other, turns out to re-enforce the oppositional structure so prominent in Byatt's texts. The ideal type of the creative genius resurfaces, together with discussions of truth, beauty and a good life.

2. Killing the Monsters in the Ivory Tower

When both university and literature become more accessible to women around the middle of the twentieth century, novels featuring female artists appropriate the narrative and structures usually asso-

ciated with the male *Künstlerroman* to explore the dialectics between university and life, teaching and doing. A.S. Byatt's *The
Game*,[11] for instance, projects the traditional theme of the divided
self of the artist figure onto a pair of sisters.[12] In their childhood
Julia and Cassandra Corbett both enjoy playing a (or rather, the
eponymous) Game, the creation of a self-contained imaginary
world of medieval myths, resembling the Brontë siblings' playworld
Angria.[13] While Julia starts publishing their stories, Cassandra, ap-
palled by her sister's "theft",[14] ends the Game and studies medieval
history at Oxford. At the outset of Byatt's novel, Julia has become a
mildly successful writer, mother and wife, Cassandra an unmarried
middle-aged medievalist still immured at Oxford. By way of the
Game, their common upbringing and their shared obsession for the
scientist and TV explorer Simon Moffitt, the two women are presented as complementary: "Cassandra and me – it's a composite creature, in a way, a sort of binary fission" (Byatt 1967: 176-177).[15]
But only the genuine artist survives; Cassandra commits suicide
after she has read her sister's new novel, *A Sense of Glory*, whose
protagonist is a thinly veiled portrait of herself as isolated and obsessed "lady don" (264).[16] This signals the freeing of Julia from the
fetters of her past and from her initial solipsism as artist, which
critics had lambasted as "one plaintive note of self pity" (80).[17] Just
as Stephen Dedalus matures over his dead mother's body,[18] Julia
frees herself by killing the don in the ivory tower. At the very end
of *The Game* she has found a new self: "[s]he was going to excise
Cassandra from her life; it was the only possible way. [...] Julia
knew she was a new woman" (285-286).

Julia's survival associates writing with vitality. Despite the moral
reservations about her literary adaptations of reality,[19] she is not
completely to blame for the suicide of her sister. According to the
underlying logic of gender constructions in *The Game*, Cassandra
was doomed ever since she entered academia, which in its discipline, boredom, isolation and sterility resembles life in a monastery.
In it, she represents the hysterical, repressed and gauche stereotype
of the bluestocking,[20] who performs her femininity awkwardly and
unconvincingly and suffers from repressed sexual fantasies. In contrast to this, Julia fits perfectly into the culture of the sixties,[21] second-wave feminism, sexual liberation and then popular ideas about
female creativity as substituting "the womb for the penis".[22] She is
shown to live life to the full, taking lovers, enjoying parties, com-

261

municating easily with others, and, last but not least, being able to express and transcend her feelings by way of literature.[23]

Admittedly, the complementarity of the sisters does not end with Cassandra's death. Her "private papers" (286) lurk unread in the trunk of the car which brings Julia to London, implying that the sisters do remain connected, just as creativity and critical thinking cannot be completely separated.[24] It is not Cassandra's academic work, however, but her diaries and letters which will keep the relationship with Julia alive, again hinting at the predominance of creative writing.

The themes of creativity, gender and academia recur in Byatt's *Possession*. The two (fictitious) nineteenth-century artists Randolph Henry Ash and Christabelle LaMotte are not only mystically connected by their interest in literature; they also have a torrid love affair, which cross-fertilises their literary texts and which produces a daughter. The novel juxtaposes nineteenth-century literature with twentieth-century academia. Initially as stale as Cassandra's Oxford in *The Game* and additionally riddled by a broad range of fashionable -isms (feminism, Lacanianism, post-structuralism), it only opens up to 'real' life when the scholars Roland Mitchell and Maud Bailey start to discover the affair between Ash and LaMotte and eventually get drawn into a Gothic romance cum detective story.[25] They leave their cave-like libraries and archives or their stuffy offices and engage with the secrets of creativity. This makes them shed their fancy theories and go back to basics: biographical readings, intuition and legwork.[26]

As the subtitle *A Romance* indicates, Roland and Maud not only unravel the lives of their objects of research, they also imitate them and fall in love with each other. Shedding post-structuralist *doxa*, Roland finally discovers the power of words and becomes a poet: "[h]e had been taught that language was essentially inadequate, that it could never speak what was there, that it only spoke itself".[27] But with his new experiences, he realises that "the words that named things, the language of poetry" (Byatt 1990: 473) are more important. With this epiphany, poems "came like rain and were real" (475). Parallel to this, his lover Maud discovers her true identity as the granddaughter of LaMotte and Ash and the legitimate inheritor of their writings. Creativity wins again; moreover, especially the ending confirms traditional gender roles. Jackie Buxton points out the paradox of this merging of a postmodern structure and conservative meanings: "[i]f *Possession* is a postmodern text then it is one that is deeply suspicious of *postmodernism* [...], what it does do as a literary text is to seduce the reader into the consumption of Victorian poetry (or its simulacrum!)".[28]

With its parodies of the different critical schools, *Possession* turns the erstwhile monastery into a "factory";[29] the segregation of the sexes gives way to permissiveness and power struggles. And Byatt's novel is not the only one to do so. Quite a few campus novels show how postmodern theories turn universities into places for ridiculously overcomplex models and what seem to be futile exercises in interpretation, when commonsense and a bit of close reading will do just as well, if not better.[30] Strategically linking truth, beauty or reality with art serves as counterpoint to the commodification of culture and de-politicised irony associated with Postmodernism.[31] In Smith's *On Beauty*, for example, art historian Howard Belsey fights a battle against the idea of creative genius, because he deems it an oppressive bourgeois concept. His state-of-the-art poststructuralism, however, is associated with inhumanity, sterility and taking the joy out of both art and life. Where his wife Kiki (or the focaliser Claire Malcolm) quotes Gertrude Stein, Howard uses jargon: "[s]he called a rose a rose. He called it an accumulation of cultural and biological constructions circulating around the mutually attracting binary poles of nature/artifice".[32] By means of his rigid attitude, Belsey establishes a reign of terrified silence in the classroom and cuts himself off from life.[33] *On Beauty*'s main plot highlights the ethical and moral repercussions of his anti-aesthetics: having affairs with the poet Claire Malcolm and his student Victoria Kipps he appears as hypocritical and not caring about the feelings of others.[34]

In their theorising, academic critics are shown to oppose creativity. This often serves as foil to highlight the vitality of literature and the artist figures. Julia Corbett creates, whereas her sister Cassandra merely edits; Ash and LaMotte live, while scholars try to press their lives into pre-conceived feminist, Lacanian or post-structuralist moulds. Writers *manqué* like Cassandra Corbett or scholars who find their true vocation as poets like Roland Mitchell indicate, however, that Englit as an academic discipline and English literature cannot be separated completely.[35] From this perspective, creative writing would look like the perfect compromise formation to unite literature and university.

Creative writing developed coextensively with the professionalisation of both literature and literary criticism. It takes up a middle position between the complex theories of the production of (literary) meanings and the myth of genial creation.[36] Because of this, writing workshops are often eyed suspiciously either as soft option (in contrast to genuine science and scholarship) or as promoting homogeneous "McPoem[s]".[37] This begs the question asked by David Lodge: "[i]s this healthy, is this wise, is it likely to nourish the production of quality writing?"[38] Literary representations of creative writing answer this with a guarded 'no'. Classes in poetry, drama or novel writing might be liberating and enjoyable for the students, but they are shown to be rather superfluous and sometimes actually detrimental to genuine artists.

In contrast to Penelope Lively's novel *Next to Nature, Art* (1982) or David Lodge's comedy *The Writing Game* (1991),[39] which both depict writing classes for interested and, more importantly, paying adults, whose teachers are mostly pompous, greedy and not very talented, creative writing at university as represented in David Lodge's *Changing Places* (1975) and *Thinks...* as well as Zadie Smith's *On Beauty* appears as sometimes pedestrian, but always well-meant. Rather ironically, after the cuts and criticism waged at the humanities (by British governments from Thatcher to Cameron),[40] creative-writing classes are presented as a growth industry cherished by students and the administration alike. In *On Beauty*, Zora Belsey adamantly tries to get one of the few places in Claire Malcolm's poetry class at Wellington College, despite her lack of talent and interest,[41] because "shit like that counts when it comes to grad school – she's a *name*, and it's stupid, but it makes a difference" (Smith 2005: 199; emphasis in the text). In *Thinks...*, writer in residence Helen Reed is surprised to learn that creative-writing classes are big business at the University of Gloucester. The Vice Chancellor, Sir Stanley Hibberd, admits:

> "I didn't rate creative writing an academic subject when I came here. But when I looked at the books, I was converted."
> "You mean, books by former students?" says Helen.
> "No, no! I mean the accounts," says Sir Stan, laughing heartily. "I don't have much time for reading, I'm afraid."[42]

Just like at Wellington, the participants are carefully hand-picked, "winnowed from a mass of eager applicants" (Lodge 2001: 12), indicating exclusiveness and attractiveness.

Notwithstanding the growing importance of creative writing, the novels emphasise the ambiguity of the enterprise for both teachers and students. In *On Beauty*, Claire Malcolm seems to compensate for her loss of creativity by teaching. Surrounded by her students, she tiredly wonders: "[h]ow had she ever ended up here, in one of these institutions, these universities, where one must make an argument for everything, even an argument for wanting to write about a chestnut tree?" (Smith 2005: 219) The answer might be: money. Wellington is willing to pay for the cultural capital of the star poet (150). Similarly, Helen Reed agrees to take the temporary post as writer in residence because "I need the money" (Lodge 2001: 40). Gloucester also offers her a space to deal with the death of her husband and her writer's block.[43] Hence, both Claire Malcolm and Helen Reed seem to prove Bernard Shaw's quip that those who can, do, those who cannot, teach.[44] But despite these similarities, the portraits of the artists in Lodge's and Smith's novels have slightly different functions: the readers follow Helen's recovery and gain glimpses into her life, her psyche and the creative process. Claire Malcolm's class becomes the battlefield for an ideological war at Wellington College with mainly negative consequences for young artists, shedding light on the connection between exclusion, ethics and art.

3.1 Write Thinking

Novelist Helen Reed is one of the two protagonists of *Thinks...*. In spite of the supposedly random, multi-perspectival and postmodern collection of stream-of-consciousness dictations, diaries and e-mails, the novel tells a conventional enough story:[45] Helen meets the cognitive scientist Ralph Messenger, has a brief affair and eventually parts amiably from him and Gloucester. In the happy ending, Helen overcomes both the grief for her husband and her writer's block. Moreover, she manages to write a new novel "set in a not-so-new greenfields university, and entitled *Crying is a Puzzler*" (340). The title refers to a quote by Charles Darwin, which she and Messenger discussed at the beginning of her stay (69; 79; 138-

140); thus, very probably, the new novel deals with her time at Gloucester. Although the readers do not learn much about the finished book (the extradiegetic narrator only gives the information that it "was written in the third person, past tense, with an omniscient and sometimes intrusive narrator", 340), they do get insights into the events and processes leading to the writing of it, mainly by means of Helen's diary.

For Helen, the diary serves as intimate dialogue between two selves, "my neurotic self and my more rational observing, recording self" (14; see also 103; 258). This split imitates the textual strategies of 'real' diaries; in addition, it can be seen as representation of the divided self of the conventional artist hero. At the same time, it also ties in with the ventriloquism and the fluid narratorial voices attributed to texts written by women.[46] Being allowed a look at these private musings gives the readers a privileged view of Helen's constructions of 'reality'. She intentionally uses her diary to keep her "muscles exercised" (171) and as quarry for her fiction (186). The diary entries already have a literary quality; they are articulate and imbued with a will for style. At one point, for example, Helen imitates the "solidity of specification" of Henry James, because a scene she witnessed reminds her of James's *The Ambassadors* (231; 234). Helen's wish to leave Gloucester triggers a detailed description, in which her escape fantasy attains a very concrete textual reality:

> creeping out of the house before it's light, like a thief, loading my things into the car, shutting the boot lid softly, softly, so as not to alert anybody [...] driving away along the empty service road, scarves of mist round the throats of streetlamps, slowing down at the exit barrier to give a wave to the security man yawning in his brightly-lit glazed sentry box. (13)[47]

Another short narrative rewrites the past as "Mills & Boon" romance (17). While these passages offer brief flights of fancy, Helen's account of her affair with Ralph Messenger uses a sustained third-person intradiegetic perspective. Motivated by the wish to distance herself from what happened and to come to grips with her feelings, Helen turns her experiences into a piece of proto-fiction:[48]

> ([...] I still shrink from examining this experience with the straight unflinching gaze of the first person. Let me try it another way ...)

> For that was what she had become, a woman of pleasure, a scarlet
> woman, a woman of easy virtue, a woman no better than she should be
> – or so she would have been described in the pages of an old novel. Not
> in a modern one, of course. (258)

Fiction appears as a mixture of reality, imagination and other literary texts. Like Julia Corbett, Helen bases her novels on personal
experience and the observation of other people, adding "narrative
mileage" (211) to the mundane, because fiction, according to her,
"needs conflict, disappointment, transgression" (*ibid.*). While her
earlier novels mainly draw on the lives of friends and acquaintan-
ces, keeping a comfortable emotional distance, *Eye of the Storm* and
especially *Crying is a Puzzler* appear to be more autobiographical
and therapeutic. As with Julia Corbett, really having "something to
write about. From the heart" (212) is cathartic for the author and
appears to also enhance the quality of the literary text, as the critical
praise and literary success for Helen's last two novels seem to
imply.

Having the urge to write and having something to write about
unites Helen with her students. Quite a few of them have given up
well-paid jobs or borrowed money in order to hone their skills as
fledgling novelists. The works-in-progress are often autobiographical, like, for instance,

> Chuck Romero's *Bildungsroman* about a young man losing his virginity
> and finding his vocation in Providence, Rhode Island (where Chuck
> comes from); Farat Khan's interlinked short stories about cultural and
> generational conflict in the Asian community of Leicester (where she
> comes from). (82-83; emphasis in the text)

At the same time, they are also influenced by literary trends and generic patterns: the *Bildungsroman*, postcolonial novels or, in the
case of Frieda Sinclair, the new Scottish school, which has obviously inspired her "unflinching tales of young women dancing,
drinking, shagging and puking in clubs from Inverness to Ibiza"
(82).

At the beginning of her stay, Helen wonders whether she can
"possibly give them value for money" (15) and the sessions in
which students discuss their own texts seem to bear out the opinion
of Jasper Richmond, the Head of the English Department: "I always
think good students educate each other" (12). What Helen does

manage to do, however, is to make the young artists "stretch their literary muscles – trying things they wouldn't risk in their own work" (111) by means of parodies/pastiches on a set theme. *Thinks...* features examples of two of these exercises: "What is it like to be a Bat?" and "Mary the Colour Scientist", inspired by philosophical thought experiments on the problem of human consciousness, which Ralph Messenger had talked about when Helen visited him at the Centre for Cognitive Science. Apart from creatively dealing with one of the central themes of *Thinks...*, the parodies in the styles of Martin Amis, Irvine Welsh, Salman Rushdie and Samuel Beckett highlight the intertextual web which underlies all writing.[49] They make the literary models, which the students had used unconsciously in their own work, explicit. Style – and not only the story told – creates meaning and seems to undermine too facile gender attributions. Helen, the creation of David Lodge, imitates Henry James; Frieda Sinclair imitates Irvine Welsh and Alan Warner, whose texts in turn feature female characters as protagonists. By way of this postmodern hall of mirrors, *Thinks...* cherishes the plurivocality, heterogeneity and multiculturalism of literature (albeit with a preference for the old masters) which also seems to dissolve gender binaries.

Whereas Helen is rather pleased with the outcome of her exercises and convinced about them as teaching tools, the success of her creative-writing class as a whole remains more doubtful. At the end, the by now very omniscient narrator does not divulge on the careers or non-careers of the students and the novel suggests a double perspective. From the artists' point of view, as Sandra Pickering states and Helen's struggle with her new novel demonstrates, "[y]ou have to go on writing, no matter what" (307). But, do readers have to read the stories? Both Messenger and Reed have their doubts:

> [i]t's frightening to think of how many novels I must have read in my lifetime, and how little I retain of the substance of most of them. Should I really be encouraging these bright young people to add their quotient to the dust-heap of forgotten pseudo-lives? (84)

Implicitly, *Thinks...* also begs the question whether the students need an expensive university education to acquire the art of fiction. The sketchy portrait of Helen Reed as young artist indicates that technical expertise can also be gained by closely studying literary texts. As with Stephen Dedalus, academia here offers an important space of transition. Helen read English at Oxford and started a doctoral thesis on point of view in Henry James (43). And this, as the diary and the interspersed comments on her novels bear witness, also influenced her style. It also does not really matter how one flexes one's "literary muscles" (111; 171), whether with the help of a diary or by writing parodies. All that does seem to matter are talent, stamina and motivation. Zadie Smith's *On Beauty* appears to endorse a similar premise. Additionally, it emphasises the connections between social exclusion and talent as well as the ethics of both creativity and scholarship.

3.2 Ethics and Aesthetics

Unlike Helen Reed, Claire Malcolm is a fully tenured member of the faculty at Wellington College, which – in contrast to the University of Gloucester – is a venerated American liberal arts college with a long history and an excellent reputation. Not everyone can afford the fees there, especially not members of the working class and/or ethnic minorities. Claire Malcolm undercuts this exclusiveness by opening her classes to non-students, arguing that

> [t]here are a *lot* of talented kids in this town who don't have the advantages of Zora Belsey – who can't *afford* college, who can't *afford* our summer school, who are looking at the army as their next best possibility, [...], an army that's presently *fighting a war* – (Smith 2005: 160; emphasis in the text)

With this decision, Claire takes an openly political stance,[50] and becomes a party in the "culture war" (156) between liberals and conservatives, personified and personalised by the rivalry between Howard Belsey, who supports political correctness and affirmative action, and his archenemy Monty Kipps.

Although Claire sides with Howard (and has a brief affair with him), their attitudes towards life, literature and teaching completely differ. Beauty for her not only exists, but should be the basis of life. Her philosophy of the "fittingness" of things pertains both to the creative process and the leading of a fully human and ethical life:

when your chosen pursuit and your ability to achieve it – no matter how small or insignificant both might be – are matched exactly, are fitting. *This*, Claire argued, is when we become truly human, fully ourselves, beautiful. (214; emphasis in the text)[51]

While Howard aims at cowing students into awe with his theories, Claire wants to bring out the best in them, to enhance their creative potential and to point out the great tradition of great literature:

> [i]t was Claire's great gift as a teacher to find something worth in all these efforts and to speak to their authors as if they were already household names in poetry-loving homes across America. And what a thing it is, at nineteen years old, to be told that a new Daisy poem is a perfect example of the Daisy oeuvre, that it is indeed evidence of a Daisy at the height of her powers, exercising all the traditional, much loved, Daisy strengths! [...] Claire would finish by reading a poem by a great, usually dead poet [...]. You walked out of that class if not shoulder to shoulder with Keats and Dickinson and Eliot and the rest, then at least in the same echo chamber, in the same roll-call of history. (259)

The slightly ironical tone of the passage belies doubts about the efficacy of creative writing, though. In contrast to Gloucester University, the class is part of Wellington's B.A. course and none of the participants actually envisions a career as writer yet. The regular students are self-confident, "smooth and bright" (211) young things impressed by Claire Malcolm's reputation as poet, their egos pleasantly tickled by getting her attention. But do they? In a moment of exhaustion, Claire perceives students as a deindividualised mass, "[e]very year more students, same but different" (216). And are the classes beneficial for genuine creativity? As in *Thinks...* the answer is 'probably not'.

While the likes of Zora and Daisy at least enjoy themselves, Carl Thomas, a young African-American Spoken Word artist, seems to lose his creative impetus due to his contact with Wellington. After a triumphant performance of his poetry at the bohemian Bus Stop, Claire and her class discover him as "Keats with a knapsack" (230) and invite him to join the writing group. At first, he seems to profit from all the new knowledge about styles and genres. He becomes aware of the formal framework of poetry, starts to feel proud about his own texts and puts more effort into their composition (259-261). But in the end, his misgivings about everything Wellingtonian –

"[h]e was still not sure that this whole Wellington thing wasn't a kind of sick joke being played on him" (260) – prove right.[52]

When he becomes the symbolic centre of the "culture war", he is offered a post as librarian and archivist at the Black Studies Department. Where the creative-writing class gave him a first glimpse into Literature (with very large capitals), his new job offers him a basic version of academic work. As in *The Game* and *Possession*, some of its aspects are complementary to artistic creativity. Carl loses himself in the history of hip hop, and just as in Claire's class, becomes aware of traditions and structures. At first, it seems as if he thus discovers the true joys of academia: a job that allows him to follow his favourite pastimes – "[m]oney for buying records! Getting paid to listen to music!" (373) – working overtime, driven by curiosity and the wish to communicate his findings to others.[53] He starts to systematise the hip-hop collection and writes catalogue entries which evolve into long articles, "[i]t was like suddenly he had a typing disease" (375). This new-found enthusiasm makes him abandon his own poetry, which at least Levi Belsey interprets as sellout: "this ex-Carl, this played-out fool, this shell of a brother in whom all that was beautiful and thrilling and true had utterly evaporated" (389).[54] When he gets entangled in the erotic web of the Kippses and Belseys and on top of that is also wrongly accused of having stolen a painting from Monty Kipps's office, Carl leaves Wellington and Boston for good, feeling resentful and betrayed, "[p]eople like me are just toys to people like you... I'm just some experiment for you to play with" (418).

By juxtaposing prize-winning high culture with popular culture, "outside the centripetal pull of canon formation",[55] *On Beauty* highlights two opposing poles of the creative spectrum and implicitly indicates the necessary balance between them. Likewise, Smith's novel adapts E.M. Forster's *Howards End* (1910) to a multicultural, transnational setting. The parallels in the plot, the intertextual references, and the ironical narrator point towards Smith's indebtedness to literary tradition,[56] a position coming close to what Claire Malcolm practises as both writer and teacher. The pastiche of styles, the detailed presentation of idiolects and sociolects, the importance the novel awards hip-hop and rap subculture indicate the dissolution of boundaries between high and popular culture which can not be found in *Howards End*.[57] Claire and Carl as artist figures personify the attempt to "Only Connect...",[58] or rather to deconstruct binaries, amongst others, male/female, moral/amoral, "white/ black, thin/fat, Mozart/hip-hop, Rembrandt/Haitian art, and beautiful/ugly".[59]

3.3 Stereotypes of the Artist as Other

When novels represent female artists who teach creative writing, they revert to stereotypes (or prototypes) from the past. Both Helen Reed and Claire Malcolm recall the generation of the sixties and seventies. Like Julia Corbett in *The Game*, Helen has to deal with the restrictions of family life and male prejudice, abandoning her PhD thesis after the birth of her first child and working through a post-natal depression. She seems to represent the pre-women's lib writer, burdened by a Catholic upbringing and traditional gender roles,[60] becoming a typical "lady novelist",[61] who usually maintains the rules of decorum and whose style seems very traditional. Claire Malcolm became famous in the early seventies as young, precocious "woman poet" (218), writing about sex and orgasm (53; 218), rubbing shoulders with members of the Beat Generation and international pop culture, such as Allen Ginsberg, Lawrence Ferlinghetti and Mick Jagger. Despite her early fame, she feels restricted as well, "*examined*, very picked over, not just mentally but also personally and *physically* ... and I suppose I felt somewhat ... disembodied from myself" (218; emphasis in the text). During her time at Wellington, she still suffers from the "trauma of her girlhood" and occasionally feels like "a stranger to herself" (226), sharing Helen's divided perspective as expressed in her diary.

Both characters fulfil comical clichés about artists and academics alike. Seen from the perspective of the efficient administrator Lydia, Claire Malcolm appears rather ditzy and unpractical:

> [h]ow was it possible that a woman who lost her own office keys sometimes three times in a week and did not know where the supplies cupboard was after five years at the college could yet hold a title as grandiose as Downing Professor of Comparative Literature and be paid what Lydia knew she was paid because it was Lydia who sent out the pay subs? And then, on top of it all, have an inappropriate workplace affair. Lydia knew it had something to do with art, but, personally, she didn't buy it. Academic degrees she understood – Jack's two Ph.D.s, in Lydia's mind, made up for all the times he tipped the coffee into his own filing cabinet. But poetry? (150; emphasis in the text)

Poetry and personal idiosyncrasies seem to go together quite well and point towards the role of the artist standing above the mundane, material and administrative. It fits in with Claire's bohemian lifestyle in the seventies, her affair with Howard Belsey and her pose as urbane and sophisticated artiste who introduces her students to subcultural venues and the best of world literature at the same time. The veneration for the classics – in literature, art and music – unites her with Helen Reed. Reed's predilection for Henry James, Vivaldi and the pleasures of the English countryside as well as her ignorance of e-mails, TV series and cognitive science make her appear as equally disconnected from contemporary life.

Representing these female writers as slightly old-fashioned and from a generation still trying to liberate themselves from the restraints of traditional gender roles serves as contrastive foil which implicitly corroborates a narrative of progress. Within the novels Claire and Helen highlight the comparatively carefree lives of the younger writers. In both *Thinks...* and *On Beauty* the female students are not noticeably hampered by questions of gender or confronted with the derision and condescension which used to haunt female artists.[62] In *On Beauty*, questions of class and ethnicity predominate; *Thinks...* emphasises the personal dramas of its white middle-class protagonists.

On the meta-level, the juxtaposition of Claire and Helen's writings with the texts they are written in highlights postmodern sophistication and – again – progress, most explicitly in *Thinks...* with its clever pastiche which distinguishes itself from Helen Reed's old-fashioned *Crying is a Puzzler*, a bit more guardedly in *On Beauty* with its inclusion and validation of popcultural texts not to be found in Claire's echo chamber. The novels incorporate and appropriate the traditional forms cherished by Helen and Claire – by way of the diary entries in *Thinks...*, Claire's pantoun "On Beauty" in *On Beauty* as well as by all the intertextual references –, and go beyond them.

Although the tensions between literature and 'reality' reflected by the young and old artists alike suggest an autobiographical impetus for writing, the clear gap between the artist figures and the novels they appear in problematises a too simplistic search for the "true selves" of Lodge and Smith.[63] Furthermore, the literary merits of both fictive authors seem to be somewhat below those of their creators. As Craig Raine observes in an interview with David

Lodge, Helen Reed's diary entries imply that she is "a writer poised somewhere between the mediocre and the passable" and that the truly "brilliant bits" come in the third-person narration.[64] Likewise, Claire Malcolm's fame seems to stem from "the sexualized verse of her youth" (218) and her life with famous men. *On Beauty* portrays her as someone who performs, but no longer practices, being an artist. On the whole, genuine autonomy and agency are attributed to the narrator or the author and not the characters.[65]

4. Conclusion

Pitting academia against life and criticism against true creativity, the novels by Byatt, Lodge and Smith enter into a competition about ways of world-making and making sense of life, the universe and everything, which literature, science and the humanities claim for themselves.[66] While new media like TV are dismissed out of hand as something fascinating but superficial and morally doubtful,[67] the novels concede the universities a certain value as receptacles of old knowledge, but not as producers of new meanings. Real life happens elsewhere and only literature can provide true insights into it. This dichotomy between artist and scholar is represented as lethal sibling rivalry, as the opposition between fact factory and romance and/or as petty feuds and sterile affairs versus a fulfilled life. Hence, all the artists more or less follow in Stephen Dedalus's footsteps. Only after they have left campus are they able to write genuine literature.

The dense intertextuality in *Possession, Thinks...* and *On Beauty* suggests that the cultural archive of English or world literature is necessary for creation, and this is also one of the accepted functions of universities, preserving the canon and teaching students how to love art and literature. But once the intellectuals declare the death of the author, the unconscious ideological implications of a text, or the end of creative genius, the authors write back, sometimes killing off their academics, often pointing out that analysing a text equals not really loving it and extinguishing its truth and beauty. The complexity of critical theories is both parodied and matched by a complexity of the textual structure of the novels, using shifting and overlapping timeframes and/or plurivocal narrators. But the postmodern sophistication of the surface structure overlaps with a decidedly un-postmodern attitude towards the construction of reality, truth and – last but not least – gender.

In campus novels published from the nineties onwards, creativity and centrality are conceded mainly to men. In *Possession* it is Roland Mitchell who finds his poetic voice while Maud Bailey merely finds her true ancestry.[68] Ralph Messenger's jovial honesty gains precedence over Helen Reed's primness in the course of *Thinks...* and the sympathy for the novelist is controlled by a rather condescending view on her literary merits which also reinscribes patriarchal heteronormative gender roles.[69] Claire Malcolm only plays a minor part in the family drama of the Belseys and the Kippses in *On Beauty* and her status as creative artist is quickly superseded by the raw talent of Carl Thomas.

The struggle for a "room of one's own", a female voice and a story to tell prominent in second-wave narratives recur as nostalgic reflections of a time long gone; the uniformly bright young things writing nowadays (Lodge 2001: 84; Smith 2005: 211) live in a more liberal culture and often freely decide to (seemingly naturally) replicate the tried and tested roles of their parent generation.[70]

Implicitly, this also means the return of genial creation as counterweight to the cerebral world of academia. Writers like Julia Corbett, Helen Reed or Claire Malcolm are a far cry from the traditional Hero With Creative Genius in the mould of Stephen Dedalus. The female artists are more aware of their limitations and not able to completely free themselves. The notion that "Art was a gift from God, blessing only a handful of masters" (Smith 2005: 44) is either not mentioned at all or associated with conservative patriarchalism as in *On Beauty*, where Monty Kipps praises Art in the same breath as he denounces equality and multiculturalism. But by allowing insights into the writers' workshops – via diary entries, excerpts from their texts, their teaching in class and their emphasis on tradition, form and technique – without explaining how and why literary texts finally come into being, the novels create an interpretative gap. By its conspicuous absence, they highlight the "mysterious process of creativity",[71] which leads from ideas and the flexing of muscles to the finished text. In their complex layers of textuality, the novels acknowledge the opening up of the field of literature. Art is no longer only reserved to the privileged few "masters", and with the female artist figures and the memories of their struggles the novels inscribe themselves into the history of female liberation. Nevertheless, true artists – whatever their gender, social, sexual or ethnic background – still appear as endowed with the certain *je ne sais quoi* which cannot be taught.

Notes

1 Wilde (1970: 349).
2 Watson & Kearful (2007: 88); see also Beebe (1964); Klaiber (2004: 35-40); Zwierlein (2010) for examples of the topos of the genial artist.
3 Joyce (2000: 273).
4 Huf (1983: 3); see also Beebe (1964: 267).
5 Although we have to take his genius more or less at face value (or to construe it extratextually by interpreting Stephen as portrait of his creator Joyce): both *Portrait of the Artist* and *Ulysses* (1922) present Stephen more ruminating about his role as artist and about art than actually creating it. Moreover, if he does so, the reader hardly ever gets to read and thereby to evaluate it.
6 Gerald Manley Hopkins quoted in Gubar (1985: 293).
7 Ezra Pound quoted in Zwierlein (2010: 12).
8 According to Watson & Kearful (2007: 87) the first creative-writing course was offered in Iowa in 1897.
9 *Ibid.*, 88.
10 Eagleton (2005: 3-5; 99-100); Waugh (2006: 198-200); Anjaria (2008: 32-35).
11 For a more sustained analysis of *The Game* and *Possession*, see Lena Steveker's contribution in the present volume.
12 For the theme of the divided self, see Beebe (1964: 7).
13 Todd (1997: 10); Schuhmann (2001: 81).
14 Byatt (1967: 84). Further references to this edition will be included in the text.
15 Todd (1997: 10).
16 See Schuhmann (2001: 85).
17 What Byatt would call a "me-novel" (quoted in Schuhmann 2001: 79); see also Todd (1997: 11).
18 Beebe (1964: 277; 283-284); see Huf (1983: 102) for a juxtaposition of Stephen as selfish genius with stereotypically suffering female artists.
19 Schuhmann (2001: 86).
20 Embodied, e.g., by Margaret Peel in Kingsley Amis's *Lucky Jim* (1954), see Dubber (1991: 156); Eagleton (2005: 98-99); Horlacher (2007: 469).
21 Schuhmann (2001: 76).
22 Gubar (1985: 308).
23 The opening chapters very tellingly, albeit somewhat unsubtly, introduce Julia as hostess at the end of a party (Byatt 1967: 7) and Cassandra alone at

her desk at work on her Malory edition, writing about chastity in the *Morte d'Arthur* (*ibid.*, 16).

24 Alfer & Noble (2001: 2).

25 Robbins (2006: 263).

26 Todd (1997: 28-29). On the meta-level, however, the efficacy of these methods seems doubtful: all the clues have been planted and all the romances, Gothic novels, fairy tales and detective plots have been construed by A.S. Byatt. Thus, what seems like fate or true scholarship is an effect of intricate plotting and meticulous writing, indicating scepticism towards modern scholarship and celebrating literary imagination.

27 Byatt (1990: 473). Further references to this edition will be included in the text; see also Bentley (2008: 147).

28 Buxton (2001: 102; emphasis in the text). For a more positive reading, see Eagleton (2005: 110-114).

29 The "Ash Factory", to be precise; see Byatt (1990: 10; 26-27).

30 See Schwend (1995); Antor (1996: 666-668); Horlacher (2007).

31 Eagleton (1990: 374-379).

32 Smith (2005: 225). Further references to this edition will be included in the text.

33 See Lopez (2010: 354-358).

34 Wall (2008: 760-761; 769-771).

35 Alfer & Noble (2001: 76).

36 Bach (2007: 120-121); Herholz (2011).

37 Watson & Kearful (2007: 89).

38 Lodge (2002a: 99).

39 For an analysis of *Next to Nature, Art*, see Marion Gymnich's contribution in the present volume; for an analysis of *The Writing Game*, see Bach (2007).

40 Extensively dealt with in campus novels. Probably the most famous example is David Lodge's *Nice Work* (1988), for further instances see Antor (1996: 678-693) and Robbins (2006: 260-264).

41 As Claire Malcolm puts it: "Zora Belsey couldn't write a poem if Emily Dickinson herself rolled out of her grave, put a gun to the girl's head and demanded one" (Smith 2005: 158). Taking the class does not change this. Zora's poems are said to be "the kind that appear to have been generated by a random word-generating machine" (*ibid.*, 258).

42 Lodge (2001: 132; see also 47). Further references to this edition will be included in the text.

43 The colleague she stands in for, also seems to go through a phase of creative crisis: "Russell Marsden, critic, anthologist, and author in his precocious youth of two Mervyn Peakish novels, one good, the other not so good, who has run the course since its inception, and has retreated to his rustic cottage in the Dordogne to finish, or possibly [...] to start, an impatiently awaited third novel" (*ibid.*, 11).

44 Shaw (1931: 213). The original reads "[h]e who can, does; he who cannot teaches".

45 Tönnies (2005: 60).

46 Waugh (2006: 203-205).

47 Ironically, or thanks to Lodge's composition, this resembles Helen's actual departure at the end of the semester, also highlighted by the narrator: "[i]t struck her that she was enacting the fantasy she had entertained in her first depressed weeks on the campus" (Lodge 2001: 339).

48 See also Lodge (2002b: 288).

49 Apart from providing sheer fun for erudite readers.

50 Wall (2008: 765).

51 *Ibid.*, 766.

52 Lopez (2010: 363) sees the class more critically as taming the raw force of Carl's texts, but overlooks the positive effects on his self-esteem.

53 Carl is the only character in *On Beauty* actually shown to do research. Kipps and Belsey only teach or give public lectures.

54 Sommer (2007: 185).

55 Anjaria (2008: 43).

56 For the details of the adaptation, see Lanone (2007); Anjaria (2008: 39-42); Tynan (2008: 73-83); Fischer (2008). They also point out and analyse the references to, amongst others, Elaine Scarry's philosophical text *On Beauty and Being Just* (1999), Zadie Smith's husband Nick Laird's poem "On Beauty", Zora Neale Hurston's novel *Their Eyes Were Watching God* (1937) and her study of Haitian culture, *Tell My Horse* (1938). I would like to suggest another intertext: the figure of Howard Belsey also bears strong similarities with Howard Kirk from Malcolm Bradbury's *The History Man* (1975), which go beyond their shared first name. Both have working-class origins and assume a left-wing political stance. In the course of both novels, they are discovered as frauds, manipulators and adulterers.

57 Lanone (2007: 189).

58 The epigraph of *Howards End*.

59 Anjaria (2008: 38); Tynan (2008: 75). Although *On Beauty* is highly critical towards post-structuralist theory, the imperative to connect and to undermine strict binaries resembles Jacques Derrida's notions of deconstruction as a process of decentering, oscillation and shifting meanings or Homi Bhabha and Stuart Hall's theories on cultural hybridity. Hector Hyppolite's painting *Maîtresse Erzulie* (1948) symbolises this stance of both/and, which replaces the canonical and ideological binaries of either/or: "[s]he represents love, beauty, purity, the ideal female and the moon ... and she's the *mystère* of jealousy, vengeance and discord, *and*, on the other hand, of love, perpetual help, goodwill, health, beauty and fortune" (Smith 2005: 175; emphasis in the text); see Lanone (2007: 195); Fischer (2008: 113-114).

60 Although, according to the chronology, she met her husband and married in the supposedly permissive seventies.

61 Lodge (2002b: 288).

62 See Huf (1983); Klaiber (2004); Eagleton (2005) for examples.
63 Beebe (1964: 5).
64 Lodge (2002b: 286-287).
65 Sell (2007: 167).
66 Robbins (2006: 250).
67 Most clearly in *The Game*, where TV star Simon Moffitt is associated with snakes, plagiarism and a narcissistic asexuality.
68 Buxton (2001: 102).
69 For the dominance of Messenger, see Lodge (2002b: 287-288); much of what Horlacher (2007) says about the covert conservatism of Lodge's campus trilogy, *Changing Places, Small World* (1984) and *Nice Work* also applies to *Thinks....*
70 In *Thinks...* Helen Reed and Sandra Pickering even fall for and write about the same man, Helen's husband Martin.
71 Lodge (1996: 178).

Bibliography

Alfer, Alexa & Michael J. Noble: "Introduction". – In A.A. & M.J.N. (Eds.): *Essays on the Fiction of A.S. Byatt. Imagining the Real*, Westport, 2001, pp. 1-13.

Anjaria, Ulka: "*On Beauty* and Being Postcolonial. Aesthetics and Form in Zadie Smith". – In Tracey L. Walters (Ed.): *Zadie Smith. Critical Essays*, New York *et al.*, 2008, pp. 31-55.

Antor, Heinz: *Der englische Universitätsroman. Bildungskonzepte und Erziehungsziele*, Heidelberg, 1996.

Bach, Susanne: "'Punk-Tuition' for 'Harry Krishner'. Creative Writing in Literature". – In Sabine Volk-Birke & Julia Lippert (Eds.): *Anglistentag Halle 2006. Proceedings*, Trier, 2007, pp. 119-128.

Beebe, Maurice: *Ivory Towers and Sacred Founts. The Artist as Hero in Fiction from Goethe to Joyce*, New York, 1964.

Bentley, Nick: *Contemporary British Fiction*, Edinburgh, 2008.

Buxton, Jackie: "'What's Love Got to Do With It?' Postmodernism and *Possession*". – In Alexa Alfer & Michael J. Noble (Eds.): *Essays on the Fiction of A.S. Byatt. Imagining the Real*, Westport, 2001, pp. 89-104.

Byatt, Antonia Susan: *The Game*, London, 1967.

–: *Possession*, London, 1990.

Dubber, Ulrike: *Der englische Universitätsroman der Nachkriegszeit*, Würzburg, 1991.

Eagleton, Mary: *Figuring the Woman Author in Contemporary Fiction*, Houndmills, 2005.

Eagleton, Terry: *The Ideology of the Aesthetic*, Oxford, 1990.

Fischer, Susan Alice: "'Gimme Shelter'. Zadie Smith's *On Beauty*". – In Tracey L. Walters (Ed.): *Zadie Smith. Critical Essays*, New York *et al.*, 2008, pp. 107-121.

Gubar, Susan: "'The Blank Page' and the Issues of Female Creativity" [1982]. – In Elaine Showalter (Ed.): *The New Feminist Criticism. Essays on Women, Literature, and Theory*, New York, 1985, pp. 292-313.

Herholz, Gerd: "Lässt sich der handwerkliche Teil des (literarischen) Schreibens lernen und lehren?", *Ruhrbarone*, 20 July 2011, http://www.ruhrbarone.de/laesst-sich-der-handwerkliche-teil-des-literarischen-schreibens-lernen-und-lehren/ (accessed 20 July 2011).

Horlacher, Stefan: "'Slightly Quixotic'. Comic Strategies, Sexual Role Stereotyping and the Functionalization of Femininity in David Lodge's Trilogy of Campus Novels Under Special Consideration of *Nice Work* (1988)", *Anglia* 125:3, 2007, 465-483.

Huf, Linda: *A Portrait of the Artist as a Young Woman. The Writer as Heroine in American Fiction*, New York, 1983.

Joyce, James: *A Portrait of the Artist as a Young Man*, London, 2000 [1916].

Klaiber, Isabell: *Gender und Genie. Künstlerkonzeptionen in der amerikanischen Erzählliteratur des 19. Jahrhunderts*, Trier, 2004.

Lanone, Catherine: "Mediating Multi-Cultural Muddle. E.M. Forster Meets Zadie Smith", *Études Anglaises* 60:2, 2007, 173-197.

Lodge, David: "Creative Writing. Can It/Should It Be Taught?" – In D.L.: *The Practice of Writing*, London, 1996, pp. 170-178.

–: *Thinks...*, London, 2001.

–: "Literary Criticism and Literary Creation". – In D.L.: *Consciousness and the Novel. Connected Essays*, London, 2002a, pp. 92-113.

–: "A Conversation About *Thinks...*". – In D.L.: *Consciousness and the Novel. Connected Essays*, London, 2002b, pp. 283-300.

Lopez, Gemma: "After Theory. Academia and the Death of Aesthetic Relish in Zadie Smith's *On Beauty* (2005)", *Critique* 51:4, 2010, 350-365.

Robbins, Bruce: "What the Porter Saw. On the Academic Novel". – In James F. English (Ed.): *A Concise Companion to Contemporary British Fiction*, Oxford *et al.*, 2006, pp. 248-266.

Schuhmann, Kuno: "In Search of Self and Self-Fulfilment. Themes and Strategies in A.S. Byatt's Early Novels". – In Alexa Alfer & Michael J. Noble (Eds.): *Essays on the Fiction of A.S. Byatt. Imagining the Real*, Westport, 2001, pp. 75-87.

Schwend, Joachim: "Angewandte Literaturwissenschaft? *Nice Work* als Schlüsselroman für das literarische und kritische Werk von David Lodge", *Anglistik* 6:2, 1995, 76-92.

Sell, Jonathan P.A.: "Experimental Ethics. Autonomy and Contingency in the Novels of Zadie Smith". – In Susana Onega & Jean-Michel Ganteau (Eds.): *The Ethical Component in Experimental British Fiction Since the 1960s*, Newcastle, 2007, pp. 150-170.

Shaw, George Bernard: "Maxims for Revolutionists". – In G.B.S.: *Man and Superman*, London, 1931 [1903], pp. 209-225.

Smith, Zadie: *On Beauty*, London, 2005.

Sommer, Roy: "The Aesthetic Turn in 'Black' Literary Studies. Zadie Smith's *On Beauty* and the Case for an Intercultural Narratology". – In R. Victoria Arana (Ed.): *"Black" British Aesthetics Today*, Newcastle, 2007, pp. 176-192.

Todd, Richard: *A.S. Byatt*, Plymouth, 1997.

Tönnies, Merle: "A New Self-Conscious Turn at the Turn of the Century? Postmodernist Metafiction in Recent Works by 'Established' British Writers". – In Christoph Ribbat (Ed.): *Twenty-First Century Fiction. Readings, Essays, Conversations*, Heidelberg, 2005, pp. 57-82.

Tynan, Maeve: "'Only Connect'. Intertextuality and Identity in Zadie Smith's *On Beauty*". – In Tracey L. Walters (Ed.): *Zadie Smith. Critical Essays*, New York *et al.*, 2008, pp. 73-89.

Wall, Kathleen: "Ethics, Knowledge, and the Need for Beauty. Zadie Smith's *On Beauty* and Ian McEwan's *Saturday*", *University of Toronto Quarterly* 77:2, 2008, 757-788.

Watson, Ian & Frank J. Kearful: "Creative Writing. Past, Present, Future". – In Sabine Volk-Birke & Julia Lippert (Eds.): *Anglistentag Halle 2006. Proceedings*, Trier, 2007, pp. 87-93.

Waugh, Patricia: "The Woman Writer and the Continuities of Feminism". – In James F. English (Ed.): *A Concise Companion to Contemporary British Fiction*, Oxford *et al.*, 2006, pp. 188-208.

Wilde, Oscar Fingal O'Flahertie Wills: *The Critic as Artist*. – In O.F.O.F.W. W.: *The Artist as Critic*. Ed. Richard Ellmann, London, 1970 [1891], pp. 340-408.

Zwierlein, Anne-Julia: "Introduction. Gender and Creation. Surveying Gendered Myths of Creativity, Authority, and Authorship". – In A.-J.Z. (Ed.): *Gender and Creation. Surveying Gendered Myths of Creativity, Authority, and Authorship*, Heidelberg, 2010, pp. 11-23.

Barbara Puschmann-Nalenz (Bochum)

Re-Writing the Story of the Swallow, the Nightingale and the Hoopoe. Emma Tennant's Novel *The Ballad of Sylvia and Ted*

1. Introduction

The aphorism ascribed to American novelist William Faulkner that all a reader needed to know about an author was "[h]e wrote books, then he died" may be seen as a contribution to the Barthesian "Death of the Author".[1] In the case of Sylvia Plath, whose suicide at the age of 30 and its circumstances made her universally known almost overnight, it takes on a special significance. Her death made her come alive to the public and finally rendered her a famous poet, a victim of the concepts provided by the "feminine mystique" and an icon of feminism as well.

The Ballad of Sylvia and Ted (2001) follows two contrasting literary patterns: that of fictional biography and of mythology. The tension between these subgenres of narrative fiction constitutes, I will argue, much of the appeal of this novel. Both paradigms have a long tradition in Emma Tennant's oeuvre and it is my aim to reveal the effects and function of their use in this biographical novel about a female artist, who posthumously became one of the most celebrated Anglo-American women writers of the twentieth century.

Diverging characteristics mark biography and myth, yet they also share important features. In both cases, much of what they contain is borrowed even beyond the habits of intertextual strategies:[2] in a biographical novel, events, dialogues, relationships and developments are taken from publications following historical research or the reports of eye witnesses, from other non-fictional writings like newspaper articles or police investigations. Historical facts and the theme of the individual's place in contemporary society prevail against the imaginary and the universal; they connect it to the nonfiction novel. Concerning the retelling of a fairy tale or a myth, in contrast, the intertext is communal, legendary, non-mimetic and unspecific in regard to time. The collective cultural or religious heritage levels or extinguishes the singularity of an individual, and both non-mimetic forms narrate the impossible, a characteristic which Antonsen's recent poetological study mentions as outstanding among literary texts.[3]

Thus a description of a text such as *The Ballad* as pastiche can become meaningful; reading it as a narrative cloned from Plath's biography on the one hand and the myth of Tereus, Procne and Philomela, to which is added the fairy tale of Little Red Riding Hood, on the other does not do wrong by the author. Inserting non-mimetic texts in order to shed new light on the lives and deaths of Sylvia Plath, Ted Hughes and writer Assia Wevill distinguishes this novel from the biographical narrative *Wintering. A Novel of Sylvia Plath* (2003) by Kate Moses or from Plath biographies by Edward Butscher, Peter Steinberg or Linda Wagner-Martin, to name only a few from recent years.

Emma Tennant here also alludes to her own re-write, namely the short story "Philomela" (1988), which, in contrast to *The Ballad*, presents a coherent feminist retelling of Ovid's tale. In the *Metamorphoses* Procne, daughter of the king of Athens, and married to Tereus, king of Thrace, misses her sister Philomela at her husband's court, so that Tereus travels to Athens to fetch her. But he falls in love with Philomela and rapes her (in other versions he seduces her) and cuts out her tongue, so that she cannot inform anybody. After his return he tells his wife that Philomela is dead. One day, however, Procne receives a tapestry woven by her sister, which depicts the crime Tereus committed and shows that she is still alive. Philomela is freed by her sister and reunited with her at Tereus' court. In revenge the two sisters kill Itylus, the son of Tereus and Procne, cook him, and serve him as a meal to his father. When he realises what he has eaten he tries to kill the two women. In Ovid's tale they are metamorphosed into a nightingale (Philomela), a swallow (Procne), and a hoopoe (Tereus). In Tennant's short story no metamorphosis takes place; Tereus is left to his own tortures. Procne's final words are: "[y]ou destroyed us long ago".[4]

2. Mythologisation and Biography

In applying the ancient myths of separateness, violation, infidelity, revenge and cannibalism to Plath, Hughes and Wevill Tennant gives new meanings and legendary dimensions to well-known biographical events. The actions and deeds become monstrous and beyond comprehension; this is already indicated by the title, since the (folk)ballad is a genre narrating the unusual and momentous. To readers, the most obvious disclosure, however, is the insight that Sylvia herself is a myth. The ignorance, erasure or blurring of Plath's poetic achievements at the time of her death and today by the never-ending construction of her life, her personality, her marriage and death, Assia's death and the causality connecting them provides an example of the presence/absence theme in literature and vigorously contradicts, as several critics have remarked, the notion of the "Death of the Author", in Plath's case with dramatic irony: her physical death subverts the Barthesian author's disappearance; she is more alive in the minds of people because she is dead.[5] Feminist scholars have attacked Roland Barthes for minimising the role of (female) authors, marginalising women writers as always and eliminating the importance of gender for literature.[6]

In exploring the integration of myth and fairy tale into this novel, special attention will be given to the relation between the repeated conjuring of the myth and Plath's existence as a female artist, i.e. the question as to whether the condition of authorship is also illuminated by the story of Philomela, Procne and Tereus.[7] If Plath's autobiographical novel *The Bell Jar* (1963) mirrors the obsession with the female self and by its title unconsciously (?) points at suffocation as the author's termination of her life, *The Ballad of Sylvia and Ted* dramatises the situation and conflicts of a double or triple authorship in – literally and metaphorically – confined spaces. It addresses gender boundaries and their (de)construction and, I claim, it problematises the constitutive role of art for the identity of the female writer. Is not Tennant's novel, readers may ask themselves, another effort to reproduce the author's person and identity as a woman in the creation of yet another work, Emma Tennant's work? By inscribing non-mimetic texts that focus on female identity in a patriarchal society on a life-story, Tennant transforms the author into an archetype. "Such texts are about creation against and in the midst of destruction", says Sharon Rose Wilson's recent study about how women writers such as Margaret Atwood, Jean Rhys, Doris Lessing and Iris Murdoch use myth and fairy tales as intertexts.[8]

Such a reading of this portrayal of Plath's life and death as a universal parable about the struggle and defeat of female self-assertion against gender-related compulsions would in its own way be as polemical as Tennant's earlier "rebellious understanding of the myth [in "Philomela"]".[9] Ovid's eventual metamorphosis of the protagonists is eliminated in this short story; instead, the heroic, murderous strength of female characters that reveals extreme cruelty set against male dominance is underlined, so that "Philomela" becomes "a story of survival".[10]

Ovid's original version of the myth not only bestows survival on the transformed characters, but glorifies them. His metamorphosis resurges in the course of and at the end of *The Ballad*: while in Tennant's story "Philomela" the title figure is raped by Tereus, Ovid has him seduce her – which is what Ted certainly does with Sylvia and other women. In the novel a child is also murdered by her mother, namely Assia's child fathered by Ted, but as in *Metamorphoses* the story of two equally betrayed women and their male idol ends on the conciliatory, aestheticising note of the ancient poem. Unlike "Philomela", *The Ballad* cannot be truly perceived as a feminist counter-narrative.

In the novel, the art of narration achieves what its female artists were unable to do in real life: to transcend boundaries and constraints without being hurt or doing harm, to shed the stifling or tormenting psychological and social imprisonment and, finally, to escape love's torture. In Ovid's tale of violence and shock a further act of vengeance is prevented by having the sisters change into a swallow and a nightingale in order to let them escape from the sword of the disgraced Tereus, who then becomes a hoopoe.[11] All three survive, and all three are immortalised.

Following Ovid in the novel's epilogue, Emma Tennant's narrative dissolves the immediate connection between the ending and the biographical plot of the novel: the three involved in the tragic love triangle are posthumously transfigured into the birds that are seen by many people flying high above the trees and the city.[12]

The metamorphosis of a young American woman with academic distinctions who is married to a gifted poet does not take place by means of her own literary works while she is alive; the transformation can only occur through narratives which imagine and impersonate her. Posthumously, she becomes a myth; her picture could serve Roland Barthes's explanations of mythologies as well as Garbo's face. "Few twentieth-century writers can be said to have had a greater impact on the public cultural awareness than Sylvia Plath".[13] Tennant's intertextual use of Ovid's work causes us to realise the continuous mythologisation of Plath and her life. What is mythologised, however, is much less the artist than the woman rendered artefact through other narratives.

Ina Schabert, in her theory of literary biography points out the special qualities of biographical narratives and signals that what some of Tennant's reviewers criticise as disconcerting is fully intended by an author and can gain extraordinary significance:

> [f]ictional biography aims at a narrative that can harbour unresolved complexity and make room for the different, even discrepant, sometimes very strange views on a person that have been gathered during the author's long immersion into all kinds of source materials.[14]

Among the "strange views" on the biographee expressed in *The Ballad* is the position of each character in this love triangle, the construction/discovery of symbolic sisterhood between the two women and the monstrous quality of acts and figures.

In the following, I will investigate the relation between the text of Plath's fictional biography, Tennant's method of using pastiche, and the non-mimetic textual "clones", a term created for literary works in the title of Moraru's study on the postmodern obsession with citation, revision and simulacra especially but not exclusively in fiction by American authors E.L. Doctorow, Robert Coover and Paul Auster.[15]

First allusions to the myth of Tereus are included in the novel's opening chapter "The Oceanic Feeling", which tells the story of Sylvia's process of individuation at the age of two and a half years, while she is staying with her maternal grandparents for several weeks on the Atlantic coast when her younger brother is born. The over-dramatisation of this event by the third-person narrator has been criticised by reviewers,[16] but the method marks the attempt to adopt the magic thinking of a very small child for the narrative perspective and is as such quite persuasive. Moreover, magnification as strategy starts here and continues throughout the novel.

Hints at cannibalism and ritual murder, "mythemes" or fragments from mythology,[17] signify the abrupt end of the child's oneness with the world that could dangerously engulf her, and certainly indicate the end of blithe happiness. From the beach she is called to "[t]he kitchen, dark and deep in Sylvia's mind, with a priestess and a hissing cauldron and a secret about to rise steaming from the pot" (Tennant 2001: 14).

This frightening image is a divination of something terrible yet to come, of the "underworld" of the dead in the chapter "Persephone", into which Sylvia descends in her first suicide attempt.[18] The terrifying image is repeated in one of the rare shifts to Ted's perspective and there alludes to the myth of Tereus in a temporal prolepsis preceding Ted's encounter and unfaithfulness with Assia in Devon much later:

> [t]he myth unfolds before him: betrayed wife, cauldron on a leaping fire, the young son she has thrown in to stew there, ready for her adulterous husband to feast on. Her revenge. But the crime hasn't been committed yet. (110)

From the very beginning images of death accompany the child Sylvia, but they are also present in the childhood of her later rival Assia Gutman in Berlin in 1935. It is Dr Gutman, her father, who is frightened when his wife Lisa reads the fairy tale of Little Red Riding Hood to their little daughter. A Jewish surgeon, he is aware of the danger they live in, and Assia realises the terror spreading around her one evening in a scene which shows her that people like her father and his friends are regarded as wolves, as evil creatures in a nightmarish city which has for her turned into the dark, chilly wood of the fairy tale (21-22). Although her father can save her and her mother at the very last moment by emigrating to Palestine, the reality they leave behind proves more alarming even than the fairy tale.

The endeavour to construct the early years of a protagonist from inside impacts on the reader by the magic used for this representation of childhood fears. In Sylvia's case it also implies – to the irritation of some readers – that the arrival of a sibling can have similarly menacing dimensions for a child as the fright caused by a historical situation.

In the narrative each girl's childhood includes the forebodings of horror and death, even though the contrast between them for the chronicler of their lives is striking. Conjuring up history mixed with or symbolised through the non-mimetic is the method by which this novel continues to follow the life-stories of the female protagonists, while the male child Ted fulfils the role of the archetypal hunter and indiscriminate killer. Historical events remain in the background and may suddenly emerge by association, like the death by electrocution of Julius and Ethel Rosenberg in the same summer in which Sylvia tries to take her own life (31) and in which the attempt is made to cure her psychological condition by electroshocks.

When Ina Schabert states that "the combining of historiography and imaginative comprehension in one book is destructive to both",[19] she expresses a hazard that can also be felt by readers of *The Ballad*. Time and again historical awareness overwhelms the biographee's imagination in her fantasies about her own father Otto Plath and his German past (is he the wolf-figure in the tale of Little Red Riding Hood? And how did Assia's ancestors fare in her father's country?). Historiography and imaginative comprehension prove mutually deconstructive in this book.

A second problem inherent in biographical fiction is equally epitomised by *The Ballad*: the attempt to empathise with the female protagonists prevails, but its tentativeness cannot remain concealed. Implicitly 'empathetic fallacy' is made thematic by the myths which are used to interpret another self. "None of us can enter into another person's mind; to believe so is fiction".[20] Myths, by definition ahistorical and collective, definitely counteract the historical particularity of persons and facts. The two kinds of discourse – non-mimetic fiction and history – are too divergent not to work against each other, so that the formal result is an overlaying or interspersing of biography with mythology instead of an amalgamation. In addition, this novel does not follow the structure of one myth, but uses citations of various mythemes wherever they appear appropriate, possibly ornamental or explanatory.[21] The question arises as to whether an increased meaning of the historical is disclosed by using the mythological.

In spite of a formal diffusion caused by the inclusion of mythology a dichotomy of these two modes of literary representation, the historical and the mythological, is averted by the author so that *The Ballad* belongs to those postmodern narratives that "work to destabilize the border between these contraries, and it does so by pointing out the central problematic of this border: historical *identity*".[22] The novel turns the characters into archetypes and yet underlines the idiosyncrasies of the historical figures, such as Plath's obsession with household chores and country life, her nervousness often bordering on hysteria and her self-inflicted ordeals, like staying outside in the cold during the last days of her life.

This inherent contradiction is illustrated in the scene where Sylvia and Ted meet in Cambridge for the first time. Her self-fashioning as femme fatale (42) before she goes to a party at the Women's Union to celebrate the first issue of a new little magazine publishing recent poetry culminates in the primeval chase of sexual desire Ted and Sylvia deliver in the kitchen, "of Dionysus let loose" (45), with Sylvia becoming "a vampire" (46). Mythological figures best express what happens to the individual here: something impersonal, archetypal overcomes them. In *The Ballad* Tennant introduces myths from Celtic/Teutonic culture, the folk fairy tale, legends and classical literary texts like set pieces in her performance of Plath's, Hughes's and Wevill's life.

Another example of renewed mythologisation is the representation of an evening at Smith College, Massachusetts, where Sylvia first discovers her husband's infidelity during the reading of *Oedipus* with Ted as Creon. The mythological figures, and later Sylvia, Assia and Ted as mythologised characters, become the symbols of all women destroyed by betrayal and the feminine mystique; Ted as the ominous seducer, adulterous husband and destroyer of two women writers develops into the Bluebeard figure of Tennant's *Burnt Diaries* (1999).[23] He eventually calls himself the murderer of a genius (162), not without a tinge of self-pity and gloomy ennoblement.

The archetypal contrast is immediately established between Sylvia, the fair woman, and Assia, the dark one who signifies passion, and who is moreover Jewish, a stranger and shrouded by mystery:

> [f]or Assia is certainly the 'other', the reverse side of the coin, the dark, forbidden country across the world from America, where Sylvia, in her brightness, fair as day, stands for order, discipline, and unacknowledged cruelty. (111)

The unfolding of the story of Tereus, king of Thrace, and of the two women who in the myth are sisters, not strangers, follows. They become sisters in Sylvia's dream (118-122), which presents a paradox: the "reverse side of the coin" is the other, but proves inseparable, even part of her own identity. "Sylvia slept and dreamed – of twins, of sisters, of another who is also herself" (122). The metaphorical sisterhood in Tennant's novel secures survival of the female self; the enigma of the dream shows that the other is the alter ego (118). Therefore, marriage becomes the obstacle in finding Procne's/Sylvia's own self again. That its removal can only be accomplished by an act of destruction or self-destruction is unquestionable. In her sleep the heterodiegetic narrator tells her story to Sylvia, while the other woman, to whom she is insolubly bound, is asleep in the guest room:

> [y]ou were fated to marry, and now that you know yourself to be no longer yourself, you are fated for the time that remains to you to seek out the other – for it is only when you find and come to terms with her that you will find yourself again.
>
> This is easier said than done. Even if it means the committing of an act of desperation, of self-immolation or the harming of another, you cannot live beside yourself as marriage has taught you to do. You must return to inhabit your being. (*Ibid.*)

The narrator goes beyond the identification of Sylvia with Procne by turning Assia into Philomela, the object of the man's desire, a woman who became mute in an act of atrocity and thus not able to verbalise her story. Her suffering is stifled to the degree where not even the tapestry sent to Sylvia tells her about it. At least for the present, Assia has become the victor, taking away husband and home (125); the affliction of Sylvia's rival/sister remains a secret – readers are led to suppose that it exists. Later the narrator will give her a voice and grant other voices to tell about her pain, but only after Sylvia's death when Assia, whose identity as a writer is minimised, experiences the same fate.

3. Woman Artist: Woman and Artist, or Woman versus Artist?

As a result of our investigation we have to conclude that the use of myth does not lead to an increased performance in the representation of the female artist figure; instead it shows once more the suppressive potential of marriage in a patriarchal society and the self-liberation from these fetters as indispensable for the female protagonist to re-inhabit her being. This can only be achieved "in unison" (118) with the other woman. Whether female identity includes working as an artist or whether being an artist enhances being a woman (instead of contradicting it), *The Ballad* shows that Sylvia is defeated.[24] Her revolt against the suppression of her art by marriage springs up a few days before her death when the internal focalisation shifts to Professor Trevor Thomas, who lives in the same house on Fitzroy Road in London – that representative of the sixties' mainstream conservative society to whom Sylvia has become a nuisance and a riddle, since

> everything in life is impossible for this wife and mother who was so keen to point out to him the other night that she is in fact the author of a novel and not just Mrs. Hughes. Why should he care if her husband went off with a wicked woman? It all sounds invented [...]. (153)

In and by the narrative, her being a writer is made subordinate to her womanhood to a degree where "it all" can only be understood as fiction. Not the female author is marginalised here, but the author in the female character. Tennant's Sylvia is above all a woman, a married woman, and a mother, too; if there can be an augmentation or a climax of femininity in the traditional sense – she fulfils it. To regain her identity she has to overcome what separates her from her supposed rival, who by imagination will prove "as close, as affectionate and loyal as a sister" (118). The myth of Philomela, Procne and Tereus is used in an affirmative way by Tennant's novel to define and represent Plath's life in the end. A woman fights against conventions of a society that hurts and suppresses her, but it is less the artistic potential and achievement that is marked as constitutive for her self than what she shares with other women. What they have in common, not what distinguishes her from other women, is probed by Tennant, and the myth only enhances this universalising tendency. Tennant either renounces the possibility of focusing on the outstanding, unique essence in this biography or she is induced by her "mythomania" to establish the myth as signifier and thereby emphasise the universal.[25]

Assia, also a writer, though a minor one, undergoes an equally generalised representation when she is identified with the figure of Little Red Riding Hood, her red colour the colour of life, sex and blood. At first the fairy tale serves to point out a historical situation of mortal danger which also threatens the lives of the Gutman family; afterwards it addresses her nature as 'a dangerous woman', but before the end "the story has twisted and contorted again, so there can be no happy ending" (158) after Sylvia's death and Assia's abortion of her and Hughes's first child.

The novel's closure shows a polyphonic representation of what happens after Sylvia's suicide while before an omniscient authorial voice and Sylvia's perspective dominated. In the last part, "The Chill", Tennant uses *The Canterbury Tales* as a model for her sequence of "The Nurse's Tale", "The Secretary's Tale" and "The House Sitter's Tale", disregarding chronology, focusing on Assia's life immediately after Sylvia's death and once more years later before her own suicide after Hughes's desertion. Finally it shifts to Sylvia's friend Elizabeth, who came to Devon in the spring and to whom the author had dedicated *The Bell Jar* published a few weeks before her suicide. Each character takes a different view of the situation. The man, physically the only survivor of the three, becomes a Bluebeard figure, with his own tragedy to live with.

Eventually the epilogue, barely six lines long, returns to the myth of Philomela and adds to the multiperspectival part "The Chill" Ovid's metamorphosis of the three figures. Not only are they idealised by it; transfigured, they are not dead, and they can no longer violate and harm each other. After the void left by Sylvia's suicide and the horror that her fate should repeat itself in Assia, the myth here does give additional greater meaning to the story in contrast to the closure of Tennant's short story "Philomela":[26] to posterity the nightingale, the swallow and the hoopoe convey beauty, harmony, love and animation art alone can achieve.

4. Life into Art

It is on the metafictional level that this biographical novel imposingly foregrounds art and the female artist, confirming a statement by Henry James as to the relation of life and art: "[i]t is art that *makes* life".[27] The headline of Vanessa Thorpe's review, "Sylvia,

Ted and Emma, too" not only alludes to Tennant's own affair with Hughes – she is part of a new triangle – but may also be taken as an indication of the transfiguration which Tennant, the author, tries to accomplish for Sylvia and Ted. If the imaginary level – the person of the biographee – fails to connect with the symbolic signifier – the myth of Procne, Philomela and Tereus –, which seems to me a reason why many readers are dissatisfied with the novel, it is because meanwhile our knowledge of Plath's works together with the revelations of tragedy in her life prevent this connection. This immortalisation by aestheticising does not seem to fit completely: it rests disconnected from the historically verified. Art and life are opposites in Tennant's text.

Two metaphors of the life of the artist as a young thing form another sharp contrast: while the image of the bell jar symbolised the imprisoning reality experienced by Plath's protagonist Esther Greenwood, the birds flying high in the sky as symbols of freedom are a poet's transformation of the artists into a glorified existence beyond real life.[28]

5. Biography without Myth

A very short glimpse at another text, Kate Moses's *Wintering. A Novel of Sylvia Plath* leaves the reader amazed at the abundance of details describing the last weeks of Sylvia's life, including numerous flashbacks. While Plath as a person oppressed by concepts of femininity she wants to fulfil predominates the fictional level of Emma Tennant's book, Kate Moses ostentatiously foregrounds Plath's work: apart from the book title the more than forty chapter headlines are titles of her poems – most of which were published by Hughes, who suppressed some of hers and replaced them by several of his own   a symbolic act? – four years after her suicide. The celebration of *Ariel* in 1966 by the press always included the story of her marriage, her death and the question of guilt. Plath the woman was and remained at least as important as Plath the author.[29]

The time of Moses's novel covers the last two months of Plath's life, from 12 December 1962 to 11 February 1963. The time of the mind, however, goes back especially to Court Green in Devon, where the story of her betrayal started, showing scenes of a marriage and of child-rearing, of the perfect mother, wife, housewife, hostess, and disciplined writer. Ostentatiously shown complete fulfilment followed by complete breakdown – this is also the cliché Plath has become in the public mind, blaming, amongst others, Hughes, her mother, her father, herself, college, American society for her suicide.

While Tennant in using mythology aims at a reduction to those archetypal human situations and simultaneously at elation beyond the singular, Kate Moses tries through numerous details to vividly evoke the tension resulting from what Plath wanted and what she could bear. The reader at the end of *Wintering* feels that it was all too much for the heroic protagonist – no woman, deserted and ill, could live up to her own expectations and bear such a burden as life had prepared for her. We remember or imagine the ghastly cold of 1962/1963 and the lack of care and comfort in those years, and we may deeply sympathise with her and shake our heads at so much indifference towards a betrayed young woman with small children and wonderful gifts. This novel dramatically portrays the particular circumstances of her life and seeks to represent the characters' interiority. The semi-fictional level is nowhere transcended or questioned. Sylvia survives because she dies a heroic death after fighting till the end, and Kate Moses only contributes further to the "Cult of Plath".[30]

Wintering offers – in terms of storytelling – a simpler and more modest representation of Sylvia Plath and her life than *The Ballad*, even though Kate Moses's approach is certainly not unambitious. The literary complexity of Tennant's much shorter novel results in a message that occupies the more demanding reader's mind: that art can achieve immortality in spite of defeat and despair of the artist, that after 2000 years the poetical transformation by a myth is being revived in order to reveal hidden meanings in a contemporary fictionalised biography. While Kate Moses accumulates detailed information about the last years and weeks of Sylvia's life, Tennant gives her existence an interpretation which elevates her misery to archetypal validity. By evoking images from mythology and fairy tale Tennant's novel enriches biography with elements of Magic Realism which have a distancing and at the same time exciting effect on the reader's involvement. Thus, *The Ballad* is rendered the more imaginative narrative of the two, in spite of the obvious difficulty in uniting myth and biography. The accumulation of knowledge about the woman artist in *Wintering* does not have the same force of expression achieved in the experiment of showing the significance of Sylvia's existence through the myth of Procne, Philomela and Tereus.

Notes

1 Without pointing to its source Faulkner's often-cited phrase is also quoted by Julian Barnes in *Nothing to be Frightened of* (2008: 178).
2 For the theory of intertextuality and its use by Tennant, see Barta (2007: 9-44) and Friend (2004: n.p.).
3 See Antonsen (2007).
4 Tennant (1988: 110).
5 Boileau (forthcoming); Maack (1996: 80); Huf (1983: 126).
6 See Carlier (2000: 392).
7 Ted Hughes translated selected tales from Ovid's *Metamorphoses*, where the myth was included, in his later career and published them as *Tales from Ovid* (Middlebrook 2004: 46).
8 Wilson (2008: 159).
9 Friend (2004: n.p.).
10 *Ibid.*
11 In ancient Hebrew and Persian poetry the hoopoe signifies the love messenger between King Solomon and the Queen of Sheba (see Goethe 1962: 31, where the hoopoe celebrates life over the dead).
12 Tennant (2001: 176). Further references to this edition will be included in the text. Although the end corresponds to the closure of Ovid's poem the original finishes on a more martial than placid note as Tereus' identity as a warrior is emphasised: "Tereus [...] is himself changed into a bird. Upon his head a stiff crest appears, and a huge beak stands forth instead of his long sword. He is the hoopoe, with the look of one armed for war" (1960: 6, ll. 424-674; 670-674).
13 Boileau (forthcoming).
14 Schabert (1990: 35). For criticism of the novel's 'remoteness' from Plath and her works, see reviews by Crumey (2001) and Thorpe (2001).
15 See Moraru (2001).
16 See, e.g., Crumey (2001).
17 Schmid (1996: 56).
18 Angela Carter once called the material supplied by non-mimetic texts the "scrapyard of mythology", where you may take what you can use (quoted in Schmid 1996: 40; n. 30).
19 Schabert (1990: 64).
20 Bernard Crick quoted in Schabert (1990: 63). If scholars sometimes feel that Tennant is not doing justice by the historical figures in her novel this is

expressed in title and essay by Diane Middlebrook "Misremembering Ted Hughes".

21 For a structural typology and the formal aspects in the use of myths see Schmid (1996: 44-49).
22 Keener (2001: 1; emphasis in the text).
23 See Middlebrook (2004: 41-42).
24 For the then prevailing public opinion on the female artist, see Hatterer (1966).
25 See Schmid (1996).
26 See *ibid.*, 46.
27 Letters of Henry James, quoted in Beebe (1964: 199; emphasis in the text).
28 Huf (1983: 12) defines frequent "images of flight" as "indicating that the woman artist conceives of her escape from her prison in Icarian terms" – yet another ancient myth, which serves as a motif already in James Joyce's *A Portrait of the Artist as a Young Man* (1916). It corroborates my earlier results that it is not Sylvia Plath who uses the image of freedom flight, but that Tennant's work of art bestows in the epilogue this end upon her and her fellow captives.
29 Moses (2003: 312-313).
30 Huf (1983: 126).

Bibliography

Antonsen, Jan Erik: *Poetik des Unmöglichen. Narratologische Untersuchungen zu Phantastik, Märchen und mythischer Erzählung*, Paderborn, 2007.

Barnes, Julian: *Nothing to be Frightened of*, London, 2009 [2008].

Barta, Angelika: *Re-constructing Woman. Intertextualität und weibliche Identität/en in den Romanen Emma Tennants*, Trier, 2007.

Beebe, Maurice: *Ivory Towers and Sacred Founts. The Artist as Hero in Fiction from Goethe to Joyce*, New York, 1964.

Boileau, Nicolas P.: "Sylvia Plath through the Looking-Glass. Too Beautiful to Be Dead" (unpublished paper given at the ESSE-10 conference 2010), forthcoming.

Carlier, J.C.: "Roland Barthes's Resurrection of the Author and Redemption of Biography", *Cambridge Quarterly* 29:4, 2000, 386-393.

Crumey, Andrew: Review of *The Ballad of Sylvia and Ted*, *Scotland on Sunday*, June 10 2001, http://findarticles.com/p/news-articles/scotland-on-sunday-edinburgh/mi_7924/is_2001_June_10/reviews/ai_n33026340/ (accessed 23 August 2010).

Friend, Maria Losada: "Updating the Classics. Ovid, Emma Tennant's 'Philomela' and the Intertextual Link", *Barcelona English Language and Literature Studies* (BELLS) 13, 2004, http://www.ub.edu/filoan/bells.html (accessed 10 December 2010).

Goethe, Johann Wolfgang: "Gruss". – In J.W.G.: *Westöstlicher Divan*, [1819] "Buch der Liebe", *Goethes Werke, Volume II*, Hamburg, 1962 [1949], pp. 7-125.

Hatterer, Laurence: "The Woman Artist". – In L.H.: *The Artist in Society*, New York, 1966, pp. 172-178.

Huf, Linda: *A Portrait of the Artist as a Young Woman. The Writer as Heroine in American Literature*, New York, 1983.

Keener, John F.: *Biography and the Postmodern Historical Novel*, Lewiston, 2001.

Maack, Annegret: "Translating Nineteenth-Century Classics. Emma Tennant's Intertextual Novels". – In Irmgard Maassen & Anna Maria Stuby (Eds.): *(Sub)versions of Realism. Recent Women's Fiction in Britain*, Heidelberg, 1996, pp. 70-82.

Middlebrook, Diane: "Misremembering Ted Hughes". – In Paul John Eakin (Ed.): *The Ethics of Life Writing*, Ithaca, 2004, pp. 40-50.

Moraru, Christian: *Rewriting. Postmodern Narrative and Cultural Critique in the Age of Cloning*, Albany, 2001.

Moses, Kate: *Wintering. A Novel of Sylvia Plath*, New York, 2003.

Ovid (Publius Ovidius Naso): *Metamorphoses, Volume I*. Trans. Frank Justus Miller, London, 1960.

Schabert, Ina: *In Quest of the Other Person. Fiction as Biography*, Tübingen, 1990.

Schmid, Susanne: *Jungfrau und Monster. Frauenmythen im englischen Roman der Gegenwart*, Berlin, 1996.

Tennant, Emma: "Philomela". – In Malcolm Bradbury (Ed.): *The Penguin Book of Modern British Short Stories*, Harmondsworth, 1988, pp. 102-110.

–: *The Ballad of Sylvia and Ted*, Edinburgh, 2001.

Thorpe, Vanessa: "Sylvia, Ted and Emma, too", *The Observer*, 10 June 2001 http://www.guardian.co.uk/books/2001/jun/10/fiction.tedhughes/print (accessed 23 August 2010).

Wilson, Sharon Rose: *Myths and Fairy Tales in Contemporary Women's Fiction. From Atwood to Morrison*, London, 2008.

Renate Brosch (Stuttgart)

The Figure of the Artist in David Lodge's and Colm Tóibín's Biofictions of Henry James

The biographical novel has become a very fashionable genre in recent years. Its hybrid nature highlights the paradoxical quest to deconstruct and at the same time reconstruct historical figures.[1] The immense popularity of these fictions may be a symptom of a declining faith or loss of confidence in purely fictional stories, as David Lodge suggests.[2] It may also attest to a desire to reintroduce narratives of core subjectivity into our postmodern notions of discursively and performatively constructed subjects. Playing a postmodern game with a famous figure from the past must be particularly interesting for writers when the life they are retelling is that of a writer as well.

The two novels under discussion in the following are *Author, Author* by David Lodge and *The Master* by Colm Tóibín, fictional biographies of Henry James published in 2004. One would be hard pressed to think of an author whose life was more exclusively devoted to his writing, hardly a promising subject for a contemporary novel. But both succeed – though in vastly different ways – in translating this lack of event into compelling narratives. In retelling James's life, both novels engage with questions about the interdependence of art and life which were central to cultural debates in the period of his writing life.

In this paper I first discuss the way these two novels fictionalise the male artist James and then consider how they represent the female artist Constance Fenimore Woolson. A remarkable common denominator in these two otherwise quite different biofictions is the effort to sexualise these artists' lives from a present-day perspective. Though both seize the opportunity the genre offers to imaginatively fill the gaps in documentary and autobiographical records, their invention is not very original, at least as far as the female figure is concerned. Both novels understand the blanks in James's life to result from a decided subjugation of the demands of friends to those of art, an interpretive move which is compounded by a foregrounding of sexual desire in their portrait of the female artist.

Both novels demonstrate an astonishing revival of interest in an author who never achieved popularity with a mass audience during his life or since, though in recent years, film adaptations of his novels and stories have enjoyed a measure of popularity.[3] For literary critics and philosophers, by contrast, James has proved a subject of abiding fascination. James's virtuoso deployment of point of view, an innovation anticipating modernist narrative experiments, can be seen in relation to changes in philosophy, psychology, the visual arts and communication technologies.[4] Nothing much happens in his narratives where men and women regularly reject chances in love for some ulterior purpose. But until they do so, a world of conjectures, speculations, manipulations and deceptions is going on primarily in fictional consciousness. James dramatises the uncertainty about reality which became part of the modernist epistemological dilemma. He expresses the relativity of truth, the improbability of capturing it in words and the impossibility of conveying it to others. The enduring fascination for literary scholars lies in an aesthetically pleasing and intellectually challenging conflation of these matters in terms of content, formal structure and message: the penchant for covert, sometimes voyeuristic observation in his main characters is underscored by the stylistic preference given to the distorting mirror of subjective point of view and translated into a moral questioning of our failure to arrive at an intersubjective truth.

James made the discrepancy between the communal and the individual world clear through perfecting homodiegetic focalisation. In his famous critical essay "The Art of Fiction" (1885) he insists on the inseparability of story from narrative; the telling of the story is inextricably part of the story. James's narrative technique allows us readers to share the main character's interiority, in all its limitations and fallacies. His novels have been seen to persistently explore the theme of renunciation or alternatively to mercilessly depict non-commitment and lack of solidarity. His protagonist John Marcher in "The Beast in the Jungle" (1903) is perhaps the most famous example of disturbing egocentricity. He spends his life convinced that some "rare and strange, possibly prodigious and terrible" destiny awaits him, his "beast in the jungle" which is lying in wait to pounce on him.[5] When his friend May Bartram dies, he suddenly realises that to have missed the experience of love, to have rejected the one person who loved him and to have done absolutely nothing but wait has been his unique fate. Neither of the two novels by Tóibín and Lodge can resist the temptation to make the obvious connection between James himself and his character Marcher; both expose the petty nature of the author and enlarge his flaws under the lens of a presentist vision.[6]

Both novels single out failure as the overarching leitmotif. James's spectacular failure as a playwright drives the plot, and his failure as a human being is the dominant theme. Both novels use pivotal scenes in order to focus on the defeat James had to face in his venture into drama. He was too agonised by opening-night nerves to go to the debut of his play *Guy Domville* (1895) at the St James's Theatre and so he attended Oscar Wilde's *An Ideal Husband* which had just begun its run at the Haymarket. Lodge dramatises his experience by ingeniously cutting back and forth between the delighted audience's reaction to Wilde's epigrammatic wit and James's turgid melodrama rapidly alienating his audience.[7] Finally, unable to bear the suspense, James left Wilde's play and made his way back just in time for the final curtain. Shouts of "author, author" rang out and James was persuaded to step out of the wings for what he took to be a complimentary curtain call only to be confronted with a barrage of angry boos and catcalls. Both novels depict the fiasco as a heartrending public humiliation, a traumatic calamity James would remember to his dying day.

The texts trace the path from this brutal confirmation of self-doubt that had been gathering for some time. It proved the turning point of his career. James gave up drama, and with an almost superhuman determination consecrated himself again to writing fiction. It was 1895 and the major works of his late phase, now considered his masterpieces, *What Maisie Knew* (1897), *The Wings of the Dove* (1902), *The Ambassadors* (1903), *The Golden Bowl* (1904), and "The Turn of the Screw" (1898) were still to be written. The exhaustion and depression that followed his attempt to win fame in the theatre led to the resolution to dramatise his fiction, with which James made the transition to his innovative late style.

Besides public failure, there is the emotional failure in personal relationships. Both novels thematise the ethics of fiction by dealing centrally with the way James used his friends and relatives as material for his works. The story of failure in human decency is simultaneously the story of the advancement of art. Neither of the two authors treats James's personal weaknesses sparingly, but both represent these shortcomings as a necessary condition for his literary achievement. The desire to be popular and the devotion to art are found to be as mutually exclusive as marriage and creativity for James.[8] This correlation recalls Leon Edel's magisterial five-volume biography:

> in James's equation, they were formulated as art and passion – and in his existence they could not be reconciled. The solution: renunciation. One renounced love, or was deprived of it. Accepted, it could prove ruinous.[9]

The two novels follow this Freudian line of argument; they delineate James's deep emotional investment in his imagined characters at the expense of real people, suggesting that he transferred the energies he withheld in real life to his art, i.e. that he sublimated his sexuality in order to create art.

As he neared old age, James became increasingly protective about the image he would present to posterity, specifically writing volumes of autobiography in order to manipulate the reading of his personality. He wanted to determine exactly the direction future biographers would take, and the enquiry he specifically wished to prevent was into his sexuality. As Eve Kosofsky Sedgwick argues, not telling and not describing one's sexual identity still represents an articulation of sexuality, in James's case one characterised by "homosexual panic" that was "damaging to both its male subject and its female non-object".[10]

To invent the author's life is the privilege of the genre of fictional biography, and doubly legitimate in an author whose late work insists that fictional invention actually constitutes the self.[11] Because it is invented, fictional biography can expand our understanding of the person; it can test the truth of evidence against the truth of the imagination. In view of this license, the similarity in one departure from documented evidence that both these very different novels make is remarkable. Though both follow quite closely the facts of James's life, relying on a formidable amount of research, their imaginations concerning James's relationship with a female fellow writer, Constance Fenimore Woolson, clearly run on the same track.

The two novels were published in 2004 within a few months of each other. Considering that the authors were writing at the same time without knowledge of their common subject, the correspondence in their interpretation of the relationship between James and Woolson is astonishing. Both see his breach of promise that they live together part of the year in Venice as the cause for Woolson's suicide, coming as it did after an apparent yielding up of his cautious and protracted non-commitment. James had a habit of alternating between generous impulses and sudden revulsions "that must have been grueling for the woman in proportion to [his] outrageous gift and moral magnetism".[12] Both novels stress James's tendency to recoil from relationships that became too intense and both blame his inability to commit himself for her death, emphasising his feelings of guilt in long chapters of internal focalisation which render the intensity of his self-reproach.

Moreover, both Lodge and Tóibín use the same images to expand on the meaning that they attribute to the 'affair': James is rowed out under cover of darkness to a remote place in the Venetian lagoon to dispose of the deceased Woolson's clothes, but the dresses keep rising to the surface like bodies of the undead.[13] This memorable metaphor of James's guilty conscience plays on a psychonarrative of submerged sexuality in his relation with Woolson. Of course, these similarities cannot be mere coincidence.

Earlier biographies initiated these particular interpretations. Both novels depend not only on Edel's, but to an even larger extent on Lyndall Gordon's biography published in 1998. For Gordon, James was not the generous, urbane and tolerant observer that he styled himself, but wilful, ruthless and "hard as nails".[14] His biography deals exclusively with James's relations to his cousin Minnie Temple and to Constance Fenimore Woolson. Minnie, his companion in the early New England days, and his close friend Woolson both held strong affection for James. According to Gordon, both these women died a premature death which can be related in some way to James's rejection of them. Both at some point hoped and proposed to the author their desire to join his life in Europe only to be repulsed. *The Master* relies heavily on Gordon's study, presenting the two women as victims of James's failure in love. Lodge is more moderate in his condemnation, blaming James only for the suicide of Woolson.

Gordon follows up Edel's insinuation of an erotic element in Woolson's relations to James. Edel describes Woolson as a "plain", "elderly" spinster with an "exalted notion of her own literary powers" who chased him around the continent hungry for romance.[15] Though Gordon presents this image in more respectful terms and grounds his characterisation of Woolson in the findings of feminist criticism, the whole point of his study is to claim that James was responsible for her death. When the effusions of devoted interest which James habitually expressed in his letters revealed themselves as not more than imaginary intentions, Woolson's latent depression was exacerbated and this disappointment, Gordon claims, became the cause of her suicide in 1894.[16] This romantic conclusion, it is important to note, cannot ever be more than psychologically sensitive speculation. Very little is known of Woolson's attitude to Henry James, since an agreement between them to burn their letters ensured a paucity of information concerning their relationship that must leave their biographers guessing (only four letters survived). And the exact circumstances of Woolson's death in Venice will probably never be ascertained.

For Lodge's and Tóibín's purposes, however, the absence of facts provides a perfect receptacle for a narrative of culpability and regret. But their representations of the female writer differ significantly from their source. Gordon's biography insists that Temple and Woolson were not submissive, helpless muses to the master. Woolson especially, Gordon points out, was a respected author in her own right whose innovative fables of artists precede those of James. For Gordon, all art depends in some way on collaboration; hence, he emphasises that James's narratives devolved more than he cared to acknowledge from communication with his literary friend. By erasing the traces of his relationship to Woolson, James was not covering up any sexual implications. Instead, thus Gordon, he cancelled out an influence "more intimate than sex" which would disturb the image, which he promoted of himself, of the solitary genius soaring above social ties.[17]

Woolson had been an admirer of James since the eighteen seventies and been trying to get to know him personally for some time before their meeting actually took place in 1880, shortly after her transfer to Europe. With him and some of his friends she wanted to feel part of a community of like-minded and mutually supportive artists.[18] At the time Woolson was drawn to Europe for its opportunities of travel and freedom, American women abroad were beginning to receive critical scrutiny. In fact, the press portrayed the typical American girl as a young woman without protection or restraint. American women cavorting all over Europe in search of husbands were a common image in public discourse, a discourse which also engaged in discussions of cultural difference by representing American women as more independent and spoilt than those of European countries. The majority of commentators condemned these 'fast girls' for lack of decorum and ridiculed their bold self-assertion. The publication of *Daisy Miller* (1879) at this cultural moment therefore hit a sensitive nerve. While some critics in America felt offended by James's portrayal of Daisy, others defended it as "an important lesson to women not to exercise their freedom".[19]

Woolson agreed with this latter view and scrupulously avoided any semblance of flirtation herself. According to Gordon, "[h]er energy went with a self-reliance that scorned the social favours James cultivated".[20] In Woolson James met a writer absorbed in writing even more completely than himself.[21] Like other female writers at the time whose talent and passion for art transgressed the conventional notions of femininity, Woolson made a conscious choice to remain reclusive and to forgo the social rounds James revelled in. Like many nineteenth-century women writers, she saw the sheltered calm of women's lives as an opportunity rather than a handicap, permitting a freedom of thought that might be less accessible in the more strenuous lives of men. Like many female writers, she also preferred subterfuge to submission, shunning publicity in order to remain a 'perfect lady' in the eyes of the public. And her civilised seclusion allowed James to keep the extent of their friendship secret.

She did not let James perceive a determination of will equal to his own which shaped her work. Instead, she offered him her intelligent artistic sensibility of judgement and taste. Like James, Woolson was interested in the cultural differences between America and Europe, and the influence of the continental environment on Americans. As expatriate Americans and writers these two may have felt an affinity that was the natural consequence of similar tastes, opinions, and a similar interest in chronicling the 'international scene'. Woolson's impeccable reserve and genuine modesty about her art must have appealed to him. In her first surviving letter to James she stated, "a woman, after all, can never be a complete artist".[22] Subsequently, Woolson habitually deferred to his intellectual and artistic superiority. Woolson may have disavowed special status because, at the same time, she was aligning her fiction with the particular realist aesthetic embodied in James's work.

The debates about professional female writing which were carried on at the time may have made her deferential attitude advisable.[23] Women's association with high culture was complicated by a gendered discourse of creativity which reacted to the success of female authors in the literary market. At a time of burgeoning readerships and an explosion of the literary print market, many women authors produced one best-selling novel after another. Literary criticism, however, was still largely in the hands of elitist male cultural arbiters who tended to view professional women as usurpers of male public authority. Some of these voiced essentialist notions about women's incapacity for artistic production.[24] Some were belligerent in their defense of the literary domain against the "damned mob of scribbling women", as Nathaniel Hawthorne put it.[25] The majority of more moderate commentators held that female artists could only excel in certain circumscribed areas of art, expending some sophisticated rhetoric on the particular suitability of the 'female mind' to spiritual and affective concerns in contrast to the more abstract, detached and profound enquiry iniquitous to men.

Towards the end of the nineteenth century especially, there was a critical backlash as women's literature was increasingly associated with mass production and middlebrow domestic fiction.[26] James himself contributed to this gendered discourse on art in some of his literary criticism. Rivalry may have increased the severity of his tone in the case of writers interested in the 'liberated' American girls he often depicted himself. Whether motivated by envy of commercial success or a genuine dislike of popular novels, James sought to preserve a boundary between high and low art and to relegate his female competitors to the latter. Women at the time had to realise that female genius was unavailable, not because it could not exist but because the definition of genius was a male-based construct.[27] In this situation Woolson, with great common sense, took care to appear non-threatening to her male peers. As far as we know, her voluntary subordination to James as mentor may have resulted in a productive artistic exchange for both. But her enthusiastic embrace of Europe as a place where women could enjoy the freedom and independence necessary for an artist's life must have palled, as it did for many American women artists and writers.[28]

Woolson developed a method of subtextually encoding her opinions into her stories, preferring to make her objection to British Imperialism as well as to discrimination and injustice not too overt.[29] With regard to gender issues she deployed a similar subterfuge. Woolson's significant contribution to *fin-de-siècle* literature lies in her subtle reinterpretation of the topic of the female artist, a subject which mattered personally to female authors and became a major concern for many. She uses this subject matter to dramatise ideas of emancipation as well as to interrogate the double marginalisation which female artists had to face, as women and as artists.[30] Woolson's fine artistic stories, "Miss Grief" (1880), "The Street of the Hyacinth" (1882), "At the Chateau of Corinne" (1887), focus on the roles of woman and artist as a source of irreconcilable conflict.[31] Europe is depicted as lacking in opportunities for women to develop their creative potential.[32] The silencing of Woolson's female artists is blatant, her artistic heroines "are buried alive by their voicelessness".[33] She suggests that it is not the ravages of love or the pressures of domesticity that destroy female artistic ambition. Instead she perceptively integrates the core themes of contemporary discourses in showing that it is the male rejection of the mere possibility of female genius which makes the combination of love and the pursuit of art impossible.

Though both *Author, Author* and *The Master* espouse the picture of Woolson as an independent artistic spirit which feminist research has made available, they choose to concentrate on the feelings involved, naturally for biofictions, primarily those of their main protagonist. Both highlight the emotional rather than the artistic aspect of James's relationship with Woolson. In these stories the friendship is complicated with subterranean emotions and unexpressed expectations. As is perhaps inevitable in biofictions, the relationship between James and Woolson is personalised in both novels, so that the cultural background with its particular pressures on the female artist hardly plays a role. Instead, the problems that beset women writers at the time are transformed into problems resulting from James's personal shortcoming only. In order to dramatise, both novelists choose to emotionalise Woolson's expectations regarding James. Unsurprisingly perhaps, the two male authors concur completely in what they imagine the female artist needs and desires – it must be the love of their 'hero'. Their astonishing congruence in this detail is probably due to common source material as well as a convenient conformity to dominant discourses. It is clearly James who is at fault in both narratives; the female artist is transformed into a victim of the male author. This move enlists a predictable sympathy for marginalised and subjected women in contemporary readers.

Apart from this strategy, the two novels are not at all alike. The historical background sketched above is more prominent in Lodge's novel than in Tóibín's. *Author, Author* is more external in focus, presenting a vivid portrait of the literary talent and culture of the period. Lodge follows the ups and downs of James's professional career and explicitly raises issues of the literary marketplace. Lodge presents a James character driven by the desire to reach large audiences and to increase his dwindling revenues. He is attentive to the quotidian aspects of a writer's life and describes the anxieties and preoccupations of artists – aesthetics, creative inspiration, book sales, gossip, and reputation. He also explores the agonising self-doubts that tormented James when Woolson, like his long-term friend George du Maurier, turned out bestsellers that far outdistanced his own works in readership and profitability.[34] Understandably, his thoughts about these fellow writers are tinged by occasional bouts of jealousy and resentment of their success. That James was unable to completely banish envy and disdain from his friendship with George du Maurier did not impair the happiness of this friendship in the long run. Lodge succeeds in rendering very poignantly the simplicity of James's affection for du Maurier as well as the subtle sophistication in his judgements of his friend's work.

Author, Author is much closer to 'real' biography. It is more interested in the problems and difficulties in the relationship of artists in very different circumstances. The two writers James and Woolson discuss their work, their reviews and sales. In the beginning James is gratified by the extravagance of Woolson's admiration ("[m]y work is coarse besides yours. Of entirely another grade. The two should not be mentioned on the same day").[35] Later, James is alarmed when he discovers in Woolson's story "A Florentine Experiment" (1880) a witty female author and her patronising male mentor whose conversations are obviously modelled on their own dialogues. The novel then follows the growth of intimacy as James's esteem for Woolson's professional opinion increases. Like Tóibín's novel, it describes at length James's tactics of withdrawal when he panics on account of Woolson's official introduction into his circle of friends (Lodge 2004: 72).

The character James that Lodge creates has little in common with Tóibín's James. In *Author, Author* James is naturally loquacious and social and, even in his "treacherous years",[36] deeply respected by a circle of intelligent admirers. This social side of the author is elided or at least muted in Tóibín's exquisitely written novel in which unrelieved interior focalisation imprisons James in his solitary consciousness. Tóibín invents the mind of James, a mind tense with repressed sexual anxieties, obsessed with the dead, and incapable of affection. His James persists in strategies of avoidance that include family, homeland, and politics.[37] Because of his selfish avoidance of involvement he must absorb other people's emotions and experiences for his literary works. This representation of James elaborates Gordon's notion of cannibalistic authorship which "preyed upon living human beings" and conducted experiments in human chemistry with "merciless clairvoyance".[38]

In consequence, the perception of Woolson as an artist is less important in *The Master*: "[s]he did not talk about her work to him, but he learned by implication and accident that the completion of each of her books brought with it a nervous collapse of which she lived in dread".[39] Tóibín's James divines a world of unvoiced unhappiness in his friend: "she was immensely clever and she was lonely" (Tóibín 2004: 232). The novel makes clear that Woolson had a lot to offer James; she emerges as his most sensitive friend and kindred soul, mildly tolerant of his hectoring condescension. He can depend on her perception of his needs as well as her delicate endeavour to forgo any appearance of commitment. But her fictionalised qualities – sensitivity, tolerance, intelligence and modesty – are those of a female character rather than an artist.

The use of interior focalisation is an effective instrument in this case since the neglect of Woolson as an artist, a neglect which recalls the omission of women writers from the canon of literature in earlier historiography, can be explained away as James's perception. It would then merely aggravate the deficiency of character that Tóibín is at pains to present. Interior focalisation also serves well the foregrounding of James's homosexuality.[40] This is by no means a new idea; Edel's biography already hints that it was homosexual rather than heterosexual desire that James suppressed in his celibate life. In the past decade, in the wake of masculinity and queer studies, Edel's biography has come in for a fair amount of criticism for refusing to explore James's homosexuality further and for suppressing the episodes of the writer's life in which he had close relationships to young men.[41] This criticism, articulated in particular by Stephen Novick, was in turn prepared for by Sedgwick's incisive study *Epistemology of the Closet* (1991). Sedgwick wonders why critics so long preserved religious silence on James's homosexuality. She supposes that the motivation for their "active incuriosity" was the desire to protect the author from "homophobic misreadings" or "anachronistically gay readings".[42]

Tóibín offers us the latter. *The Master*'s image is "symptomatic" in that it represents the affective life of James not as heteronormative but at the same time not transgressive in the way it has been defined in recent cultural histories.[43] His life is queered not in the sense of an oppositional sexuality but rather as instance of an evolving new and contradictory masculinity in a cultural situation of gender crisis. But it is also anachronistic in its negative image of the closet homosexual.

The Master starts with a scene in which the young James could have accepted the love of a male suitor. He describes the emotional intensity of the scene and the pain James foresees following his rejection of the offer of love, later returning again and again in memory to this initial failure of nerve. It seems clear that James must regret his deliberately repressed life, as does Marcher in "The Beast in the Jungle". In his 2001 collection of essays about gay writers and artists, *Love in a Dark Time. And Other Explorations of Gay Lives and Literature*, Tóibín remarks that "The Beast in the Jungle"

> becomes much darker when you know about James's life [...]. You realize that the catastrophe the story led you to expect was in fact the very life that James chose to live, or was forced to live [...]. In "The Beast in the Jungle" James's solitary existence is shown in its most frightening manifestation: a life of pure coldness.[44]

For Tóibín, therefore, James stands as the negative prototype – "a figure who, because of his self-repression, not only didn't have a 'gay life', but had no life at all".[45]

In view of the greatly increased gay visibility and "landslide levels of acceptance" for gays in recent years, Steven Seidman speaks of "the disappearing closet".[46] The change in cultural discourses has made it equally possible to decry closet homosexuals as it is to mobilise against a marginalising system. The championing of gay identity and celebration of gay pride which the last decades have witnessed may have led to impatience with those who prefer to accommodate themselves in a heteronormative society by preserving the habit of concealment. In light of Seidman's work, it has been claimed that the closet persists most prominently in the imaginary of Western literature.[47] Tóibín's literary image of the closet exhibits his vehement objection to a secretiveness that once frustrated him too, as he admits in his essays.

In Tóibín's novel, a connection is established between closet homosexuality and a general failure as a human being. His James is barely likable, a solipsistic "beast-in-the-jungle" type unable to maintain intimate relationships; a sterile, thin-lipped, inhibited personality who opts for spectatorship instead of emotion and fulfilment. And his preference for detached observation is not just a technique of the artist but fundamental to his emotionally crippled personality.

The coldness and failure of passion, which Tóibín sees at the core of James's work and nature, are linked to his failed sexuality in elaborate metaphors of indoor spaces which suggest the constriction of the closet. His James is a necrophiliac who can only love deeply once a person is deceased. "Sometimes in the night he dreamed about the dead" is the novel's first sentence (1). In each chapter, present-day incidents evoke memories of the dead that impact on his art. In the

> impressionistic ambling between past and present, a distinctive and perhaps too repetitive pattern begins to emerge: each memory that is triggered or captured may lead to the creation of a work of literature by Henry the artist, but each memory tends also to lead you to a scene of moral failure on the part of Henry the man.[48]

Consider the following translation of the haunting memory of Minnie Temple into a literary character:

> [h]e felt a sharp and unbearable idea staring at him, like something alive and fierce and predatory in the air, whispering to him that he had pre-

311

ferred her dead rather than alive, that he had known what to do with her once life was taken from her, but he had denied her when she asked him gently for help. (121)[49]

The lack of sympathy in Tóibín's characterisation contrasts strangely with his statements as a chronicler of gay lives. In *Love in a Dark Time* he writes about the way in which the homosexuals of an earlier generation were forced to lead double, lying lives: "[i]t is duplicitous and slippery, and it requires a great deal of sympathy and understanding".[50]

As Woolson perceptively remarked: "[m]en, as a general thing, are not generous to each other. I told you that once before and you laughed it to scorn".[51] Her opinion is borne out by Tóibín's vision of "James the cold fish, the artistic vampire living off the lifeblood of his innocent and truly suffering victims".[52] In *Author, Author* the subtext of homosexual panic that Sedgwick discerned in James's decision to stay in the closet is not denied but also not fore-grounded. Instead, Lodge's rendering of James as a celibate bachelor by choice puts the emphasis on asexuality. This emphasis deprives his novel of the sentimental appeal which Tóibín's representation of James's suppressed homosexual yearnings possesses. But Lodge's novel is ultimately the more generous, leaving a margin for compassion in its firm historical grounding of James's behaviour. Near the end of the novel Lodge imagines visiting the writer's deathbed and reassuring him of his celebrated place in the literary future:

> [h]ow pleasing to tell him that after a few decades of relative obscurity he would become an established classic [...], that all of his major works and most of his minor ones would be constantly in print, scrupulously edited, annotated, and studied in schools, colleges and universities around the world. [...] And what fun to tell him that millions of people all over the world would encounter his stories in theatrical and cine-matic and television adaptations. (Lodge 2004: 375)

The aim of Tóibín's novel is not just to recreate and resuscitate, but to murder and dissect; his debunking of "the master" is premised on a very present-day obsession with sex and on the notion that a happy life necessitates sexual fulfilment. As one critic puts it, Tóibín "exemplifies the prurience" of the contemporary literary imagination, "and its assumption that you can't really understand someone until you comprehend the nature of their couplings – or lack thereof".[53] Tóibín refuses to acknowledge that James may have been quite a happy person, because for him art was the highest satisfaction, "he just keeps showing you the damage that art causes without really suggesting what its compensatory value might be – for James or, indeed, for us".[54]

What readers of James love about his novels is the demand they make on intellectual and moral speculation. James's texts are charged with overtones and hidden meanings conveying a turmoil of the mind that invites readers to imaginatively engage with and question the decisions made. As Martha Nussbaum argues, James's novels make special demands for an ethical reading. His stylistic subtlety and delicate use of easily missed nuances remind readers of their own fallible and partial views.[55] By contrast, the subjectivity so explicitly spelt out by Tóibín undermines the artistry he sets out to portray. Moreover, the suffering he depicts so powerfully appears as poetic justice for lack of passion and lack of courage, thus encouraging the reader's moral condemnation rather than moral questioning.

Notes

1 Middeke (1999: 4).
2 Lodge (2006: 10).
3 E.g. *Portrait of a Lady*, dir. Jane Campion (1996); *The Wings of the Dove*, dir. Iain Softley (1997); *Washington Square*; dir. Agnieszka Holland (1997); *The Golden Bowl*, dir. James Ivory (2000).
4 Brosch (2000).
5 James (1915: 18).
6 Perhaps I should make a personal confession at this point: as an ardent Jamesian I am probably ill-equipped to do justice to these two novels, since the supreme accomplishment of James's art rarely rises to the surface in either of them. Lodge seems modestly aware of the discrepancy, and in his many quotations from notebooks, letters and novels James's brilliance and singularity are humblingly evident; see Hollinghurst (2004).
7 Lodge's representation of this unusual intersection of two very different writers uncannily presages his own painful discovery when he found out about Tóibín's novel and was forced to endure comparisons that generally favoured the latter. He records this experience with admirable candour in *The Year of Henry James* (2006).

8   Matterson (2008: 138).
9   Edel (1972: 112).
10 Sedgwick (2008: 3; 188).
11 Person (2003: 2).
12 Sedgwick (2008: 196).
13 This particular scene also crops up in a third novel about James, Emma Tennant's *Felony* (2002), which investigates James's "The Aspern Papers" (1888) and its sources. All three novelists have taken the episode from Lyndall Gordon's *A Private Life of Henry James* (1998), which describes this otherwise unattested event.
14 Gordon (1998: 7).
15 Quoted in Boyd (2004: 190).
16 Gordon (1998: 257).
17 *Ibid.*, 8.
18 Boyd (2004: 118).
19 *Ibid.*, 117.
20 Gordon (1998: 163).
21 *Ibid.*, 165.
22 Quoted in *ibid.*, 171.
23 Recent feminist criticism has presented a more nuanced picture of the ideology of the separate spheres in emphasising the fluidity of the concept, which could authorise and cultivate women's professional ambition, so as to gradually transform the female ideal and to challenge the perception of work as degrading for women. Gradually the "refining work" of beneficiary female influence on society came to include a contribution to its public culture; see Zakreski (2006: 8). Partly, but not insignificantly, such refining work took place in the field of artistic professions.
24 Morrien (2000: 136).
25 See Boyd (2004: 9).
26 *Ibid.*
27 *Ibid.*, 149.
28 *Ibid.*, 125.
29 Brehm & Dean (2004: xvii).
30 Morrien (2000: 137).
31 Boyd (2004: 122).
32 *Ibid.*, 120.
33 *Ibid.*, 149.
34 In *Author, Author* James's long friendship with George du Maurier actually takes up more room than his relationship with Woolson. Du Maurier turned to writing fiction when his eyesight was failing and with his novel *Trilby* (1894) – a sentimental thriller about an artist's model – he wrote the bestseller of the nineteenth century. Ironically, he had offered the story to James first, who rejected it.
35 Lodge (2004: 71). Further references to this edition will be included in the text.

36 Edel (1985: 423).

37 This is James contemplating the Civil War in which he did not take part: "[w]hen everyone else had fire in their blood, he was calm. So calm that he could neither read nor think, merely bask in the freedom that the afternoon offered, savour, as deeply as he could, this quiet and strange treachery, his own surreptitious withdrawal from the world", Tóibín (2004: 183). As Laura Miller comments, Tóibín makes us feel that the greatness of James's mind was an immense littleness; see Miller (2004).

38 Gordon (1998: 5).

39 Tóibín (2004: 230). Further references to this edition will be included in the text.

40 According to Stephen Matterson, Tóibín is to be praised for his reticence and caution, for not taking full advantage of the liberties that fictional biography offers; see Matterson (2008: 135). This is an unusual understanding of reticence when the whole point of the novel is to sexualise the image of James.

41 See Novick (1996). In the course of an acrimonious exchange, Novick disclosed letters that Edel apparently knew of but omitted in his biography which revealed the closeness of his attachment to Paul Joukowsky and Hendrik C. Anderson; see Matterson (2008: 136).

42 Sedgwick (2008: 197).

43 Kaplan (2007: 78).

44 Tóibín (2002: 35).

45 Mendelsohn (2004: 4).

46 Seidman (2004: 1-2; 6).

47 Winning (2011: 54).

48 Mendelsohn (2004: 12).

49 Tóibín cites part of a letter that the real-life Minny Temple wrote to James ("[t]hink, my dear, of the pleasure we would have together in Rome"), but he omits the postscript, in which she admits that her fantasy of travelling with him in Europe is just that: "I am really not strong enough to go abroad with even the kindest of friends", quoted in Edel (1985: 105).

50 Tóibín (2002: 17).

51 James (1980: 530).

52 Mendelsohn (2004: 13).

53 Gioia (n.d.).

54 Mendelsohn (2004: 14).

55 See Nussbaum (1985: 522).

Bibliography

Boyd, Anne: *Writing For Immortality. Women and the Emergence of High Literary Culture in America*, Baltimore, 2004.

Brehm, Victoria & Sharon L. Dean: "Introduction". – In V.B. & S.L.D. (Eds.): *Constance Fenimore Woolson. Selected Stories and Travel Narratives*, Knoxville, 2004, pp. xv-xxvii.

Brosch, Renate: *Krisen des Sehens. Henry James und die Veränderung der Wahrnehmung im 19. Jahrhundert*, Tübingen, 2000.

Edel, Leon: *Henry James. The Master*, Philadelphia, 1972.

–: *Henry James. A Life*, New York, 1985.

Gioia, Ted: "The Master", *The New Canon*, http://www.Thenewcanon.com/the_master.html (accessed 1 June 2011).

Gordon, Lyndall: *A Private Life of Henry James. Two Women and His Art*, London, 1998.

Hollinghurst, Allan: "The Middle Fears", *The Guardian*, 4 September 2004, http://www.guardian.co.uk/books/2004/sep/04/fiction.henryjames (accessed 1 June 2011).

James, Henry: *The Beast in the Jungle*, London, 1915.

–: *Henry James Letters. 1883-1995*. Ed. Leon Edel, Cambridge, 1980.

Kaplan, Cora: *Victoriana. Histories, Fictions, Criticism*, Edinburgh, 2007.

Lodge, David: *Author, Author. A Novel*, London, 2004.

Matterson, Stephen: "Dreaming About the Dead. *The Master*". – In Paul Delaney (Ed.): *Reading Colm Tóibín*, Dublin, 2008, pp. 131-148.

Mendelsohn, Daniel: "The Passion of Henry James", *The New York Times*, 20 June 2004, 1-14, http://www.nytimes.com/2004/06/20/books/the-passion-of-henry-james.html (accessed 1 June 2011).

Middeke, Martin: "Introduction". – In M.M. & Werner Huber (Eds.): *Biofictions. The Rewriting of Romantic Lives in Contemporary Fiction and Drama*, Rochester, 1999, pp. 1-26.

Miller, Laura: "*The Master* by Colm Tóibín", *Salon*, 7 July 2004, http://dir.salon.com/story/books/review/2004/07/07/master/ (accessed 1 June 2011).

Morrien, Rita: "Können Frauen sublimieren? Zur Verflechtung von sexueller und künstlerischer Entfaltung in Clara Viebigs *Es lebe die Kunst* und Grete Meisel Hess' *Fanny Roth. Eine Jung Frauengeschichte*". – In Karin Tebben (Ed.): *Frauen – Körper – Kunst. Literarische Inszenierungen weiblicher Sexualität*, Göttingen, 2000, pp. 136-154.

Novick, Sheldon M.: *Henry James. The Young Master*, New York, 1996.

Nussbaum, Martha: "Finely Aware and Richly Responsible. Moral Attention and the Moral Task of Literature", *The Journal of Philosophy* 82:10, 1985, 516-529.

Person, Leland S.: *Henry James and the Suspense of Masculinity*, Philadelphia, 2003.

Sedgwick, Eve Kosofsky: *Epistemology of the Closet*, Berkeley, 2008 [1990].

Seidman, Steven: *Beyond the Closet. The Transformation of Gay and Lesbian Life*, New York, 2004.

Tóibín, Colm: *Love in a Dark Time. And Other Explorations of Gay Lives and Literature*, New York, 2002.

–: *The Master*, London, 2004.

Winning, Joanne: "Writing in and Beyond the Closet". – In Hugh Stevens (Ed.): *The Cambridge Companion to Gay and Lesbian Writing*, Cambridge, 2011, pp. 50-64.

Zakreski, Patricia: *Representing the Female Artistic Labour 1848-1890. Refining Work for the Middle-Class Woman*, Aldershot, 2006.

Contributors' Addresses

Prof. Dr. Christiane Bimberg, Technische Universität Dortmund, Institut für Anglistik und Amerikanistik, Emil-Figge-Str. 50, 44227 Dortmund, Germany.

Prof. Dr. Renate Brosch, Universität Stuttgart, Institut für Literaturwissenschaft: Anglistik/Amerikanistik, Kepplerstrasse 17, 70174 Stuttgart, Germany.

Prof. Dr. Peter Childs, Dean of Research, Professor of Modern English Literature, University of Gloucestershire, Dunholme, The Park, Cheltenham, GL50 2RH, United Kingdom.

Prof. Dr. Jean-Michel Ganteau, Professor of British Literature, Directeur du master d'Etudes anglophones, Directeur de l'Ecole Doctorale 58, Directeur de la publication *Etudes britanniques contemporaines*, Université Montpellier 3 Paul Valérie, Route du Mende, 34199 Montpellier CEDEX 5, France.

Prof. Dr. Brigitte Glaser, Georg-August-Universität Göttingen, Seminar für Englische Philologie, Käte-Hamburger-Weg 3, 37073 Göttingen, Germany.

Prof. Dr. Marion Gymnich, Rheinische Friedrich-Wilhelms-Universität Bonn, Institut für Anglistik, Amerikanistik und Keltologie, Regina-Pacis-Weg 5, 53113 Bonn, Germany.

Alexa Keuneke, M.A., Ruhr-Universität Bochum, Englisches Seminar, Universitätsstraße 150, 44780 Bochum, Germany.

PD Dr. Uwe Klawitter, Ruhr-Universität Bochum, Englisches Seminar, Universitätsstraße 150, 44780 Bochum, Germany.

Prof. Dr. Silvia Mergenthal, Universität Konstanz, Fachbereich Literaturwissenschaft/Anglistik, Fach D 161, 78457 Konstanz, Germany.

Prof. Dr. Susana Onega, Departmento de Filología Inglesa y Alemana, Facultad de Filosofía y Letras, 50009 Universidad de Zaragoza, Spain.

Prof. Dr. Anette Pankratz, Ruhr-Universität Bochum, Englisches Seminar, Universitätsstraße 150, 44780 Bochum, Germany.

Dr. Barbara Puschmann-Nalenz, Ruhr-Universität Bochum, Englisches Seminar, Universitätsstraße 150, 44780 Bochum, Germany.

Prof. Dr. Ingrid von Rosenberg, Kolberger Platz 2, 14199 Berlin, Germany.

Prof. Dr. Christian Schmitt-Kilb, Universität Rostock, Institut für Anglistik/Amerikanistik, August-Bebel-Str. 28, 18051 Rostock, Germany.

Dr. Lena Steveker, Universität des Saarlandes, Anglistik, Amerikanistik und Anglophone Kulturen, Campus C5 3, 66123 Saarbrücken, Germany.